Pentaho Data Integration Beginner's Guide

Second Edition

Get up and running with the Pentaho Data Integration
tool using this hands-on, easy-to-read guide

María Carina Roldán

[PACKT]
PUBLISHING

open source*
community experience distilled

BIRMINGHAM - MUMBAI

ᴜata Integration Beginner's Guide

ᴇdition

First published: April 2010

Second Edition: October 2013

Production Reference: 1171013

Published by Packt Publishing Ltd.
Livery Place
35 Livery Street
Birmingham B3 2PB, UK.

ISBN 978-1-78216-504-0

www.packtpub.com

Cover Image by Suresh Mogre (suresh.mogre.99@gmail.com)

Credits

Author

María Carina Roldán

Reviewers

Tomoyuki Hayashi

Gretchen Moran

Acquisition Editors

Usha Iyer

Greg Wild

Lead Technical Editor

Azharuddin Sheikh

Technical Editors

Sharvari H. Baet

Aparna K

Kanhucharan Panda

Vivek Pillai

Project Coordinator

Navu Dhillon

Proofreaders

Simran Bhogal

Ameesha Green

Indexer

Mariammal Chettiyar

Graphics

Ronak Dhruv

Yuvraj Mannari

Production Coordinator

Conidon Miranda

Cover Work

Conidon Miranda

About the Author

María Carina Roldán was born in Esquel, Argentina, and earned her Bachelor's degree in Computer Science at at the Universidad Nacional de La Plata (UNLP) and then moved to Buenos Aires where she has lived since 1994.

She has worked as a BI consultant for almost fifteen years. She started working with Pentaho technology back in 2006. Over the last three and a half years, she has been devoted to working full time for Webdetails—a company acquired by Pentaho in 2013—as an ETL specialist.

Carina is the author of *Pentaho 3.2 Data Integration Beginner's Book, Packt Publishing, April 2009*, and the co-author of *Pentaho Data Integration 4 Cookbook, Packt Publishing, June 2011*.

I'd like to thank those who have encouraged me to write this book: firstly, the Pentaho community. They have given me such rewarding feedback after my other two books on PDI; it is because of them that I feel compelled to pass my knowledge on to those willing to learn. I also want to thank my friends! Especially Flavia, Jaqui, and Marce for their encouraging words throughout the writing process; Silvina for clearing up my questions about English; Gonçalo for helping with the use of PDI on Mac systems; and Hernán for helping with ideas and examples for this new edition.

I would also like to thank the technical reviewers—Gretchen, Tomoyuki, Nelson, and Paula—for the time and dedication that they have put in to reviewing the book.

About the Reviewers

Tomoyuki Hayashi is a system engineer who mainly works for the intersection of open source and enterprise software. He has developed a CMIS-compliant and CouchDB-based ECM software named NemakiWare (`http://nemakiware.com/`).

He is currently working with Aegif, Japan, which provides advisory services for content-oriented applications, collaboration improvement, and ECM in general. It is one of the most experienced companies in Japan that supports the introduction of foreign-made software to the Japanese market.

Gretchen Moran works as an independent Pentaho consultant on a variety of business intelligence and big data projects. She has 15 years of experience in the business intelligence realm, developing software and providing services for a number of companies including Hyperion Solutions and the Pentaho Corporation.

Gretchen continues to contribute to Pentaho Corporation's latest and greatest software initiatives while managing the daily adventures of her two children, Isabella and Jack, with her husband, Doug.

www.PacktPub.com

Support files, eBooks, discount offers and more

You might want to visit www.PacktPub.com for support files and downloads related to your book.

Did you know that Packt offers eBook versions of every book published, with PDF and ePub files available? You can upgrade to the eBook version at www.PacktPub.com and as a print book customer, you are entitled to a discount on the eBook copy. Get in touch with us at service@packtpub.com for more details.

At www.PacktPub.com, you can also read a collection of free technical articles, sign up for a range of free newsletters and receive exclusive discounts and offers on Packt books and eBooks.

http://PacktLib.PacktPub.com

Do you need instant solutions to your IT questions? PacktLib is Packt's online digital book library. Here, you can access, read and search across Packt's entire library of books.

Why Subscribe?

- ◆ Fully searchable across every book published by Packt
- ◆ Copy and paste, print and bookmark content
- ◆ On demand and accessible via web browser

Free Access for Packt account holders

If you have an account with Packt at www.PacktPub.com, you can use this to access PacktLib today and view nine entirely free books. Simply use your login credentials for immediate access.

Table of Contents

Preface

Pentaho Data Integration (also known as Kettle) is an engine along with a suite of tools responsible for the processes of Extracting, Transforming, and Loading—better known as the ETL processes. PDI not only serves as an ETL tool, but is also used for other purposes such as migrating data between applications or databases, exporting data from databases to flat files, data cleansing, and much more. PDI has an intuitive, graphical, drag-and-drop design environment, and its ETL capabilities are powerful. However, getting started with PDI can be difficult or confusing. This book provides the guidance needed to overcome that difficulty, covering the key features of PDI. Each chapter introduces new features, allowing you to gradually get involved with the tool.

By the end of the book, you will have not only experimented with all kinds of examples, but will have also built a basic but complete datamart with the help of PDI.

How to read this book

Although it is recommended that you read all the chapters, you don't have to. The book allows you to tailor the PDI learning process according to your particular needs.

The first five chapters along with *Chapter 10, Creating Basic Task Flows*, cover the core concepts. If you don't know PDI and want to learn just the basics, reading those chapters will suffice. If you need to work with databases, you could include *Chapter 8, Working with Databases*, in the roadmap.

If you already know the basics, you can improve your PDI knowledge by reading *Chapter 6, Transforming Your Data by Coding, Chapter 7, Transforming the Rowset*, and *Chapter 11, Creating Advanced Transformations and Jobs*.

If you already know PDI and want to learn how to use it to load or maintain a data warehouse or datamart, you will find all that you need in *Chapter 9, Performing Advanced Operations with Databases*, and *Chapter 12, Developing and Implementing a Simple Datamart*.

Finally, all the appendices are valuable resources for anyone reading this book.

What this book covers

Chapter 1, Getting Started with Pentaho Data Integration, serves as the most basic introduction to PDI, presenting the tool. This chapter includes instructions for installing PDI and gives you the opportunity to play with the graphical designer (Spoon). The chapter also includes instructions for installing a MySQL server.

Chapter 2, Getting Started with Transformations, explains the fundamentals of working with transformations, including learning the simplest ways of transforming data and getting familiar with the process of designing, debugging, and testing a transformation.

Chapter 3, Manipulating Real-world Data, explains how to apply the concepts learned in the previous chapter to real-world data that comes from different sources. It also explains how to save the results to different destinations: plain files, Excel files, and more. As real data is very prone to errors, this chapter also explains the basics of handling errors and validating data.

Chapter 4, Filtering, Searching, and Performing Other Useful Operations with Data, expands the set of operations learned in previous chapters by teaching the reader a great variety of essential features such as filtering, sorting, or looking for data.

Chapter 5, Controlling the Flow of Data, explains different options that PDI offers to combine or split flows of data.

Chapter 6, Transforming Your Data by Coding, explains how JavaScript and Java coding can help in the treatment of data. It shows why you may need to code inside PDI, and explains in detail how to do it.

Chapter 7, Transforming the Rowset, explains the ability of PDI to deal with some sophisticated problems—for example, normalizing data from pivoted tables—in a simple fashion.

Chapter 8, Working with Databases, explains how to use PDI to work with databases. The list of topics covered includes connecting to a database, previewing and getting data, and inserting, updating, and deleting data. As database knowledge is not presumed, the chapter also covers fundamental concepts of databases and the SQL language.

Chapter 9, Performing Advanced Operations with Databases, explains how to perform advanced operations with databases, including those especially designed to load data warehouses. A primer on data warehouse concepts is also given in case you are not familiar with the subject.

Chapter 10, Creating Basic Task Flows, serves as an introduction to processes in PDI. Through the creation of simple jobs, you will learn what jobs are and what they are used for.

Chapter 11, Creating Advanced Transformations and Jobs, deals with advanced concepts that will allow you to build complex PDI projects. The list of covered topics includes nesting jobs, iterating on jobs and transformations, and creating subtransformations.

Chapter 12, Developing and Implementing a Simple Datamart, presents a simple datamart project, and guides you to build the datamart by using all the concepts learned throughout the book.

Appendix A, Working with Repositories, is a step-by-step guide to the creation of a PDI database repository and then gives instructions on to work with it.

Appendix B, Pan and Kitchen – Launching Transformations and Jobs from the Command Line, is a quick reference for running transformations and jobs from the command line.

Appendix C, Quick Reference – Steps and Job Entries, serves as a quick reference to steps and job entries used throughout the book.

Appendix D, Spoon Shortcuts, is an extensive list of Spoon shortcuts useful for saving time when designing and running PDI jobs and transformations.

Appendix E, Introducing PDI 5 Features, quickly introduces you to the architectural and functional features included in Kettle 5—the version that was under development when this book was written.

Appendix F, Best Practices, gives a list of best PDI practices and recommendations.

Appendix G, Pop Quiz Answers, contains answers to pop quiz questions.

What you need for this book

PDI is a multiplatform tool. This means that no matter what your operating system is, you will be able to work with the tool. The only prerequisite is to have JVM 1.6 installed. It is also useful to have Excel or Calculator, along with a nice text editor.

Having an Internet connection while reading is extremely useful as well. Several links are provided throughout the book that complement what is explained. Additionally, there is the PDI forum where you may search or post doubts if you are stuck with something.

Who this book is for

This book is a must-have for software developers, database administrators, IT students, and everyone involved or interested in developing ETL solutions, or more generally, doing any kind of data manipulation. Those who have never used PDI will benefit the most from the book, but those who have, will also find it useful.

This book is also a good starting point for database administrators, data warehouse designers, architects, or anyone who is responsible for data warehouse projects and needs to load data into them.

You don't need to have any prior data warehouse or database experience to read this book. Fundamental database and data warehouse technical terms and concepts are explained in easy-to-understand language.

Conventions

In this book, you will find several headings that appear frequently.

To give clear instructions on how to complete a procedure or task, we use:

Time for action – heading

1. Action 1
2. Action 2
3. Action 3

Instructions often need some extra explanation so that they make sense, so they are followed with:

What just happened?

This heading explains the working of tasks or instructions that you have just completed.

You will also find some other learning aids in the book, including:

Pop quiz – heading

These are short multiple-choice questions intended to help you test your own understanding.

Have a go hero – heading

These practical challenges and give you ideas for experimenting with what you have learned.

You will also find a number of styles of text that distinguish between different kinds of information. Here are some examples of these styles, and an explanation of their meaning.

Code words in text are shown as follows: "You may notice that we used the Unix command `rm` to remove the `Drush` directory rather than the DOS `del` command."

A block of code is set as follows:

```
# * Fine Tuning
#
key_buffer = 16M
key_buffer_size = 32M
max_allowed_packet = 16M
thread_stack = 512K
thread_cache_size = 8
max_connections = 300
```

When we wish to draw your attention to a particular part of a code block, the relevant lines or items are set in bold:

```
# * Fine Tuning
#
key_buffer = 16M
key_buffer_size = 32M
max_allowed_packet = 16M
thread_stack = 512K
thread_cache_size = 8
max_connections = 300
```

Any command-line input or output is written as follows:

```
cd /ProgramData/Propeople

rm -r Drush

git clone --branch master http://git.drupal.org/project/drush.git
```

New terms and **important words** are shown in bold. Words that you see on the screen, in menus or dialog boxes for example, appear in the text like this: "On the **Select Destination Location** screen, click on **Next** to accept the default destination."

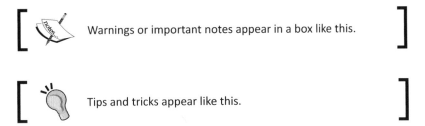

> Warnings or important notes appear in a box like this.

> Tips and tricks appear like this.

Reader feedback

Feedback from our readers is always welcome. Let us know what you think about this book—what you liked or may have disliked. Reader feedback is important for us to develop titles that you really get the most out of.

To send us general feedback, simply send an e-mail to feedback@packtpub.com, and mention the book title through the subject of your message.

If there is a topic that you have expertise in and you are interested in either writing or contributing to a book, see our author guide on www.packtpub.com/authors.

Customer support

Now that you are the proud owner of a Packt book, we have a number of things to help you to get the most from your purchase.

Downloading the example code

You can download the example code files for all Packt books you have purchased from your account at http://www.packtpub.com. If you purchased this book elsewhere, you can visit http://www.packtpub.com/support and register to have the files e-mailed directly to you.

Errata

Although we have taken every care to ensure the accuracy of our content, mistakes do happen. If you find a mistake in one of our books—maybe a mistake in the text or the code—we would be grateful if you would report this to us. By doing so, you can save other readers from frustration and help us improve subsequent versions of this book. If you find any errata, please report them by visiting http://www.packtpub.com/submit-errata, selecting your book, clicking on the **errata submission form** link, and entering the details of your errata. Once your errata are verified, your submission will be accepted and the errata will be uploaded to our website, or added to any list of existing errata, under the Errata section of that title.

Piracy

Piracy of copyright material on the Internet is an ongoing problem across all media. At Packt, we take the protection of our copyright and licenses very seriously. If you come across any illegal copies of our works, in any form, on the Internet, please provide us with the location address or website name immediately so that we can pursue a remedy.

Please contact us at `copyright@packtpub.com` with a link to the suspected pirated material.

We appreciate your help in protecting our authors, and our ability to bring you valuable content.

Questions

You can contact us at `questions@packtpub.com` if you are having a problem with any aspect of the book, and we will do our best to address it.

1

Getting Started with Pentaho Data Integration

Pentaho Data Integration or **PDI** *is an engine along with a suite of tools responsible for the processes of* **Extracting, Transforming,** *and* **Loading;** *also known as* **ETL** *processes. This book is meant to teach you how to use PDI.*

In this chapter, you will:

- ◆ Learn what Pentaho Data Integration is
- ◆ Install the software and start working with the PDI graphical designer
- ◆ Install MySQL, a database engine that you will use when you start working with databases

Pentaho Data Integration and Pentaho BI Suite

Before introducing PDI, let's talk about Pentaho BI Suite. The **Pentaho Business Intelligence Suite** is a collection of software applications intended to create and deliver solutions for decision making. The main functional areas covered by the suite are:

- ◆ **Analysis**: The analysis engine serves multidimensional analysis. It's provided by the **Mondrian OLAP** server.
- ◆ **Reporting**: The reporting engine allows designing, creating, and distributing reports in various known formats (HTML, PDF, and so on), from different kinds of sources.

- ◆ **Data Mining**: Data mining is used for running data through algorithms in order to understand the business and do predictive analysis. Data mining is possible thanks to the **Weka Project**.

- ◆ **Dashboards**: Dashboards are used to monitor and analyze **Key Performance Indicators (KPIs)**. The **Community Dashboard Framework (CDF)**, a plugin developed by the community and integrated in the Pentaho BI Suite, allows the creation of interesting dashboards including charts, reports, analysis views, and other Pentaho content, without much effort.

- ◆ **Data Integration**: Data integration is used to integrate scattered information from different sources (applications, databases, files, and so on), and make the integrated information available to the final user. Pentaho Data Integration—the tool that we will learn to use throughout the book—is the engine that provides this functionality.

All of this functionality can be used standalone but also integrated. In order to run analysis, reports, and so on, integrated as a suite, you have to use the **Pentaho BI Platform**. The platform has a solution engine, and offers critical services, for example, authentication, scheduling, security, and web services.

This set of software and services form a complete BI Platform, which makes Pentaho Suite the world's leading open source Business Intelligence Suite.

Exploring the Pentaho Demo

Despite being out of the scope of this book, it's worth to briefly introduce the Pentaho Demo. The **Pentaho BI Platform Demo** is a pre-configured installation that allows you to explore several capabilities of the Pentaho platform. It includes sample reports, cubes, and dashboards for Steel Wheels. Steel Wheels is a fictional store that sells all kind of scale replicas of vehicles. The following screenshot is a sample dashboard available in the demo:

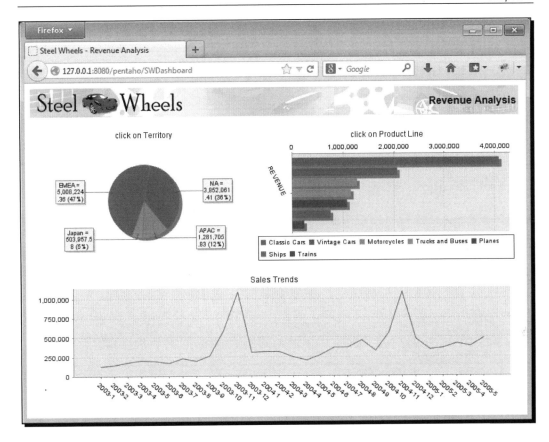

The Pentaho BI Platform Demo is free and can be downloaded from http://sourceforge.net/projects/pentaho/files/. Under the **Business Intelligence Server** folder, look for the latest stable version. By the time you read the book, Pentaho 5.0 may already have arrived. At the time of writing this book, the latest stable version is 4.8.0, so the file you have to download is **biserver-ce-4.8.0-stable.zip** for Windows and **biserver-ce-4.8.0-stable.tar.gz** for other systems.

> You can find out more about Pentaho BI Suite Community Edition at http://community.pentaho.com/projects/bi_platform. There is also an Enterprise Edition of the platform with additional features and support. You can find more on this at www.pentaho.org.

Pentaho Data Integration

Most of the Pentaho engines, including the engines mentioned earlier, were created as community projects and later adopted by Pentaho. The PDI engine is not an exception—Pentaho Data Integration is the new denomination for the business intelligence tool born as **Kettle**.

 The name Kettle didn't come from the recursive acronym Kettle Extraction, Transportation, Transformation, and Loading Environment it has now. It came from KDE Extraction, Transportation, Transformation, and Loading Environment, since the tool was planned to be written on top of KDE, a Linux desktop environment, as mentioned in the introduction of the book.

In April 2006, the Kettle project was acquired by the Pentaho Corporation and Matt Casters, the Kettle founder, also joined the Pentaho team as a Data Integration Architect.

When Pentaho announced the acquisition, James Dixon, Chief Technology Officer said:

> *We reviewed many alternatives for open source data integration, and Kettle clearly had the best architecture, richest functionality, and most mature user interface. The open architecture and superior technology of the Pentaho BI Platform and Kettle allowed us to deliver integration in only a few days, and make that integration available to the community.*

By joining forces with Pentaho, Kettle benefited from a huge developer community, as well as from a company that would support the future of the project.

From that moment, the tool has grown with no pause. Every few months a new release is available, bringing to the users improvements in performance, existing functionality, new functionality, ease of use, and great changes in look and feel. The following is a timeline of the major events related to PDI since its acquisition by Pentaho:

- **June 2006**: PDI 2.3 is released. Numerous developers had joined the project and there were bug fixes provided by people in various regions of the world. The version included among other changes, enhancements for large-scale environments and multilingual capabilities.

- **February 2007**: Almost seven months after the last major revision, PDI 2.4 is released including remote execution and clustering support, enhanced database support, and a single designer for jobs and transformations, the two main kind of elements you design in Kettle.

- **May 2007**: PDI 2.5 is released including many new features; the most relevant being the advanced error handling.

- **November 2007**: PDI 3.0 emerges totally redesigned. Its major library changed to gain massive performance. The look and feel had also changed completely.

- **October 2008**: PDI 3.1 arrives, bringing a tool which was easier to use, and with a lot of new functionality as well.

- **April 2009**: PDI 3.2 is released with a really large amount of changes for a minor version: new functionality, visualization and performance improvements, and a huge amount of bug fixes. The main change in this version was the incorporation of dynamic clustering.

- **June 2010**: PDI 4.0 was released, delivering mostly improvements with regard to enterprise features, for example, version control. In the community version, the focus was on several visual improvements such as the mouseover assistance that you will experiment with soon.

- **November 2010**: PDI 4.1 is released with many bug fixes.

- **August 2011**: PDI 4.2 comes to light not only with a large amount of bug fixes, but also with a lot of improvements and new features. In particular, several of them were related to the work with repositories (see *Appendix A, Working with Repositories* for details).

- **April 2012**: PDI 4.3 is released also with a lot of fixes, and a bunch of improvements and new features.

- **November 2012**: PDI 4.4 is released. This version incorporates a lot of enhancements and new features. In this version there is a special emphasis on Big Data—the ability of reading, searching, and in general transforming large and complex collections of datasets.

- **2013**: PDI 5.0 will be released, delivering interesting low-level features such as step load balancing, job transactions, and restartability.

Using PDI in real-world scenarios

Paying attention to its name, Pentaho Data Integration, you could think of PDI as a tool to integrate data.

In fact, PDI not only serves as a data integrator or an ETL tool. PDI is such a powerful tool, that it is common to see it used for these and for many other purposes. Here you have some examples.

Loading data warehouses or datamarts

The loading of a data warehouse or a datamart involves many steps, and there are many variants depending on business area, or business rules.

But in every case, no exception, the process involves the following steps:

- **Extracting** information from one or different databases, text files, XML files and other sources. The extract process may include the task of validating and discarding data that doesn't match expected patterns or rules.

- **Transforming** the obtained data to meet the business and technical needs required on the target. Transformation implies tasks as converting data types, doing some calculations, filtering irrelevant data, and summarizing.

- **Loading** the transformed data into the target database. Depending on the requirements, the loading may overwrite the existing information, or may add new information each time it is executed.

Kettle comes ready to do every stage of this loading process. The following screenshot shows a simple ETL designed with Kettle:

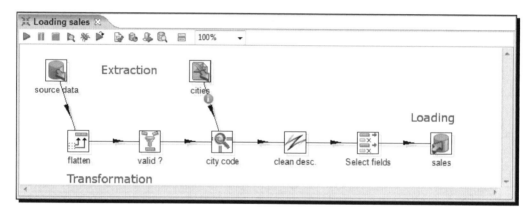

Integrating data

Imagine two similar companies that need to merge their databases in order to have a unified view of the data, or a single company that has to combine information from a main **ERP (Enterprise Resource Planning)** application and a **CRM (Customer Relationship Management)** application, though they're not connected. These are just two of hundreds of examples where data integration is needed. The integration is not just a matter of gathering and mixing data. Some conversions, validation, and transport of data have to be done. Kettle is meant to do all of those tasks.

Data cleansing

It's important and even critical that data be correct and accurate for the efficiency of business, to generate trust conclusions in data mining or statistical studies, to succeed when integrating data. Data cleansing is about ensuring that the data is correct and precise. This can be achieved by verifying if the data meets certain rules, discarding or correcting those which don't follow the expected pattern, setting default values for missing data, eliminating information that is duplicated, normalizing data to conform minimum and maximum values, and so on. These are tasks that Kettle makes possible thanks to its vast set of transformation and validation capabilities.

Migrating information

Think of a company, any size, which uses a commercial ERP application. One day the owners realize that the licenses are consuming an important share of its budget. So they decide to migrate to an open source ERP. The company will no longer have to pay licenses, but if they want to change, they will have to migrate the information. Obviously, it is not an option to start from scratch, nor type the information by hand. Kettle makes the migration possible thanks to its ability to interact with most kind of sources and destinations such as plain files, commercial and free databases, and spreadsheets, among others.

Exporting data

Data may need to be exported for numerous reasons:

◆ To create detailed business reports

◆ To allow communication between different departments within the same company

◆ To deliver data from your legacy systems to obey government regulations, and so on

Kettle has the power to take raw data from the source and generate these kind of ad-hoc reports.

Integrating PDI along with other Pentaho tools

The previous examples show typical uses of PDI as a standalone application. However, Kettle may be used embedded as part of a process or a dataflow. Some examples are pre-processing data for an online report, sending mails in a scheduled fashion, generating spreadsheet reports, feeding a dashboard with data coming from web services, and so on.

 The use of PDI integrated with other tools is beyond the scope of this book. If you are interested, you can find more information on this subject in the *Pentaho Data Integration 4 Cookbook* by Packt Publishing at http://www.packtpub.com/pentaho-data-integration-4-cookbook/book.

Pop quiz – PDI data sources

Q1. Which of the following are not valid sources in Kettle?

1. Spreadsheets.
2. Free database engines.
3. Commercial database engines.
4. Flat files.
5. None.

Installing PDI

In order to work with PDI, you need to install the software. It's a simple task, so let's do it now.

Time for action – installing PDI

These are the instructions to install PDI, for whatever operating system you may be using.

The only prerequisite to install the tool is to have JRE 6.0 installed. If you don't have it, please download it from `www.javasoft.com` and install it before proceeding. Once you have checked the prerequisite, follow these steps:

1. Go to the download page at `http://sourceforge.net/projects/pentaho/files/Data Integration`.

2. Choose the newest stable release. At this time, it is 4.4.0, as shown in the following screenshot:

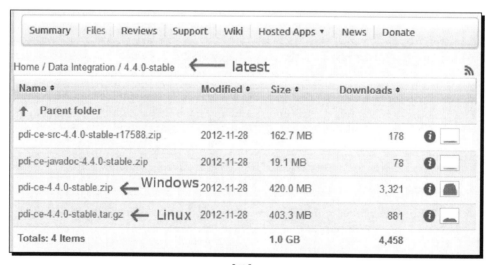

3. Download the file that matches your platform. The preceding screenshot should help you.

4. Unzip the downloaded file in a folder of your choice, that is, `c:/util/kettle` or `/home/pdi_user/kettle`.

5. If your system is Windows, you are done. Under Unix-like environments, you have to make the scripts executable. Assuming that you chose `/home/pdi_user/kettle` as the installation folder, execute:

```
cd /home/pdi_user/kettle
chmod +x *.sh
```

6. In Mac OS you have to give execute permissions to the `JavaApplicationStub` file. Look for this file; it is located in `Data Integration 32-bit.app\Contents\MacOS\`, or `Data Integration 64-bit.app\Contents\MacOS\` depending on your system.

What just happened?

You have installed the tool in just a few minutes. Now, you have all you need to start working.

Pop quiz – PDI prerequisites

Q1. Which of the following are mandatory to run PDI? You may choose more than one option.

1. Windows operating system.
2. Pentaho BI platform.
3. JRE 6.
4. A database engine.

Launching the PDI graphical designer – Spoon

Now that you've installed PDI, you must be eager to do some stuff with data. That will be possible only inside a graphical environment. PDI has a desktop designer tool named Spoon. Let's launch Spoon and see what it looks like.

Time for action – starting and customizing Spoon

In this section, you are going to launch the PDI graphical designer, and get familiarized with its main features.

1. Start Spoon.
   - If your system is Windows, run `Spoon.bat`

> You can just double-click on the `Spoon.bat` icon, or `Spoon` if your Windows system doesn't show extensions for known file types. Alternatively, open a command window—by selecting **Run** in the Windows start menu, and executing `cmd`, and run `Spoon.bat` in the terminal.

   - In other platforms such as Unix, Linux, and so on, open a terminal window and type `spoon.sh`
   - If you didn't make `spoon.sh` executable, you may type `sh spoon.sh`
   - Alternatively, if you work on Mac OS, you can execute the `JavaApplicationStub` file, or click on the `Data Integration 32-bit.app`, or `Data Integration 64-bit.app` icon

2. As soon as Spoon starts, a dialog window appears asking for the repository connection data. Click on the **Cancel** button.

> Repositories are explained in *Appendix A, Working with Repositories*. If you want to know what a repository connection is about, you will find the information in that appendix.

3. A small window labeled **Spoon tips...** appears. You may want to navigate through various tips before starting. Eventually, close the window and proceed.

4. Finally, the main window shows up. A **Welcome!** window appears with some useful links for you to see. Close the window. You can open it later from the main menu.

5. Click on **Options...** from the menu **Tools**. A window appears where you can change various general and visual characteristics. Uncheck the highlighted checkboxes, as shown in the following screenshot:

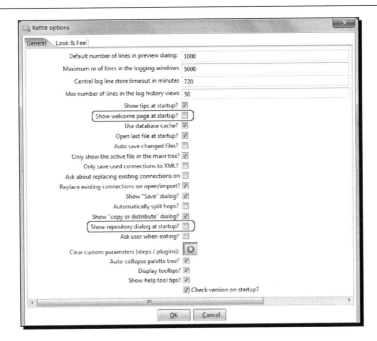

6. Select the tab window **Look & Feel**.

7. Change the **Grid size** and **Preferred Language** settings as shown in the following screenshot:

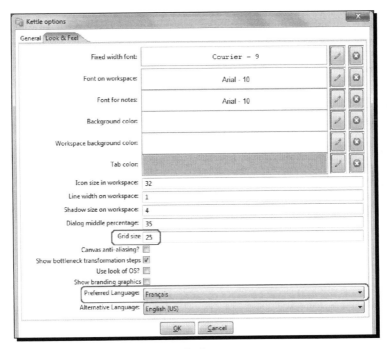

8. Click on the **OK** button.

9. Restart Spoon in order to apply the changes. You should not see the repository dialog, or the **Welcome!** window. You should see the following screenshot full of French words instead:

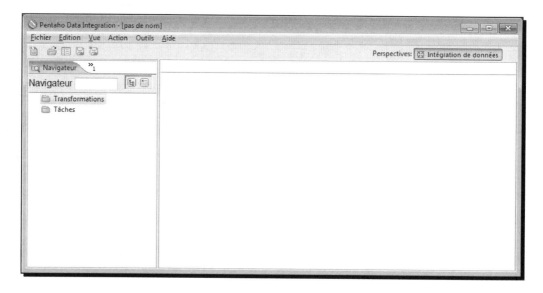

What just happened?

You ran for the first time Spoon, the graphical designer of PDI. Then you applied some custom configuration.

In the **Option...** tab, you chose not to show the repository dialog or the **Welcome!** window at startup. From the **Look & Feel** configuration window, you changed the size of the dotted grid that appears in the canvas area while you are working. You also changed the preferred language. These changes were applied as you restarted the tool, not before.

The second time you launched the tool, the repository dialog didn't show up. When the main window appeared, all of the visible texts were shown in French which was the selected language, and instead of the **Welcome!** window, there was a blank screen.

You didn't see the effect of the change in the **Grid** option. You will see it only after creating or opening a transformation or job, which will occur very soon!

Spoon

Spoon, the tool you're exploring in this section, is the PDI's desktop design tool. With Spoon, you design, preview, and test all your work, that is, **Transformations** and **Jobs**. When you see PDI screenshots, what you are really seeing are Spoon screenshots. The other PDI components which you will learn in the following chapters, are executed from terminal windows.

Setting preferences in the Options window

In the earlier section, you changed some preferences in the **Options** window. There are several look and feel characteristics you can modify beyond those you changed. Feel free to experiment with these settings.

[Remember to restart Spoon in order to see the changes applied.]

In particular, please take note of the following suggestion about the configuration of the preferred language.

[If you choose a preferred language other than English, you should select a different language as an alternative. If you do so, every name or description not translated to your preferred language, will be shown in the alternative language.]

One of the settings that you changed was the appearance of the **Welcome!** window at startup. The **Welcome!** window has many useful links, which are all related with the tool: wiki pages, news, forum access, and more. It's worth exploring them.

[You don't have to change the settings again to see the **Welcome!** window. You can open it by navigating to **Help | Welcome Screen**.]

Storing transformations and jobs in a repository

The first time you launched Spoon, you chose not to work with repositories. After that, you configured Spoon to stop asking you for the **Repository** option. You must be curious about what the repository is and why we decided not to use it. Let's explain it.

As we said, the results of working with PDI are transformations and jobs. In order to save the transformations and jobs, PDI offers two main methods:

◆ **Database repository**: When you use the database repository method, you save jobs and transformations in a relational database specially designed for this purpose.

◆ **Files**: The files method consists of saving jobs and transformations as regular XML files in the filesystem, with extension KJB and KTR respectively.

It's not allowed to mix the two methods in the same project. That is, it makes no sense to mix jobs and transformations in a database repository with jobs and transformations stored in files. Therefore, you must choose the method when you start the tool.

 By clicking on **Cancel** in the repository window, you are implicitly saying that you will work with the files method.

Why did we choose not to work with repositories? Or, in other words, to work with the files method? Mainly for two reasons:

◆ Working with files is more natural and practical for most users.

◆ Working with a database repository requires minimal database knowledge, and that you have access to a database engine from your computer. Although it would be an advantage for you to have both preconditions, maybe you haven't got both of them.

There is a third method called **File repository,** that is a mix of the two above—it's a repository of jobs and transformations stored in the filesystem. Between the File repository and the files method, the latest is the most broadly used. Therefore, throughout this book we will use the files method. For details of working with repositories, please refer to *Appendix A, Working with Repositories*.

Creating your first transformation

Until now, you've seen the very basic elements of Spoon. You must be waiting to do some interesting task beyond looking around. It's time to create your first transformation.

Time for action – creating a hello world transformation

How about starting by saying hello to the world? It's not really new, but good enough for our first practical example; here are the steps to follow:

1. Create a folder named `pdi_labs` under a folder of your choice.

2. Open Spoon.

3. From the main menu, navigate to **File | New | Transformation**.

4. On the left of the screen, under the **Design** tab, you'll see a tree of **Steps**. Expand the **Input** branch by double-clicking on it.

 Note that if you work in Mac OS a single click is enough.

5. Then, left-click on the **Generate Rows** icon and without releasing the button, drag-and-drop the selected icon to the main canvas. The screen will look like the following screenshot:

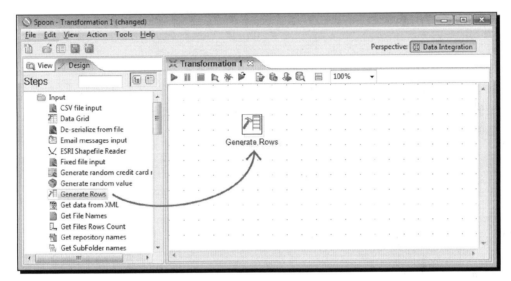

 Note that we changed the preferred language back to English.

6. Double-click on the **Generate Rows** step you just put in the canvas, and fill the textboxes, including **Step name** and **Limit** and grid as follows:

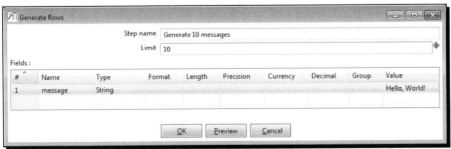

7. From the **Steps** tree, double-click on the **Flow** branch.

8. Click on the **Dummy (do nothing)** icon and drag-and-drop it to the main canvas.

9. Put the mouse cursor over the **Generate Rows** step and wait until a tiny toolbar shows up below the entry icon, as shown in the following screenshot:

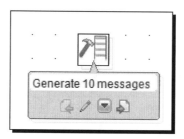

10. Click on the output connector (the last icon in the toolbar), and drag towards the **Dummy (do nothing)** step. A grayed hop is displayed.

11. When the mouse cursor is over the **Dummy (do nothing)** step, release the button. A link—a hop from now on—is created from the Generate Rows step to the **Dummy (do nothing)** step. The screen should look like the following screenshot:

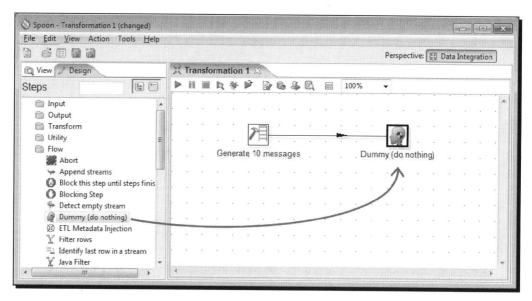

12. Right-click anywhere on the canvas to bring a contextual menu.

13. In the menu, select the **New note** option. A note editor appears.

14. Type some description such as `Hello, World!` Select the **Font style** tab and choose some nice font and colors for your note, and then click on **OK**.

15. From the main menu, navigate to **Edit | Settings....** A window appears to specify transformation properties. Fill the **Transformation name** textbox with a simple name, such as `hello world`. Fill the **Description** textbox with a short description such as `My first transformation`. Finally, provide a more clear explanation in the **Extended description** textbox, and then click on **OK**.

16. From the main menu, navigate to **File | Save**.

17. Save the transformation in the folder `pdi_labs` with the name `hello_world`.

18. Select the **Dummy (do nothing)** step by left-clicking on it.

19. Click on the Preview icon in the bar menu above the main canvas. The screen should look like the following screenshot:

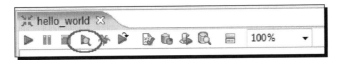

20. The **Transformation debug dialog** window appears. Click on the **Quick Launch** button.

21. A window appears to preview the data generated by the transformation as shown in the following screenshot:

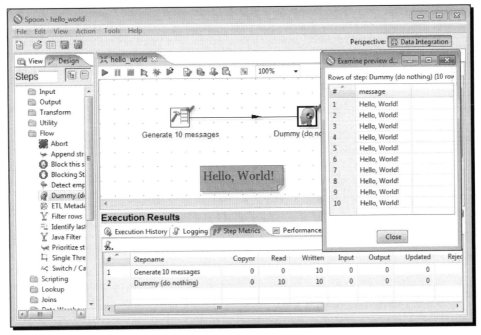

22. Close the preview window and click on the Run icon. The screen should look like the following screenshot:

23. A window named **Execute a transformation** appears. Click on **Launch**.

24. The execution results are shown at the bottom of the screen. The **Logging** tab should look as follows:

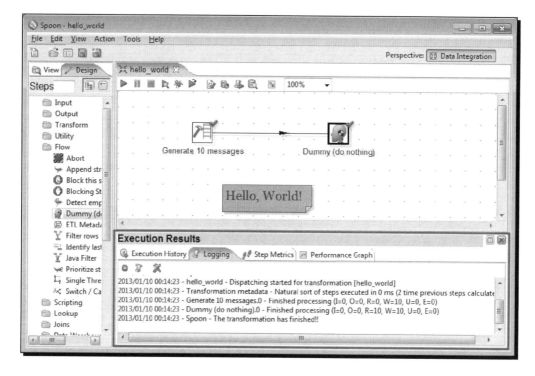

What just happened?

You have just created your first transformation.

First, you created a new transformation, dragged-and-dropped into the work area two steps: **Generate Rows** and **Dummy (do nothing)**, and connected them.

With the **Generate Rows** step you created 10 rows of data with the message `Hello World!` The **Dummy (do nothing)** step simply served as a destination of those rows.

After creating the transformation, you did a preview. The preview allowed you to see the content of the created data, this is, the 10 rows with the message **Hello World!**

Finally, you run the transformation. Then you could see at the bottom of the screen the **Execution Results** window, where a **Logging** tab shows the complete detail of what happened. There are other tabs in this window which you will learn later in the book.

Directing Kettle engine with transformations

A transformation is an entity made of steps linked by hops. These steps and hops build paths through which data flows—the data enters or is created in a step, the step applies some kind of transformation to it, and finally the data leaves that step. Therefore, it's said that a transformation is data flow oriented.

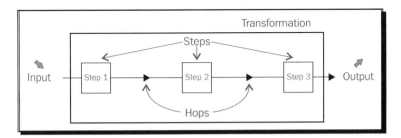

A transformation itself is neither a program nor an executable file. It is just plain XML. The transformation contains metadata which tells the Kettle engine what to do.

A step is the minimal unit inside a transformation. A big set of steps is available. These steps are grouped in categories such as the Input and Flow categories that you saw in the example.

Each step is conceived to accomplish a specific function, going from reading a parameter to normalizing a dataset.

Each step has a configuration window. These windows vary according to the functionality of the steps and the category to which they belong. What all steps have in common are the name and description:

Step property	Description
Name	A representative name inside the transformation.
Description	A brief explanation that allows you to clarify the purpose of the step. It's not mandatory but it is useful.

A **hop** is a graphical representation of data flowing between two steps: an origin and a destination. The data that flows through that hop constitute the output data of the origin step and the input data of the destination step.

Exploring the Spoon interface

As you just saw, Spoon is the tool with which you create, preview, and run transformations. The following screenshot shows you the basic work areas: **Main menu**, **Design view**, **Transformation toolbar**, and **Canvas (work area)**:

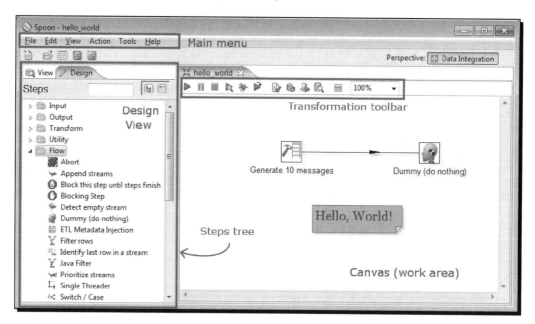

 The words canvas and work area will be used interchangeably throughout the book.

There is also an area named **View** that shows the structure of the transformation currently being edited. You can see that area by clicking on the **View** tab at the upper-left corner of the screen:

 Downloading the example code

You can download the example code files for all Packt books you have purchased from your account at http://www.packtpub.com. If you purchased this book elsewhere, you can visit http://www.packtpub.com/support and register to have the files e-mailed directly to you.

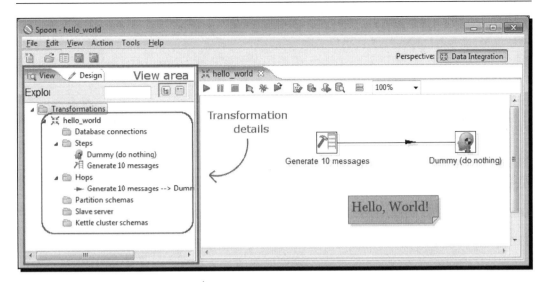

Designing a transformation

In the earlier section, you designed a very simple transformation, with just two steps and one explanatory note. You learned to link steps by using the mouseover assistance toolbar. There are alternative ways to do the same thing. You can use the one that you feel more comfortable with. *Appendix D, Spoon Shortcuts* explains all of the different options to you. It also explains a lot of shortcuts to zoom in and out, align the steps, among others. These shortcuts are very useful as your transformations become more complex.

[*Appendix F, Best Practices,* explains the benefit of using shortcuts as well as other best practices that are invaluable when you work with Spoon, especially when you have to design and develop big ETL projects.]

Running and previewing the transformation

The **Preview** functionality allows you to see a sample of the data produced for selected steps. In the previous example, you previewed the output of the **Dummy (do nothing)** step.

The Run icon effectively runs the whole transformation.

Whether you preview or run a transformation, you'll get an **Execution Results** window showing what happened. You will learn more about this in the next chapter.

Pop quiz – PDI basics

Q1. There are several graphical tools in PDI, but Spoon is the most used.

    1. True.
    2. False.

Q2. You can choose to save transformations either in files or in a database.

    1. True.
    2. False.

Q3. To run a transformation, an executable file has to be generated from Spoon.

    1. True.
    2. False.

Q4. The grid size option in the Look & Feel window allows you to resize the work area.

    1. True.
    2. False.

Q5. To create a transformation you have to provide external data (that is, text file, spreadsheet, database, and so on).

    1. True.
    2. False.

Installing MySQL

Before skipping to the next chapter, let's devote some time to the installation of MySQL.

In *Chapter 8*, *Working with Databases*, you will begin working with databases from PDI. In order to do that, you will need access to a database engine. As MySQL is the world's most popular open source database, it was the database engine chosen for the database-related tutorials in this book.

In this section, you will learn how to install the MySQL database engine both on Windows and on Ubuntu, the most popular distribution of Linux these days. As the procedures for installing the software are different, a separate explanation is given for each system.

 Mac users may refer to the Ubuntu section, as the installation procedure is similar for both systems.

Time for action – installing MySQL on Windows

In order to install MySQL on your Windows system, please follow these instructions:

1. Open an Internet browser and type `http://dev.mysql.com/downloads/installer`.

2. You will be directed to a page with the downloadable installer. Click on **Download** and the download process begins.

3. Double-click on the downloaded file, whose name should be `mysql-installer-community-5.5.29.0.msi` or similar, depending on the current version that you are running in this section.

4. In the window that shows up, select **Install MySQL Products**. A wizard will guide you through the process.

5. When asked to choose a setup type, select **Server only**.

6. Several screens follow. In all cases, leave the proposed default values. If you are prompted for the installation of missing components (for example, Microsoft .NET Framework 4 Client Profile), accept it, or you will not be able to continue.

7. When the installation is complete, you will have to configure the server. You will have to supply a password for the root user.

MySQL will not allow remote connections by default, so a simple password such as 123456 or passwd will suffice. Stronger passwords are necessary only if you plan to open up the MySQL server to external connections.

8. Optionally, you will have the choice of creating additional users. The following screenshot shows this step of the installation. In this case, we are telling the installer to create a user named pdi_user with the role of a **DB Designer**:

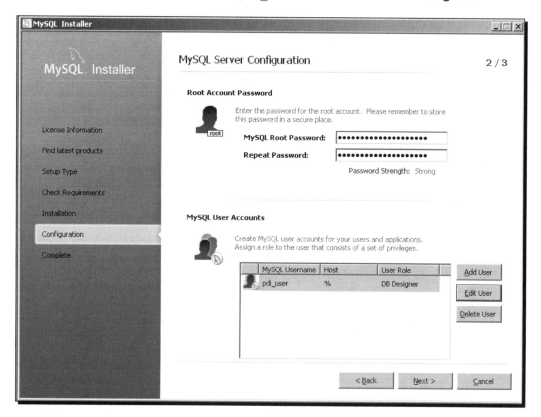

9. When the configuration process is complete, click on **Finish**.

10. MySQL server is now installed as a service. To verify that the installation has been successful, navigate to **Control Panel | Administrative Tools | Services**, and look for **MySQL**. This is what you should see:

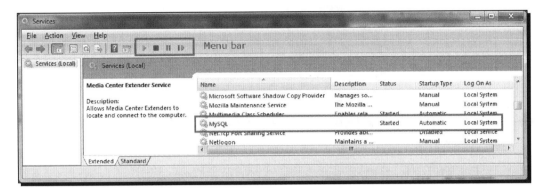

11. At any moment you can start or stop the service using the buttons in the menu bar at the top of the **Services** window, or the contextual menu that appears when you right-click on the service.

What just happened?

You downloaded and installed MySQL on your Windows system, using the **MySQL Installer** software. MySQL Installer simplifies the installation and upgrading of MySQL server and all related products. However, using this software is not the only option you have.

> For custom installations of MySQL or for troubleshooting you can visit
> `http://dev.mysql.com/doc/refman/5.5/en/windows-installation.html`.

Time for action – installing MySQL on Ubuntu

This section shows you the procedure to install MySQL on Ubuntu. Before starting, please note that Ubuntu typically includes MySQL out of the box. So if that's the case, you're done. If not, please follow these instructions:

 In order to follow the tutorial you need to be connected to the Internet

1. Open **Ubuntu Software Center**.

2. In the search textbox, type `mysql`. A list of results will be displayed as shown in the following screenshot:

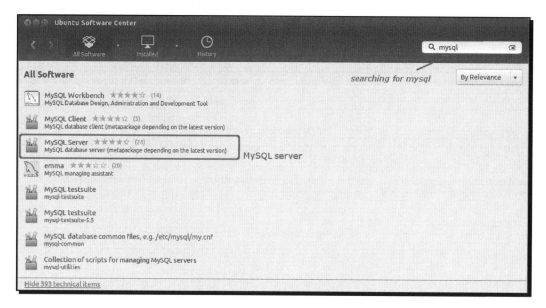

3. Among the results, look for **MySQL Server** and click on it. In the window that shows up, click on **Install**. The installation begins.

 Note that if MySQL is already installed, this button will not be available.

4. At a particular moment, you will be prompted for a password for the root user—the administrator of the database engine. Enter a password of your choice. You will have to enter it twice.

5. When the installation ends, the MySQL server should start automatically. To check if the server is running, open a terminal and run this:

    ```
    sudo netstat -tap | grep mysql
    ```

6. You should see the following line or similar:

    ```
    tcp    0    0 localhost:mysql         *:*         LISTEN    -
    ```

7. At any moment, you can start the service using this command:

    ```
    /etc/rc.d/init.d/mysql start
    ```

8. Or stop it using this:

    ```
    /etc/rc.d/init.d/mysql stop
    ```

What just happened?

You installed MySQL server in your Ubuntu system. In particular, the screens that were displayed belong to Version 12 of the operating system.

 The previous directions are for a standard installation. For custom installations you can visit this page `https://help.ubuntu.com/12.04/serverguide/mysql.html`. For instructions related to other operating systems or for troubleshooting information you can check the MySQL documentation at `http://dev.mysql.com/doc/refman/5.5/en/windows-installation.html`.

Have a go hero – installing a visual software for administering and querying MySQL

Beside the MySQL server, it's recommended that you install some visual software that will allow you to administer and query MySQL. Now it's your time to look for a software of your choice and install it.

One option would be installing the official GUI tool: MySQL Workbench. On Windows, you can install it with the MySQL Installer. In Ubuntu, the installation process is similar to that of the MySQL server.

Another option would be to install a generic open source tool, for example, SQuirrel SQL Client, a graphical program that will allow you to work with MySQL as well as with other database engines. For more information about this software, visit this link: `http://squirrel-sql.sourceforge.net/`.

Summary

In this chapter, you were introduced to Pentaho Data Integration. Specifically, you learned what Pentaho Data Integration is and you installed the tool. You also were introduced to Spoon, the graphical designer tool of PDI, and created your first transformation.

As an additional exercise, you installed a MySQL server. You will need this software when you start working with databases in *Chapter 8, Working with Databases*.

Now that you have learned the basics, you are ready to begin experimenting with transformations. That is the topic of the next chapter.

2

Getting Started with Transformations

In the previous chapter, you used the graphical designer Spoon to create your first transformation: Hello world. Now you're ready to begin transforming data, and at the same time get familiar with the Spoon environment.

In this chapter, you will:

- ◆ Learn the simplest ways of transforming data
- ◆ Get familiar with the process of designing, debugging, and testing a transformation
- ◆ Explore the available features for running transformations from Spoon
- ◆ Learn basic PDI terminology related with data
- ◆ Get an introduction to handling runtime errors

Designing and previewing transformations

In the first chapter, you created a Hello world transformation, previewed the data, and also ran the transformation. As you saw, the preview functionality allows you to see a sample of the data produced for selected steps and the Run option effectively runs the whole transformation. In this section, you will experiment the Preview option in detail. You will also deal with errors that may appear as you develop and test a transformation.

Time for action – creating a simple transformation and getting familiar with the design process

In this exercise, you will create a simple transformation that takes a list of projects with the start and end dates, and calculates the time that it took to complete each project.

1. Start Spoon.

2. From the main menu, navigate to **File | New | Transformation**.

3. Expand the **Input** branch of the **Steps** tree. Remember that the **Steps** tree is located in the **Design** tab to the left of the work area.

4. Drag-and-drop the **Data Grid** icon on the canvas.

5. Double-click on the **Data Grid** icon and enter projects in the **Step name** field.

6. Fill in the grid as shown in the following screenshot:

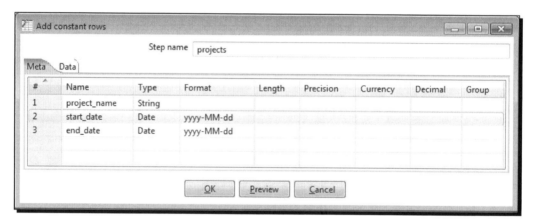

7. Click on the **Data** tab, and fill the grid as shown in the following screenshot:

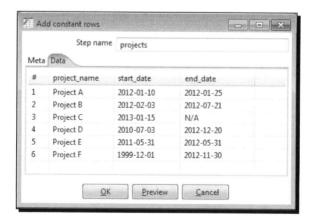

8. Click on **Preview** and in the small window that appears, click on **OK**.

9. Oops! It seems that something went wrong. The following **ERROR** window appears:

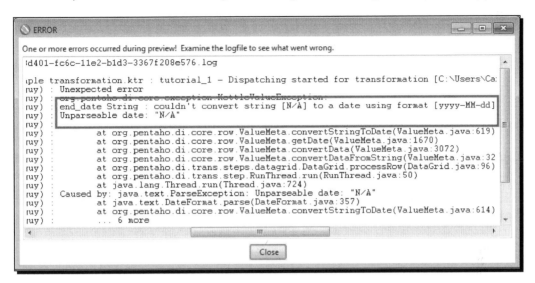

10. Great! Now you know what the error was: Kettle tried to convert the string N/A to a date. You can easily fix it: delete the N/A value, leaving the cell empty.

11. Try the preview again. This time you should see a preview window with the six rows of data you typed into the grid. Then close the window.

12. Now expand the **Transform** branch of steps. Look for the **Calculator** step and drag-and-drop it to the work area.

13. Create a hop from the **Data Grid** step towards the **Calculator** step. Remember that you can do it using the mouseover assistance toolbar.

 Don't miss this step! If you do, the fields will not be available in the next dialog window.

14. Double-click on the **Calculator** step and fill in the grid as shown in the following screenshot:

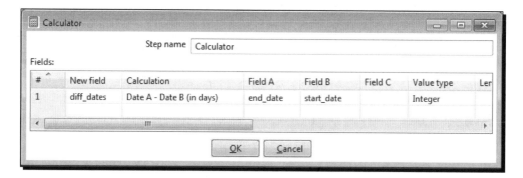

15. Click on **OK** to close the window.

16. Now add a new step: **Number range**. This step is also inside the **Transform** branch of steps.

 If you have difficulty in finding a step, you can type the search criteria in the textbox on top of the **Steps** tree. Kettle will filter and show only the steps that match your search.

17. Link the **Calculator** step to the **Number range** step with a new hop. Make sure that the arrow goes from the **Calculator** step towards the **Number range** step, and not the other way.

18. Double-click on the **Number range** step and fill in the grid as shown in the following screenshot. Then click on **OK**:

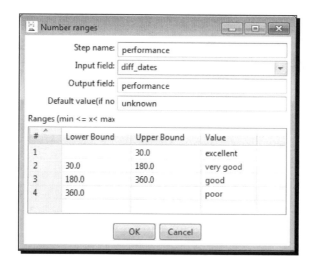

19. Finally, from the **Scripting** branch, add a **User Defined Java Expression** step.

20. Create a hop from the **Number range** step towards this new step. When you create the hop, you will be prompted for the kind of hop. Select **Main output of step**:

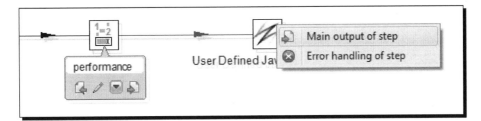

 If you unintentionally select the wrong option, don't worry. Right-click on the hop and a contextual menu will appear. Select **Delete hop**, and create the hop again.

21. Double-click on the **User Defined Java Expression** step or UDJE for short, and fill in the grid as shown in the following screenshot:

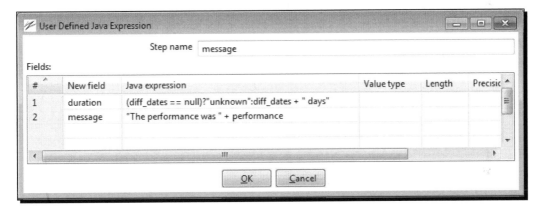

22. Click on **OK** to close the window. Your final transformation should look like the following screenshot:

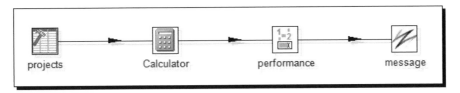

23. Now, let's do a preview at each step to see what the output in each case is. Let's start with the **Calculator** step. Select it and run a preview. You already know how to do it: click on the Preview icon in the transformation toolbar and then click on **Quick Launch**. You'll see the following screenshot:

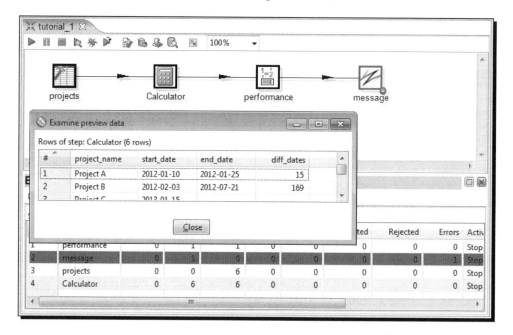

24. Something was wrong with the UDJE step! Well, we don't know what the error was, but don't worry. Let's do this, step-by-step. Click on the hop that leaves the **Number range** step to disable it. It will become light gray.

25. Select the **Calculator** step and try the preview again. As you disabled the hop, the steps beyond it will not be executed and you will not have the error, but a grid with the following results:

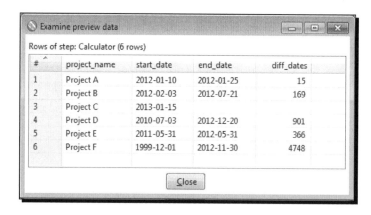

26. Now close the preview window, select the **Number range** step, and do a new preview. Again, you should see a grid with the results, but this time with a new column named `performance`.

27. Now it's time to see what was wrong with the **User Defined Java Expression** step. Enable the hop that you had disabled. You can do that by clicking on it again.

28. Select the UDJE step and try to run a preview. You will see an error window telling you that there weren't any rows to display. Close the preview window and switch to the **Logging** tab. In the logging table, you will see the error. The message, however, will not be very verbose. You'll just see: `Errors detected!`

29. Let's try another option. Before we do that, save the transformation.

30. Now run the transformation. You can do it by clicking on the Run icon on the transformation toolbar, or by pressing *F9*.

31. Click on **Launch**.

32. This time, the error is clear:

```
Please specify a String type to parse [java.lang.String] for
    field [duration] as a result of formula [(diff_dates ==
    null)?"unknown":diff_dates + " days"]
```

33. We forgot to specify the data types for the fields defined in the UDJE step. Fix the error by editing the step, and selecting `String` from the `Value type` column for both fields: `duration` and `message`.

34. Close the window, make sure the UDJE step is selected, and run a final preview. The error should have disappeared and the window should display the final data:

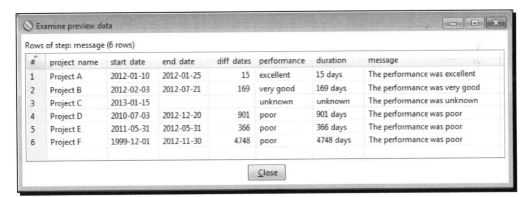

What just happened?

You created a very simple transformation that performed some calculations on a set of dummy data.

◆ A **Data Grid** step allowed you to create the starting set of data to work with. In the **Meta** tab, you defined three fields: a string named `project_name`, and two dates, `start_date` and `end_date`. Then, in the **Data** tab, you were prompted to fill in a grid with values for those three fields. You filled in the grid with six rows of values. A handy Preview icon allowed you to see the defined dataset.

◆ After that **Data Grid** step, you used a **Calculator** step. With this step, you created a new field: `diff_dates`. This field was calculated as **Date A - Date B (in days)**. As you must have guessed, this function expected two parameters. You provided those parameters in the `Field A` and `Field B` columns of the configuration window. You also told Kettle that the new field should be an integer. In this case, you only created one field, but you can define several fields in the same **Calculator** step.

◆ After that, you used a **Number range** step. This step simply creates a new field, `performance`, based on the value of a field coming from a previous step: `diff_dates`.

◆ Finally, you used a UDJE to create some informative messages: `duration`, `performance`, and `message`. As in the **Calculator** step, this step also allows you to create a new field per row. The main difference between both kind of steps is that while the **Calculator** step has a list of predefined formulas, the UDJE allows you to write your own expressions using Java code.

As you designed the transformation, you experimented with the preview functionality that allows you to get an idea of how the data is being transformed. In all cases, you were able to see the **Execution Results** window with the details of what was going on.

Besides that, you learned how to deal with errors that may appear as you create a transformation and test your work.

There is something important to note about the preview functionality you experimented with in this section.

> When you select a step for previewing, the objective is to preview the data as it comes out from that step. The whole transformation is executed unless you disable a part of it.

That is why you disabled the last step while running the preview of the **Calculator** step. By disabling it, you avoid the error that appeared the first time you ran the preview.

> Don't feel intimidated if you don't understand completely how the used steps work. By now, the objective is not to fully dominate Kettle steps, but to understand how to interact with Spoon. There will be more opportunities throughout the book to learn about the use of the steps in detail.

Getting familiar with editing features

Editing transformations with Spoon can be very time-consuming if you're not familiar with the editing facilities that the software offers. In this section, you will learn a bit more about two editing features that you already faced in the last section: using the mouseover assistance toolbar and editing grids.

Using the mouseover assistance toolbar

The **mouseover assistance toolbar**, as shown in the following screenshot, is a tiny toolbar that assists you when you position the mouse cursor over a step. You have already used some of its functionality. Here you have the full list of options.

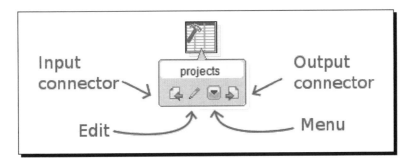

The following table explains each button in this toolbar:

Button	Description
Edit	It's equivalent to double-clicking on the step to edit it.
Menu	It's equivalent to right-clicking on the step to bring up the contextual menu.
Input connector	It's an assistant for creating hops directed toward this step. If the step doesn't accept any input (that is, a Data Grid step), the Input connector function is disabled.
Output connector	It's an assistant for creating hops leaving this step. It's used just like the Input connector, but the direction of the created hop is the opposite.

Depending on the kind of source step, you might be prompted for the kind of hop to create. For now, just select the **Main output of step** option just as you did in the section when created the last hop.

Working with grids

Grids are tables used in many instances in Spoon to enter or display information. You already edited grids in the configuration window of the Data Grid, Calculator, Number range, and UDJE steps.

Grids can be used for entering different kinds of data. No matter what kind of grid you are editing, there is always a contextual menu that you may access by right-clicking on a row. That menu offers editing options such as copy, paste, or move rows of the grid.

 When the number of rows in the grid are more, use shortcuts! Most of the editing options of a grid have shortcuts that make editing easier and quicker. You'll find a full list of shortcuts for editing grids in *Appendix D, Spoon Shortcuts*.

Understanding the Kettle rowset

Transformations deal with datasets, that is, data presented in a tabular form, where:

◆ Each column represents a field. A field has a name and a data type. The data type can be any of the common data types—Number (float), String, Date, Boolean, Integer, and Big number—or can also be of type Serializable or Binary.

 In PDI 5, you will see two new and very interesting data types: Internet Address and Timestamp.

◆ Each row corresponds to a given member of the dataset. All rows in a dataset have the same structure, that is, all rows have the same fields, in the same order. A field in a row may be null, but it has to be present.

A Kettle dataset is called rowset. The following screenshot is an example of rowset. It is the result of the preview in the Calculator step:

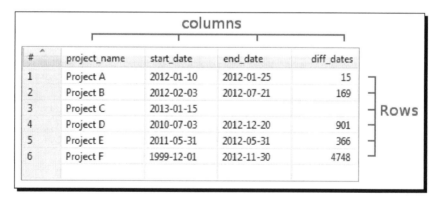

In this case, you have four columns representing the four fields of your rowset: project_ name, start_date, end_date, and diff_dates. You also have six rows of data, one for each project.

As we've already said, besides a name, each field has a data type. If you move the mouse cursor over a column title and leave it there for a second, you will see a small pop up telling you the data type of that field. For a full detail of the structure of the dataset, there is another option: select the **Calculator** step and press the space bar. A window named **Step fields and their origin** will appear:

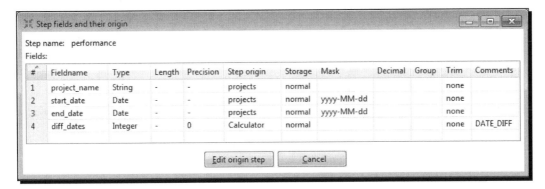

#	Fieldname	Type	Length	Precision	Step origin	Storage	Mask	Decimal	Group	Trim	Comments
1	project_name	String	-	-	projects	normal				none	
2	start_date	Date	-	-	projects	normal	yyyy-MM-dd			none	
3	end_date	Date	-	-	projects	normal	yyyy-MM-dd			none	
4	diff_dates	Integer	-	0	Calculator	normal				none	DATE_DIFF

Step name: performance

Edit origin step   *Cancel*

Alternatively, you could open this window from the contextual menu available in the mouseover assistance toolbar, or by right-clicking on the step. In the menu you have to select the **Show output fields** option.

In this window you don't only see the name and type of the fields, but also some extra columns, for example, the mask and the length of each field.

As the name of the option suggests, this is the description of the fields that leaves the step towards the following step.

If you selected **Show input fields** instead, you would see the metadata of the incoming data, that is, data that left the previous step.

One of the columns in these windows is Step origin. This column gives the name of the step where each field was created or modified. It's easy to compare the input fields against the output fields of a step. For example, in the **Calculator** step you created the field diff_dates. This field appears in the output fields of the step but not in the input list, as expected.

Looking at the results in the Execution Results pane

The **Execution Results** pane shows you what is happening while you preview or run a transformation. This pane is located below the canvas. If not immediately visible, it will appear when a transformation is previewed or run.

If you don't see this pane, you can open it by clicking on the last icon in the transformation toolbar.

The Logging tab

The **Logging** tab shows the execution of your transformation, step-by-step. By default, the level of the logging detail is **Basic logging** but you can choose among the following options: **Nothing at all, Error logging only, Minimal logging, Basic logging, Detailed logging, Debugging,** or **Rowlevel (very detailed)**. This is how you change the log level:

- If you run a transformation, just select the proper option in drop-down list available in the **Execute a transformation** window besides the **Log level** label.

- If you preview a transformation, instead of clicking on **Quick Launch**, select **Configure**. The **Execute a transformation** window appears allowing you to choose the desired level.

You should choose the option depending on the level of detail that you want to see, from **Nothing at all** to **Rowlevel (very detailed)**, which is the most detailed level of log. In most situations, however, you will be fine with the default value.

The Step Metrics tab

The **Step Metrics** tab shows, for each step of the transformation, the executed operations and several status and information columns. For us, the most relevant columns in this tab are:

Column	Description
Read	Contains the number of rows coming from previous steps.
Written	Contains the number of rows leaving from this step toward the next.
Input	Number of rows read from a file or table.
Output	Number of rows written to a file or table.
Errors	Errors in the execution. If there are errors, the whole row will become red.
Active	Gives the current status of the execution.

Recall what you did when you were designing your transformation. When you first did a preview on the Calculator step, you got an error. Go back to the *Time for action – creating a simple transformation and getting familiar with the design process* section in this chapter and look at the screenshot that depicts that error. The line for the UDJE step in the **Execution Results** window shows one error. The Active column shows that the transformation has been stopped. You can also see that the icon for that step changed: a red square indicates the situation.

When you ran the second preview on the Calculator step, you got the following results: in the Data Grid step the number of written rows is six which is the same as the number of read rows for the Calculator step. This step in turn writes 6 rows that travel toward the Number range step. The Number range step reads and also writes 6 rows, but the rows go nowhere because the hop that leaves the step was disabled. As a consequence, the next step, the UDJE, doesn't even appear in the window.

Finally, as we didn't work with files or databases, the `Input` and `Output` rows are zero in all cases.

Have a go hero – calculating the achieved percentage of work

Take as starting point the transformation you created in the earlier section, and implement the following:

1. Add a new field named `estimated`. The field must be a number, and will represent the number of days that you estimated for finishing the project.

     Add the field in the **Meta** tab of the **Data Grid** step, and then the values in the **Data** tab. Do a preview to see that the field has been added as expected.

2. Create a new field named `achieved` as the division between the amount of days taken to implement the project and the estimated time.

     You can use the same **Calculator** step that you used for calculating the `diff_dates` field.

3. Calculate the performance with a different criterion. Instead of deciding the performance based on the duration, calculate it based on the achieved percentage.

     In order to craft a true percentage, provide proper values for the `Length` and `Precision` columns of the new field, as length gives the total number of significant figures, and precision provides the number of floating point digits. For detailed examples on the use of these properties, you can take a look at the section *Numeric Fields* in *Chapter 4, Filtering, Searching, and Other Useful Operations*.

4. Modify the messages that were created in the last step, so they show the new information.

Have a go hero - calculating the achieved percentage of work (second version)

Modify the transformation of the previous section. This time, instead of using the Calculator step, do the math with UDJE.

The following are a few hints that will help you with the UDJE step:

◆ Here you have a Java expression for calculating the difference (in days) between dateA and dateB:

```
(dateB.getTime() - dateA.getTime())/ (1000 * 60 * 60 * 24)
```

◆ In UDJE, the expressions cannot reference a field defined in the same step. You should use two different UDJE steps for doing that.

Running transformations in an interactive fashion

In the previous section, you created a transformation and learned some basics about working with Spoon during the design process. Now you will continue learning about interacting with Spoon. This time you will create a new transformation and then run it.

Time for action – generating a range of dates and inspecting the data as it is being created

In this section, you will generate a rowset with one row by date in a date range.

As you progress, feel free to preview the data that is being generated even if you're not told to do so. This will help you understand what is going on. Testing each step as you move forward makes it easier to debug and craft a functional transformation.

1. Create a new transformation.
2. From the **Input** group of steps, drag to the canvas a **Generate Rows** step.

3. Double-click on the step and fill in the grid as shown in the following screenshot:

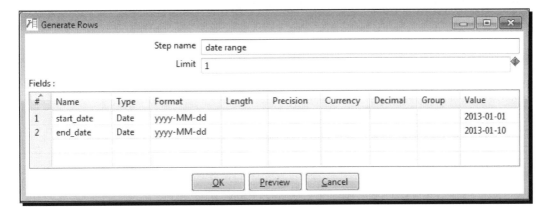

4. Note that you have to change the default value for the **Limit** textbox. Close the window.

5. From the **Transform** category of steps, add a **Calculator** step, and create a hop that goes from the **Generate Rows** step to this one.

6. Double-click on the **Calculator** step and add a field named diff_dates as the difference between end_date and start_date. That is, configure it exactly the same way as you did in the previous section.

7. Do a preview. You should see a single row with three fields: the start date, the end date, and a field with the number of days between both.

8. Now add a **Clone row** step. You will find it inside the **Utility** group of steps.

9. Create a hop from the **Calculator** step towards this new step.

10. Edit the **Clone row** step.

11. Select the **Nr clone in field?** option to enable the **Nr Clone field** textbox. In this textbox, type diff_dates.

12. Now select the **Add clone num to** option to enable the **Clone num field** textbox. In this textbox, type delta.

13. Run a preview. You should see the following:

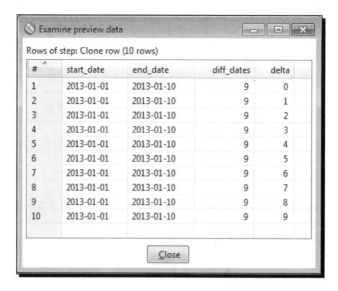

14. Add another **Calculator** step, and create a hop from the **Clone row** step to this one.

15. Edit the new step, and add a field named `a_single_date`. As `Calculation` select **Date A + B Days**. As `Field A` select **start_date**, and as `Field B` select **delta**. Finally, as `Value type` select **Date**. For the rest of the columns, leave the default values.

16. Now add two **Select values** steps. You will find them in the **Transform** branch of the **Steps** tree.

17. Link the steps as shown in the following screenshot. When you create the hop leaving the first **Select values** step you will be prompted for the kind of hop. Select **Main output of step**:

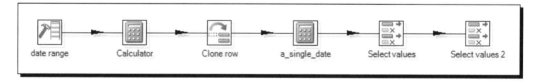

18. Edit the first of the **Select values** steps and select the **Meta-data** tab.

19. Under **Fieldname** type or select `a_single_date`. As `Type` select **String**. As `Format` type or select **MM/dd/yy**.

20. Close the window, and edit the second **Select values** step.

21. In the **Select & Alter** tab (which appears selected by default), under **Fieldname** type `a_single_date`.

22. Close the window and save your work.

23. Select the first of the **Select values** steps, and do a preview. You should see this:

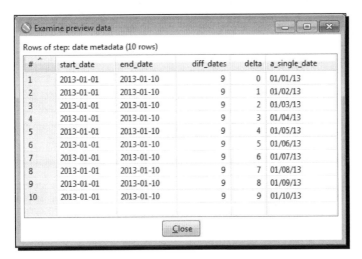

24. Try a preview on the second **Select values** step. You should only see the last column:
`a_single_date`.

 If you don't obtain the same results, check carefully that you followed the steps exactly as explained. If you hit errors in the middle of the section, you know how to deal with them. Take your time, read the log, fix the errors, and resume your work.

Now that you have an idea of what the transformation does, do the following modifications:

1. Edit the **Generate Rows** step and change the date range. As `end_date`, type `2023-12-31`.

2. From the **Utility** group of steps, drag to the work area a **Delay row** step.

3. Drag the step to the hop between the **Clone row** step and the second **Calculator** step until the hop changes the width:

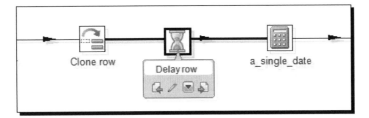

4. A window will appear asking you if you want to split the hop. Click on **Yes**. The hop will be split in two: one from the **Clone row** step to the **Delay row** step, and a second one from this step to the **Calculator** step.

 You can configure Kettle to split the hops automatically. You can do it by selecting the **Don't ask again?** checkbox in this same window, or by navigating to the **Tools | Options...** menu.

5. Double-click on the **Delay row** step, and configure it using the following information : as **Timeout**, type `500`, and in the drop-down list select **Milliseconds**. Close the window.

6. Save the transformation, and run it. You will see that it runs at a slower pace. This delay was deliberately caused by adding the **Delay row** step. We did this on purpose, so you could try the next steps.

7. Click on the second **Calculator** step. A pop-up window will show up describing the execution results of this step in real time. Control-click two more steps: the **Generate Rows** step and the **Clone row** step. You will see the following screenshot:

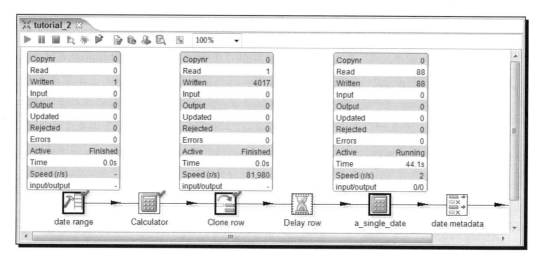

8. Now let's inspect the data itself. Right-click on the second **Calculator** step and navigate to **Sniff test during execution | Sniff test output rows**. A window will appear showing the data as it's being generated.

9. Now do the same in the second **Select values** step. A new window appears also showing the progress, but this time you will only see one column.

What just happened?

In this section, you basically did two things. First, you created a transformation and had the opportunity to learn some new steps. Then, you ran the transformation and inspected the data as the transformation was being executed. Let's explain these two tasks in detail.

The transformation that you created generated a dataset with all dates in between a given range of dates. How did you do it? First of all, you created a dataset with a single row with two fields: the start and end dates. But you needed as many rows as the dates between those reference dates. You did this trick with two steps. First, a **Calculator** step that calculated the difference between the dates, and then a **Clone row** step that not only cloned the single row as many times as you needed (diff_dates field), but also numerated those cloned rows (delta field). Then you used that delta field to create the desired field by adding start_date and delta.

After having your date field, you used two **Select values** steps: the first to convert the date to a string in a specific format MM/dd/yy, and the second for keeping just this field, and discarding all the others.

After creating the transformation, you added a **Delay row** step, to deliberately delay each row of data for 500 milliseconds. If you didn't do this, the transformation would run so fast that it wouldn't allow you to do the sniff testing. The **sniff testing** is the possibility of seeing the rows that are coming into or out of a step in real time. While the transformation was running, you experimented with this feature for sniffing the output rows. In the same way, you could have selected the **Sniff test input rows** option to see the incoming rows of data.

 Note that sniff testing slows down the transformation and its use is recommended just for debugging purposes.

Finally, in the **Execution Results** window, it's worth noting two columns that we hadn't mentioned before:

Column	Description
Time	The time that it's taking for the execution of each step.
Speed (r/s)	The speed calculated in rows per second.

As you put a delay of 500 milliseconds for each row, it's reasonable to see that the speed is 2 rows per second.

Adding or modifying fields by using different PDI steps

As you saw in the last transformation, once the data is created in the first step, it travels from step to step through the hops that link those steps. The hop's function is just to direct data from an output buffer to an input one. The real manipulation of data, as well as the modification of a stream by adding or removing fields occurs in the steps. In this section and also in the first section of this chapter, you used the Calculator Step to create new fields and add them to your dataset. The Calculator step is one of the many steps that PDI has to create new fields by combining existent ones. Usually, you will find these steps under the **Transform** category of the **Steps** tree. In the following table you have a description of some of the most used steps. The examples reference the first transformation you created in this chapter:

Step	Description	Example
Add constants	Add one or more fields with constant values.	If the start date was the same for all the projects, you could add that field with an Add constants step instead of typing the value for each row.
Add sequence	Add a field with a sequence. By default, the generated sequence will be 1, 2, 3 ... but you can change the start, increment, and maximum values to generate different sequences.	You could have created the delta field with an Add sequence step instead of using the Clone row step.
Number ranges	Create a new field based on ranges of values. Applies to a numeric field.	You used this step in the first section for creating the performance based on the duration of the project.
Replace in string	Replaces all occurrences of a text in a string field with another text.	The names of the projects include the word Project. With this step you could remove the word or replace it with a shorter one. The final name for Project A could be `Proj.A` or simply `A`.
Split Fields	Splits a single field into two or more. You have to give the character that acts as a separator.	Split the name of the project into two fields: the first word (that in this case is always Project) and the rest. The separator would be a space character.
Value Mapper	Creates a correspondence between the values of a field and a new set of values.	Suppose that you want to create a flag named `finished` with values Yes/No. The value should be No if the end date is absent, and Yes in other case. Note that you could also define the flag based on the performance field: the flag is No when the performance is unknown, and Yes for the rest of the values.

Step	Description	Example
User Defined Java Expression	Creates a new field by using a Java expression that involves one or more fields. This step may eventually replace any of the previous steps, but it's only recommended for those familiar with Java.	You used this step in the first section for creating two strings. You also had the chance of using it to do some math (refer the *Have a go hero - calculating the achieved percentage of work* section).

Any of these steps when added to your transformation, is executed for every row in the stream. It takes the row, identifies the fields needed to do its tasks, calculates the new field(s), and adds it to the dataset.

 For more details on a particular step, don't hesitate to visit the Wiki page for steps at:
`http://wiki.pentaho.com/display/EAI/`
`Pentaho+Data+Integration+Steps`.

The Select values step

Despite being classified as member of the Transform category, just like most of the steps mentioned in the previous section, the Select values step is a very particular step and deserves a separate explanation. This step allows you to select, rename, and delete fields, or change the metadata of a field. The configuration window of the step has three tabs:

- **Select & Alter**
- **Remove**
- **Meta-data**

 You may use only one of the Select values step tabs at a time. Kettle will not restrain you from filling more than one tab, but that could lead to unexpected behavior.

The **Select & Alter** tab which appears selected by default lets you specify the fields that you want to keep. You used it in the previous section for keeping just the last created field: the date field. This tab can also be used to rename the fields or reorder them. You may have noticed that each time you add a new field, this tab is added at the end of the list of fields. If for any reason you want to put it in another place, this is the step for doing that.

The **Remove** tab is useful to discard undesirable fields. This tab is useful if you want to remove just a few fields. For removing many, it's easier to use the **Select & Alter** tab, and specify not the fields to remove, but the fields to keep.

Removing fields by using this tab is expensive from a performance point of view. Please don't use it unless needed!

Finally, the **Meta-data** tab is used when you want to change the definition of a field. In the earlier section, you used it in the first **Select values** step. In this case, you changed the metadata of the field named `a_single_date`. The field was of the `Date` type, and you changed it to a `String`. You also told Kettle to convert the date using MM/dd/yy as the format. For example, the date `January 31st 2013` will be converted to the string `01/31/13`. In the next section, you will learn more about date formats.

Getting fields

The Select values step is just one of several steps that contain field information. In these cases, the grids are usually accompanied by a **Get Fields** button. The **Get Fields** button is a facility to avoid typing. When you press that button, Kettle fills the grid with all the available fields.

 Every time you see a **Get Fields** button, consider it as a shortcut to avoid typing. Kettle will bring the fields available to the grid, and you will only have to check the information brought, and do minimal changes.

The name of the button is not necessarily **Get Fields**.

 In the case of the Select values step, depending on the selected tab, the name of the button changes to **Get fields to select**, **Get fields to remove**, or **Get fields to change**, but the purpose of the button is the same in all cases.

Date fields

As we've already said, every field in a Kettle dataset must have a data type. Among the available data types, namely `Number` (float), `String`, `Date`, `Boolean`, `Integer`, and `BigNumber`, `Date` is one of the most used.

Look at the way you defined the start and end date in the earlier section. You told Kettle that these were `Date` fields, with the format **yyyy-MM-dd**. What does it mean? To Kettle, it means that when you provide a value for that field, it has to interpret the field as a date, where the four first positions represent the year, then there is a hyphen, then two positions for the month, another hyphen, and finally two positions for the day. This way, Kettle knows how to interpret, for example, the string `2013-01-01` that you typed as the start date. Something similar occurred with the date fields in the Data Grid step you created in the previous section.

Generally speaking, when a `Date` field is created, like the fields in the example, you have to specify the format of the date so Kettle can recognize in the values the different components of the date. There are several formats that may be defined for a date; all of them combinations of letters that represent date or time components.

 These format conventions are not Kettle specific, but based on this class in the Java library.

The following table shows the main letters used for specifying date formats:

Letter	Meaning
y	Year
M	Month
d	Day
H	Hour (0-23)
m	Minutes
s	Seconds

There is also the opposite case: a `Date` type converted to a `String` type, such as that in the first Select values step of the earlier section. In this case, the format doesn't indicate how to interpret a given text, but which format to apply to the date when converted to a string. In other words, it indicates how the final string should look. It's worth mentioning a couple of things about this conversion. Let's explain this taking as an example the date `January 31st, 2012`:

- A format does not have to have all the pieces for a date. As an example, your format could be simply `yyyy`. With this format, your full date will be converted to a string with just four positions representing the year of the original date. In the given example, the date field will be converted to the string `2012`.

- In case you don't specify a format, Kettle sets a default format. In the given example, this default will be `2012/01/31 00:00:00.000`.

 As we've already said, there are more combinations to define the format to a `Date` field. For a complete reference, check the Sun Java API documentation, located at:
`http://java.sun.com/javase/7/docs/api/java/text/`
`SimpleDateFormat.html`

Pop quiz – generating data with PDI

For each of the following rowsets, can the data be generated with:

1. A Data Grid step.
2. A Generate Rows step.
3. Any of the above options.

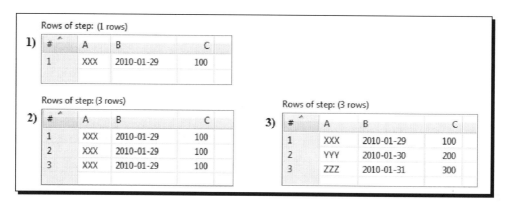

Have a go hero – experiencing different PDI steps

Taking as a starting point the transformation that you created in the first section, try implementing each of the examples provided in the section named *Adding or modifying fields by using different PDI steps*.

Have a go hero – generating a rowset with dates

Create a transformation that generates the following dataset:

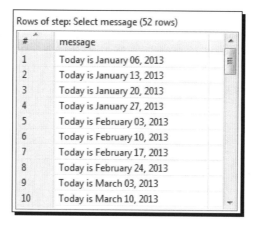

The dataset has only one field of type `String`. There is one row for each Sunday starting from **January 06, 2013** and ending at **December 29, 2013**. The transformation in the last section can serve as a model.

The following are a few hints that will help you:

- For knowing how many rows to generate, do a little more math in the calculator
- For generating the dates, combine the use of the **Clone row** and **Add sequence** steps
- For generating the message, change the metadata of the date to string using the proper format (if necessary visit the format documentation), and then construct the string by using either a UDJE or a Calculator step

Handling errors

So far, each time you got an error you had the opportunity to discover what kind of error it was and fix it. This is quite different form real scenarios, mainly for two reasons:

- Real data has errors—a fact that cannot be avoided. If you fail to heed it, the transformations that run with test or sample data will probably crash when running with real data.
- In most cases, your final work is run by an automated process and not by a user from Spoon. Therefore, if a transformation crashes, there will be nobody who notices and reacts to that situation.

In the next section, you will learn the simplest way to trap errors that may occur, avoiding unexpected crashes. This is the first step in the creation of transformations ready to be run in a production environment.

Time for action – avoiding errors while converting the estimated time from string to integer

In this section, you will create a variation of the first transformation in this chapter. In this case, you will allow invalid data as source, but will take care of it:

1. Create a transformation.
2. Add a **Data Grid** step and fill in the **Meta** tab just like you did in the first section: add a string named `project_name` and two dates with the format **yyyy-MM-dd**, named **start_date** and **end_date**. Also add a fourth field of type `String`, named `estimated`.

3. Now also fill in the **Data** tab with the same values you had in that first section. For the `estimated` field, type the following values: `30, 180, 180, 700, 700, ---`.

> You can avoid typing all of this in again! Instead of adding and configuring the step from scratch, open the transformation you created in the first section, select the **Data Grid** step, copy it by pressing *Ctrl + C*, and paste it into the new transformation by pressing *Ctrl + V*. Then enter the new information, the metadata, and the data for the new field.

4. Now add a **Select values** step and create a hop from the **Data Grid** step towards it.

5. Double-click on the **Select values** step and select the **Meta-data** tab.

6. Under **Fieldname** type or select `estimated`, and under `Type` select `Integer`.

7. Close the window.

8. Now, just like you did in the first section, add a **Calculator** step to calculate the field named `diff_dates` as the difference between the dates.

9. In the **Calculator** step, also define a new field named `achieved`. As `Calculation`, select **A / B**. As `Field A` and `Field B` select or type **diff_dates** and **estimated**, respectively. As `Value type`, select `Number`. Finally, as `Conversion mask` type `0.00%`.

10. Create a hop from the **Select values** step to the **Calculator** step. When asked for the kind of hop to create, select **Main output of step**.

11. Drag to the canvas a **Write to log** step. You will find it in the **Utility** category of steps.

12. Create a new hop from the **Select values** step, but this time the hop has to go to the **Write to log** step. When asked for the kind of hop to create, select **Error handling of step**. Then, the following **Warning** window appears:

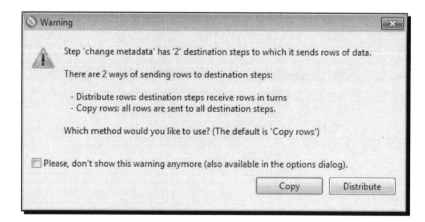

13. Click on **Copy**.

For now, you don't have to worry about these two offered options. You will learn about them in *Chapter 5, Controlling the Flow of Data*.

14. Now your transformation should look like as shown in the following screenshot:

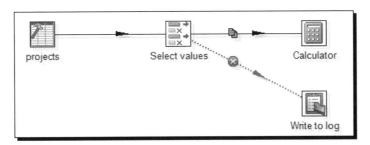

15. Double-click on the **Write to log** step. In the **Write to log** textbox type `There was an error changing the metadata of a field`.

16. Click on **Get Fields**. The grid will be populated with the name of the fields coming from the previous step.

17. Close the window and save the transformation.

18. Now run it. Look at the **Logging** tab in the **Execution Results** window. The log will look like the following screenshot:

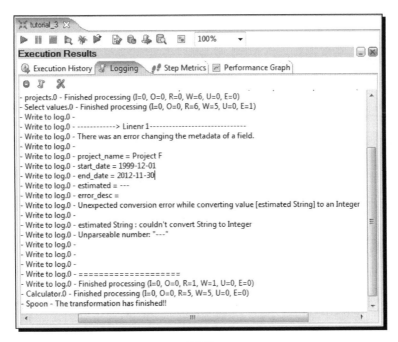

19. Do a preview of the **Calculator** step. You will see all of the lines except that line containing the invalid estimated time. In these lines, you will see the two fields calculated in this step.

20. Do a preview on the **Write to log** step. You will only see the line that had the invalid estimated time.

What just happened?

In this section, you learned one way of handling errors. You created a set of data, and intentionally introduced an invalid number for the `estimated` field. If you defined the `estimated` field as an `Integer`, Kettle would throw an error. In order to avoid that situation, you did the following:

1. Defined the field as a string. The `String` type has no limitations for the kind of text to put in it.

2. Then you changed the metadata of this field, converting it to an integer.

If you had done only that, nothing would have changed. The error would have appeared anyway, not in the Data Grid, but in the Select values step. So, this is how you handled the error. You created an alternative stream, represented with the hop in red, where the rows with errors go. As you could see both in the preview and in the **Execution Results** windows, the rows with valid values continued their way towards the **Calculator** step, while the row whose estimated value could not be converted to `Integer` went to the **Write to log** step. In the **Write to log** step you wrote an informative message as well as the values for all the fields, so it is easy to identify which row was the one that caused this situation.

The error handling functionality

With the error handling functionality, you can capture errors that otherwise would cause the transformation to halt. Instead of aborting, the rows that cause the errors are sent to a different stream for further treatment.

You don't need to implement error handling in every step. In fact, you cannot do that because not all steps support error handling. The objective of error handling is to implementing it in the steps where it is more likely to have errors. In the previous section, you faced a typical situation where you should consider handling errors. Changing the metadata of fields works perfectly, just as long as you know that the data is good, but it might fail when executing against real data. Another common use of error handling is when working with JavaScript code, or with databases. You will learn more on this later on in this book.

In the previous section, you handled the error in the simplest way. There are some options that you may configure. The next section teaches you how to personalize the error handling option.

Time for action – configuring the error handling to see the description of the errors

In this section, you will adapt the previous transformation so that you can capture more detail about the errors that occur:

1. Open the transformation from the previous section, and save it with a different name. You can do it from the main menu by navigating to **File | Save as...**, or from the main toolbar.

2. Right-click on the **Select values** step and select **Define Error handling....** The following dialog window appears:

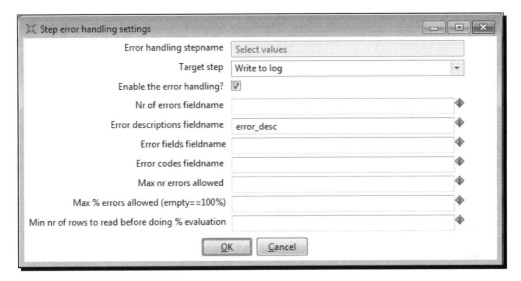

3. In the **Error descriptions fieldname** textbox, type `error_desc` and click on **OK**.

4. Double-click on the **Write to log** step and, after the last row, type or select `error_desc`.

5. Save the transformation.

6. Do a preview on the **Write to log** step. You will see a new field named `error_desc` with the description of the error.

7. Run the transformation. In the Execution Window, you will see the following code:

```
Write to log.0 - ------------> Linenr 1----------------------
Write to log.0 - There was an error changing the metadata of a
field.
Write to log.0 -
Write to log.0 - project_name = Project F
```

```
Write to log.0 - start_date = 1999-12-01
Write to log.0 - end_date = 2012-11-30
Write to log.0 - estimated = ---
Write to log.0 - error_desc =
Write to log.0 - Unexpected conversion error while converting
value [estimated String] to an Integer
Write to log.0 -
Write to log.0 - estimated String : couldn't convert String to
Integer
Write to log.0 - Unparseable number: "---"
Write to log.0 -
```

Downloading the example code

You can download the example code files for all Packt books you have purchased from your account at http://www.packtpub.com. If you purchased this book elsewhere, you can visit http://www.packtpub.com/support and register to have the files e-mailed directly to you.

What just happened?

You modified a transformation that captured errors, by changing the default configuration of the error handling. In this case, you added a new field containing the description of the errors. You also wrote the value of the new field to the log.

Personalizing the error handling

The **Error handling setting** window gives you the chance to overwrite the default values of the error handling. Basically, this window allows you to do two kinds of things: configure additional fields describing the errors, and control the number of errors to capture.

The first textboxes are meant to be filled with the names of the new fields. As an example, in the previous section you filled the textbox **Error descriptions fieldname** with the word error_desc. Then, you could see that the output dataset of this step had a new field named error_desc with a description of the error.

The following table shows all the available options for fields describing the errors:

Field	Description
Nr of errors fieldname	Name of the field that will have the number of errors
Error descriptions fieldname	Name of the field that will have the error description
Error fields fieldname	Name of the field that will have the name of the field(s) that caused the errors
Error codes fieldname	Name of the field that will have the error code

As you saw, you are not forced to fill in all these textboxes. Only the fields for which you provide a name will be added to the dataset. These added fields can be used as any other field. In the previous section, for example, you wrote the field to the log just as you did with the rest of the fields in your dataset.

The second thing that you can do in this setting window is control the number of errors to capture. You do it by configuring the following settings:

- **Max nr errors allowed**
- **Max % errors allowed (empty==100%)**
- **Min nr of rows to read before doing % evaluation**

The meaning of these settings is quite straightforward, but let's make it clear with an example. Suppose that you set **Max nr errors allowed** to 10, **Max % errors allowed (empty==100%)** to 20, and **Min nr of rows to read before doing % evaluation** to 100. The result will be that after 10 errors, Kettle will stop capturing errors, and will abort. The same will occur if the number of rows with errors exceeds 20 percent of the total, but this control will only be made after having processed 100 rows.

Note that by default, there is no limit in the number of errors to be captured.

Finally, you might have noticed that the window also had an option named **Target step**. This option gives the name of the step that will receive the rows with errors. This option was automatically set when you created the hop to handle the error, but you can also set it by hand.

Have a go hero – trying out different ways of handling errors

Modify the transformation that handles errors in the following way:

1. In the **Data Grid** step, change the start and end dates so they are both strings. Then, change the metadata to date by using the **Select values** step.

2. Modify the settings of the **Error handling dialog** window, so besides the description of the error, you have a field with the number of errors that occurred in each row.

3. Also change the settings so Kettle can handle a maximum of five errors.

4. Add more rows to the initial dataset, introducing both right and wrong values. Make sure you have rows with more than one error.

5. Test your work!

Summary

In this chapter, you created several transformations. As you did it, you got more familiar with the design process, including dealing with errors, previewing, and running transformations. You had the opportunity of learning several Kettle steps, and you also learned how to handle errors that may appear. At the same time, you learned the basic terminology related to data and transformations.

In all the sections of this chapter, you worked with dummy data. Now, you are prepared to work with real world data. You will learn how to do that in the next chapter.

3

Manipulating Real-world Data

In the previous chapter, you started working with the graphical designer Spoon. However, all the examples were based on dummy data. In this chapter, you will start creating transformations to explore data from the real world.

Data is everywhere; in particular, you will find data in files. Product lists, logs, survey results, and statistical information are just a few examples of the different kind of information usually stored in files. In this chapter, you will:

- ◆ Create transformations to get data from different kinds of files
- ◆ Learn how to send data from Kettle to plain files

You will also get the chance to learn more basic features of PDI, for example, working with variables.

Reading data from files

Despite being the most primitive format used to store data, files are broadly used and they exist in several flavors such as fixed width, comma separated values, spreadsheets, or even free format files. PDI has the ability to read data from all kinds of files. In this section let's see how to use PDI to get data from text files.

Time for action – reading results of football matches from files

Suppose you have collected several football results in plain files. Your files look like this:

```
Date;Venue;Country;Matches;Country
07/09/12 15:00;Havana;Cuba;0:3;Honduras;
07/09/12 19:00;Kingston;Jamaica;2:1;USA;
07/09/12 19:30;San Salvador;El Salvador;2:2;Guyana;
07/09/12 19:45;Toronto;Canada;1:0;Panama;
07/09/12 20:00;Guatemala City;Guatemala;3:1;Antigua and Barbuda;
07/09/12 20:05;San Jose;Costa Rica;0:2;Mexico;
11/09/12 19:00;St. John's;Antigua and Barbuda;0:1;Guatemala;
11/09/12 19:30;San Pedro Sula;Honduras;1:0;Cuba;
11/09/12 20:00;Mexico City;Mexico;1:0;Costa Rica;
11/09/12 20:00;Georgetown;Guyana;2:3;El Salvador;
11/09/12 20:05;Panama City;Panama;2:0;Canada;
11/09/12 20:11;Columbus;USA;1:0;Jamaica;
-- qualifying for the finals in Brazil 2014 --
-- USA, September
```

You don't have one, but many files, all with the same format. You now want to unify all the information in one single file. Let's begin by reading the files:

1. Create a folder named `pdi_files`. Inside it, create the subfolders `input` and `output`.

2. Use any text editor to type the file shown, and save it under the name `usa_201209.txt` in the folder named `input` that you just created. Or you can use the file available in the downloadable code.

3. Start Spoon.

4. From the main menu navigate to **File | New | Transformation**.

5. Expand the **Input** branch of the **Steps** tree.

6. Drag-and-drop to the canvas the icon **Text file input**.

7. Double-click on the **Text file input** icon, and give the step a name.

8. Click on the **Browse...** button, and search for the file `usa_201209.txt`.

9. Select the file. The textbox **File or directory** will be temporarily populated with the full path of the file, for example, `C:\pdi_files\input\usa_201209.txt`.

10. Click on the **Add** button. The full text will be moved from the **File or directory** textbox to the grid. The configuration window should appear as follows:

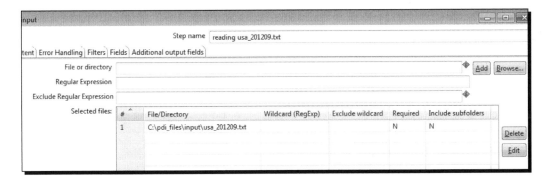

11. Click on the **Content** tab, and fill it in, as shown in the following screenshot:

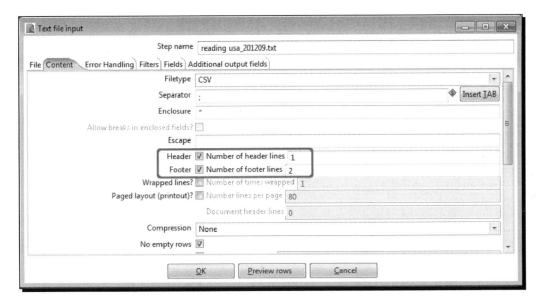

12. Click on the **Fields** tab.

13. Click on the **Get Fields** button. The screen should look like the following screenshot:

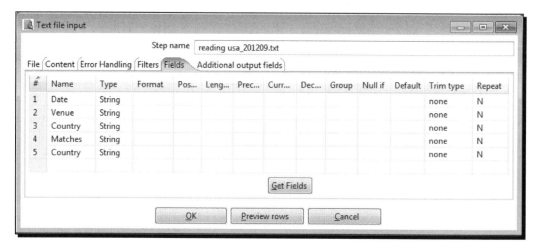

> By default, Kettle assumes DOS format for the file. If you created the file in a UNIX machine, you will be warned that the DOS format for the file was not found. If that's the case, you can change the format in the **Content** tab.

14. In the small window that propose you a number of sample lines, click on **Cancel**. You will see that the grid was filled with the list of fields found in your file, all of the type `String`.

15. Click on the **Preview rows** button, and then click on the **OK** button. The previewed data should look like the following screenshot:

Note that the second field named `Country` was renamed as `Country_1`. This is because there cannot be two Kettle fields with the same name.

16. Now it's time to enhance the definitions a bit. Rename the columns as: `match_date`, `venue`, `home_team`, `results`, and `away_team`. You can rename the columns just by overwriting the default values in the grid.

17. Change the definition of the `match_date` field. As `Type` select `Date`, and as `Format` type `dd/MM/yy HH:mm`.

18. Run a new preview. You should see the same data, but with the columns renamed. Also the type of the first column is different. This is not obvious by looking at the screen but you can confirm the type by moving the mouse cursor over the column as you learned to do in the previous chapter.

19. Close the window.

20. Now expand the **Transform** branch of steps and drag to the canvas a **Select values** step.

21. Create a hop from the **Text file input** step to the **Select values** step.

22. Double-click on the **Select values** step, and use it to remove the venue step. Recall that you do it by selecting or typing the field name in the **Remove** tab.

23. Click on **OK**.

24. Now add a **Dummy (do nothing)** step. You will find it in the **Flow** branch of steps.

25. Create a hop from the **Select values** step to the **Dummy (do nothing)** step. Your transformation should look like the following screenshot:

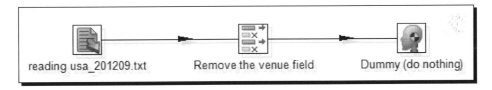

26. Configure the transformation by pressing *Ctrl + T* or *Ctrl + T* on Mac, and giving the transformation a name and a description.

27. Save the transformation by pressing *Ctrl + S* or *Ctrl + S* on Mac.

28. Select the **Dummy (do nothing)** step.

29. Click on the **Preview** button located in the transformation toolbar.

30. Click on the **Quick Launch** button. The following window appears, showing the final data:

What just happened?

You created a very simple transformation that read a single file with the results of football matches.

By using a **Text file input** step, you told Kettle the full path of your file, along with the characteristics of the file so that Kettle was able to read it correctly. In particular you configured the **Content** tab to specify that the file had a header and footer made up by two rows (rows that should be ignored). As separator you left the default value (;), but if your file had another separator you could have changed the separator character in this tab. Finally, you defined the name and type of the different fields.

After that, you used a **Select values** step to remove unwanted fields. A **Dummy (do nothing) step** was used simply as the destination of the data. You used this step to run a preview and see the final results.

Input files

Files are one of the most used input sources. PDI can take data from several types of files, with almost no limitations.

When you have a file to work with, the first thing you have to do is to specify where the file is, what it looks like, and which kind of values it contains. That is exactly what you did in the first section of this chapter.

With the information you provide, Kettle can create the dataset to work within the current transformation.

Input steps

There are several steps which allow you to take a file as the input data. All those steps are under the Input step category; Text file input, Fixed file input, and Microsoft Excel Input are some of them.

Despite the obvious differences that exist between these types of files, the way to configure the steps has much in common. These are the main properties you have to specify for an input step:

- **Name of the step**: It is mandatory and must be different for every step in the transformation.

- **Name and location of the file**: These must be specified of course. It is not mandatory but desirable the existence of the file at the moment you are creating the transformation.

- **Content type**: This data includes delimiter character, type of encoding, whether a header is present or not, and so on. The list depends on the kind of file chosen. In each case, Kettle proposes default values, so you don't have to enter too much data.

- **Fields**: Kettle has the facility to get the definitions automatically by clicking on the **Get Fields** button. However, not always the data types, or size, or formats guessed by Kettle are the expected. So, after getting the fields you may change what you consider more appropriate.

- **Filtering**: Some steps allow you to filter the data, skip blank rows, read only the first N rows, and so on.

After configuring an input step, you can preview the data just as you did, by clicking on the **Preview rows** button. This is useful to discover if there is something wrong in the configuration. In that case, you can make the adjustments and preview again, until your data looks fine.

> In order to read CSV text files there is an alternative step: CSV file input. This step has a simple but less flexible configuration, but as a counterpart, it provides better performance. One of its advantages is the presence of an option named **Lazy conversion**. When checked, this flag prevents Kettle from performing unnecessary data type conversions, increasing the speed for reading files.

Reading several files at once

In the previous exercise, you used an input step to read one file. But suppose you have several files, all with the very same structure. That will not be a problem, because with Kettle it is possible to read more than a file at a time.

Time for action – reading all your files at a time using a single text file input step

Suppose that the names of your files are usa_201209.txt, usa_201210.txt, europe_201209.txt, and europe_201210.txt. To read all your files follow the listed steps:

1. Open the transformation created in the last section.

2. Double-click on the **Input** step and add the rest of the files in the same way you added the first. At the end, the grid will have as many lines as added files.

3. Click on the **Preview rows** button. Your screen will look like the following screenshot:

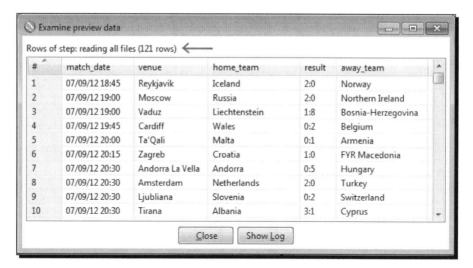

What just happened?

You read several files at once. By putting the names of all the files into the grid, you could get the content of every specified file one after the other.

Time for action – reading all your files at a time using a single text file input step and regular expressions

You can do the same thing that you did previously by using a different notation. Follow these instructions:

1.   Open the transformation that reads several files and double-click on the **Input** step.

2.   Delete the lines with the names of the files.

3.   In the first row of the grid, under the `File/Directory` column, type the full path of the input folder, for example `C:\pdi_files\input`.

4.   Under the `Wildcard (RegExp)` column type `(usa|europe)_[0-9]{6}\.txt`.

5.   Click on the **Show filename(s)...** button. You will see the list of files that match the expression:

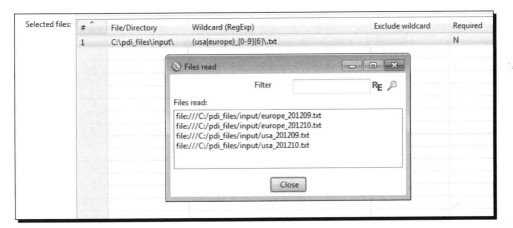

6.   Close the tiny window and click on **Preview rows** to confirm that the rows shown belong to the files that match the expression you typed.

What just happened?

In this case, all the filenames follow a pattern: `usa_201209.txt`, `usa_201210.txt`, and so on. So, in order to specify the names of the files you used a regular expression. In the column `File/Directory` you put the static part of the names, while in the `Wildcard (RegExp)` column you put the regular expression with the pattern that a file must follow to be considered: the name of the region which should be either `usa` or `europe`, followed by an underscore and the six numbers representing the period, and then the extension `.txt`. Then, all files that matched the expression were considered as input files.

Regular expressions

There are many places inside Kettle where you may have to provide a regular expression. A regular expression is much more than specifying the known wildcards ? and *.

In the following table you have some examples of regular expressions you may use to specify filenames:

The following regular expression	matches	examples
`.*\.txt`	Any TXT file	`thisisaValidExample.txt`
`test(19|20)\d\d-(0[1-9]|1[012])\.txt`	Any TXT file beginning by test followed by a date such as yyyy-mm	`test2013-12.txt` `test2013-01.txt`
`(?i)test.+\.txt`	Any TXT file beginning by test, upper, or lower case	`TeSTcaseinsensitive.tXt`

> Please note that the * wildcard does not work the same as it does on the command line. If you want to match any character, the * has to be preceded by a dot.

Here you have some useful links in case you want to know more about regular expressions:

- Read about regular expressions at `http://www.regular-expressions.info/quickstart.html`

- Read the Java Regular Expression tutorial at `http://java.sun.com/docs/books/tutorial/essential/regex/`

- Read about Java Regular Expression pattern syntax at `http://java.sun.com/javase/7/docs/api/java/util/regex/Pattern.html`

Troubleshooting reading files

Despite the simplicity of reading files with PDI, obstacles and errors appear. Many times the solution is simple, but difficult to find if you are new to PDI. The following table gives you a list of common problems and possible solutions to take into account while reading and previewing a file:

Problem	Diagnostic	Possible solutions
You get the message **Sorry, no rows found to be previewed.**	This happens when the input file does not exist or is empty. It may also happen if you specified the input files with regular expressions and there is no file that matches the expression.	Check the name of the input files. Verify the syntax used, check that you didn't put spaces or any strange character as part of the name. If you used regular expressions, check the syntax. Also verify that you put the filename in the grid. If you just put it in the **File or directory** textbox, Kettle will not read it.
When you preview the data you see a grid with blank lines.	The file contains empty lines, or you forgot to get the fields.	Check the content of the file. Also check that you got the fields in the **Fields** tab.
You see the whole line under the first defined field.	You didn't set the proper separator and Kettle couldn't split the different fields.	Check and fix the separator in the **Content** tab.
You see strange characters.	You left the default content but your file has a different format or encoding.	Check and fix the **Format and Encoding** option in the **Content** tab. If you are not sure of the format you can specify mixed.
You don't see all the lines you have in the file.	You are previewing just a sample (100 lines by default). Or you put a limit to the number of rows to get. Another problem may be that you set wrong number of header or footer lines.	When you preview, you see just a sample. This is not a problem. If you raise the previewed number of rows and still have few lines, check the **Header**, **Footer**, and **Limit** options in the **Content** tab.
Instead of rows of data you get a window headed **ERROR** with an extract of the log.	Different errors may occur, but the most common has to do with problems in the definition of the fields.	You could try to understand the log and fix the definition accordingly. For example, if you see: **Couldn't parse field [Integer] with value [Honduras], format [null] on data row [1].** The error is that PDI found the text **Honduras** in a field that you defined as `Integer`. If you made a mistake, you can fix it. On the contrary, if the file has errors, you could read all fields as `String` and then handle the errors as you learned to do in *Chapter 2, Getting Started with Transformations*.

Have a go hero – exploring your own files

Try to read your own text files from Kettle. You must have several files with different kinds of data, different separators, with or without a header or footer. You can also search for files over the Internet; it has plenty of files there to download and play with. After configuring the input step, do a preview. If the data is not shown properly, fix the configuration and preview again until you are sure that the data is read as expected. If you have trouble reading the files, please refer to the section *Troubleshooting reading files* for diagnosis and possible ways to solve the problems.

Pop quiz – providing a list of text files using regular expressions

Q1. In the previous exercise you read four different files by using a single regular expression: `(usa|europe)_[0-9]{6}\.txt`. Which of the following options is equivalent to that one? In other words, which of the following serves for reading the same set of files? You can choose more than one option.

1. Replacing that regular expression with this one: `(usa|europe)_[0-9][0-9]` `[0-9][0-9][0-9][0-9]\.txt`.

2. Filling the grid with two lines: one with the regular expression `usa_[0-9]{6}\.` `txt` and a second line with this expression: `europe_[0-9]{6}\.txt`.

Q2. Try reproducing the previous sections using a CSV file input step instead of a Text file input step. Identify whether the following statements are true or false:

1. There is no difference in using a Text file input step or a CSV file input step.

2. It is not possible to read the sample files with a CSV file input.

3. It is not possible to read more than one file at a time with a CSV file input.

4. It is not possible to specify a regular expression for reading files with a CSV file input.

Have a go hero – measuring the performance of input steps

The previous Pop quiz was not the best propaganda for the CSV file input step! Let's change that reputation by doing some tests.

In the material that you can download from the book's website there is a transformation that generates a text file with 10 million rows of dummy data.

Run the transformation for generating that file (you can even modify the transformation to add new fields or generate more data).

Create three different transformations for reading the file:

1. With a Text file input step.
2. With a CSV file input step. Uncheck the **Lazy conversion** flag which is on by default.
3. With a CSV file input step, making sure that the **Lazy conversion** option is on.

Run one transformation at a time and take note of the metrics. No matter how slow or fast your computer is, you should note that the CSV file input step performs better than the Text file input step, and even better when using the **Lazy conversion** option.

Sending data to files

Now you know how to bring data into Kettle. You didn't bring the data just to preview it. You probably want to do some transformations on the data, and send it to a final destination, for example, another plain file. Let's learn how to do this task.

Time for action – sending the results of matches to a plain file

In the previous section, you read several files with the results of football matches. Now you want to send the data coming from all files to a single output file:

1. Open the transformation that you created in the last section and save it under a different name.
2. Delete the **Dummy (do nothing)** step by selecting it and pressing *Del*.
3. Expand the **Output** branch of the **Steps** tree.
4. Look for the **Text file output** step and drag this icon to the work area.
5. Create a hop from the **Select values** step to this new step.
6. Double-click on the **Text file output** step icon and give it a name.
7. As **Filename** type C:/pdi_files/output/matches.

 Note that the path contains forward slashes. If your system is Windows, you may use back or forward slashes. PDI will recognize both notations.

8. In the **Content** tab, leave the default values.

9. Select the **Fields** tab and configure it as shown in the following screenshot:

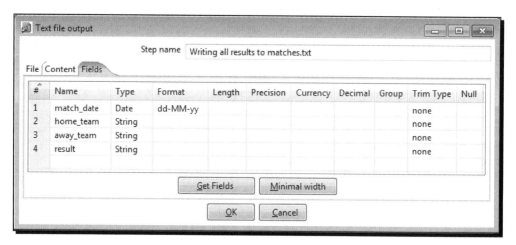

#	Name	Type	Format	Length	Precision	Currency	Decimal	Group	Trim Type	Null
1	match_date	Date	dd-MM-yy						none	
2	home_team	String							none	
3	away_team	String							none	
4	result	String							none	

10. Click on **OK**. Your screen will look like the following screenshot:

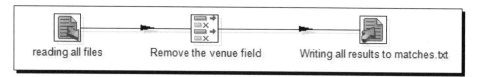

reading all files   Remove the venue field   Writing all results to matches.txt

11. Give the transformation a name and description, and save it.

12. Run the transformation by pressing *F9* and then click on **Launch**.

13. Once the transformation is finished, look for the new file. It should have been created as `C:/pdi_files/output/matches.txt` and will appear as shown:

```
match_date;home_team;away_team;result
07-09-12;Iceland;Norway;2:0
07-09-12;Russia;Northern Ireland;2:0
07-09-12;Liechtenstein;Bosnia-Herzegovina;1:8
07-09-12;Wales;Belgium;0:2
07-09-12;Malta;Armenia;0:1
07-09-12;Croatia;FYR Macedonia;1:0
07-09-12;Andorra;Hungary;0:5
07-09-12;Netherlands;Turkey;2:0
07-09-12;Slovenia;Switzerland;0:2
07-09-12;Albania;Cyprus;3:1
07-09-12;Montenegro;Poland;2:2
...
```

If your system is Linux or similar, or if your files are in a different location, change the paths accordingly.

What just happened?

You gathered information from several files and sent all data to a single file.

Output files

We saw that PDI could take data from several types of files. The same applies to output data. The data you have in a transformation can be sent to different kinds of files. All you have to do is redirect the flow of data towards an Output step.

Output steps

There are several steps which allow you to send the data to a file. All those steps are under the Output category; Text file output and Microsoft Excel Output are some of them.

For an output step, just like you do for an input step, you also have to define:

◆ **Name of the step**: It is mandatory and must be different for every step in the transformation.

◆ **Name and location of the file**: These must be specified. If you specify an existing file, the file will be replaced by a new one (unless you check the **Append** checkbox, present in some of the output steps, for example, the Text file output step used in the last section).

◆ **Content type**: This data includes a delimiter character, type of encoding, whether to use a header, and so on. The list depends on the kind of file chosen. If you check **Header** (which is selected by default), the header will be built with the names of the fields.

 If you don't like the names of the fields as header names in your file, you may use a Select values step to rename those fields before sending them to a file.

◆ **Fields**: Here you specify the list of fields that have to be sent to the file, and provide some format instructions. Just like in the input steps, you may use the **Get Fields** button to fill the grid. In this case, the grid is going to be filled based on the data that arrives from the previous step. You are not forced to send every data coming to the Output step, nor to send the fields in the same order, as you can figure out from the example in the previous section.

> If you leave the **Fields** tab empty, Kettle will send all the fields coming from the previous step to the file.

Have a go hero – extending your transformations by writing output files

Supposing that you read your own files in the previous section, modify your transformations by writing some or all the data back into files, but this time changing the format, headers, number, or order of fields, and so on. The objective is to get some experience, to see what happens. After some tests, you will feel confident with input and output files, and ready to move forward.

Have a go hero – generate your custom matches.txt file

Modify the transformation that generated the `matches.txt` file. This time your output file should look similar to this:

```
match_date|home_team|away_team
07-09|Iceland (2)|Norway (0)
07-09|Russia (2)|Northern Ireland (0)
07-09|Liechtenstein (1)|Bosnia-Herzegovina (8)
07-09|Wales (0)|Belgium (2)
07-09|Malta (0)|Armenia (1)
07-09|Croatia (1)|FYR Macedonia (0)
...
```

> In order to create the new fields you can use some or all of the next steps: Split Fields, UDJE, Calculator, and Select values. Besides, you will have to customize the Output step a bit, by changing the format of the date field, changing the default separator, and so on.

Getting system information

So far, you have been learning how to read data from files with known names, and send data back to files. What if you don't know beforehand the name of the file to process? There are several ways to handle this with Kettle. Let's learn the simplest.

Time for action – reading and writing matches files with flexibility

In this section, you will create a transformation very similar to the one you created in the previous section. In this case, however, you will interact with Spoon by telling it one-by-one which source files you want to send to the destination file:

1. Create a new transformation.

2. From the **Input** category of steps, drag to the work area a **Get System Info** step.

3. Double-click the step and add a new line to the grid. Under Name type filename. As Type select **command line argument 1**, as shown in the following screenshot:

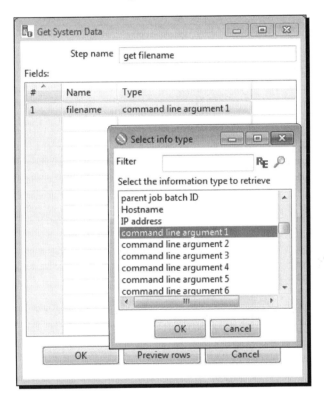

4. Click on **OK**.

5. Add a **Calculator** step and create a hop from the previous step toward this step.

6. Double-click on the **Calculator** step and fill in the grid as shown in the following screenshot:

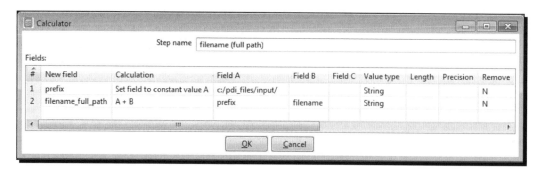

7. Save the transformation.

8. Select the **Calculator** step, and press *F10* to run a preview. In the **Transformation debug** dialog, click on **Configure**.

9. Fill in the **Arguments** grid by typing the name of one of your input files under the Value column. Your window will look like the following screenshot:

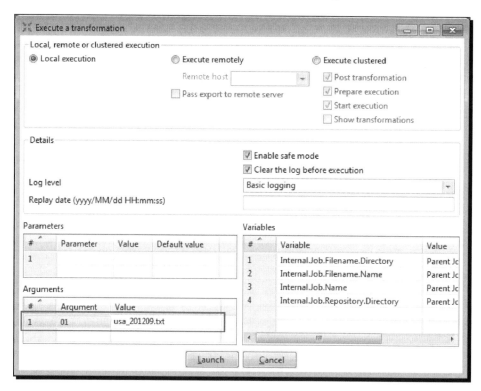

10. Click on **Launch**. You will see a window displaying the full path of your file, for example, `c:/pdi_files/input/usa_201209.txt`.

11. Close the preview window, add a **Text file input** step, and create a link from the **Calculator** step towards this step.

12. Double-click on the **Text file input** step and fill the lower grid as shown in the following screenshot:

Accept filenames from previous steps

Accept filenames from previous step	☑
Pass through fields from previous step	☐
Step to read filenames from	filename (full path) ▼
Field in the input to use as filename	filename_full_path

13. Fill in the **Content** and **Fields** tabs just like you did before. It's worth saying that the **Get Fields** button will not populate the grid as expected, because the filename has not been provided. In order to avoid typing the fields manually you can refer to the following tip:

Instead of configuring the tabs again, you can open any of the transformations, copy the **Text file input** step and paste it here. Leave the **Contents** and **Fields** tabs untouched and just configure the **File** tab as explained previously.

14. Click on **OK**.

15. Add a **Select values** step to remove the venue field.

16. Finally, add a **Text file output** step and configure it in the same way that you did in the previous section, but this time, in the **Content** tab select the **Append** checkbox.

Again, you can save time by copying the steps from the transformation you created before and pasting them here.

17. Save the transformation and make sure that the `matches.txt` file doesn't exist.

18. Press *F9* to run the transformation.

19. In the first cell of the **Arguments** grid type the name of one of the files. For example, you can type `usa_201209.txt`.

20. Click on **Launch**.

21. Open the `matches.txt` file. You should see the data belonging to the `usa_201209.txt` file.

22. Run the transformation again. This time, as the name of the file type `usa_201210.txt`.

23. Open the `matches.txt` file again. This time you should see the data belonging to the `usa_201209.txt` file, followed by the data in the `usa_201210.txt` file.

What just happened?

You read a file whose name is known at runtime, and fed a destination file, by appending the contents of the input file.

The Get System Info step tells Kettle to take the first command-line argument, and assume that it is the name of the file to read. Then the Calculator step serves for building the full path of the file.

In the Text file input step, you didn't specify the name of the file, but told Kettle to take as the name of the file, the field coming from the previous step, that is, the field built with the Calculator step.

The destination file is appended with new data every time you run the transformation.

> This is an advice regarding the configuration of the Text file input step: When you don't specify the name and location of a file (like in the previous example), or when the real file is not available at design time, you will not be able to use the **Get Fields** button, nor be able to to see if the step is well configured. The trick is to configure the step by using a real file identical to the expected one. After the step is configured, change the name and location of the file as needed.

The Get System Info step

The Get System Info step allows you to get different types of information from the system. In this exercise, you read a command-line argument. If you look at the available list, you will see a long list of options including up to ten command-line arguments, dates relative to the present date (`Yesterday 00:00:00`, `First day of last month 23:59:59`, and so on), information related to the machine where the transformation is running (`JVM max memory`, `Total physical memory size (bytes)`, and so on), and more.

In this section, you used the step as the first in the flow. This causes Kettle to generate a dataset with a single row, and one column for each defined field. In this case, you created a single field, `filename`, but you could have defined more if needed.

There is also the possibility of adding a Get System Info step in the middle of the flow. Suppose that after the Select values step you add a Get System Info step with the system date. That is, you define the step as shown in the following screenshot:

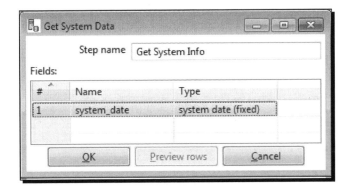

This will cause Kettle to add a new field with the same value, in this case the system date, for all rows, as you can see in the following screenshot:

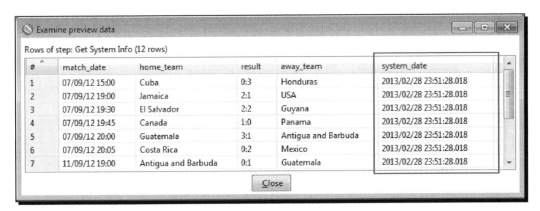

Running transformations from a terminal window

In the previous exercise, you specified that the name of the input file will be taken from the first command-line argument. That means that when executing the transformation, the filename has to be supplied as an argument. Until now, you only ran transformations from inside Spoon. In the last exercise, you provided the argument by typing it in a dialog window. Now it is time to learn how to run transformations with or without arguments, from a terminal window.

Time for action – running the matches transformation from a terminal window

Let's suppose that the name of your transformation is `matches.ktr`. In order to run the transformation from a terminal, follow these instructions:

1. Open a terminal window, and go to the directory where Kettle is installed. If your system is Windows, and supposing that Kettle is installed in `C:\pdi-ce`, type:

```
C:\pdi-ce>Pan.bat /file=c:\pdi_labs\matches.ktr europe_201210.txt
```

2. On Unix, Linux, and other types of systems, supposing that Kettle is installed under `/home/your_dir/pdi-ce/`, type:

```
/home/your_dir/pdi-ce/pan.sh /file=/home/your_dir/pdi_labs/
matches.ktr europe_201210.txt
```

3. If your transformation is in another folder, modify the command accordingly.

4. While the transformation runs you will be able to see the progress in the terminal:

5. Check the output file. The contents of `europe_201210.txt` should be at the end of the `matches.txt` file.

What just happened?

You executed a transformation with **Pan**, the program that runs transformations from terminal windows. As a part of the command you specified the full path of the transformation file and provided the name of the file to process, which was the only argument expected by the transformation. As a result, you got the same output as if you had run the transformation from Spoon: a small file appended to the global file.

When you are designing transformations, you run them with Spoon; you don't use Pan. Pan is mainly used as part of batch processes, for example, processes that run every night in a scheduled fashion.

 Appendix B, Pan and Kitchen – Launching Transformations and Jobs from the Command Line gives you all the details about using Pan.

Have a go hero – finding out system information

Create a transformation that writes to the log the following information:

- System date
- Information about Kettle: version, build version, and build date
- Name of the transformation you're running

Run the transformation both from Spoon and from a terminal window.

XML files

XML files or documents are not only widely used to store data, but also to exchange data between heterogeneous systems over the Internet. PDI has many features that enable you to manipulate XML files. In this section, you will learn to get data from those files.

Time for action – getting data from an XML file with information about countries

In this section, you will build an Excel file with basic information about countries. The source will be an XML file that you can download from the book's website.

1. Open the `kettle.properties` file located in a folder named `.kettle` inside your home directory. If you work under Windows, that folder could be `C:\Documents and Settings\<your_name>\` or `C:\Users\<your_name>\` depending on the Windows version.

2. If you work under Linux (or similar) or Mac OS, the folder will most probably be `/home/<your_name>/`.

 Note that the `.kettle` folder is a system folder, and as such, may not display using the GUI file explorer on any OS. You can change the UI settings to display the folder, or use a terminal window.

3. Add the following line (for Windows systems):

    ```
    LABSOUTPUT=c:/pdi_files/output
    ```

    Or this line (for Linux or similar systems):

    ```
    LABSOUTPUT=/home/your_name/pdi_files/output
    ```

4. Make sure that the directory named `output` exists.

5. Save the file, restart Spoon and create a new transformation.

6. Give the transformation a name and save it in the same directory where you have all the other transformations.

7. From the book's website, download the `resources` folder containing a file named `countries.xml`. Save the folder in your working directory. For example, if your transformations are in `pdi_labs`, the file will be in `pdi_labs/resources/`.

 The previous two steps are important. Don't skip them! If you do, some of the following steps will fail.

8. Take a look at the file. You can edit it with any text editor, or you can double-click on it to see it within a web explorer. In any case, you will see information about countries. This is just the extract for a single country:

    ```
    <?xml version="1.0" encoding="UTF-8"?>
    <world>
    ...
    ```

```
<country>
  <name>Argentina</name>
  <capital>Buenos Aires</capital>
  <language isofficial="T">
    <name>Spanish</name>
    <percentage>96.8</percentage>
  </language>
  <language isofficial="F">
    <name>Italian</name>
    <percentage>1.7</percentage>
  </language>
  <language isofficial="F">
    <name>Indian Languages</name>
    <percentage>0.3</percentage>
  </language>
</country>
...
</world>
```

9. From the **Input** steps, drag to the canvas a **Get data from XML** step.

10. Open the configuration window for this step by double-clicking on it.

11. In the **File or directory** textbox, press *Ctrl + Space* or *Shift + command + Space* in Mac. A drop-down list appears containing a list of defined variables:

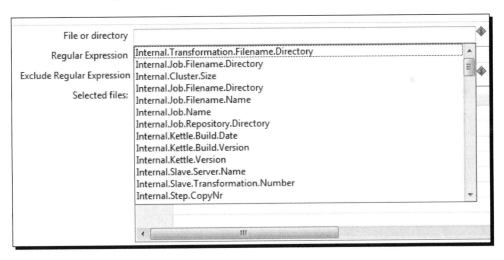

12. Select **Internal.Transformation.Filename.Directory**. The textbox is filled with this text.

13. Complete the text so you can read this: `${Internal.Transformation.Filename.Directory}/resources/countries.xml`.

14. Click on the **Add** button. The full path is moved to the grid.

15. Select the **Content** tab and click on **Get XPath nodes**.

16. In the list that appears, select **/world/country/language**.

17. Select the **Fields** tab and fill in the grid as shown in the following screenshot:

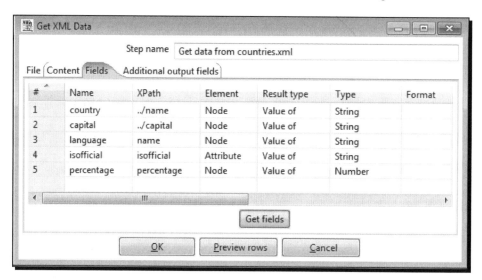

18. Click on **Preview rows**, and you should see something like the following screenshot:

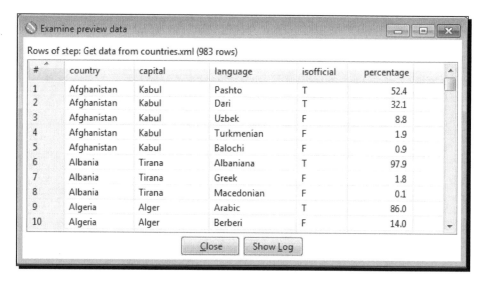

19. Click on **OK**.

20. From the **Output** steps, drag to the canvas a **Microsoft Excel Output** step.

21. Create a hop from the **Get data from XML** step to the **Microsoft Excel Output** step.

22. Open the configuration window for this step by double-clicking on it.

23. In the **Filename** textbox press *Ctrl + Space*.

24. From the drop-down list, select **${LABSOUTPUT}**.

> If you don't see this variable, please verify that you spelled the name correctly in the `kettle.properties` file, saved the file, and restarted Spoon.

25. Beside that text, type `/countries_info`. The complete text should be: `${LABSOUTPUT}/countries_info`.

26. Select the **Fields** tab and then click on the **Get fields** button to fill in the grid.

27. Click on **OK**. This is your final transformation:

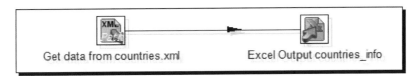

Get data from countries.xml   Excel Output countries_info

28. Save and run the transformation.

29. Check that the file `countries_info.xls` has been created in the `output` folder, and contains the information you previewed in the input step.

What just happened?

You got information about countries from an XML file and saved it in a more readable format for the common people: an Excel sheet.

To get the information you used a **Get data from XML** step. As the source file was taken from a folder relative to the folder where you stored the transformation, you set the directory to `${Internal.Transformation.Filename.Directory}`. When the transformation runs, Kettle replaces `${Internal.Transformation.Filename.Directory}` with the real path of the transformation, for example, `c:/pdi_labs/`.

In the same way, you didn't put a fixed value for the path of the final Excel file. As the folder you used `${LABSOUTPUT}`. When the transformation ran, Kettle replaced `${LABSOUTPUT}` with the value you wrote in the `kettle.properties` file. Then, the output file was saved in that folder, for example, `c:/pdi_files/output`.

What is XML?

XML stands for **EXtensible Markup Language**. It is basically a language designed to describe data. XML files or documents contain information wrapped in tags. Look at this piece of XML taken from the `countries` file:

```
<?xml version="1.0" encoding="UTF-8"?>
<world>
 . . .
  <country>
    <name>Argentina</name>
    <capital>Buenos Aires</capital>
    <language isofficial="T">
      <name>Spanish</name>
      <percentage>96.8</percentage>
    </language>
    <language isofficial="F">
      <name>Italian</name>
      <percentage>1.7</percentage>
    </language>
    <language isofficial="F">
      <name>Indian Languages</name>
      <percentage>0.3</percentage>
    </language>
  </country>
 . . .
</world>
```

The first line in the document is the XML declaration. It defines the XML version of the document, and should always be present.

Below the declaration is the body of the document. The body is a set of nested elements. An element is a logical piece enclosed by a start tag and a matching end tag, for example, `<country> </country>`.

Within the start tag of an element, you may have attributes. An attribute is a markup construct consisting of a name/value pair, for example, `isofficial="F"`.

This is the most basic terminology related to XML files. If you want to know more about XML, you can visit `http://www.w3schools.com/xml/`.

PDI transformation files

Despite the KTR extension, PDI transformations are just XML files. As such, you are able to explore them inside and recognize different XML elements. Look the following sample text:

```
<?xml version="1.0" encoding="UTF-8"?>
<transformation>
  <info>
    <name>hello_world</name>
    <description>My first transformation</description>
    <extended_description>PDI Beginner&apos;s Guide (2nd edition)
  Chapter 1</extended_description>
  ...
</transformation>
```

This is an extract from the `hello_world.ktr` file. Here you can see the root element named `transformation` and some inner elements, for example, `info` and `name`.

Note that if you copy a step by selecting it in the Spoon work area and press *Ctrl + C*, and then paste it to a text editor, you can see its XML definition. If you copy it back to the canvas, a new identical step will be added to your transformation.

Getting data from XML files

In order to get data from an XML file, you have to use the Get data from XML input step. To tell PDI which information to get from the file. it is required that you use a particular notation named XPath.

XPath

XPath is a set of rules used for getting information from an XML document. In XPath, XML documents are treated as trees of nodes. There are several kinds of nodes: elements, attributes, and texts are some of them. As an example, `world`, `country`, and `isofficial` are some of the nodes in the sample file.

Among the nodes, there are relationships. A node has a parent, zero or more children, siblings, ancestors, and descendants depending on where the other nodes are in the hierarchy.

In the sample countries file, `country` is the parent of the elements `name`, `capital` and `language`. These three elements are children of `country`.

To select a node in an XML document you have to use a path expression relative to a current node.

The following table has some examples of path expressions you may use to specify fields. The examples assume that the current node is `language`:

Path expression	Description	Sample expression
`node_name`	Selects all child nodes of the node named `node_name`.	`percentage` This expression selects all child nodes of the node `percentage`. It looks for the node `percentage` inside the current node `language`.
`.`	Selects the current node.	`language`
`..`	Selects the parent of the current node.	`../capital` This expression selects all child nodes of the node `capital`. It doesn't look in the current node (`language`), but inside its parent which is `country`.
`@`	Selects an attribute.	`@isofficial` This expression gets the attribute `isofficial` in the current node `language`.

 Note that the expressions `name` and `../name` are not the same. The first expression selects the name of the language, while the second selects the name of the country.

For more information on XPath, visit the link `http://www.w3schools.com/XPath/`.

Configuring the Get data from the XML step

In order to specify the name and location of an XML file you have to fill in the **File** tab just as you do in any file input step. What is different here is how you get the data.

The first thing you have to do is select the path that will identify the current node. This is optimally the repeating node in the file. You select the path by filling in the **Loop XPath** textbox in the **Content** tab. You can type it by hand, or you can select it from the list of available paths by clicking on the **Get XPath nodes** button.

Once you select a path, PDI will generate one row of data for every found path.

In the *Time for action – getting data from an XML file with information about countries* section, you selected **/world/country/language**. Then PDI generates one row for each **/world/country/language** element in the file.

After selecting the loop XPath, you have to specify the fields to get. In order to do that, you have to fill in the grid in the **Fields** tab by using XPath notation, as explained previously.

Note that if you press the **Get fields** button, PDI will fill the grid with the child nodes of the current node. If you want to get some other node, you have to type its XPath by hand.

Also note the notation for the attributes. To get an attribute you can use the @ notation as explained, or you can simply type the name of the attribute without @ and select **Attribute** under the `Element` column, as you did in this section.

Kettle variables

In the previous section, you used the string `${Internal.Transformation.Filename.Directory}` to identify the folder where the current transformations were saved. You also used the string `${LABSOUTPUT}` to define the destination folder of the output file.

Both strings, `${Internal.Transformation.Filename.Directory}` and `${LABSOUTPUT}` are Kettle variables, that is, keywords linked to a value. You use the name of a variable, and when the transformation runs, the name of the variable is replaced by its value.

The first of these two variables is an environment variable, and it is not the only one available. Other known environment variables are: `${user.home}`, `${java.io.tmpdir}` and `${java.home}`. All these variables, whose values are auto-populated by Kettle by interrogating the system environment, are ready to use any time you need.

The second variable is a variable you defined in the `kettle.properties` file. In this file, you may define as many variables as you want. The only thing you have to keep in mind is that those variables will be available inside Spoon only after you restart it.

> You also have the possibility of editing the `kettle.properties` file from Spoon. The option is available in the main menu **Edit | Edit the kettle. properties file**. If you use this option to modify a variable, the value will be available immediately.

If you defined several variables in the `kettle.properties` file and care about the order in which you did it, or the comments you may have put in the file, it's not a good idea to edit it from Spoon.

> You have to know that when you edit the `kettle.properties` file from Spoon, Kettle will not respect the order of the lines you had in the file, and it will also add to the file a lot of pre-defined variables. So if you want to take control over the look and feel of your file you shouldn't use this option.

These two kinds of variables, environment variables and variables defined in `kettle.properties` are the most primitive kind of variables found in PDI. All of these variables are string variables and their scope is the Java Virtual Machine. This mainly means that they will always be ready for being used in any job or transformation.

How and when you can use variables

Any time you see a red dollar sign by the side of a textbox, you may use a variable. Inside the textbox you can mix variable names with static text, as you did in *Time for action – getting data from an XML file with information about countries* section when you put the name of the destination as `${LABSOUTPUT}/countries_info`.

To see all the available variables, you have to position the cursor in the textbox, press *Ctrl + Space* , and a full list is displayed so you can select the variable of your choice. If you place the mouse cursor over any of the variables for a second, the actual value of the variable will be shown.

If you know the name of the variable, you don't need to select it from the list. You may type its name, by using any of these notations: `${<name>}` or `%%<name>%%`.

Have a go hero – exploring XML files

Now you can explore by yourself. On the book's website, there are some sample XML files. Download them and try this:

- Read the `customer.xml` file and create a list of customers
- Read the `tomcat-users.xml` file and get the users and their passwords
- Read the `areachart.xml` and get the color palette, that is, the list of colors used

 The customer file is included in the Pentaho Report Designer software package. The others come with the Pentaho BI package. This software has many XML files for you to use. If you are interested, you can download the software from `http://sourceforge.net/projects/pentaho/files/`.

Summary

In this chapter, you learned how to get data from files and put data back into the files. Specifically you learned how to get data from plain and XML files, put data into text and Excel files, and get information from the operating system, for example, command-line arguments. Besides, you saw an introduction to Kettle variables and learned to run transformations from a terminal with the Pan command.

You are now ready to learn more advanced and very useful operations, for example, sorting or filtering data. This will be covered in the next chapter.

4

Filtering, Searching, and Performing Other Useful Operations with Data

In the previous chapters, you learned the basics of transforming data. The kind of operations that you learned are useful but limited. This chapter expands your knowledge by teaching you a variety of essential features, such as sorting or filtering data, among others.

In this chapter, you will learn about:

- ◆ Filtering and sorting data
- ◆ Grouping data by different criteria
- ◆ Looking up for data outside the main stream of data
- ◆ Data cleaning

Sorting data

Until now, you worked with data, transforming it in several ways, but you were never worried about the order in which the data came. Do you remember the file about matching games that you read in the previous chapter? It would be interesting, for example, to see the data ordered by date, or by team. As another example, in *Chapter 2, Getting Started with Transformations*, we had a list of projects and we created a field with the achieved percentage of work. It would have been ideal to see the project sorted by that new field. In this quick tutorial, you will learn how to do that kind of sorting.

Time for action – sorting information about matches with the Sort rows step

In *Chapter 3, Manipulating Real-world Data*, you created a file with information about football matches. The following lines of code show a variant of that file. The information is the same, and only the structure of the data has changed:

```
region;match_date;type;team;goals
europe;07-09;home;Iceland;2
europe;07-09;away;Norway;0
europe;07-09;home;Russia;2
europe;07-09;away;Northern Ireland;0
europe;07-09;home;Liechtenstein;1
europe;07-09;away;Bosnia-Herzegovina;8
europe;07-09;home;Wales;0
europe;07-09;away;Belgium;2
europe;07-09;home;Malta;0
europe;07-09;away;Armenia;1
...
```

Now you want to see the same information, but sorted by date and team.

1. First of all, download this sample file from the Packt Publishing website (www.packtpub.com/support). The name of the file is matches.txt.

2. Now create a transformation, give it a name and description, and save it in a folder of your choice.

3. By using a **Text file input** step, read the file. Provide the name and location of the file, check the **Content** tab to see that everything matches your file, and fill in the **Fields** tab with the shown columns: region, match_date, type, team, goals.

 If you will not use the match_date field for date operations (for example, adding dates), you don't have to define the first column as a Date. The same is valid for the goals column: You only need to define the column as Integer if you plan to do math with it. In the other case, a String is enough.

4. Do a preview just to confirm that the step is well configured.

5. Add a **Select values** step to select and reorder the columns as follows: `team`, `type`, `match_date`, `goals`.

6. From the **Transform** category of steps add a **Sort rows** step, and create a link from the Select values step towards this new step.

7. Double-click on the Sort rows step and configure it, as shown in the following screenshot:

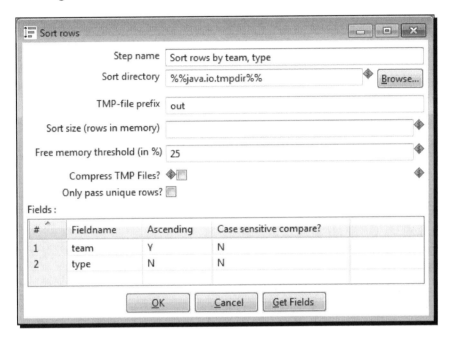

8. Click on **OK**.

9. At the end, add a **Dummy** step. Your transformation should look like this:

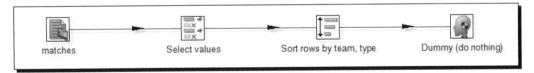

10. Save the transformation.

11. Select the last step and do a preview. You should see this:

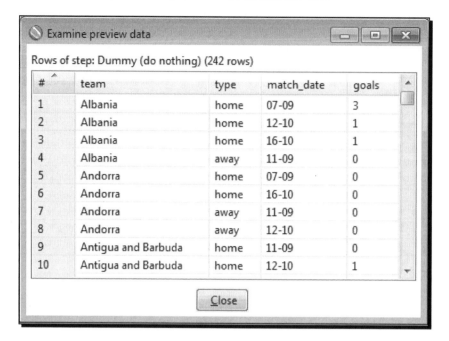

What just happened?

You read a file with a list of football match results and sorted the rows based on two columns: team (ascendant) and type (descendant). Using this method, your final data was ordered by team. Then, for any given team, the home values were first, followed by the away values. This is due to the ascending flag that is you set N under the **Ascending** column.

Note that the Select values step is not mandatory here. We just used it for having the columns team and type to the left, so the sorted dataset was easy to read.

Sorting data

For small datasets, the sorting algorithm runs mainly using the JVM memory. When the number of rows exceeds the specified sort size, it works differently. Suppose that you put 5000 as the value of the **Sort size** field. Every 5000 rows, the process sorts them and writes them to a temporary file. When there are no more rows, it does a merge sort on all of those files and gives you back the sorted dataset. You can conclude that for huge datasets a lot of reading and writing operations are done on your disk, which slows down the whole transformation. Fortunately, you can change the number of rows in memory (one million by default) by setting a new value in the **Sort size (rows in memory)** textbox. The bigger this number, the faster the sorting process. In summary, the amount of memory allocated to the process will offset the speed gained, and as soon as the JVM has to start using swap space, the performance will degrade.

Note that a sort size that works in your system may not work in a machine with a different configuration. To avoid that risk you can use a different approach. In the Sort rows configuration window you can set a Free memory threshold (in %) value. The process begins to use temporary files when the percentage of available memory drops below the indicated threshold. The lower the percentage, the faster the process.

You cannot, however, just set a small free memory threshold and expect that everything runs fine

As it is not possible to know the exact amount of free memory, it's not recommended to set a very small free memory threshold. You definitely should not use that option in complex transformations, or when there is more than one sort going on, as you could still run out of memory.

The final steps were added just to preview the result of the transformation. You could have previewed the data by selecting the Sort rows step. The idea, however, is that after this test, you can replace the Dummy step with any of the output steps you already know, or delete it and continue transforming the data.

You have used the Dummy step several times but still nothing has been said about it. Mainly because it does nothing! However, you can use it as a placeholder for testing purposes, as in the previous exercise.

Have a go hero – listing the last match played by each team

Read the `matches.txt` file and, as output, generate a file with the following structure and data: one team by row, along with information about its last played football match. The output should be something like this:

```
team;match_date;goals
Albania;16-10;1
Andorra;16-10;0
Antigua and Barbuda;16-10;1
Armenia;12-10;1
Austria;16-10;4
Azerbaijan;16-10;0
Belarus;16-10;2
Belgium;16-10;2
Bosnia-Herzegovina;16-10;3
Bulgaria;16-10;0
```

Use two **Sort rows** steps. Use the first for sorting as needed. In the second Sort rows step experiment with the flag named **Only pass unique rows? (verifies keys only)**.

As it's not really intuitive, let's briefly explain the purpose of this flag.

The **Only pass unique rows?** flag filters out duplicate rows leaving only unique occurrences. The uniqueness is forced on the list of fields by which you sorted the dataset. When there are two or more identical rows, only the first is passed to the next step(s).

This flag behaves exactly as a step that we haven't seen, but one that you can try as well: the **Unique rows** step, which you will find in the **Transform** category of steps. This step discards duplicate rows and keeps only unique occurrences. In this case, the uniqueness is also forced on a specific list of fields.

Calculations on groups of rows

So far, you have learned how to do operations for every row of a dataset. Now you are ready to go beyond this. Suppose that you have a list of daily temperatures in a given country over a year. You may want to know the overall average temperature, the average temperature by region, or the coldest day in the year. When you work with data, these kinds of calculations are a common requirement. In this section, you will learn how to address these requirements with Kettle.

Time for action – calculating football match statistics by grouping data

Let's continue working with the football matches file. Suppose that you want to take that information to obtain some statistics, for example, the maximum number of goals per match in a given day. To do this, follow these instructions:

1. Create a new transformation, give it a name and description, and save it.

2. By using a **Text file input** step, read the `matches.txt` file, just like you did it in the previous section.

3. Do a preview just to confirm that the step is well configured.

4. Add a **Sort rows** step to the transformation, and sort the fields by `region` and `match_date` in ascending order.

5. Expand the **Statistics** category of steps, and drag a **Group by** step to the canvas. Create a hop from the Sort rows step to this new step.

6. Edit the Group by step and fill in the configuration window as shown in the following screenshot:

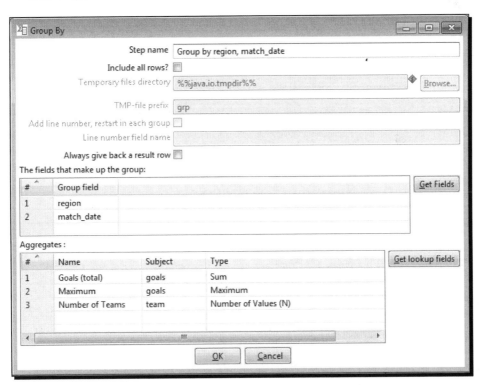

7. When you click on the **OK** button, a window appears to warn you that this step needs the input to be sorted on the specified keys, in this case, the `region` and `match_date` fields. Click on **I understand**, and don't worry because you already sorted the data in the previous step.

8. Add a final **Dummy** step.

9. Select the Dummy and the Sort rows steps, left-click on one and holding down the *Ctrl* key —cmd key on Mac — left-click the other.

10. Click on the Preview button. You will see this:

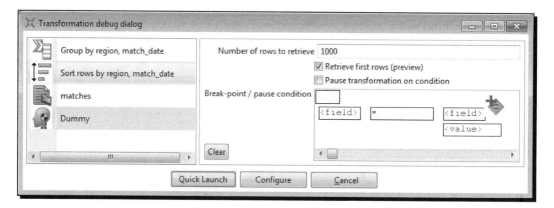

11. Click on **Quick Launch**.

12. The following window appears:

13. Double-click on the Sort rows option. A window appears with the data coming out of the Sort rows step.

14. Double-click on the Dummy option. A window appears with the data coming out of the Dummy step.

15. If you rearrange the preview windows, you can see both preview windows at a time, and understand better what happened with the numbers. The following would be the data shown in the windows:

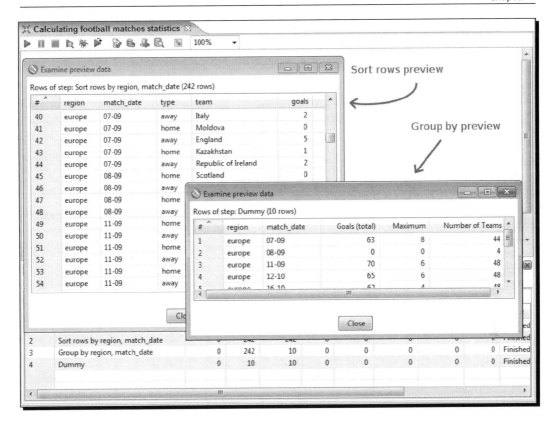

What just happened?

You opened a file with results from several matches, and got some statistics from it.

After reading the file, you ordered the data by region and match date with a Sort rows step, and then you ran some statistical calculations:

- First, you grouped the rows by region and match date. You did this by typing or selecting `region` and `match_date` in the upper grid of the Group by step.

- Then, for every combination of region and match date, you calculated some statistics. You did the calculations by adding rows in the lower grid of the step, one for every statistic you needed.

Let's see how it works. As the Group by step was preceded by a Sort rows step, the rows came to the step already ordered. When the rows arrive at the Group by step, Kettle creates groups based on the fields indicated in the upper grid; in this case, the region and match_date fields. The following screenshot shows this idea:

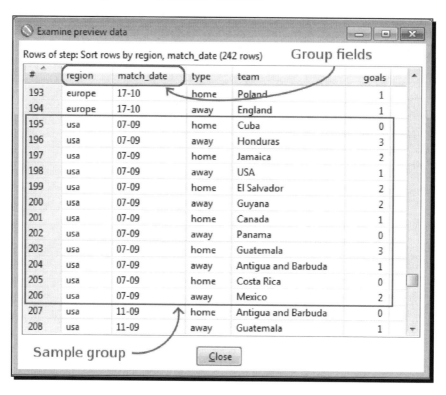

Then, for every group, the fields that you put in the lower grid are calculated. Let's see, for example, the group for the region usa and match date 07-09. There are 12 rows in this group. For these rows, Kettle calculated the following:

♦ **Goals (total)**: The total number of goals converted in the region usa on 07-09. There were 17 (0+3+2+1+2+2+1+0+3+1+0+2) goals.

♦ **Maximum**: The maximum number of goals converted by a team in a match. The maximum among the numbers in the preceding bullet point is 3.

♦ **Teams**: The number of teams that played on a day in a region—12.

The same calculations were made for every group. You can verify the details by looking at the preview windows or the preceding screenshot.

Look at the **Step Metrics** tab in the **Execution Results** area of the following screenshot:

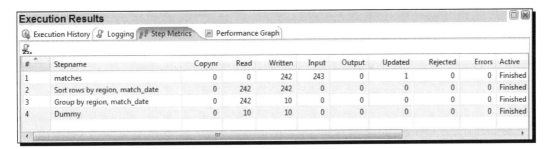

#	Stepname	Copynr	Read	Written	Input	Output	Updated	Rejected	Errors	Active
1	matches	0	0	242	243	0	1	0	0	Finished
2	Sort rows by region, match_date	0	242	242	0	0	0	0	0	Finished
3	Group by region, match_date	0	242	10	0	0	0	0	0	Finished
4	Dummy	0	10	10	0	0	0	0	0	Finished

Note that 242 rows enter the Group by step, and only 10 came out of that step towards the Dummy step. That is because after the grouping, you no longer have the details of the matches. The output of the Group by step is your new data now: one row for every group created.

Group by Step

The **Group by** step allows you to create groups of rows and calculate new fields over those groups.

In order to define the groups, you have to specify which field or fields are the keys. For every combination of values for those fields, Kettle builds a new group.

In the previous section, you grouped by two fields: `region` and `match_date`. Then for every pair (`region`, `match_date`), Kettle created a different group, generating a new row.

The Group by step operates on consecutive rows. The step traverses the dataset and each time the value for any of the grouping field changes, it creates a new group. The step works in this way, even if the data is not sorted by the grouping field.

 As you probably don't know how the data is ordered, it is safer and recommended that you sort the data by using a Sort rows step just before using a Group by step.

Once you have defined the groups, you are free to specify new fields to be calculated for every group. Every new field is defined as an aggregate function over some of the existent fields.

Let's review some of the fields that you created in the previous section:

- The `Goals (total)` field is the result of applying the `Sum` function over the field named goals.
- The `Maximum` field is the result of applying the `Maximum` function over the field `goals`.

- The `Number of Teams` field is the result of applying the `Number of Values (N)` function over the field `team`.

> Note that for a given region and date, it's supposed that a team only played a single match. That is, it will only appear once in the rows for that group. Therefore, you can safely use this function. If you can't make that assumption, you can use the `Number of Distinct Values (N)` function instead, which would count 1 for each team, even if it appears more than once.

Finally, you have the option to calculate aggregate functions over the whole dataset. You do this by leaving the upper grid blank. Following with the same example, you could calculate the number of teams that played and the average number of goals converted by a team in a football match. This is how you do it:

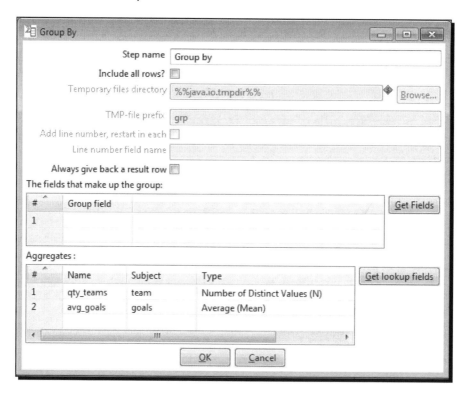

This is what you get:

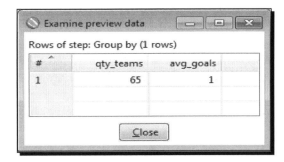

In any case, as a result of the Group by step, you will no longer have the detailed rows, unless you check the **Include all rows?** checkbox.

Numeric fields

As you know, there are several data types in Kettle. Among This section has been removed as it is badly phrased and the sentence makes sense without it the most used are String, Date, and Number. There is not much to say about the String fields, and we already discussed the Date type in *Chapter 2, Getting Started with Transformations*. Now it's time to talk about numeric fields, which are present in almost all Kettle transformations. In the preceding transformation, we read a file with a numeric field. As discussed in the *Time for action – sorting information about matches with the Sort rows step* section, if you don't intend to use the field for math, you don't need to define it as a numeric field. In the *Time for action – Calculating football matches statistics by grouping data* section, however, the numeric field represented goals, and you wanted to do some calculations based on the values. Therefore, we defined it as an integer, but didn't provide a format. When your input sources have more elaborate fields, for example, numbers with separators, dollar signs, and so on—see as an example the transformations about projects in *Chapter 2, Getting Started with Transformations*—you should specify a format to tell Kettle how to interpret the number. If you don't, Kettle will do its best to interpret the number, but this could lead to unexpected results.

On the other hand, when writing fields to an output destination, you have the option of specifying the format in which you want the number to be written. The same occurs when you change the metadata from a numeric field to a String: you have the option of specifying the format to use for doing the conversion.

There are several formats you may apply to a numeric field. The format is basically a combination of predefined symbols, each with a special meaning.

These format conventions are not Kettle specific, but Java standard. The following are the most used symbols:

Symbol	Meaning
#	Digit. Leading zeros are not shown.
0	Digit. If the digit is not present, zero is displayed in its place.
.	Decimal separator.
-	Minus sign.
%	Field has to be multiplied by 100 and shown as a percentage.

These symbols are not used alone. In order to specify the format of your numbers, you have to combine them. Suppose that you have a numeric field whose value is 99.55. The following table shows you the same value after applying different formats to it:

Format	Result
#	100
0	100
#.#	99.6
#.##	99.55
#.000	99.550
000.000	099.550

If you don't specify a format for your numbers, you may still provide a **length** and **precision**. Length is the total number of significant figures, while precision is the number of floating point digits.

If you neither specify the format nor length or precision, Kettle behaves as follows: while reading, it does its best to interpret the incoming number; when writing, it sends the data as it comes, without applying any format.

For a complete reference on number formats, you can check the Sun Java API documentation at `http://java.sun.com/javase/7/docs/api/java/text/DecimalFormat.html`.

Have a go hero – formatting 99.55

Create a transformation to see for yourself the different formats for the number 99.55. Test the formats shown in the preceding table, and try some other options as well.

To test this, you will need a dataset with a single row and a single field: the number. You can generate it with a Generate rows step.

Pop quiz — formatting output fields

Recall the transformation that you created in the first section of this chapter. You did not do any math, so you were free to read the `goals` field as a numeric or as a String field. Suppose that you define the field as a Number and, after sorting the data, you want to send it back to a file. How do you define the field in the Text file output step if you want to keep the same look and feel it had in the input? (You may choose more than one option):

1. As a Number. In the format, you put #.

2. As a String. In the format, you put #.

3. As a String. You leave the format blank.

Have a go hero – listing the languages spoken by a country

Read the file containing the information on countries, which you used in *Chapter 3, Manipulating Real-world Data.* Build a file where each row has two columns: the name of a country, and the list of languages spoken in that country.

 Us a Group by step, and as aggregate function use the option **Concatenate strings separated by ,**.

Filtering

Until now, you have learned how to do several kinds of calculations which enriched the set of data. There is still another kind of operation that is frequently used, and does not have anything to do with enriching the data, but with discarding the data. It is called filtering unwanted data. Now, you will learn how to discard rows under given conditions. As there are several kinds of filters that we may want to apply, let's split this section into two parts: *Counting frequent words by filtering* and *Refining the counting task by filtering even more*.

Time for action – counting frequent words by filtering

On this occasion, you have some plain text files, and you want to know what is said in them. You don't want to read them, so you decide to count the times that the words appear in the text, and see the most frequent ones to get an idea of what the files are about. The first of our two tutorials on filtering is about counting the words in the file.

Before starting, you'll need at least one text file to play with. The text file used in this tutorial is named smcng10.txt, and is available for you to download from Packt Publishing's website, www.packtpub.com.

Let's work.

This section and the following sections have many steps. So, feel free to preview the data from time-to-time. In this way, you make sure that you are doing well, and understand what filtering is about, as you progress in the design of your transformation.

1. Create a new transformation.

2. By using a **Text file input** step, read your file. The trick here is to put as a **Separator**, a sign you are not expecting in the file, such as |. By doing so, of the whole lines would be recognized as a single field. Configure the **Fields** tab by defining a single String field named line.

3. This particular file has a big header describing the content and origin of it. We are not interested in those lines, so in the **Content** tab, as **Header** type 378, which is the number of lines that precedes the specific content we're interested in.

4. From the **Transform** category of steps, drag to the canvas a **Split field to rows** step, and create a hop from the Text file input step to this one.

5. Configure the step as follows:

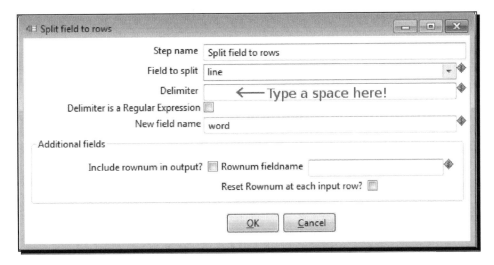

6. With this last step selected, do a preview. Your preview window should look as follows:

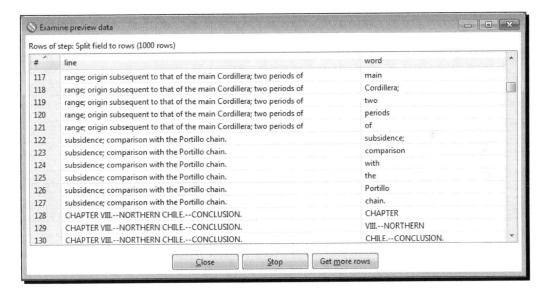

7. Close the preview window.

8. Add a **Select values** step to remove the `line` field.

 It's not mandatory to remove this field, but as it will not be used any longer, removing it will make future previews clearer.

9. Expand the **Flow** category of steps, and drag a **Filter rows** step to the work area.

10. Create a hop from the last step to the Filter rows step.

11. Edit the Filter rows step by double-clicking on it.

12. Click on the <field> textbox to the left of the = sign. The list of fields appears. Select **word**.

13. Click on the = sign. A list of operations appears. Select **IS NOT NULL**.

14. The window looks like the following screenshot:

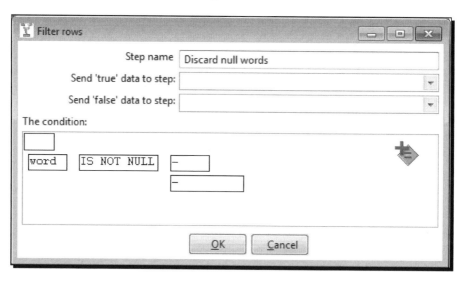

15. Click on **OK**.

16. From the **Transform** category of steps, drag a **Sort rows** step to the canvas.

17. Create a hop from the Filter rows step, to the Sort rows step. When asked for the kind of hop, select **Main output of step**, as shown in the following screenshot:

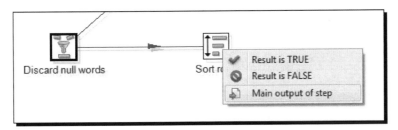

18. Use the last step to sort the rows by word (ascending).

19. From the **Statistics** category, drag-and-drop a **Group by** step on the canvas, and add it to the stream, after the Sort rows step.

20. Configure the grids in the Group by configuration window, as shown in the following screenshot:

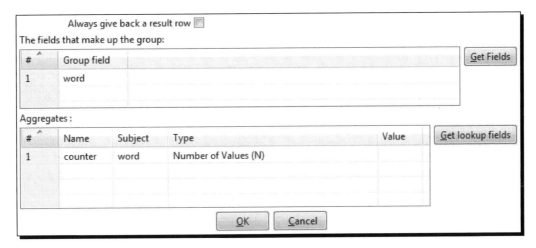

21. With the Group by step selected, do a preview. You will see this:

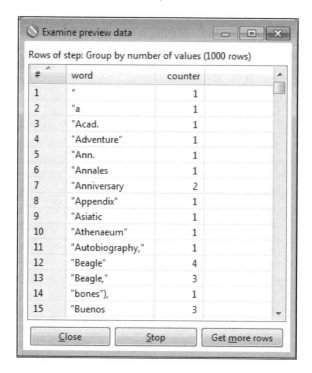

What just happened?

You read a regular plain file, and counted the words appearing in it.

The first thing you did was read the plain file, and split the lines so that every word became a new row in the dataset. For example, as a consequence of splitting the line:

```
subsidence; comparison with the Portillo chain.
```

The following rows were generated:

#	line	word
122	subsidence; comparison with the Portillo chain.	subsidence;
123	subsidence; comparison with the Portillo chain.	comparison
124	subsidence; comparison with the Portillo chain.	with
125	subsidence; comparison with the Portillo chain.	the
126	subsidence; comparison with the Portillo chain.	Portillo
127	subsidence; comparison with the Portillo chain.	chain.

Thus, a new field named `word` became the basis for your transformation, and therefore you removed the `line` field.

First of all, you discarded rows with null words. You did it by using a filter with the condition `word IS NOT NULL`.

Then, you counted the words by using the Group by step you learned in the previous tutorial. Doing it this way, you got a preliminary list of the words in the file, and the number of occurrences of each word.

Time for action – refining the counting task by filtering even more

This is the second tutorial on filtering. As discussed in the previous tutorial, we have a plain file and want to know what kind of information is present in it. In the previous section, we listed and counted the words in the file. Now, we will apply some extra filters in order to refine our work.

1. Open the transformation from the previous section.

2. Add a **Calculator** step, link it to the last step, and calculate the new field `len_word` representing the length of the words. To do this use the calculator function **Return the length of a string A**. As **Field A** type or select `word`, and as **Type** select **Integer**.

3. Expand the **Flow** category and drag another **Filter rows** step to the canvas.

4. Link it to the Calculator step and edit it.

5. Click on the <field> textbox and select **counter**.

6. Click on the = sign, and select **>**.

7. Click on the <value> textbox. A small window appears.

8. In the **Value** textbox of the little window type 2.

9. Click on **OK**.

10. Position the mouse cursor over the icon at the upper right-hand corner of the window. When the text **Add condition** shows up, click on the icon, as shown in the following screenshot:

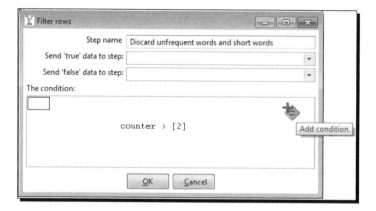

11. A new blank condition is shown below the one you created.

12. Click on **null = []** and create the following condition: `len_word>3`, in the same way that you created the condition `counter>2`.

13. Click on **OK**.

14. The final condition looks like this:

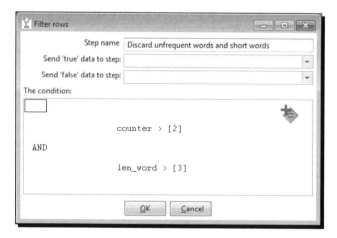

15. Close the window.

16. Add one more Filter rows step to the transformation and create a hop from the last step toward this one.

17. Configure the step in this way: at the left side of the condition select **word**, as comparator select **IN LIST**, and at the right side of the condition, inside the value textbox, type `a;an;and;the;that;this;there;these`.

18. Click on the upper-left square above the condition, and the word **NOT** will appear. The condition will look as shown in the following screenshot:

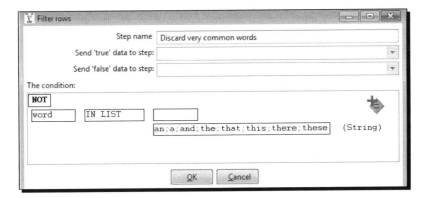

19. Add a **Sort rows** step, and sort the rows by `counter` descending.

20. Add a Dummy step at the end of the transformation.

21. With the Dummy step selected, preview the transformation. This is what you should see now:

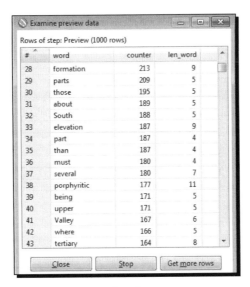

What just happened?

This section was the second part of the two devoted to learning how to filter data. In the first part, you read a file and counted the words in it. In this section, you discarded the rows where the word was too short (length less than 4), or appeared just once (counter less than 3), or was too common (compared to a list you typed).

Once you applied all of those filters, you sorted the rows descending by the number of times a word appeared in the file, so you could see which the most frequent words were.

Scrolling down the preview window to skip some prepositions, pronouns, and other common words that have nothing to do with a specific subject, you found words such as shells, strata, formation, South, elevation, porphyritic, Valley, tertiary, calcareous, plain, North and rocks. If you had to guess, you would say that this was a book or article about Geology, and you would be right. The text taken for this exercise was from the book *Geological Observations on South America* by Charles Darwin.

Filtering rows using the Filter rows step

The **Filter rows** step allows you to filter rows based on conditions and comparisons.

The step checks the condition for every row, then applies a filter letting only the rows for which the condition is `true` pass. The other rows are lost.

 If you want to keep those rows, there is a way. You just will learn how to do it later in the book.

In the last two tutorials, you used the Filter rows step several times, so you already have an idea of how it works. Let's review it:

When you edit a Filter rows step, you have to enter a condition. This condition may involve one field, such as `word IS NOT NULL`. In this case, only the rows where the words are neither null nor with empty values will pass. The condition may involve one field and a constant value such as `counter > 2`. This filter allows only the rows with a word that is more than twice in the file to pass. Finally, the condition may have two fields, such as `line CONTAINS word`.

You can also combine conditions, as follows:

```
counter > 2
AND
len_word>3
```

or even create sub-conditions, such as:

```
    (
    counter > 2
AND
    len_word>3
    )
OR
    (word in list geology; sun)
```

In this example, the condition let the word `geology` pass even if it appears only once. It also let the word `sun` pass, despite its length.

When editing conditions, you always have a contextual menu which allows you to add and delete sub-conditions, change the order of existent conditions, and more.

Maybe you wonder what the **Send 'true' data to step:** and **Send 'false' data to step:** textboxes are for. Be patient, you will learn how to use them in *Chapter 5, Controlling the Flow of Data*.

As an alternative to this step, there is another step for the same purpose: it's the **Java Filter** step. You also find it in the **Flow** category. This step can be useful when your conditions are too complicated, and it becomes difficult or impossible to create them in a regular Filter rows step. This is how you use it: in the Java Filter configuration window, instead of creating the condition interactively, you write a Java expression that evaluates to true or false. As an example, you can replace the second Filter row step in the section with a Java Filter step, and in the **Condition (Java expression)** textbox type `counter>2 && len_word > 3`. The result would have been the same as with the Filter row step.

Have a go hero – playing with filters

Now it is your turn to try filtering rows. Modify the transformation you just created in the following way: add a sub-condition to avoid excluding some words, just like the one in the preceding example, `word in list geology; sun`. Change the list of words and test the filter to see that the results are as expected.

Looking up data

Until now, you worked with a single stream of data. When you did calculations or created conditions to compare fields, you only involved fields of your stream. Usually this is not enough, and you need data from other sources. In this section, you will learn how to look up data outside your stream.

Time for action – finding out which language people speak

An International Musical Contest will take place and 24 countries will participate; each presenting a duet. Your task is to hire interpreters so the contestants can communicate in their native language. In order to do that, you need to find out the language they speak:

1. Create a new transformation.

2. By using a **Get data from XML** step, read the file with information about countries that you used in *Chapter 3, Manipulating Real-world Data*, `countries.xml`.

 To avoid configuring the step again, you can open the transformation that reads this file, copy the Get data from XML step, and paste it here.

3. Drag to the canvas a **Filter rows** step.

4. Create a hop from the Get data from XML step to the Filter rows step.

5. Edit the Filter rows step and create this condition: `isofficial= T`.

6. Click on the Filter rows step and do a preview. The list of previewed rows will show the countries along with the official languages, as shown in the following screenshot:

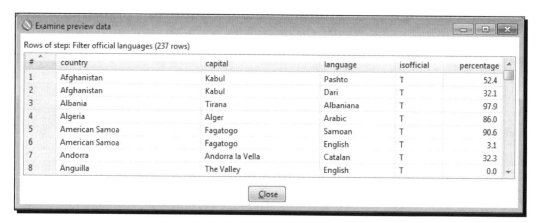

#	country	capital	language	isofficial	percentage
1	Afghanistan	Kabul	Pashto	T	52.4
2	Afghanistan	Kabul	Dari	T	32.1
3	Albania	Tirana	Albaniana	T	97.9
4	Algeria	Alger	Arabic	T	86.0
5	American Samoa	Fagatogo	Samoan	T	90.6
6	American Samoa	Fagatogo	English	T	3.1
7	Andorra	Andorra la Vella	Catalan	T	32.3
8	Anguilla	The Valley	English	T	0.0

7. Now let's create the main flow of data.

8. From the Packt Publishing website, `www.packtpub.com`, download the list of contestants. It looks like this:

```
ID;Country Name;Duet
1;Russia;Mikhail Davydova
;;Anastasia Davydova
2;Spain;Carmen Rodriguez
```

```
;;Francisco Delgado
3;Japan;Natsuki Harada
;;Emiko Suzuki
4;China;Lin Jiang
;;Wei Chiu
5;United States;Chelsea Thompson
;;Cassandra Sullivan
6;Canada;Mackenzie Martin
;;Nathan Gauthier
7;Italy;Giovanni Lombardi
;;Federica Lombardi
```

9. In the same transformation, drag to the canvas a **Text file input** step and read the downloaded file.

 The ID and Country fields have values only in the first of the two lines for each country. In order to repeat the values in the second line, use the flag **Repeat** in the **Fields** tab. Set it to Y.

10. Expand the **Lookup** category of steps.

11. Drag to the canvas a **Stream lookup** step.

12. Create a hop from the Text file input you just created, to the Stream lookup step.

13. Create another hop from the Filter rows step to the Stream lookup step. When asked for the kind of hop, choose **Main output of step**. So far you have this:

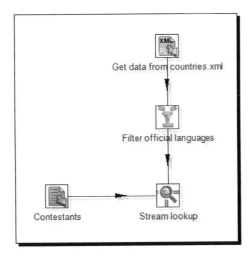

14. Edit the Stream lookup step by double-clicking on it.

15. In the **Lookup step** drop-down list, select **Filter official languages**, the step that brings the list of languages.

16. Fill in the grids in the configuration window as follows:

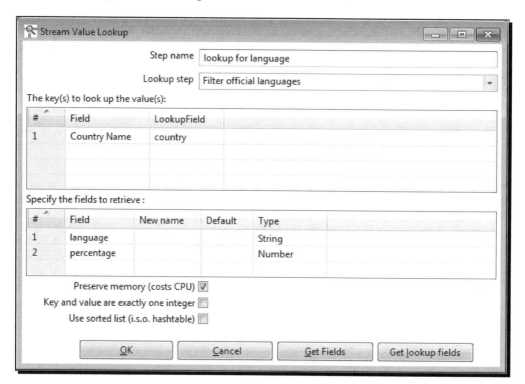

Note that Country Name is a field coming from the text file stream, while the country field comes from the countries stream.

17. Click on **OK**.

18. The hop that goes from the Filter rows step to the Stream lookup step changes its look and feel. The icon that appears over the hop shows that this is the stream where the Stream lookup step is going to look up, as shown in the following screenshot:

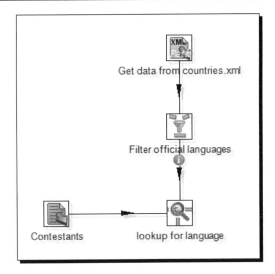

19. By using a **Select values** step, rename the fields Duet, Country Name, and language, to Name, Country, and Language.

20. Drag to the canvas a **Text file output** step and create the file people_and_ languages.txt with the selected fields.

21. Save the transformation.

22. Run the transformation and check the final file that should look like this:

```
Name|Country|Language
Mikhail Davydova|Russia|
Anastasia Davydova|Russia|
Carmen Rodriguez|Spain|Spanish
Francisco Delgado|Spain|Spanish
Natsuki Harada|Japan|Japanese
Emiko Suzuki|Japan|Japanese
Lin Jiang|China|Chinese
Wei Chiu|China|Chinese
Chelsea Thompson|United States|English
Cassandra Sullivan|United States|English
Mackenzie Martin|Canada|French
Nathan Gauthier|Canada|French
Giovanni Lombardi|Italy|Italian
Federica Lombardi|Italy|Italian
```

What just happened?

First of all, you read a file with information about countries and the languages spoken in those countries.

Then, you read a list of people along with the country they come from. For every row in this list, you told Kettle to look for the country (the `Country Name` field), in the countries stream (the `country` field), and to give you back a language and the percentage of people who speak that language (`language` and `percentage` fields). Let's explain it with a sample row: the row for `Francisco Delgado` from `Spain`. When this row gets to the Stream lookup step, Kettle looks in the list of countries for a row with the country `Spain`. It finds it. Then, it returns the value of the columns `language` and `percentage`, `Spanish` and `74.4`.

Now take another sample row: the row with the country `Russia`. When the row gets to the Stream lookup step, Kettle looks for it in the list of countries, but it does not find it. So, what you get as language is a null string.

Whether the country is found or not, two new fields are added to your stream: the fields `language` and `percentage`.

Finally, you exported all of the information to a plain text file.

The Stream lookup step

The **Stream lookup** step allows you to look up data in a secondary stream.

You tell Kettle which of the incoming streams is the stream used to look up, by selecting the right choice in the **Lookup step** list.

The upper grid in the configuration window allows you to specify the names of the fields that are used to look up.

In the left column, **Field**, you indicate the field of your main stream. You can fill in this column by using the **Get Fields** button, and deleting all the fields you don't want to use for the search.

In the right column, **LookupField**, you indicate the field of the secondary stream.

When a row of data comes to the step, a lookup is made to see if there is a row in the secondary stream for which, for every pair in the upper grid, the value of **Field** is equal to the value of **LookupField**. If there is one, the lookup will be successful.

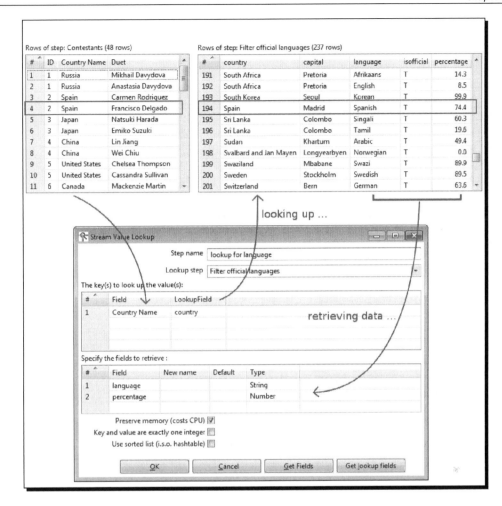

In the lower grid, you specify the names of the secondary stream fields that you want back as result of the lookup. You can fill in this column by using the **Get lookup fields** button, and deleting all the fields that you don't want to retrieve.

After the lookup, new fields are added to your dataset—one for every row of this grid.

For the rows for which the lookup is successful, the values for the new fields will be taken from the lookup stream.

For the others, the fields will remain null, unless you set a default value.

It's important that you are aware of the behavior of this step:

> Only one row is returned per key. If the key you are looking for appears more than once in the lookup stream, only one will be returned. As an example, think that when there is more than one official language spoken in a country, you get just one. Sometimes you don't care, but on some occasions this is not acceptable and you have to try some other methods.

There is a possible solution to this drawback in the following *Have a go hero – selecting the most popular of the official languages* section. You will also learn other ways to overcome this situation later in the book.

Have a go hero – selecting the most popular of the official languages

As already discussed, when a country has more than one official language, the lookup step picks any of them. Take for example, the contestant for `Canada`. `Canada` has two official languages, and `English` the most frequently used (60.4%). However, the lookup step returned `French`. So, the proposal here is to change the transformation in one of the following ways (or both—create two different transformations—if you really want to practice!):

- Alter the countries stream, so for each country only the most relevant official language is considered.

 Use a combination of a Sort rows and a Group by step. As **Type**, use **First value** or **Last value**.

- Alter the countries stream so that for each country instead of one official language by row, there is a single row with the list of official languages concatenated by `-`.

 Use a Group by step. As **Type** use **Concatenate strings separated by**, and use the **Value** column for typing the separator.

Have a go hero – counting words more precisely

The section where you counted the words in a file worked pretty well, but you may have noticed that it has some details you can fix or enhance.

You discarded a very small list of words, but there are many more that are common in English, such as prepositions, pronouns, and auxiliary verbs. So here is the challenge: get a list of commonly used words and save it in a file. Instead of excluding words from a small list as you did with a Filter rows step, exclude the words that are present in your words file.

 Use a combination of a Stream lookup step and a Filter rows step, which discards the words if they were found in the words file.

Data cleaning

Data from the real world is not always as perfect as we would like it to be. On one hand, there are cases where the errors in data are so critical that the only solution is to report them or even abort a process. There is, however, a different kind of issue with data: minor problems that can be fixed somehow, as in the following examples:

- You have a field that contains years. Among the values, you see 2912. This can be considered as a typo, and assume that the proper value is 2012.

- You have a string that represents the name of a country, and it is supposed that the names belong to a predefined list of valid countries. You see, however, values as USA, U.S.A., or United States. In your list, you have only USA as valid, but it is clear that all of these values belong to the same country, and should be easy to unify.

- You have a field that should contain integer numbers between 1 and 5. Among the values, you have numbers such as 3.01 or 4.99. It should not be a problem to round those numbers so the final values are all in the expected range of values.

In the following section, you will practice some of this cleansing task.

Time for action – fixing words before counting them

In this section, we will modify the transformation that counted words. We will clean the field words by removing leading characters.

1. Open the transformation that counted words and save it with a different name.

2. Delete (or disable) all the steps after the Group by step.

3. After the Group by step, add a **Filter rows** step with this condition: word STARTS WITH albite.

4. Do a preview on this step. You will see this:

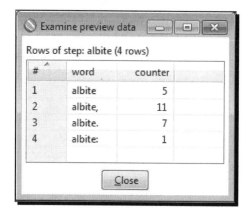

5. Now, from the **Transform** category of steps, drag a **Replace in string** step to the work area.

6. Insert the step between the Select row step and the first Filter rows step, as shown in the following screenshot:

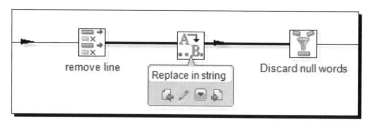

7. Double-click on the step and configure it. Under **In stream field**, type word. Under **use RegEx**, type or select Y. Under **Search**, type [\.,:]$.

8. Click on **OK**.

9. Repeat the preview on the recently added Filter rows step. You will see this:

What just happened?

You modified the transformation that counted words by cleaning some words.

In the source file, you had several occurrences of the word `albite`, but some of them had a leading character as `.`, `,` `;` or `:`. This caused the transformation to consider them as different words, as you saw in the first preview. Simply by using the Replace in string step you removed those symbols, and then all the occurrences of the word were grouped together, which lead to a more precise final count.

Let's briefly explain how the Replace in string step works. The function of the step is to take a field and replace its value with all of the occurrences of a string with a different string. In this case, you wanted to modify the word field by deleting the leading symbols (. , ; :); in other words, replacing them with `null`.

In order to tell Kettle which string to replace, you provided a regular expression: `[\.,:]$` This expression represents any of the following characters . , : at the end of the field and not in another place.

In order to remove these symbols, you left the **Replace with** column empty.

By leaving the **Out stream field** column empty, you have overwritten the field with the new value.

Cleansing data with PDI

While validation means mainly rejecting data, data cleansing detects and tries to fix not only invalid data, but also the data that is considered illegal or inaccurate in a specific domain.

Data cleansing, also known as data cleaning or data scrubbing, may be done manually or automatically depending on the complexity of the cleansing.

Knowing in advance the rules that apply, you can do an automatic cleaning by using any PDI step that suits. The following are some steps particularly useful:

Step	Purpose
If field value is null	If a field is `null`, it changes its value to a constant. It can be applied to all fields of a same data type, or to particular fields.
Null if...	Sets a field value to `null` if it is equal to a constant value.
Number range	Creates ranges based on a numeric field. An example of its use is converting floating numbers to a discrete scale as 0, 0.25, 0.50, and so on.
Value Mapper	Maps values of a field from one value to another. For example, you can use this step to convert yes/no, true/false, or 0/1 values to Y/N.

Step	Purpose
Replace in string	Replaces all occurrences of a string inside a field, with a different string. This was the step used in the section for removing leading symbols.
String operations	Useful for trimming, removing special characters, and more.
Stream lookup	Looks up values coming from another stream. In data cleansing, you can use it to set a default value if your field is not in a given list.
Database lookup	Same as Stream lookup, but looking in a database table.
Unique rows	Removes double consecutive rows and leaves only unique occurrences.

For examples that use these steps or for getting more information about them, please refer to *Appendix D, Job Entries and Steps Reference*.

Have a go hero – counting words by cleaning them first

If you take a look at the results in the previous section, you may notice that some words appear more than one in the final list, because of special signs such as . ,) , or ", or because of lower or uppercase letters. Look, for example, how many times the word rock appears: rock (99 occurrences), rock, (51 occurrences), rock. (11 occurrences), rock." (1 occurrence), rock: (6 occurrences), rock; (2 occurrences). You can fix it and make the word rock to appear only once. Before grouping the words, remove all extra signs and convert all of the words to lower or uppercase, so they are grouped as expected.

 Try one or more of the following steps: **Formula**, **Calculator**, **User Defined Java Expression**, or any of the steps mentioned in the preceding table.

Summary

In this chapter, we learned some of the most used and useful ways of transforming data.

Specifically, you learned about filtering and sorting data, calculating statistics on groups of rows, and looking up data.

You also learned what data cleansing is about. After learning about the basic manipulation of data, you may now create more complex transformations, where the streams begin to split and merge. That is the core subject of the next chapter.

5

Controlling the Flow of Data

In the previous chapters, you learned to transform your data in many ways. Now suppose you collect results from a survey. You receive several files with the data and those files have different formats. You have to merge those files somehow, and generate a unified view of the information. Not only that, you want to remove the rows of data whose content is irrelevant. Finally, based on the rows that interest you, you want to create another file with some statistics. This kind of requirement is very common, but requires more background in PDI.

In this chapter, you will learn how to implement this kind of task with Kettle. In particular, we will cover the following topics:

- ◆ Copying and distributing rows
- ◆ Splitting the stream based on conditions
- ◆ Merging streams

You will also apply these concepts in the treatment of invalid data.

Splitting streams

Until now, you have been working with simple and straight flows of data. Often, the rows of your dataset have to take different paths and those simple flows are not enough. This situation is handled very easily, and you will learn how to do it in this section.

Time for action – browsing new features of PDI by copying a dataset

Before starting, let's introduce the Pentaho BI Platform Tracking site. At the Tracking site, you can see the current Pentaho roadmap and browse their issue-tracking system. The PDI page for that site is `http://jira.pentaho.com/browse/PDI`.

In this exercise, you will export the list of proposed new features for PDI, from the site and generate detailed and summarized files from that information.

Access to the main Pentaho Tracking site page is at: `http://jira.pentaho.com`.

 At this point, you may want to create a user ID. Logging is not mandatory, but beneficial if you want to create new issues or comment on existing ones.

1. In the menu at the top of the screen, select **Issues**. A list of issues will be displayed.

2. At the top, you will have several drop-down listboxes for filtering. Use them to select the following filters:

    ☐ **Project: Pentaho Data Integration - Kettle**

    ☐ **Issue Type: New Feature**

    ☐ **Status: Open**

3. As you select the filters, they are automatically applied and you can see the list of issues that match the filters:

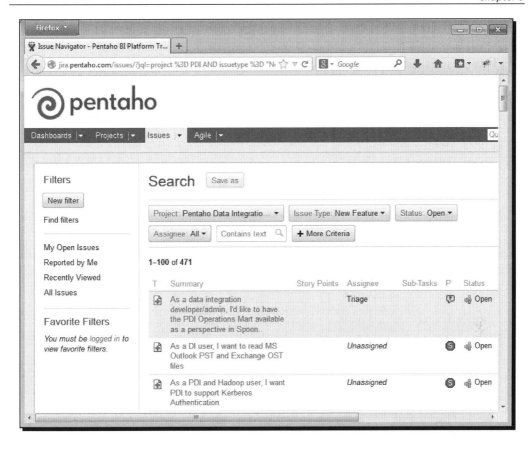

4. Above the list of search criteria, click on the **Views** icon and a list of options will be displayed. Among the options, select **Excel (Current fields)** to export the list to an Excel file.

5. Save the file to the folder of your choice.

 The Excel file exported from the JIRA website is a Microsoft Excel 97-2003 Worksheet. PDI does not recognize this version of worksheets. So, before proceeding, open the file with Excel or Calc and convert it to Excel 97/2000/XP.

6. Create a transformation.

7. Read the file by using a **Microsoft Excel Input** step. After providing the filename, click on the **Sheets** tab and fill it as shown in the following screenshot, so it skips the header rows and the first column:

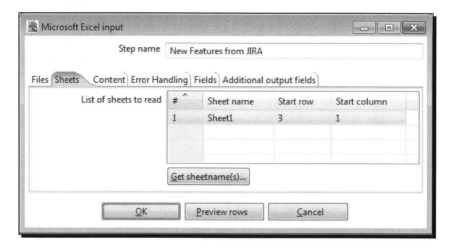

8. Click on the **Fields** tab and fill in the grid by clicking on the **Get fields from header row...** button.

9. Click on **Preview rows** just to be sure that you are reading the file properly. You should see all the contents of the Excel file except the first column and the three heading lines.

10. Click on **OK**.

11. Add a **Filter rows** step to drop the rows where the `Summary` field is null. That is, the filter will be `Summary IS NOT NULL`.

12. After the **Filter rows** step, add a **Value Mapper** step. When asked for the kind of hop, select **Main output of step**. Then fill the Value Mapper configuration window as shown in the following screenshot:

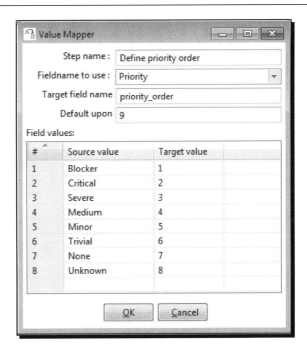

13. After the Value Mapper step, add a **Sort rows** step and order the rows by `priority_order` (ascending), `Summary` (ascending).

14. Select this last step and do a preview. You will see this:

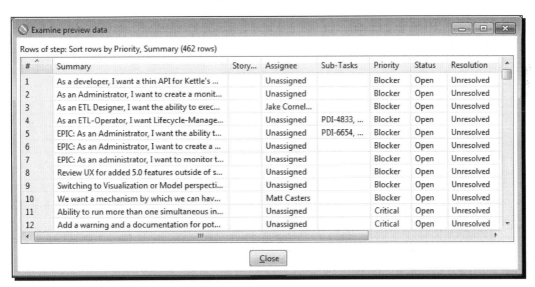

Take into account that the issues you see may not match the ones shown here as you derived your own source data from the JIRA system, and it changes all the time.

So far, you read a file with JIRA issues and after applying minor transformations, you got the dataset shown previously. Now it's time to effectively generate the detailed and summarized files as promised at the beginning of the section.

1. After the Sort rows step, add a **Microsoft Excel Output** step, and configure it to send the `priority_order` and `Summary` fields to an Excel file named `new_features.xls`.

2. Drag to the canvas a **Group by** step.

3. Create a new hop from the Sort rows step to the Group by step.

4. A warning window appears asking you to decide whether to copy or distribute rows. Click on **Copy**.

5. The hops leaving the Sort rows step change to show you the decision you made. So far, you have this:

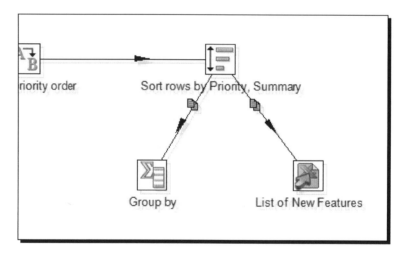

6. Configure the Group by steps as shown in the following screenshot:

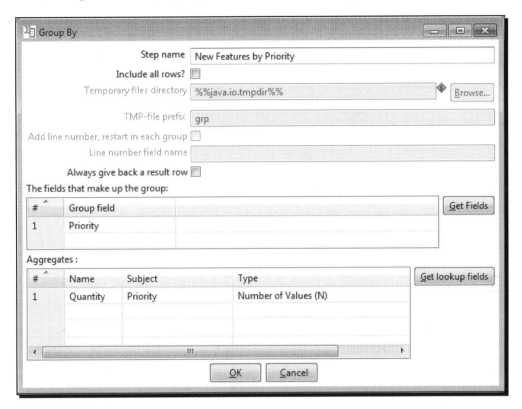

7. Add a new **Microsoft Excel Output** step to the canvas, and create a hop from the Group by step to this new step.

8. Configure the Microsoft Excel Output step to send the fields `Priority` and `Quantity` to an Excel file named `new_features_summarized.xls`.

9. Save the transformation, and then run it.

10. Verify that both files `new_features.xls` and `new_features_summarized.xls` have been created. The first file should look like this:

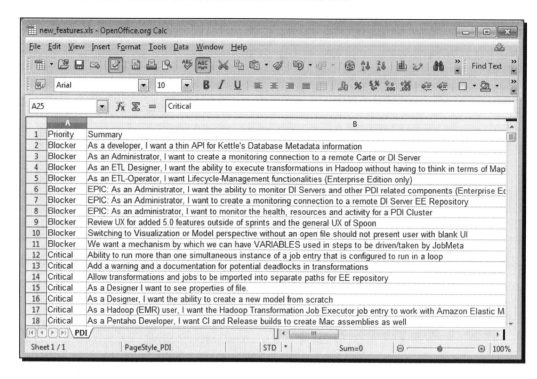

11. And the second file should look like this:

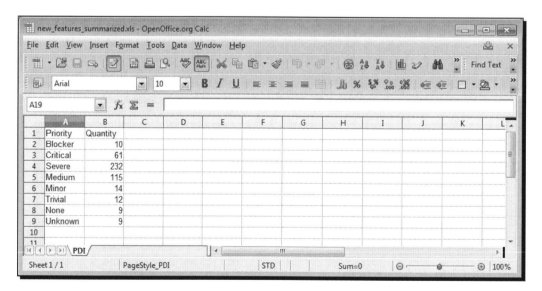

What just happened?

After exporting an Excel file with the PDI new features from the JIRA site, you read the file and created two Excel files: one with a list of the issues and another with a summary of the list.

The first steps of the transformation are well known: read a file, filter null rows, map a field, and sort.

 Note that the mapping creates a new field to give an order to the `Priority` field, so that the more severe issues are first in the list while the minor priorities remain at the end of the list.

You linked the Sort rows step to two different steps. This caused PDI to ask you what to do with the rows leaving the step. By clicking on **Copy**, you told PDI to create a copy of the dataset. After that, two identical copies left the Sort rows step, each to a different destination step.

From the moment you copied the dataset, those copies became independent, each following its own way. The first copy was sent to a detailed Excel file. The other copy was used to create a summary of the fields, which then was sent to another Excel file.

Copying rows

At any place in a transformation, you may decide to split the main stream into two or more streams. When you do so, you have to decide what to do with the data that leaves the last step: copy or distribute.

To **copy** means that the whole dataset is copied to each of the destination steps. Once the rows are sent to those steps, each follows its own way.

When you copy, the hops that leave the step from which you are copying change visually to indicate the copy action.

In the section, you created two copies of the main dataset. You could have created more than two, like in this example:

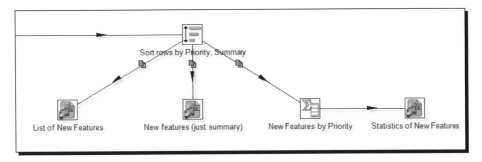

When you split the stream into two or more streams, you can do whatever you want with each one as if they had never been the same stream. The transformations you apply to any of those output streams will not modify the data in the others.

 You should not assume a particular order in the execution of steps, due to its asynchronous nature. As the steps are executed in parallel and all the output streams receive the rows in sync, you don't have control over the order in which they are executed.

Have a go hero – recalculating statistics

Recall the *Have a go hero – Selecting the most popular of the official languages* exercise Calculate some statistics about the spoken from *Chapter 4, Filtering, Searching, and Performing Other Useful Operations with Data*. You were told to create two transformations that calculated different statistics taking as starting point the same source data. Now, create a single transformation that does both tasks.

Distributing rows

As previously said, when you split a stream, you can copy or distribute the rows. You already saw that copy is about creating copies of the whole dataset and sending each of them to each output stream. To **distribute** instead means that the rows of the dataset are distributed among the destination steps. Let's see how it works through a modified exercise.

Time for action – assigning tasks by distributing

Let's suppose you want to distribute the issues among three programmers so each of them implements a subset of the new features.

1. Open the transformation created in the previous section, change the description, and save it under a different name.

2. Now delete all the steps after the Sort rows step.

3. Change the Filter rows step to keep only the unassigned issues: Assignee field equal to the string Unassigned. The condition looks like this:

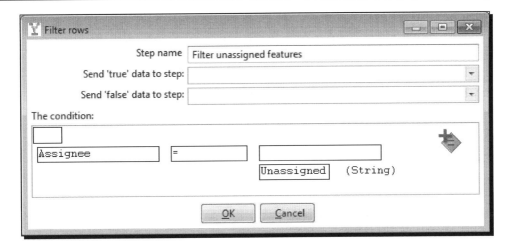

4. From the **Transform** category of steps, drag an **Add sequence** step to the canvas and create a hop from the Sort rows step to this new step.

5. Double-click on the Add sequence step and replace the content of the **Name of value** textbox with nr.

6. Drag to the canvas three **Microsoft Excel Output** steps.

7. Link the Add sequence step to one of these steps.

8. Configure the Microsoft Excel Output step to send the fields nr, Priority, and Summary to an Excel file named f_costa.xls (the name of one of the programmers). The **Fields** tab should look like this:

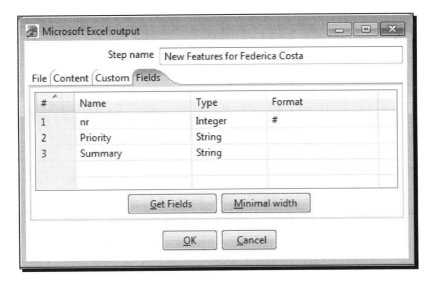

9. Create a hop from the Add sequence step to the second Microsoft Excel Output step. When asked to decide between **Copy** and **Distribute**, select **Distribute**.

10. Configure the step as before, but name the file as `b_bouchard.xls` (the second programmer).

11. Create a hop from the Add sequence step to the last Microsoft Excel Output step.

12. Configure this last step as before, but name the file as `a_mercier.xls` (the last programmer).

13. The transformation should look like this:

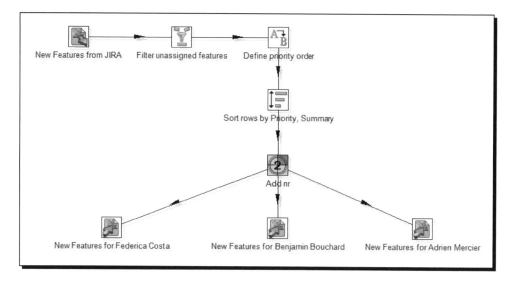

14. Run the transformation and look at the execution tab window to see what happened. If you don't remember the meaning of the different metrics, you can go back and take a look at *The Step Metrics tab* section in *Chapter 2, Getting Started with Transformations*.

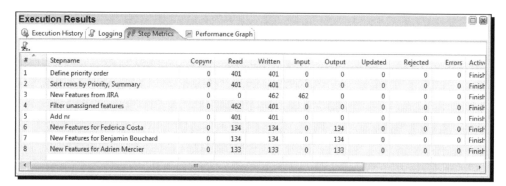

#	Stepname	Copynr	Read	Written	Input	Output	Updated	Rejected	Errors	Activ
1	Define priority order	0	401	401	0	0	0	0	0	Finish
2	Sort rows by Priority, Summary	0	401	401	0	0	0	0	0	Finish
3	New Features from JIRA	0	0	462	462	0	0	0	0	Finish
4	Filter unassigned features	0	462	401	0	0	0	0	0	Finish
5	Add nr	0	401	401	0	0	0	0	0	Finish
6	New Features for Federica Costa	0	134	134	0	134	0	0	0	Finish
7	New Features for Benjamin Bouchard	0	134	134	0	134	0	0	0	Finish
8	New Features for Adrien Mercier	0	133	133	0	133	0	0	0	Finish

Again, take into account that your numbers may not match the exact metrics shown here, as you derived your own source data from the JIRA system.

15. To see which rows were to which of the created files, open any of them. It should look like this:

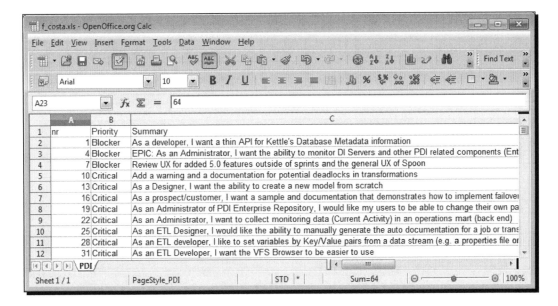

What just happened?

You distributed the issues among three programmers.

In the execution window, you could see that 401 rows leave the Add sequence step, and a third part of those rows arrive to each of the Microsoft Excel Output steps. In numbers, 134, 134, and 133 rows go to each file respectively. You verified that when you explored the Excel files.

In the transformation, you added an Add sequence step that did nothing more than add a sequential number to the rows. That sequence helps you recognize that one out of every three rows went to every file.

Here you saw a practical example for the Distribute option. When you distribute, the destination steps receive the rows in turns. For example, if you have three target steps, the first row goes to the first target step, the second row goes to the second step, the third row goes to the third step, the fourth row goes to the first step, and so on.

As you can see, when distributing, the hops leaving the steps from which you distribute are plain; they don't change its look and feel.

Despite the fact that this example clearly showed how the Distribute method works, this is not how you will regularly use this option. The Distribute option is mainly used for performance reasons. Throughout the book, you will always use the Copy option. To avoid being asked for the action to take every time you create more than one hop leaving a step, you can set the Copy option as default. You do it by opening the **PDI options** window (**Tools | Options...** from the main menu) and unchecking the option **Show "copy or distribute" dialog?**. Remember that to see the change applied you will have to restart Spoon.

Once you have changed this option, the default method is Copy rows. If you want to distribute rows, you can change the action by right-clicking on the step from which you want to copy or distribute, selecting **Data Movement...** in the contextual menu that appears, and then selecting the desired option.

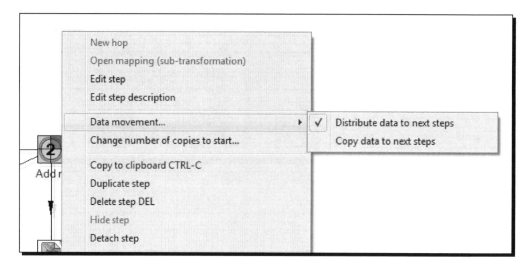

Pop quiz – understanding the difference between copying and distributing

Look at the following transformations:

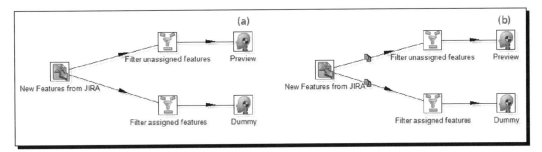

Q1. If you do a preview on the steps named Preview, which of the following is true?

1. The number of rows you see in (a) is greater than or equal to the number of rows you see in (b).

2. The number of rows you see in (b) is greater than or equal to the number of rows you see in (a).

3. The dataset you see in (a) is exactly the same you see in (b) no matter what data you have in the Excel file.

You can create a transformation and test each option to check the results for yourself. To be sure you understand correctly where and when the rows take one or other way, you can preview every step in the transformation, not just the last one.

Splitting the stream based on conditions

In the previous section, you learned to split the main stream of data into two or more streams. The whole dataset was copied or distributed among the destination steps. Now you will learn how to put conditions so the rows take one way or another depending on the conditions.

Time for action – assigning tasks by filtering priorities with the Filter rows step

Continuing with the JIRA subject, let's do a more realistic distribution of tasks among programmers. Let's assign the severe task to our most experienced programmer, and the other tasks to others.

Create a new transformation.

Read the JIRA file and filter the unassigned tasks, just as you did in the previous section.

1. Add a **Filter rows** step. Create a hop from the previous Filter rows step toward this new filter. When asked for the kind of hop, select **Main output of step**.

2. Add two **Microsoft Excel Output** steps.

3. Create a hop from the last Filter row to one of the Microsoft Excel Output steps. As the type for the hop, select **Result is TRUE**.

4. Create a hop from the last Filter row to the other Excel step. This time as the type for the hop, select **Result is FALSE**. The transformation looks as follows:

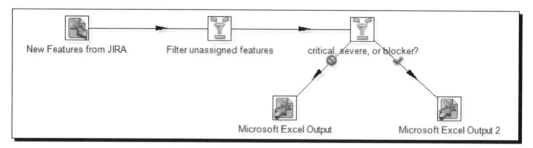

5. Double-click on the Filter rows step to edit it.

 Note that the content of the textboxes **Send "true" data to step** and **Send "false"data to step** should be the names of the destination steps - the two Microsoft Excel Output steps.

6. Enter the condition `Priority = [Critical] OR Priority = [Severe] OR Priority = [Blocker]`.

Alternatively you can use a single condition: `Priority IN LIST Critical;Severe;Blocker`.

7. Configure the Microsoft Excel Output step located at the end of the green hop. As fields, select **Priority** and **Summary**, and as the name for the file type `b_bouchard.xls` (the name of the senior programmer).

8. Configure the other Microsoft Excel Output step to send the fields **Priority** and **Summary** to an Excel file named `new_features_to_develop.xls`.

9. Click on **OK** and save the transformation.

10. Run the transformation, and verify that the two Excel files were created. The files should look like this:

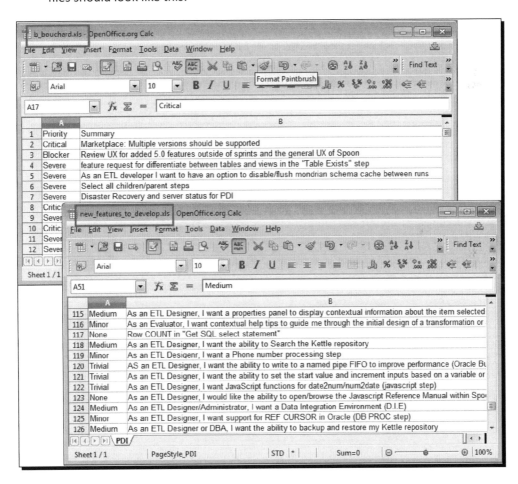

What just happened?

You sent the list of PDI new features to two Excel files: one file with the blocker, severe, and critical issues, and the other file with the rest of the issues.

In the Filter rows step, you put a condition to evaluate if the priority of a task was blocker, severe, or critical. For every row coming to the filter, the condition was evaluated.

The rows that met the condition, that is, those that had one of those three priorities, followed the green hop. This hop linked the Filter rows step with the Microsoft Excel Output step that creates the `b_bouchard.xls` file. If you take a look at the Filter rows configuration window, you can also see the name of that step in the **Send 'true' data to step** textbox.

The rows that did not meet the condition, that is, those with another priority, were sent toward the other Microsoft Excel Output step, following the red hop. This hop linked the Filter rows step with the Microsoft Excel Output step that creates the `new_features_to_develop.xls` file. In this case, you can also see the name of the Microsoft Excel Output step in the **Send 'false' data to step** textbox.

PDI steps for splitting the stream based on conditions

When you have to make a decision, and upon that decision split the stream into two, you can use the Filter rows step as you did in this last exercise. In this case, the Filter rows step acts as a decision maker: it has a condition and two possible destinations. For every row coming to the filter, the step evaluates the condition. Then, if the result of the condition is true, it decides to send the row towards the step selected in the first drop-down list of the configuration window: **Send 'true' data to step**.

If the result of the condition is false, it sends the row towards the step selected in the second drop-down list of the configuration window: **Send 'false' data to step**.

Alternatively, you can use the Java Filter step. As said in the last chapter, the purpose of both steps—Filter rows and Java Filter—is the same; the main difference is the way in which you type or enter the conditions.

Sometimes you have to make nested decisions, for example:

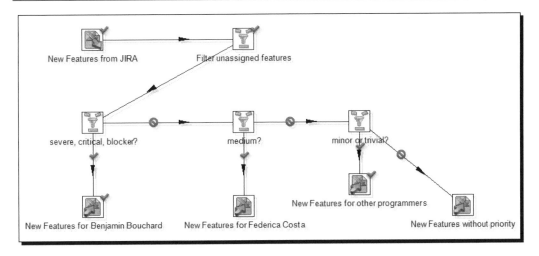

When the conditions are as simple as testing whether a field is equal to a value, you have a simpler way for creating a transformation like the one shown previously.

Time for action – assigning tasks by filtering priorities with the Switch/Case step

Let's use a Switch/Case step to replace the nested Filter rows steps shown in the previous image.

1. Create a transformation like the following:

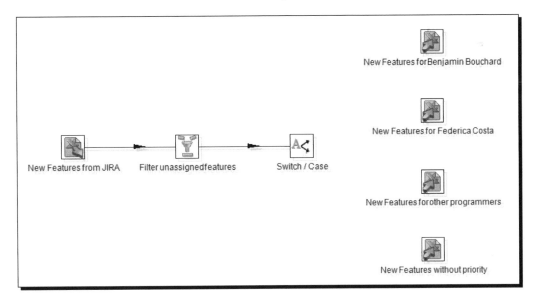

2. You will find the **Switch/Case** step in the **Flow** category of steps.

 To save time, you can take as starting point the last transformation you created. Configure the new Microsoft Excel Output steps just as you configured the others but changing the names of the output files.

3. Create a hop, leaving the Switch/Case step towards the first of the Microsoft Excel Output steps. When prompted for the kind of hop to create, select **Create a new target case for this step** as shown in the following image:

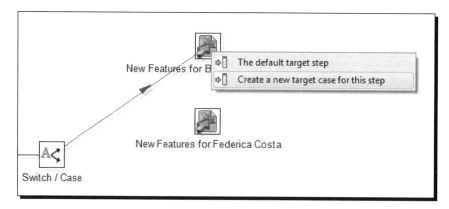

4. Create a new hop from the Switch/Case step to the second Microsoft Excel Output step, also selecting **Create a new target case for this step**.

5. Do the same again, this time linking the Switch/Case to the third Microsoft Excel Output step.

6. Finally, create a hop from the Switch/Case step to the fourth Microsoft Excel Output step, but this time select **The default target step**.

7. You still have to configure the Switch/Case step. Double-click on it. You will see this:

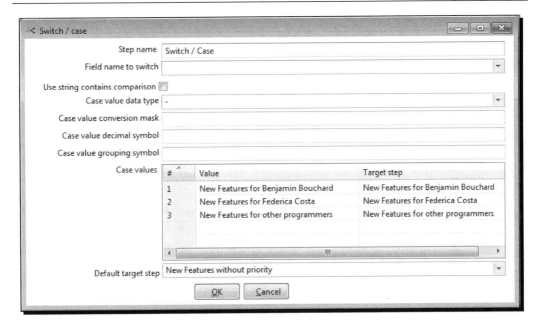

8. As **Field name to switch** select or type `Priority`.

9. Now adjust the contents of the **Case values** grid so it looks like the following:

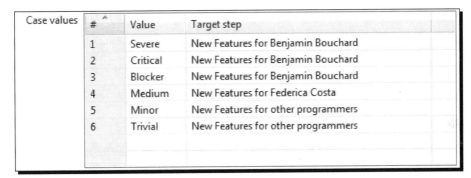

10. Save the transformation and run it.

11. Open the generated Excel files to see that the transformation distributed the task among the files based on the given conditions.

What just happened?

In this section, you learned to use the Switch/Case step. This step routes rows of data to one or more target steps based on the value encountered in a given field.

In the Switch/Case step configuration window, you told Kettle where to send the row depending on a condition. The condition to evaluate was the equality of the field set in **Field name to switch** and the value indicated in the grid. In this case, the field name to switch is **Priority**, and the values against which it will be compared are the different values for priorities: Severe, Critical, and so on. Depending on the values of the Priority field, the rows will be sent to any of the target steps. For example, the rows where the value of Priority is **Medium** will be sent towards the target step **New Features for Federica Costa**.

 Note that it is possible to specify the same target step more than once.

The **Default target step** represents the step where the rows which don't match any of the case values are sent. In this example, the rows with a priority not present in the list will be sent to the step **New Features without priority**.

Have a go hero – listing languages and countries

Open the transformation you created in the *Time for action – Finding out which language people speak* section in *Chapter 4, Filtering, Searching, and Performing Other Useful Operations with Data*. If you run the transformation and check the content of the output file, you'll notice that there are missing languages. Modify the transformation so that it generates two files: one with the rows where there is a language, that is, the rows for which the lookup succeeded, and another file with the list of countries not found in the `countries.xlm` file.

Pop quiz – deciding between a Number range step and a Switch/Case step

Continuing with the contestant exercise, suppose that the number of interpreters you will hire depends on the number of people that speak each language:

Number of people that speak the language	Number of interpreters
Less than 3	1
Between 3 and 6	2
More than 6	3

You want to create a file with the languages with a single interpreter, another file with the languages with two interpreters, and a final file with the languages with three interpreters.

Q1. Which of the following would solve your situation when it comes to splitting the languages into three output streams?

1.   Number range step followed by a Switch/Case step

2.   A Switch/Case step

3.   Both

In order to figure out the answer, create a transformation and count the number of people that speak each language. You will have to use a Sort rows step followed by a Group by step. After that, try to develop each of the proposed solutions and see what happens.

Merging streams

You have just seen how the rows of a dataset can take different paths. Here you will learn the opposite: how data coming from different places is merged into a single stream.

Time for action – gathering progress and merging it all together

Suppose that you delivered the Excel files you generated in the sections on assigning tasks by filtering priorities. You gave the b_bouchard.xls to Benjamin Bouchard, the senior programmer. You also gave the other Excel file to a project leader who is going to assign the tasks to different programmers. Now they are giving you back the worksheets with a new column indicating the progress of the development. In the case of the shared file, there is also a column with the name of the programmer who is working on every issue. Your task is now to unify those sheets.

Here is how the Excel files look:

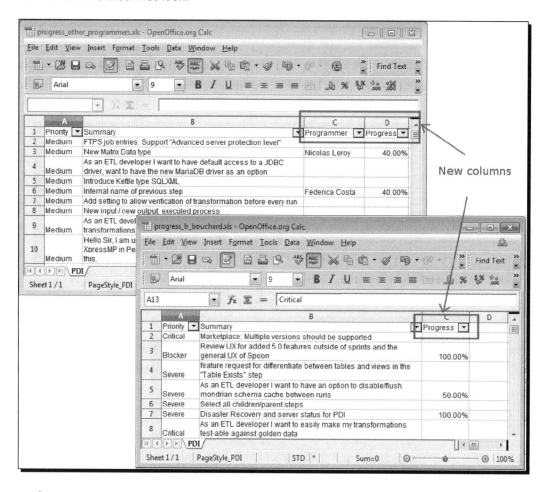

1. Create a new transformation.

2. Drag to the canvas a **Microsoft Excel Input** step and read one of the files.

3. Add a **Filter rows** step to keep only the rows where the progress is not null, that is, the rows belonging to tasks whose development has been started.

4. After the filter, add a **Sort rows** step, and configure it to order the fields by `Progress` descending.

5. Add another **Microsoft Excel Input** step, read the other file and filter and sort the rows just like you did before. Your transformation should look like this:

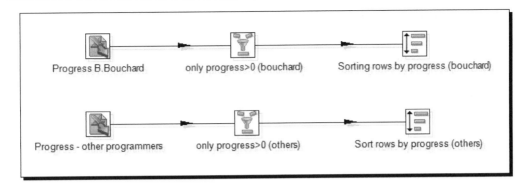

6. From the **Transform** category of steps, select the **Add constants** step and drag it on to the canvas.

7. Connect the Add Constants step to the stream that reads B. Bouchard's file by adding a hop from the Sort rows step to this one. Edit the Add constants step and add a new field named `Programmer`, with type **String** and value `Benjamin Bouchard`.

8. After this step, add a **Select values** step and reorder the fields so that they remain in this specific order: Priority, Summary, Programmer, and Progress to resemble the other stream.

9. Now from the **Transform** category, add an **Add sequence** step, create a new field named as `ID`, and link the step with the Select values step.

10. Create a hop from the Sort rows steps of the other stream to the Add sequence step. Your transformation should look like this:

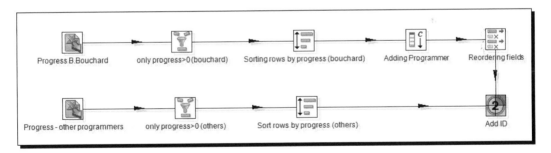

11. Select the Add sequence step and do a preview. You will see this:

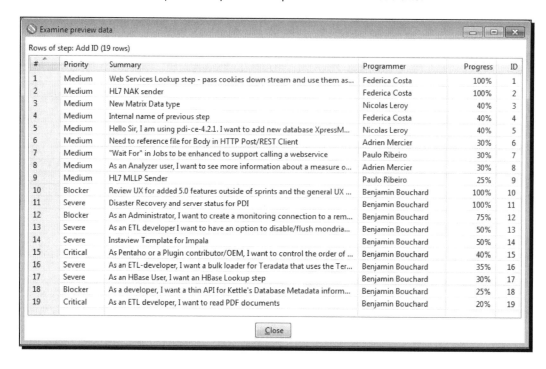

What just happened?

You read two similar Excel files and merged them into one single dataset.

First of all, you read, filtered, and sorted the files as usual.

Then, you altered the stream belonging to B. Bouchard so it looked similar to the other. You added the field `Programmer`, and reordered the fields.

After that, you used an Add sequence step to create a single dataset containing the rows of both streams, with the rows numbered. The structure of the new dataset is the same as before, plus the new field `ID` at the end.

PDI options for merging streams

You can create a union of two or more streams anywhere in your transformation. To create a union of two or more data streams, you can use any step. The step that unifies the data takes the incoming streams in any order and then it does its task, in the same way as if the data came from a single stream.

In the example, you used an Add sequence step as the step to join two streams. The step gathered the rows from the two streams and then proceeded to numerate the rows with the sequence name `ID`.

This is only one example of how you can mix streams together. As previously said, any step can be used to unify two streams. Whichever the step, the most important thing you need to bear in mind is that you cannot mix rows that have a different layout. The rows must have the same length, the same data type, and the same fields in the same order.

Fortunately, there is a **trap detector** that provides warnings at design time if a step is receiving mixed layouts.

Try this: delete the Select values step, and create a hop from the Add constants step to the Add sequence step. A warning message appears:

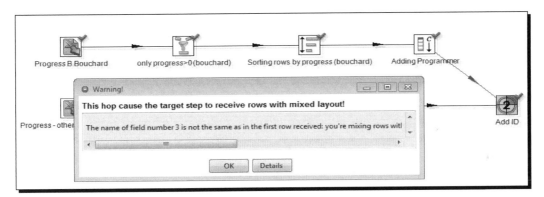

In this case, the third field of the first stream, `Programmer` (`String`), does not have the same name nor the same type as the third field of the second stream: `Progress` (`Number`).

Note that PDI warns you but doesn't prevent you from mixing rows layout when creating the transformation.

If you want Kettle to prevent you from running transformations with mixing row layout, you can check the option **Enable safe mode** in the window that shows up when you dispatch the transformation. Keep in mind that doing this will cause a performance drop.

When you use an arbitrary step to unify, the rows remain in the same order as they were in their original stream, but the streams are joined in any order. Take a look at the example's preview: The rows of Bouchard's stream and the rows of the other stream remained sorted within their original group. However, you didn't tell Kettle to put Bouchard's stream before or after the rows of the other stream. You did not decide the order of the streams; PDI decides it for you. If you care about the order in which the union is made, there are some steps that can help you. Here are the options you have:

If you want to ...	You can do this ...
Append two or more streams and don't care about the order	Use any step. The selected step will take all the incoming streams in any order, and then will proceed with the specific task.
Append two or more streams in a given order	For two streams, use the **Append streams** step from the **Flow** category. It allows you to decide which stream goes first.
	For two or more, use the **Prioritize streams** step from the **Flow** category. It allows you to decide the order of all the incoming streams.
Merge two streams ordered by one or more fields	Use a **Sorted Merge** step from the **Joins** category. This step allows you to decide on which field(s) to order the incoming rows before sending them to the destination step(s). Both input streams must be sorted on that field(s).
Merge two streams keeping the newest when there are duplicates	Use a **Merge Rows (diff)** step from the **Joins** category.
	You tell PDI the key fields, that is, the fields that tell you a row is the same in both streams. You also give PDI the fields to compare when the row is found in both streams.
	PDI tries to match rows of both streams based on the key fields. Then it creates a field that will act as a flag and fill it as follows:

- If a row was only found in the first stream, the flag is set to `deleted`.

- If a row was only found in the second stream, the flag is set to `new`.

- If the row was found in both streams, and the fields to compare are the same, the flag is set to `identical`.

- If the row was found in both streams, and at least one of the fields to compare is different, the flag is set to `changed`.

Let's try one of these options.

Time for action – giving priority to Bouchard by using the Append Stream

Suppose you want Bouchard's rows before the other rows. You can modify the transformation as follows:

1. From the **Flow** category of steps, drag to the canvas an **Append streams** step. Rearrange the steps and hops so the transformation looks like this:

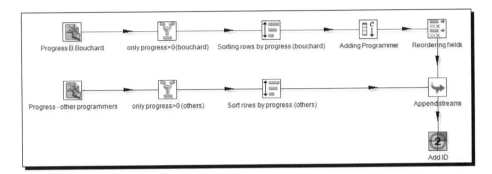

2. Edit the Append streams step, and select as the **Head hop** the one coming from Bouchard's stream. As the **Tail hop**, select the other hop. By doing this, you indicate to PDI how it has to order the streams.

3. Click on **OK**. You will notice that the hops coming to the step have changed the look and feel.

4. Preview the Add sequence step. You should see this:

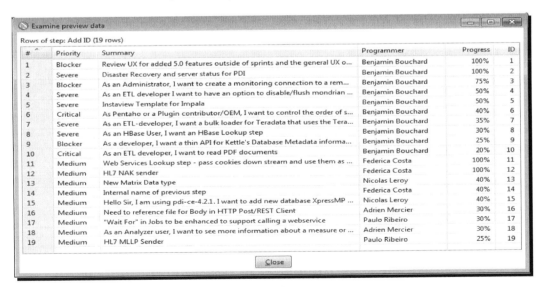

Examine preview data

Rows of step: Add ID (19 rows)

#	Priority	Summary	Programmer	Progress	ID
1	Blocker	Review UX for added 5.0 features outside of sprints and the general UX o...	Benjamin Bouchard	100%	1
2	Severe	Disaster Recovery and server status for PDI	Benjamin Bouchard	100%	2
3	Blocker	As an Administrator, I want to create a monitoring connection to a rem...	Benjamin Bouchard	75%	3
4	Severe	As an ETL developer I want to have an option to disable/flush mondrian ...	Benjamin Bouchard	50%	4
5	Severe	Instaview Template for Impala	Benjamin Bouchard	50%	5
6	Critical	As Pentaho or a Plugin contributor/OEM, I want to control the order of s...	Benjamin Bouchard	40%	6
7	Severe	As an ETL-developer, I want a bulk loader for Teradata that uses the Tera...	Benjamin Bouchard	35%	7
8	Severe	As an HBase User, I want an HBase Lookup step	Benjamin Bouchard	30%	8
9	Blocker	As a developer, I want a thin API for Kettle's Database Metadata informa...	Benjamin Bouchard	25%	9
10	Critical	As an ETL developer, I want to read PDF documents	Benjamin Bouchard	20%	10
11	Medium	Web Services Lookup step - pass cookies down stream and use them as ...	Federica Costa	100%	11
12	Medium	HL7 NAK sender	Federica Costa	100%	12
13	Medium	New Matrix Data type	Nicolas Leroy	40%	13
14	Medium	Internal name of previous step	Federica Costa	40%	14
15	Medium	Hello Sir, I am using pdi-ce-4.2.1. I want to add new database XpressMP ...	Nicolas Leroy	40%	15
16	Medium	Need to reference file for Body in HTTP Post/REST Client	Adrien Mercier	30%	16
17	Medium	"Wait For" in Jobs to be enhanced to support calling a webservice	Paulo Ribeiro	30%	17
18	Medium	As an Analyzer user, I want to see more information about a measure or ...	Adrien Mercier	30%	18
19	Medium	HL7 MLLP Sender	Paulo Ribeiro	25%	19

Close

What just happened?

You changed the transformation to give priority to Bouchard's issues.

You made it by using the Append streams step. By telling that the head hop was the one coming from Bouchard's file, you got the expected order: first the rows with the tasks assigned to Bouchard sorted by progress descending, then the rows with the tasks assigned to other programmers also sorted by progress descending.

 Whether you use arbitrary steps or some of the special steps mentioned here to merge streams, don't forget to verify the layout of the streams you are merging. Pay attention to the warnings of the trap detector and avoid mixing row layouts.

Have a go hero – sorting and merging all tasks

Modify the previous exercise so that the final output is sorted by priority. Try two possible solutions:

◆ Sort the input streams on their own and then use a Sorted Merge step

◆ Merge the stream with a Dummy step and then sort

Which one do you think would give the best performance? Why?

 Refer to the Sort rows step issues in *Chapter 4, Filtering, Searching, and Performing Other Useful Operations with Data*.

In which circumstances would you use the other option?

Treating invalid data by splitting and merging streams

It's a fact that data from the real world is not perfect; it has errors. We already saw that errors in data can cause our transformations to crash. We also learned how to detect and report errors while avoiding undesirable situations. The main problem is that in doing so, we discard data that may be important. Sometimes the errors are not so severe; in fact, there is a possibility that we can fix them so that we don't loose data. Let's see some examples:

♦ You have a field defined as a string, and that field represents the date of birth of a person. As values, you have, besides valid dates, other strings for example N/A, -, ???, and so on. Any attempt to run a calculation with these values would lead to an error.

♦ You have two dates representing the start date and end date of the execution of a task. Suppose that you have 2013-01-05 and 2012-10-31 as the start date and end date respectively. They are well-formatted dates, but if you try to calculate the time that it took to execute the task, you will get a negative value, which is clearly wrong.

♦ You have a field representing the nationality of a person. The field is mandatory but there are some null values.

In these cases and many more like these, the problem is not so critical and you can do some work to avoid aborting or discarding data because of these anomalies. In the first example, you could delete the invalid year and leave the field empty. In the second example, you could set the end date equal to the start date. Finally, in the last example, you could set a predefined default value.

Recall the *Cleansing data with PDI* section in the previous chapter. In that section, you already did some cleansing tasks. However, at that time you didn't have the skills to solve the kind of issues mentioned here. In the next section, you will see an example of fixing these kinds of issues and avoiding having to discard the rows that cause errors or are considered invalid. You will do it by using the latest learned concepts: splitting and merging streams.

Time for action – treating errors in the estimated time to avoid discarding rows

Do you remember the section named *Time for action – Avoiding errors while converting the estimated time from string to integer* from *Chapter 2, Getting Started with Transformations*. In that exercise, you detected the rows with an invalid estimated time, reported the error, and discarded the rows. In this section, you will fix the errors and keep all rows.

1. Open the transformation you created in that section and save it with a different name.
2. After the Write to log step, remove the fields estimated and error_desc. Use a **Select values** step for that purpose.
3. After that, add an **Add constants** step. You will find it under the **Transform** category.
4. Double-click on the step and add a new field. Under **Name** type estimated, under **Type** select **Integer**, and as **Value** type 180.
5. Click on **OK**.

6. Finally, create a hop from this step towards the calculator. You will have the following:

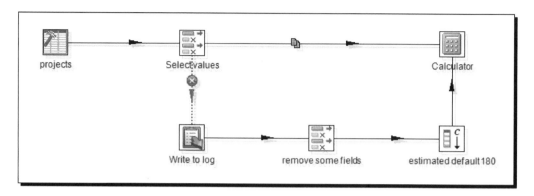

7. Select the calculator and do a preview. You will see this:

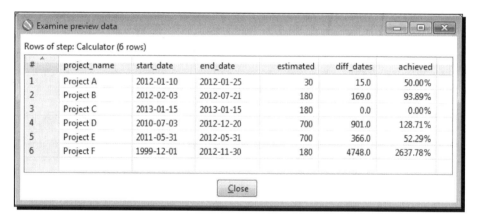

What just happened?

You modified a transformation that captured errors and discarded rows. In this new version, instead of discarding rows with a bad formatted estimated time, you fixed it proposing a default estimated time of 180 days. After fixing the error, you sent the rows back to the main stream.

If you run the transformation instead of just previewing the data, you can observe in the **Logging** tab of the **Execution Results** window that PDI captured one error and reported it. However, in the **Step Metrics** tab, you can see that the calculator receives 6 rows, the total of the rows coming out of the first step, and the data grid with all the information about projects.

Treating rows with invalid data

When you are transforming data, it is not uncommon that you detect inaccuracies or errors. The issues you find may not be severe enough to discard the rows. Maybe you can somehow guess what data was supposed to be there instead of the current values, or it can happen that you have default values for a value that is null. In any of those situations, you can do your best to fix the issues and send the rows back to the main stream. This is valid both for regular streams and for streams that are a result of error handling, as was the case in this section.

There are no rules for what to do with bad rows where you detect invalid or improper data. You always have the option to discard the bad rows or try to fix them. Sometimes you can fix only a few and discard the rest of them. It always depends on your particular data or business rules. In any case, it's common behavior to log erroneous rows for manual inspection at a later date.

Have a go hero – trying to find missing countries

As you saw in the *Time for action – Finding out which language people speak* section in Chapter 4, *Filtering, Searching, and Performing Other Useful Operations with Data*, there are missing countries in the `countries.xml` file. In fact, the countries are there, but with different names. For example, `Russia` in the contestant file is `Russian Federation` in the XML file.

Modify the transformation that looks for the language in the following way:

- Split the stream into two, one for the rows where a language was found and one for the others.

- For this last stream, use a **Value Mapper** step to rename the countries you identified as wrong (that is, rename `Russia` as `Russian Federation`).

- Look again for a language, this time with the new name.

- Finally, merge the two streams and create the output file with the result.

- It may be the case that even with this modification, you have rows with countries that are not in the list of countries and languages. Send these rows to a different stream and report the errors in the PDI log.

Summary

In this chapter, you learned different options that PDI offers to combine or split flows of data. The covered topics included copying and distributing rows, and splitting streams based on conditions. You also saw different ways to merge independent streams.

With the concepts you learned in the previous chapters, the kind of tasks you are able to do is already broad. In the next chapter, you will learn how to insert code in your transformations as an alternative to do some of those tasks, but mainly as a way to accomplish other tasks that are complicated or even unthinkable of doing with the regular PDI steps.

6

Transforming Your Data by Coding

Whatever the transformation you need to do on your data, you have a good chance of finding PDI steps able to do the job. Despite that, it may be that there are not proper steps that serve your requirements. Or that an apparently minor transformation consumes a lot of steps linked in a very confusing arrangement that is difficult to test or understand. Putting colorful icons here and there and making notes to clarify a transformation can be practical to a point, but there are some situations like the ones described above where you inevitably will have to code.

This chapter explains how to insert code in your transformations. Specifically, you will learn:

 ◆ Inserting and testing JavaScript and Java code in your transformations

 ◆ Distinguishing situations where coding is the best option, from those where there are better alternatives

Doing simple tasks with the JavaScript step

In earlier versions of Kettle, coding in JavaScript was the only way the users had for performing many tasks. In the latest versions, there are many other ways for doing the same tasks, but JavaScript is still an option. There is the JavaScript step that allows you to insert code in a Kettle transformation. In the following section, you will recreate a transformation from *Chapter 4, Filtering, Searching, and Performing Other Useful Operations with Data*, by replacing part of its functionality with JavaScript.

Time for action – counting frequent words by coding in JavaScript

In *Chapter 4, Filtering, Searching, and Performing Other Useful Operations with Data*, you created a transformation that read a file and counted frequent words. In this section, you will create a variant of that transformation by replacing some of the steps with a piece of JavaScript code.

1. Open the transformation from the section named *Counting frequent words by filtering* from *Chapter 4, Filtering, Searching, and Performing Other Useful Operations with Data*. Select the first two steps—the Text file input and the Split field to rows steps—and copy them to a new transformation.

2. From the **Scripting** category of steps, select and drag a **Modified Java Script Value** step to the work area. Create a hop from the Split field to rows step toward this. You will have the following:

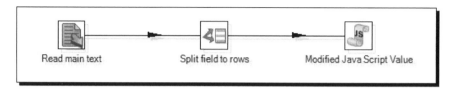

3. Double-click on the Modified Java Script Value step—MJSV from now on—and under the text `//Script here`, type the following:

```
var len_word = word.length;
var u_word = upper(word);

if (len_word > 3)
    trans_Status = CONTINUE_TRANSFORMATION;
else
    trans_Status = SKIP_TRANSFORMATION;
```

4. Click on the **Get variables** button. The lower grid will be filled with the two defined variables, `len_word` and `u_word`. Do some adjustments in the default values so it looks like the following screenshot:

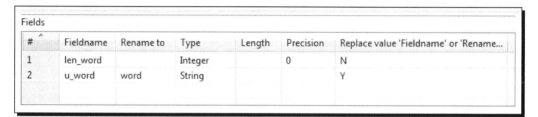

Fields

#	Fieldname	Rename to	Type	Length	Precision	Replace value 'Fieldname' or 'Rename...
1	len_word		Integer		0	N
2	u_word	word	String			Y

5. Click on the **Test script** button and a window will appear to create a set of rows for testing. Fill it as shown in the following screenshot:

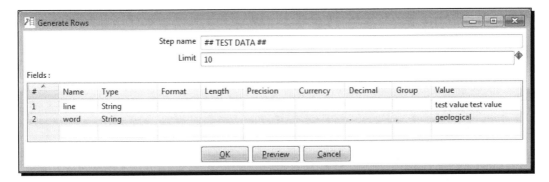

6. Click on **Preview** and a window appears showing ten identical rows with the provided sample values.

7. Close the Preview window and click on **OK** to test the code.

8. A window appears with the result of having executed the script on the test data:

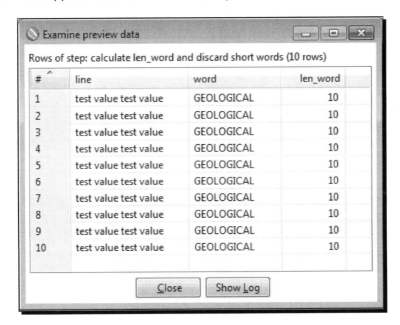

9. Close the window with the preview data and close the MJSV configuration window.

10. Save the transformation.

11. Make sure the MJSV step is selected and do a preview. You should see the following:

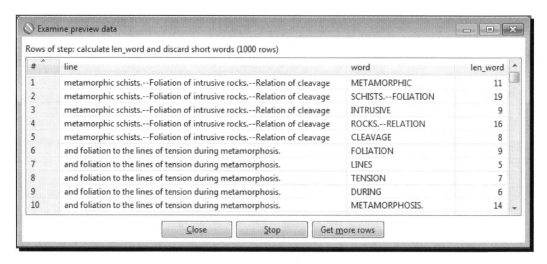

#	line	word	len_word
1	metamorphic schists.--Foliation of intrusive rocks.--Relation of cleavage	METAMORPHIC	11
2	metamorphic schists.--Foliation of intrusive rocks.--Relation of cleavage	SCHISTS.--FOLIATION	19
3	metamorphic schists.--Foliation of intrusive rocks.--Relation of cleavage	INTRUSIVE	9
4	metamorphic schists.--Foliation of intrusive rocks.--Relation of cleavage	ROCKS.--RELATION	16
5	metamorphic schists.--Foliation of intrusive rocks.--Relation of cleavage	CLEAVAGE	8
6	and foliation to the lines of tension during metamorphosis.	FOLIATION	9
7	and foliation to the lines of tension during metamorphosis.	LINES	5
8	and foliation to the lines of tension during metamorphosis.	TENSION	7
9	and foliation to the lines of tension during metamorphosis.	DURING	6
10	and foliation to the lines of tension during metamorphosis.	METAMORPHOSIS.	14

Note that you see the first 1000 rows. If you want to see more, just click on **Get more rows**.

What just happened?

You used a Modified Java Script Value step to calculate the length of the words found in a text file, and to filter the words with a length less than or equal to 3.

The code you typed was executed for every row in your dataset. Let's explain the first part of the code:

```
var len_word = word.length;
```

The first line declared a variable named `len_word` and set it to the length of the field named `word`. This variable is the same as the one you typed in the lower grid. This means that `len_word` will become a new field in your dataset, as you could see in the last preview:

```
var u_word = upper(word);
```

The second line implements something that was not in the original transformation, but was deliberately added to show you how you modify a field. In this line, you declared a variable named `u_word` and set it equal to the field `word` but converted it to uppercase. In the lower grid, you also typed this variable. In this case, however, you are not creating a new field, but replacing the original field `word`. You do it by renaming the value `u_word` to `word`, and setting the **Replace value 'Fieldname' or 'Rename to'** value to Y.

Now let's explain the second part of the code:

```
if (len_word > 3)
    trans_Status = CONTINUE_TRANSFORMATION;
else
    trans_Status = SKIP_TRANSFORMATION;
```

This piece of code is meant to keep only the words whose length is greater than 3. You accomplish it by setting the value of the predefined Kettle variable `trans_Status` to `CONTINUE_TRANSFORMATION` for the rows you want to keep, and to `SKIP_TRANSFORMATION` for the rows you want to discard. If you pay attention to the last preview, you will notice that all the words have at least a length of 3 characters.

As part of the preceding section, you also tested the code of the JavaScript step.

You clicked on the `Test script` button, and created a dataset which served as the basis for testing the script. You previewed the test dataset.

After that, you did the test itself. A window appeared showing you how the created dataset looks like after the execution of the script. The `word` field was converted to uppercase, and a new field named `len_word` was added, containing the length of the sample word as the value. Note that the length of the sample word was greater than 3. If you run a new test and type a word with 3 or less characters, nothing will appear as expected.

> The objective of the tutorial was just to show you how to replace some Kettle steps with JavaScript code. You can recreate the original transformation by adding the rest of the steps needed for doing the job of calculating frequent words.

Using the JavaScript language in PDI

JavaScript is a scripting language primarily used in website development. However inside PDI, you use just the core language; you don't run a web browser and you don't care about HTML. There are many available JavaScript engines. PDI uses the **Rhino** engine from **Mozilla**. Rhino is an open-source implementation of the core JavaScript language; it doesn't contain objects or methods related to the manipulation of web pages. If you are interested in getting to know more about Rhino, follow this link:

```
https://developer.mozilla.org/en/Rhino_Overview
```

The core language is not too different from other languages you might know. It has basic statements, block statements (statements enclosed by curly brackets), conditional statements (`if-else` and `switch-case`), and loop statements (`for`, `do-while`, and `while`). If you are interested in the language itself, you can access a good JavaScript guide by following this link:

```
https://developer.mozilla.org/En/Core_JavaScript_1.5_Guide
```

There is also a complete tutorial and reference guide at `http://www.w3schools.com/js/`. Despite being quite oriented to web development, which is not your concern here, it is clear, complete, and has plenty of examples.

 Besides the basics, you can use JavaScript for parsing both **XML** and **JSON** objects, as well as for generating them.

There are some Kettle steps that do this, but when the structure of those objects is too complex, you may prefer to do the task by coding.

Inserting JavaScript code using the Modified JavaScript Value Step

The Modified JavaScript Value step—JavaScript step for short—allows you to insert JavaScript code inside your transformation. The code you type in the script area is executed once per row coming to the step.

Let's explore its dialog window:

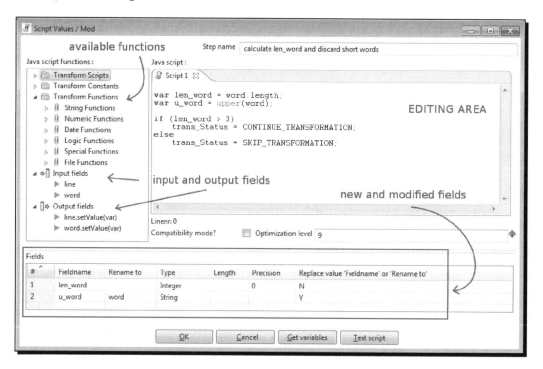

Most of the window is occupied by the editing area. It's there where you write JavaScript code using the standard syntax of the language, and the functions and fields from the tree on the left side of the window.

The **Transform Functions** branch of the tree contains a rich list of functions that are ready to use. The functions are grouped by category:

The **String**, **Numeric**, **Date**, and **Logic** categories contain usual JavaScript functions.

> This is not a full list of JavaScript functions. You are allowed to use JavaScript functions even if they are not in this list.

- The **Special** category contains a mix of utility functions. Most of them are not JavaScript functions but Kettle functions. One of those functions is `writeToLog()`, which is very useful for displaying data in the Kettle log.
- Finally, the **File** category, as its name suggests, contains a list of functions that do simple verifications or actions related to files and folders, for example, `fileExist()` or `createFolder()`.

To add a function to your script, simply double-click on it, or drag it to the location in your script where you wish to use it, or just type it.

> If you are not sure about how to use a particular function or what a function does, just right-click on the function and select **Sample**. A new script window appears with a description of the function and sample code showing how to use it.

The **Input fields** branch contains the list of the fields coming from previous steps. To see and use the value of a field for the current row, you double-click on it or drag it to the code area. You can also type it by hand, as you did in the previous section.

When you use one of these fields in the code, it is treated as a JavaScript variable. As such, the name of the field has to follow the conventions for a variable name, for instance, it cannot contain dots or start with non-character symbols.

As Kettle is quite permissive with names, you can have fields in your stream whose names are not valid for use inside JavaScript code.

If you intend to use a field with a name that does not follow the name rules, rename it just before the JavaScript step with a Select values step. If you use that field without renaming it, you will not be warned when coding; but you'll get an error or unexpected results when you execute the transformation.

Output fields is a list of the fields that will leave the step.

Adding fields

At the bottom of the JavaScript configuration window, there is a grid where you put the fields you created in the code. This is how you add a new field:

1. Define the field as a variable in the code, such as `var len_word`.

2. Fill the grid manually or by clicking on the **Get variables** button. A new row will be filled for every variable you defined in the code.

That was exactly what you did for the `len_word` and `u_word` fields.

In the JavaScript code, you can create and use all variables you need without declaring them. However, if you intend to add a variable as a field in your stream, the declaration with the `var` sentence is mandatory.

 The variables you define in the JavaScript code are not Kettle variables. Recall that you learned about Kettle variables in *Chapter 3, Manipulating Real-world Data*. JavaScript variables are local to the step, and have nothing to do with the Kettle variables you know.

Modifying fields

Instead of adding a field, you may want to change the value and eventually the data type of an existent field. You can do that but not directly in the code. That was exactly what you did with the `word` field. In the code, you defined a variable named `u_word` as the field `word` converted to uppercase:

```
var u_word = upper(word);
```

If you simply add that variable to the lower grid, Kettle adds a new field to the dataset. In this case, however, you intended to replace or modify the `word` field, not to create a new field named `u_word`. You do it by renaming `u_word` to `word` and setting the **Replace value 'Fieldname' or 'Rename to'** to `Y`.

Using transformation predefined constants

In the tree at the left side of the JavaScript window, under **Transformation Constants**, you have a list of the JavaScript predefined constants. You can use those constants to change the value of the predefined variable `trans_Status`, for example in:

```
trans_Status = SKIP_TRANSFORMATION
```

Here is how it works:

If trans_Status value is set to ...	The current row ...
SKIP_TRANSFORMATION	is removed from the dataset.
CONTINUE_TRANSFORMATION	is kept. Nothing happens to it.
ERROR_TRANSFORMATION	causes the abortion of the transformation.

In other words, you use that constant to control what will happen to the rows. In the exercise, you put:

```
if (len_word > 3)
    trans_Status = CONTINUE_TRANSFORMATION;
else
    trans_Status = SKIP_TRANSFORMATION;
```

This means that a row where the length of the word is greater than three characters will continue its way to the following steps. On the contrary, the row will be discarded.

Testing the script using the Test script button

The **Test script** button allows you to check that the script does what it is intended to do. It actually generates a transformation in the back with two steps: a **Generate Rows** step sending data to a copy of the JavaScript step.

Just after clicking on the button, you are allowed to fill the Generate Rows window with the test dataset.

Once you click on **OK** in the Generate Rows window to effectively run the test, the first thing that the test function does is to verify that the code is properly written, that is, that there are no syntax errors in the code. Try deleting the last parenthesis in the JavaScript code you wrote in the previous section and click on the **Test script** button.

When you click on **OK** to see the result of the execution; instead of a dataset, you will see an **ERROR** window. Among the lines, you will see something like this:

```
...
Unexpected error
org.pentaho.di.core.exception.KettleValueException:
Couldn't compile javascript:
missing ) after condition (script#6)
...
```

If the script is syntactically correct, what follows is the preview of the JavaScript step for the transformation in the back, that is, the JavaScript code applied to the test dataset.

If you don't see any error and the previewed data shows the expected results, you are done. If not, you can check the code, fix it, and test it again until you see that the step works properly.

Reading and parsing unstructured files with JavaScript

It's marvelous to have input files where the information is well formed, that is, the number of columns and the type of its data is precise, all rows follow the same pattern, and so on. However, it is common to find input files where the information has little or no structure, or the structure doesn't follow the matrix (*n* rows by *m* columns) you expect. This is one of the situations where JavaScript comes to the rescue.

Time for action – changing a list of house descriptions with JavaScript

Suppose you decided to invest some money in a new house. You asked a real-estate agency for a list of candidate houses for you and it gave you this:

```
...
Property Code: MCX-011
Status: Active
5 bedrooms
5 baths
Style: Contemporary
```

```
Basement
Laundry room
Fireplace
2 car garage
Central air conditioning
More Features: Attic, Clothes dryer, Clothes washer, Dishwasher

Property Code: MCX-012
4 bedrooms
3 baths
Fireplace
Attached parking
More Features: Alarm System, Eat-in Kitchen, Powder Room

Property Code: MCX-013
3 bedrooms
...
```

You want to compare the properties before visiting them, but you're finding it hard to do because the file doesn't have a precise structure. Fortunately, you have the JavaScript step that will help you to give the file some structure.

Create a new transformation.

1. Get the sample file from the Packt Publishing website, www.packtpub.com, and read it with a Text file input step. Uncheck the **Header** checkbox and create a single field named text.

2. Do a preview. You should see the content of the file under a single column named text.

3. Add a JavaScript step after the input step and double-click on it to edit it.

4. In the editing area, type the following JavaScript code to create a field with the code of the property:

```
var prop_code;

posCod = indexOf(text,'Property Code:');
if (posCod>=0)
    prop_code = trim(substr(text,posCod+15));
```

5. Click on **Get variables** to add the prop_code variable to the grid under the code.

6. Click on **OK** and with the JavaScript step selected, run a preview. You should see this:

What just happened?

You read a file where each house was described in several rows. You added to every row the code of the house to which that row belonged. In order to obtain the property code, you identified the lines with a code and then you cut the `Property Code:` text with the `substr` function, and discarded the leading spaces with `trim`.

Looping over the dataset rows

The code you wrote may seem a little strange at the beginning, but it is not really so complex. It creates a variable named `prod_code`, which will be used to create a new field for identifying the properties. When the JavaScript code detects a property header row, for example:

```
Property Code: MCX-002
```

It sets the variable `prop_code` to the code it finds in that line, in this case, `MCX-002`.

PROP_CODE

Until a new header row appears, the `prop_code` variable keeps that value. Thus, all the rows following a row, like the one shown previously, will have the same value for the variable `prop_code`.

The variable is then used to create a new field, which will contain for every row, the code for the house to which it belongs.

This is an example where you can keep values from the previous rows in the dataset to be used in the current row.

 Note that here you use JavaScript to see and use values from previous rows, but you can't modify them! JavaScript always works on the current row.

Have a go hero – enhancing the houses file

Modify the exercise from the previous section by doing the following:

After keeping the property code, discard the rows that headed each property description.

◆ Create two new fields named `Feature` and `Description`. Fill the `Feature` field with the feature described in the row (for example, `Exterior construction`) and the `Description` field with the description of that feature (for example, `Brick`). If you think that it is not worth keeping some features (for example, `Living Room`), you may discard some rows. Also discard the original field `text`. Here you have a sample house description showing a possible output after the changes:

```
prop_code; Feature; Description
MCX-023;bedrooms;4
MCX-023;baths;4
MCX-023;Style;Colonial
MCX-023;family room;yes
MCX-023;basement;yes
MCX-023;fireplace;yes
MCX-023;Heating features;Hot Water Heater
MCX-023;Central air conditioning present;yes
MCX-023;Exterior construction;Stucco
MCX-023;Waterview;yes
MCX-023;More Features;Attic, Living/Dining Room, Eat-In-Kitchen
```

Doing simple tasks with the Java Class step

The User Defined Java Class step appeared only in recent versions of Kettle. As a JavaScript step, this step is also meant to insert code in your transformations but in this case, the code is in Java. Whether you need to implement a functionality not provided in built-in steps, or want to reuse some external Java code, or to access Java libraries, or to increase performance, this step is what you need. In the following section, you will learn how to use it.

Time for action – counting frequent words by coding in Java

In this section, we will redo the transformation from the *Time for action – counting frequent words by coding in JavaScript* section, but this time we will code in Java rather than in JavaScript.

1. Open the transformation from the *Time for action – counting frequent words by coding in JavaScript* section of this chapter and save it as a new transformation.

2. Delete the JavaScript step and in its place, add a **User Defined Java Class** step. You will find it under the **Scripting** category of steps. You will have the following:

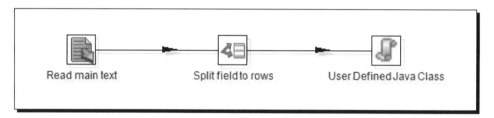

Read main text   Split field to rows   User Defined Java Class

3. Double-click on the **User Defined Java Class** step—UDJC from now on—and in the **Processor** tab, type the following:

```
public boolean processRow(StepMetaInterface smi,
    StepDataInterface sdi) throws KettleException
{
    Object[] r = getRow();
    if (r == null) {
        setOutputDone();
        return false;
    }

    if (first)
    {
        first = false;
    }
```

```
r = createOutputRow(r, data.outputRowMeta.size());

String word = get(Fields.In, "word").getString(r);
get(Fields.Out, "word").setValue(r, word.toUpperCase());

long len_word = word.length();
if (len_word > 3) {
    get(Fields.Out, "len_word").setValue(r, len_word);
    putRow(data.outputRowMeta, r);
    }

return true;
}
```

 You can save time by expanding the **Code Snippits** tree to the left of the window, and double-clicking on the option **Main** after expanding **Common use**. This action will populate the **Processor** tab with a template and you just need to modify the code so it looks like the one shown previously.

If you populate the tab with the template, you will have to fix an error present in the Main code snippet, or you will not be able to compile correctly. In the Main code snippet, replace this line:

```
r = createOutputRow(r, outputRowSize);
```

with the following line:

```
r = createOutputRow(r, data.outputRowMeta.size());
```

1. Fill in the **Fields** tab in the lower grid as shown in the following screenshot:

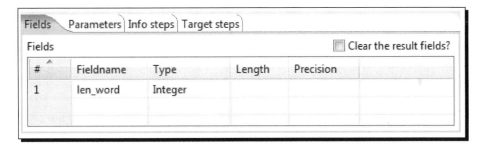

2. Click on **OK** to close the window, and save the transformation.

3. Double-click on the UDJC step again. This time you will see that the **Input fields** and **Output fields** branches of the tree on the left have been populated with the name of the fields coming in and out of the step:

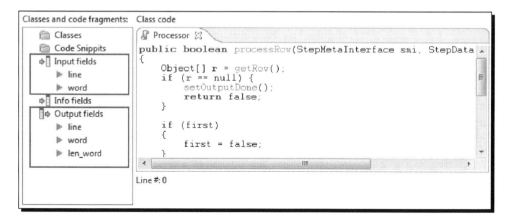

4. Now click on the **Test class** button at the bottom of the window.

5. A window appears to create a set of rows for testing. Fill it in as shown in the previous screenshot:

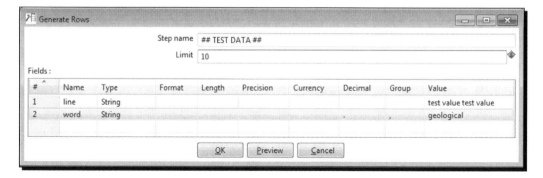

6. Click on **Preview** and a window appears showing ten identical rows with the provided sample values.

7. Click on **OK** in the Preview window to test the code.

A window appears with the result of having executed the code on the test data:

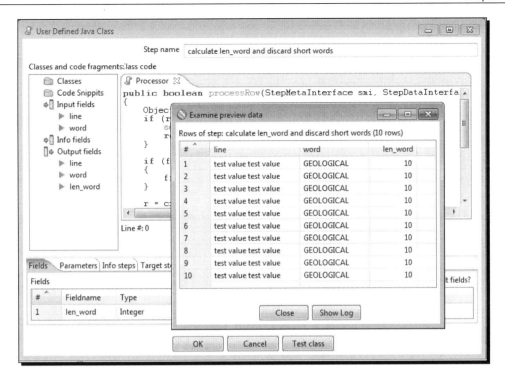

8. Close the window with the preview data and close the UDJC configuration window.

9. Save the transformation.

10. Make sure the UDJC step is selected and run a preview. You should see this:

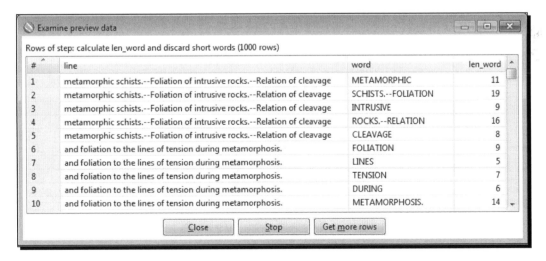

What just happened?

You used a User Defined Java Class step to calculate the length of the words found in a text file, and for filtering the words with length less or equal to 3.

The code you typed in the UDJC step was executed for every row in your dataset. Let's explain the Java code in detail:

At the beginning, you have the main function:

```
public boolean processRow(StepMetaInterface smi, StepDataInterface
    sdi) throws KettleException
{
    Object[] r = getRow();
    if (r == null) {
        setOutputDone();
        return false;
    }
}
```

The `processRow()` function, a predefined Kettle function, processes a new row.

The `getRow()` function, another predefined Kettle function, gets the next row from the input steps. It returns an Object array with the incoming row. A `null` value means that there are no more rows for processing.

The following code only executes for the first row:

```
if (first) {
    first = false;
}
```

You can use the flag first to prepare a proper environment before processing the rows. As we don't need to do anything special for the first row, we just set the `first` flag to `false`.

The next line ensures that your output row's Object array is large enough to handle any new fields created in this step.

```
r = createOutputRow(r, data.outputRowMeta.size());
```

After those mandatory lines, your specific code begins. The first line uses the `get()` method to set the internal variable `word` with the value of the `word` field.

```
String word = get(Fields.In, "word").getString(r);
```

The next line takes the uppercase value of the `word` variable and uses that string to set the value of the output field `word`.

```
get(Fields.Out, "word").setValue(r, word.toUpperCase());
```

So far your output row has the same fields as the input row, but the word field has been converted to uppercase.

Let's see the rest of the lines:

```
long len_word = word.length();
if (len_word > 3) {
    get(Fields.Out, "len_word").setValue(r, len_word);
    putRow(data.outputRowMeta, r);
    }
```

In the first line of this piece of code, we calculate the length of the word and save it in an internal variable named len_word.

If the length of the word is greater than 3, we do the following:

Create a new output field named len_word with that value:

```
get(Fields.Out, "len_word").setValue(r, len_word);
```

and send the row out to the next step:

```
putRow(data.outputRowMeta, r);
```

In summary, the output dataset differs from the original in that it has a new field named len_word, but only contains the rows where the length of the word field is greater than 3. Another difference is that the word field has been converted to uppercase.

As part of the previous section, you also tested the Java class. The method for testing is similar to the one you saw in the *Time for Action – counting frequent words by coding in JavaScript* section. You clicked on the **Test class** button and created a dataset which served as the basis for testing the code. You previewed the test dataset. After that, you did the test itself. A window appeared showing you how the created dataset looks after the execution of the code: the word field was converted to uppercase and a new field named len_word was added, containing as value the length of the sample word.

The objective of the *Time for action – counting frequent words by coding in Java* section was just to show you how to replace some Kettle steps with Java code. You can recreate the original transformation by adding the rest of the steps needed for doing the job of calculating frequent words.

Using the Java language in PDI

Java, originally developed at Sun Microsystems which then merged into Oracle Corporation, was first released in 1995 and is one of the most popular programming languages in use, particularly for client-server web applications. In particular, Kettle and the whole **Pentaho** platform have been developed using Java as the core language.

It was to be expected that eventually a step would appear that allows you to code Java inside PDI. That step is **User Defined Java Class**, which we will call **UDJC** for short. The goal of this step is to allow you to define methods and logic using Java but also to provide a way of executing pieces of code as fast as possible. Also, one of the purposes of this step when it was created was to overcome performance issues; one of the main drawbacks of JavaScript.

For allowing Java programming inside PDI, the tool uses the Janino project libraries. **Janino** is a super-small, super-fast embedded compiler that compiles Java code at runtime. To see a full list of Janino features and limitations, you can follow this link: `http://docs.codehaus.org/display/JANINO/Home`.

As previously said, the goal of the UDJC is not to do full-scale Java development but to allow you to execute pieces of Java code. If you need to do a lot of Java development, you should think of doing it in a Java IDE, exposing your code in a `jar` file, and placing that library in the Kettle classpath, namely the `libext` folder inside the Kettle installation directory. Then you can include the library at the top of the step code using the regular Java syntax, for example:

```
import my_library.util.*;
```

Also, a good choice if you find yourself writing extensive amounts of Java code is to create a new step which is a drop-in Plug and Play (PnP) operation.

> The creation of plugins is outside the scope of this book. If you are interested in this subject, a good starting point is the blog entry *Exploring the sample plugins for PDI*, by the Kettle expert Slawomir Chodnicki. You can find that entry at `http://type-exit.org/adventures-with-open-source-bi/2012/07/exploring-the-sample-plugins-for-pdi/`. If you are not familiar with the Java language and think that your requirement could be implemented with JavaScript, you could use the Modified Java Script Value step instead. Take into account that the code in the JavaScript step is interpreted, whereas the code in UDJC is compiled. This means that a transformation that uses the UDJC step will have a much better performance.

Inserting Java code using the User Defined Java Class step

The User Defined Java Class or UDJC step allows you to insert Java code inside your transformation. The code you type here is executed once per row coming to the step.

The UI for the UDJC step is very similar to the UI for the MJSV step; there is a main area to write the Java code, a left panel with many functions as snippets, the input fields coming from the previous step, and the outputs fields.

Let's explore the dialog for this step:

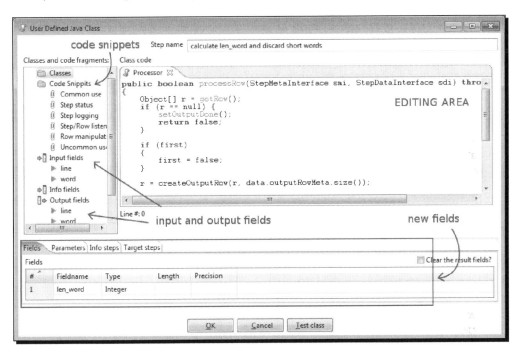

Most of the window is occupied by the editing area. Here you write the Java code using the standard syntax of the language. On the left, there is a panel with a lot of fragments of code ready to use (**Code Snippets**), and a section with sets and gets for the input and output fields. To add one of the provided pieces of code to your script, either double-click on it and drag it to the location in your script where you wish to use it, or just type it in the editing area.

> The code you see in the code snippets is not pure Java. It has a lot of Kettle predefined functions for manipulating rows, looking at the status of steps, and more.

The input and outputs fields appear automatically in the tree when the Java code compiles correctly.

Then you have some tabs at the bottom. The next table summarizes their functions:

Tab	Function	Example
Fields	To declare the new fields added by the step.	In the *Time for action – Counting frequent words by coding in Java* section, you declared and added a new field named `len_word` of `Integer` type.
Parameters	To add parameters to your code, along with their values.	You could add a parameter telling the threshold for the length of words.
Info steps	To declare additional steps that provide information to be read inside your Java code.	You could use this function to read from another stream a list of undesirable words (words to be excluded of the dataset).
Target steps	To declare the steps where the rows will be redirected, in case you want to redirect rows to more than one destination.	You may want to classify the words using different criteria (length of word, words containing/not containing strange characters, kind of word— pronoun, article, and so on) and redirect the rows to a different target step depending on the classification.

In the *Time for action – counting frequent words by coding in Java* section, you just used the **Fields** tab. For more details on the use of the **Parameters** tabs, please see the *Have a go hero – Parameterizing the Java Class* section.

The other two tabs are considered advanced and their use is outside the scope of this book. If you are interested, you can get *Pentaho Data Integration 4 Cookbook, Packt Publishing*, and browse *Chapter 9 , Getting the Most Out of Kettle,* for more details and examples of the use of these tabs.

Adding fields

Adding new fields to the dataset is really simple. This is how you do it:

◆ In the code, you define the field as an internal variable and calculate its value.

◆ Then you have to update the output row. Supposing that the name for the new field is `my_new_field` and the name of the internal variable is `my_var`, you update the output row as follows:

```
get(Fields.Out, "my_new_field").setValue(r, my_var);
```

◆ Finally, you have to add the field to the lower grid. You just add a new line for each new field. You have to provide at least the **Fieldname**, and the **Type**.

To know exactly which type to put in there, please see the *Data types equivalence* section that will follow shortly.

Modifying fields

Modifying a field instead of adding a new one is even easier. Supposing that the name of your field is `my_field`, and the value you want to set is stored in a variable named `my_var`, you just set the field to the new value by using the following syntax:

```
get(Fields.Out, "my_field").setValue(r, my_var);
```

By doing it this way, you are modifying the output row. When you send the row to the next step by using the `putRow()` method, the field already has its new value.

Sending rows to the next step

With the UDJC step, you control which rows go to the next step by using the `putRow()` method. By using this method selectively, you decide which rows to send and which rows to discard. As an example, in the *Time for action – counting frequent words by coding in Java* section, you only sent to the next step the rows where the `word` field had a length greater than `3`.

Data types equivalence

The code you type inside the UDJC step is pure Java. Therefore, the fields of your transformation will be seen as Java objects according to the following equivalence table:

Data type in Kettle	Java Class
String	Java.lang.String
Integer	Java.lang.Long
Number	Java.lang.Double
Date	Java.util.Date
BigNumber	BigDecimal
Binary	byte[]

The opposite occurs when you create an object inside the Java code and want to expose it as a new field of your transformation. For example, in the Java code, you defined the variable `len_word` as `long` but in the **Fields** tab, you defined the new output field as `Integer`.

Testing the Java Class using the Test class button

The **Test class** button in the Java Class configuration window allows you to check that the code does what it is intended to do. The way it works is quite similar to the way the JavaScript test functionality does: it actually generates a transformation in the back with two steps—a Generate Rows step sending data to a copy of the Java Class step.

Just after clicking on the button, you are allowed to fill the **Generates Rows** window with the test dataset.

Once you click on **OK** in the **Generate Rows** window to effectively run the test, the first thing that the test function does is compile the Java class. Try deleting the last parenthesis in the code and clicking on the **Test class** button. When you click on **OK** to see the result of the execution; instead of a dataset, you will see an **Error during class compilation** window. If you are lucky, you will clearly see the cause of the error as, in this case:

```
Line 23, Column 3: Operator ")" expected
```

It may be that the error is much more complicated to understand, or on the contrary, does not give you enough details. You will have to be patient, comment the parts that you suspect that are causing the problem, review the code, fix the errors, and so on, until your code compiles successfully. After that, what follows is the preview of the result of the Java Class step for the transformation in the back, that is, the Java code applied to the test dataset.

If the previewed data shows the expected results, you are done. If not, you can check the code, modify or fix it, and test it again until you see that the step works properly.

Have a go hero – parameterizing the Java Class

Modify the transformation you created in the *Time for action – counting frequent words by coding in Java* section, in the following way:

1. Add a parameter named THRESHOLD, which contains the value to use for comparing the length of the words.

 You add a parameter by adding a new line in the **Parameters** tab. For each parameter, you have to provide a name under the **Tag** column, and a value under the **Value** column.

2. Modify the Java code so it reads and uses that parameter.

You read a parameter by using the `getParameter()` function. For example, `getParameter("THRESHOLD")`.

3. Test the transformation by providing different values for the threshold.

Transforming the dataset with Java

One of the features of the Java Class step is that it allows you to customize the output dataset, and even generate an output as a dataset that is totally different in content and structure to the input one. The next section shows you an example of this.

Time for action – splitting the field to rows using Java

In this section, we will read the text file we read in the previous sections and we will split the line to rows using Java code.

1. Create a new transformation and read the sample text file. In case you can't find the file, remember that its name is `smcng10.txt` and we used it for the first time in *Chapter 4, Filtering, Searching, and Other Useful Operations with Data*.

To save time, you can copy and paste the Text file input step from any of the other transformations that read the file.

2. From the **Scripting** category, add a **User Defined Java Class** step and create a hop from the Text file input step toward this new step.

3. Double-click on the UDJC step and type the following code:

```
public boolean processRow(StepMetaInterface smi,
    StepDataInterface sdi) throws KettleException
{
    Object[] r = getRow();
    if (r == null) {
        setOutputDone();
        return false;
    }
}
```

```
if (first) {
   first = false;
}

r = createOutputRow(r, data.outputRowMeta.size());

String linein;
linein = get(Fields.In, "line").getString(r);

String word;
int len = linein.length();
int prev =0;

boolean currentSpecialChar = false;

for (int i=0;i<len;i++) {
   char ch = linein.charAt(i);
   switch(ch) {
      case ',':
      case '.':
      case ' ':
      case ';':
      case ':':
      case '-':
         if (!currentSpecialChar) {
            r = createOutputRow(r,
               data.outputRowMeta.size());
            word = linein.substring(prev,i);
            get(Fields.Out, "word").setValue(r, word);
            putRow(data.outputRowMeta, r);
         }
         prev=i+1;
         currentSpecialChar = true;
         break;
      default:
         currentSpecialChar = false;
         break;
   }
}
```

```
        if (!currentSpecialChar) {    // last word
            r = createOutputRow(r, data.outputRowMeta.size());
            word = linein.substring(prev,len);
            get(Fields.Out, "word").setValue(r, word);
            putRow(data.outputRowMeta, r);
        }
        return true;
    }
```

4. Now click on the **Test class** button. A **Generate Rows** window appears for defining a sample dataset for testing.

5. In the **Generate Rows** window, replace the default value `test value test value` with this:

`bold and naked cliffs: in many places the cliffs are high; thus, south of`

6. As **Limit**, type 14. Then click on **Preview**. A window appears showing 14 identical rows with the provided sample values.

7. Close the Preview window and click on **OK** to test the code.

8. A window appears with the result of having executed the code on the test data:

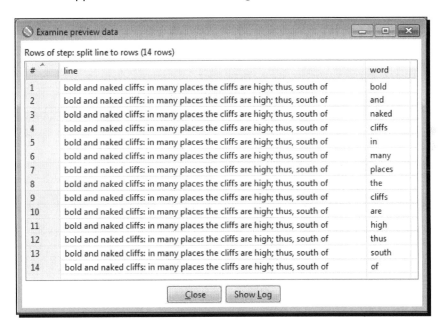

9. Close the window with the previewed data and the UDJC configuration window. Then save the transformation.

10. Make sure the UDJC step is selected and run a preview. You should see this:

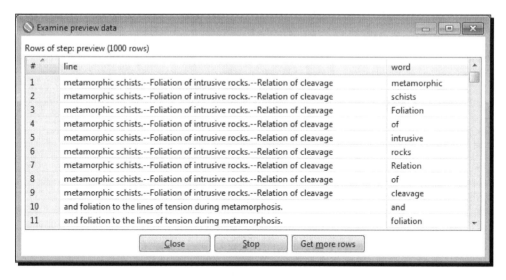

What just happened?

You used a UDJC step to split a line of text into several rows, one per word. This is an advanced version of the task implemented by the Split field to rows step: In this case, you split words based not only on a space but also on a list of separators.

Note that for each incoming row, the number of output rows varies depending on the content of the line field.

Avoiding coding by using purpose built steps

You saw through the exercises how powerful the JavaScript and Java Class steps are for helping you in your transformations. In older versions of PDI, coding JavaScript was the only means you had for doing specific tasks. In the latest releases of PDI, actual steps appeared that eliminate the need for coding in many cases. Here you have some examples of these steps:

- **Formula step**: Before the appearance of this step, there were a lot of functions—such as the right or left text functions—that you could only solve with JavaScript.

- **Analytic Query**: This step offers a way to retrieve information from rows before or after the current row.

- **Split field to rows**: This step is used to create several rows from a single string value.

Other steps have enhanced their capabilities. For example, the Calculator step has doubled the number of available calculations.

Despite the appearance of new steps, you still have the choice to do the tasks using code.

In fact, quite a lot of tasks you do with regular PDI steps may also be done with code using the JavaScript or the Java Class step as you saw in the sections of this chapter. This is a temptation to programmers who end up with transformations with plenty of code in them.

 Whenever there is a step that does what you want to do, you should prefer to use that step rather than coding.

Why should you prefer to use a specific step rather than code? There are some reasons:

♦ Coding takes more development time. You don't have to waste your time coding if there are steps that have solved your problem.

♦ Code is hard to maintain. If you have to modify or fix a transformation, it will be much easier to attack the change if the transformation is made of plenty of colorful steps with meaningful names, rather than if the transformation is made of just a couple of JavaScript or Java Class icons.

♦ A bunch of icons is self-documented. JavaScript or Java Class steps are like the Pandora's box. Until you open them, you don't know exactly what they do and whether they contain just a line of code or thousands.

♦ In the case of JavaScript, you should know that it is inherently slow. Faster alternatives for simple expressions are the **User Defined Java Expression** (also in the **Scripting** category of steps) and **Calculator** (in the **Transform** category) steps. They are typically more than twice as fast.

 The **User Defined Java Expression** (or **UDJE**) step allows you to create new fields in an easy way by typing Java expressions. You already saw several examples of its use throughout the chapters. The step doesn't replace the functionality of the UDJC syep, but it is more practical when the task to accomplish is simple.

On the contrary, there are situations where you may prefer or have to code. Let's enumerate some of them:

♦ To handle unstructured input data

♦ To manipulate complicated XML or JSON objects

♦ For accessing Java libraries

♦ When you need to use a function provided by the JavaScript or Java language and it is not provided by any of the regular PDI steps

- ◆ In the case of JavaScript, when the code saves a lot of regular PDI steps (as well as screen space), and you think it is not worth showing the details of what those steps do

- ◆ In the case of Java, for performance reasons, if you have to deal with millions of rows and very complicated operations, a Java class may be all you need for ending up with a transformation that performs very well

When you have doubts about the proper solution—to code or not to code—keep the following points in mind:

- ◆ Time to develop
- ◆ Maintenance
- ◆ Documentation
- ◆ Ability to handle unstructured data
- ◆ Number of needed steps
- ◆ Performance

Doing it this way, you will have arguments to help you decide which option is preferable. At the end, it is up to you to choose one or the other.

Pop quiz – choosing a scripting language for coding inside a transformation

Q1. If you plan to code in your transformation, you have to choose the language. You cannot mix Java and JavaScript in the same transformation.

1. True
2. False

Q2. The only available languages for coding in a transformation are Java and JavaScript.

1. True
2. False

Q3. You should avoid coding in JavaScript because the MJSV step is going to be deprecated and replaced by the UDJC step.

1. True
2. False

Summary

In this chapter, you learned to insert code in your PDI transformations. Specifically, you learned what the JavaScript and the User Defined Java Class steps are, how to modify fields and add new fields to your dataset from inside your JavaScript or Java Class steps, and how to deal with unstructured input data. You also saw a list of the pros and cons of coding inside your transformations, as well as alternative ways to do things, such as avoiding writing code when possible.

If you feel confident with all you have learned until now, you are certainly ready to move on to the next chapter. There, you will learn to solve some sophisticated problems—such as normalizing data from pivoted tables—in a simple fashion.

7
Transforming the Rowset

There are occasions when your dataset does not have the structure you like or the structure you need. The solution is not always about changing or adding fields, or about filtering or adding rows. The solution has to do with pivoting the whole dataset.

In this chapter, you will learn:

- Conversion of rows to columns, also called denormalizing
- Conversion of columns to rows, also called normalizing
- You will also be introduced to a core subject in data warehousing, called time dimensions

Converting rows to columns

In most datasets, each row belongs to a different element, such as a different match or a different student. However, there are datasets where a single row doesn't completely describe one element. Take, for example, the real-estate file from *Chapter 6, Transforming Your Data by Coding*. Every house was described through several rows. A single row gave incomplete information about the house. The ideal situation would be the one in which all the attributes for the house were in a single row. With **Pentaho Data Integration (PDI)**, you can convert the data into this alternative format. You will learn how to do it in this section.

Time for action – enhancing the films file by converting rows to columns

In this tutorial, we will work with a file that contains a list of French movies of all times. Each movie is described through several rows. This is how it looks:

```
...
Caché
Year: 2005
Director: Michael Haneke
Cast: Daniel Auteuil, Juliette Binoche, Maurice Bénichou

Jean de Florette
Year: 1986
Genre: Historical drama
Director: Claude Berri
Produced by: Pierre Grunstein
Cast: Yves Montand, Gérard Depardieu, Daniel Auteuil

Le Ballon rouge
Year: 1956
Genre: Fantasy | Comedy | Drama
...
```

In order to process the information within the file it would be better if the rows belonging to each movie were merged into a single row. Now carry out the following steps:

1. Download the `movies.txt` file from the book's website (`www.packtpub.com/support`).

2. Create a transformation and read the file with a Text file input step.

3. In the **Content** tab of the Text file input configuration step, put `:` as a separator. Also, uncheck the **Header** and **No empty rows** options.

4. In the **Fields** tab, enter two string fields: `feature` and `description`. Preview the input file to see if it is well configured. You should see two columns feature with the texts to the left of the semicolons and description with the text to the right.

5. Add a JavaScript step, create a hop from the Text file input step toward this, and edit this new step. Type the following code that will create the `film` field:

```
var film;

if (getProcessCount('r') == 1) film = '';

if (feature == null)
    film = '';
```

```
else if (film == '')
    film = feature;
```

6. Click on the **Get Variables** button to add the `film` field to the dataset.

7. Add a **Filter rows** step with the condition description `IS NOT NULL`.

8. With the **Filter rows** selected, do a preview. This is what you should see:

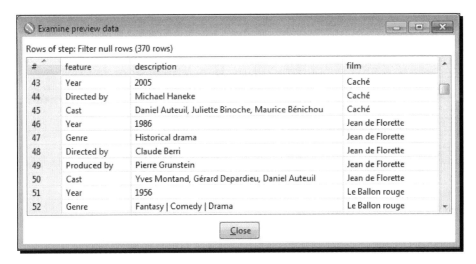

9. After the **Filter rows** step, add a **Row Denormaliser** step. You can find it under the **Transform** category. When asked for the kind of hop leaving the **Filter row** step, choose **Main output of step**.

10. Double-click on the step and fill in its fields, as shown in the following screenshot:

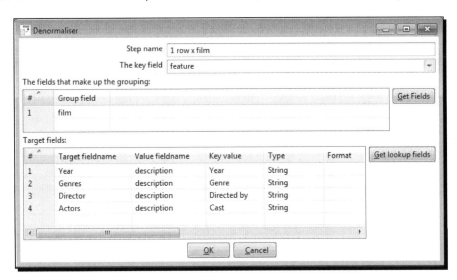

11. From the **Utility** category, select an **If field value is null** step and drag it to the canvas. Create a hop from the **Row denormaliser** step to this new step.

12. Double-click on the new step, check the **Select fields** option, and fill in the **Fields** grid as follows:

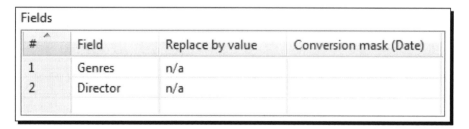

Fields

#	Field	Replace by value	Conversion mask (Date)
1	Genres	n/a	
2	Director	n/a	

13. With this last step selected, do a preview. You will see this:

Examine preview data

Rows of step: Defaults for null fields (97 rows)

#	film	Year	Genres	Director	Actors
12	Caché	2005	n/a	Michael Haneke	Daniel Auteuil, Juliette Binoche, Maurice Bénichou
13	Jean de Florette	1986	Historical drama	Claude Berri	Yves Montand, Gérard Depardieu, Daniel Auteuil
14	Le Ballon rouge	1956	Fantasy | Comedy | Drama	n/a	
15	Casque d'or	1952	Drama | Romance	Jacques Becker	Simone Signoret, Serge Reggiani, Claude Dauphin
16	Les Misérables	1925	History | Drama	Henri Fescourt	
17	Napoléon	1927	History | Biography | Drama	Abel Gance	Albert Dieudonné, Edmond Van Daële, Alexandre Koul
18	Le pornographe	2001	n/a	n/a	Jean-Pierre Leaud
19	Je rentre à la maison	2001	Comedy | Drama	Manoel de Oliveira	Michel Piccoli, Catherine Deneuve, John Malkovich
20	Les temps qui changent	2004	n/a	André Téchiné	Catherine Deneuve, Gérard Depardieu, Gilbert Melki

Close

What just happened?

You read a file with a selection of films in which each film was described through several rows.

First of all, you created a new field with the name of the film by using a small piece of JavaScript code. If you look at the code, you will notice that the empty rows are key for calculating the new field. They are used to distinguish between one film and the next, and that is the reason for unchecking the **No empty rows** option. When the code executes for an empty row it sets the film to an empty value. Then, when it executes for the first line of a film (`film == ''` in the code), it sets the new value for the `film` field. When the code executes for other lines, it does nothing, but the film already has the proper value. You can see the result of this in the preview you did after the **Filter rows** step. This step just filtered out the rows with null descriptions.

If you have difficulties in understanding the piece of JavaScript code, you can take a look at the *Reading and parsing unstructured files with JavaScript* section in the last chapter.

After that, you used a Row Denormaliser step to translate the description of films from rows to columns, so the final dataset had a single row by film.

Finally, you used a new step to replace some null fields with the text **n/a**, meaning not available.

Converting row data to column data by using the Row Denormaliser step

The Row Denormaliser Step converts the incoming dataset into a new dataset by moving information from rows to columns according to the values of a key field.

To understand how the Row Denormaliser works, let's create a diagram of the desired final dataset:

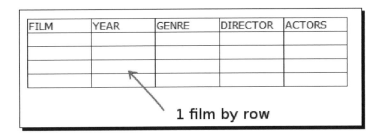

Here, a film is described by using a single row. On the contrary, in your input file the description for every film was spread in several rows.

To tell PDI how to combine a group of rows into a single one, there are three things you have to think about. They are as follows:

+ Among the input fields, there must be a **key field**. Depending on the value of that key field, you decide how the new fields will be filled. In your example, the key field is `feature`. Depending on the value of the column `feature`, you will send the value of the field `description` to some of the new fields: `Year`, `Genres`, `Director`, or `Actors`.

+ You have to group the rows together to form a related set of data. Each set of related data will eventually become a single row. The way you group will depend on the value of one or more fields. In our example, that field is `film`. All rows with the same value for the field `film` will become a single row.

◆ Decide the rules that have to be applied in order to fill in the new target fields. All rules follow this pattern:

❑ If the value for the key field is equal to A, put the value of the field B into the new field C

❑ A sample rule could be: if the value for the field `feature` (our key field) is equal to `Directed by`, put the value of the field `description` into the new field `Director`

Once you have these three things clear, all you have to do is to fill in the **Row Denormaliser** configuration window to tell PDI how to do this task.

1. Fill in the **key field** textbox with the name of the key field. In the example, the field is `feature`.

2. Fill the upper grid with the fields that make up the grouping. In this case, it is `film`.

 The dataset must be sorted on the grouping fields. If not, you will get unexpected results.

3. Finally, fill in the lower grid. This grid contains the rules for the new fields. Fill it in following this example:

To add this rule...	Fill a row like this...
If the value for the key field is equal to A, put the value of the field B into the new field C.	**Key value**: A **Value fieldname**: B **Target fieldname**: C

This is how you fill the row for the sample rule:

To add this rule...	Fill a row like this...
If the value for the field `feature` (our key field) is equal to `Directed by`, put the value of the field `description` into the new field `Director`.	**Key value**: Directed by **Value fieldname**: description **Target fieldname**: Director

For every rule, you must fill in a different row in the target fields' grid.

Let's see how the Row Denormaliser works for the following sample rows:

feature	description	film
Directed by	Claude Berri	Manon Des Sources
Produced by	Pierre Grunstein	Manon Des Sources
Genre	Drama | Romance	Manon Des Sources
Cast	Yves Montand, Daniel Auteuil, Emmanuelle Béart	Manon Des Sources

PDI creates an output row for the film `Manon Des Sources`. Then, it processes every row looking for values to fill the new fields.

Let's take the first row. The value for the key field `feature` is `Directed by`. PDI searches in the grid of `Target fields`, and if there is an entry where `Key value` is `Directed by`, PDI finds it:

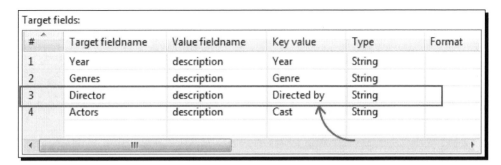

Target fields:

#	Target fieldname	Value fieldname	Key value	Type	Format
1	Year	description	Year	String	
2	Genres	description	Genre	String	
3	Director	description	Directed by	String	
4	Actors	description	Cast	String	

Then, PDI puts the value of the field description as the content for the target field `Director`. The output row is now as follows:

film	Year	Genres	Director	Actors
Manon Des Sources			Claude Berri	

Now, take the second row. The value for the key field `feature` is `Produced by`.

PDI searches in the target fields' grid to see if there is an entry where `Key value` is `Produced by`. It doesn't find it, and the information for this source row is discarded.

The following screenshot shows the rule applied to the third sample row. It also shows how the final output row looks:

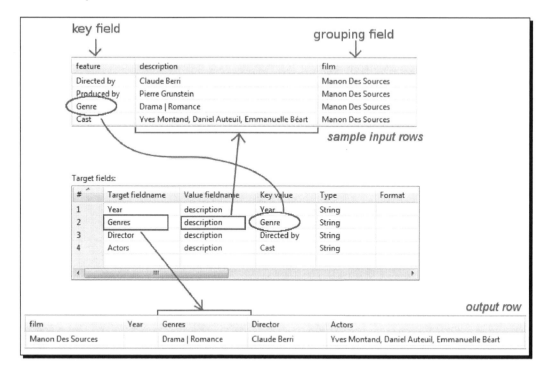

Note that it is not mandatory that the rows will be present for every key value entered in the target fields' grid. If an entry in the grid is not used, the target field is created anyway, but it remains empty.

In this sample film, the year was not present, hence the field Year remained empty.

Have a go hero – houses revisited

Take the output file of the *Have a go hero – enhancing the houses* section from *Chapter 6, Transforming Your Data by Coding*.

Alternatively, you can use the output data of the sample file available in the downloadable code bundle. Create a transformation that reads that file and generates the following output:

#. ▲	prop_code	Style of the House	Fireplace	Bathrooms	Bedrooms
1	MCX-001	Colonial	No	4	7
2	MCX-002	Colonial	Yes	5	5
3	MCX-003	Colonial	Yes	5	4
4	MCX-004	unknown	No	3	4
5	MCX-005	unknown	No	4	4
6	MCX-006	Colonial	Yes	6	4
7	MCX-007	Colonial	Yes	5	3
8	MCX-008	Colonial	Yes	4	5
9	MCX-009	Colonial	Yes	5	5
10	MCX-010	unknown	Yes	5	5
11	MCX-011	Contemporary	Yes	5	5
12	MCX-012	unknown	Yes	3	4
13	MCX-013	Contemporary	Yes	4	3
14	MCX-014	unknown	Yes	5	4
15	MCX-015	Tudor	Yes	3	5
16	MCX-016	Colonial	No	4	5
17	MCX-017	Tudor	Yes	3	4
18	MCX-018	Ranch	No	2	3
19	MCX-019	unknown	No	3	4
20	MCX-020	Contemporary	Yes	4	6
21	MCX-021	unknown	No	5	7
22	MCX-022	Colonial	Yes	4	4
23	MCX-023	Colonial	Yes	4	4

Aggregating data with a Row Denormaliser step

In the previous section, you learned how to use the Row Denormaliser step to combine several rows into one. The Row Denormaliser step can also be used to take a dataset as input and generate a new dataset as an output with aggregated or consolidated data. Let's see how the Row Denormaliser step works with an example.

Time for action – aggregating football matches data with the Row Denormaliser step

Let's now work with the football matches files that you came across in *Chapter 2, Getting Started with Transformations*, and *Chapter 3, Manipulating Real-world data*.

In this tutorial, we will calculate the total and average number of goals converted in a match date-wise. You will calculate the numbers for both the USA and for Europe.

1. Create a new transformation.
2. Read the football matches files just as you did in the tutorials of *Chapter 2, Getting Started with Transformations*, and *Chapter 3, Manipulating Real-world data*. This time, however, we will add a new field. In the **Text file input** configuration window select the **Additional output fields** tab.

3. In the **Short filename field** textbox, type the word `filename`.

4. Do a preview. You should see this:

5. Add a **Split Fields** step and create a hop from the Text file input step toward this.

6. Use the step for splitting the field `filename` into two fields of type **String**: `region` and `unused`. As a separator, type an underscore (_).

7. Add a **Split Fields** step and a **Calculator** step, and link them as follows:

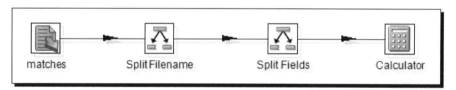

8. Use the **Split Fields** step for splitting the result field into two fields of type Integer: `home_t_goals` and `away_t_goals`. As a separator, use a colon (:).

9. Then, use the **Calculator** for creating a field named goals of type `Integer`, with the sum of the new fields above. As operation, under the Calculation field, select *A + B*.

10. Run a preview. You will see this:

11. Now, add a **Sort rows** step and use it to sort the data by `match_date` in ascending order.

12. Finally, add a **Row Denormaliser** step.

13. Double-click on it and configure it. For **The key field** select **region**.

14. In the first grid, as **Group field** select or type `match_date`.

15. Fill the **Target fields** grid, as shown in the following screenshot, and then close the window:

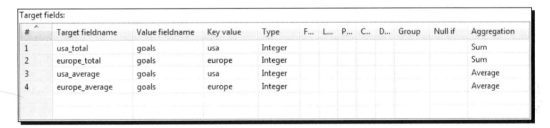

16. Add a **Select Values** step for selecting just the fields that we are interested in: `match_date`, `usa_total`, `europe_total`, `usa_average`, and `europe_average`.

17. With the **Select Values** step selected, do a preview. You will see this:

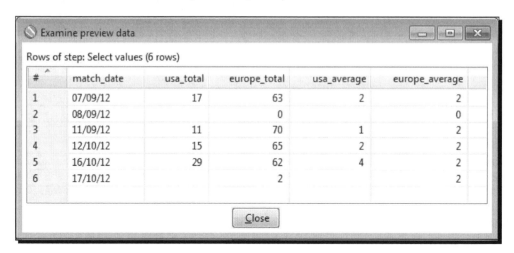

Rows of step: Select values (6 rows)

#	match_date	usa_total	europe_total	usa_average	europe_average
1	07/09/12	17	63	2	2
2	08/09/12		0		0
3	11/09/12	11	70	1	2
4	12/10/12	15	65	2	2
5	16/10/12	29	62	4	2
6	17/10/12		2		2

Close

What just happened?

You read the football matches file, grouped the data by match date, and then created four new columns: two with the total and average goals scored in the USA sorted by match and date, and two with the same statistics, but for Europe.

Using Row Denormaliser for aggregating data

The purpose for which you used the Row Denormaliser step in this tutorial was different from the purpose in the previous tutorial. In this case, you put the dates in rows, and created four fields: two for the region USA, two for the region Europe. In the cells, you put sums and averages. The final dataset was a kind of a cross tab like those you create with the DataPilot tool in Open Office, or the Pivot in Excel. The big difference is that here, the final dataset is not interactive, because in essence PDI is not.

 If you want, you can eventually export this output to Excel for an interactive final dataset.

Another difference is that here you have to know the names or elements for the columns in advance. To compensate for it, PDI has some advantages, for example, allowing you to normalize complex data or data coming from many different kinds of sources.

Let's explain how the Row Denormaliser step works in these cases. Basically, the way it works is quite the same as before. The step groups the rows by the grouping fields, and creates a new output row for each group.

The novelty here is the **aggregation** of values, that is, the combination of measures by using different operations, mainly summary statistics, for example, sum or minimum. When more than one row in the group matches the value for the key field, PDI calculates the new output field as the result of applying an aggregate function to all the values. The aggregate functions available are a subset of those in the Group by step: sum, average, minimum, and so on. Take a look at the following sample rows:

match_date	venue	home_team	home_t_goals	away_t_goals	away_team	region	unused	goals
07/09/12	Havana	Cuba	0	3	Honduras	usa	201209.txt	3
07/09/12	Kingston	Jamaica	2	1	USA	usa	201209.txt	3
07/09/12	San Salvador	El Salvador	2	2	Guyana	usa	201209.txt	4
07/09/12	Toronto	Canada	1	0	Panama	usa	201209.txt	1
07/09/12	Guatemala City	Guatemala	3	1	Antigua and Barbuda	usa	201209.txt	4
07/09/12	San Jose	Costa Rica	0	2	Mexico	usa	201209.txt	2

All these rows have usa as the value for the key field region. According to the rule of the Row Denormaliser step, the values for the field goals of these rows go to the new target fields usa_total and usa_average, but aggregated; usa_total is defined as the sum of the original values, while usa_average is defined as the average.

So, the output data for this sample group is as follows:

match_date	usa_total	europe_total	usa_average	europe_average
07/09/12	17		2	

The value for the new field usa_total is 17, the sum of 3, 3, 4, 1, 4, and 2, the values of the field goals for the input rows where region was usa. In the same way, the value for the new field usa_average is 2; the average of those values.

Note the difference between the Row Denormaliser and the Group by step for aggregating. With the Row Denormaliser step, you generate a new different field for each interesting key value. Using the Group by step for the tutorial, you couldn't have created the four columns shown earlier.

Have a go hero – calculating statistics by team

Create a new transformation, read the football matches files, and generate the following output, where the cells represent the number of goals by month, by region:

#	region	September	October
1	europe	133	129
2	usa	28	44

Normalizing data

Some datasets are nice to view but complicated for further processing. Take a look at the following extract of one of the matches files we were working with:

```
Date;Venue;Country;Matches;Country
07/09/12 15:00;Havana;Cuba;0:3;Honduras;
07/09/12 19:00;Kingston;Jamaica;2:1;USA;
07/09/12 19:30;San Salvador;El Salvador;2:2;Guyana;
07/09/12 19:45;Toronto;Canada;1:0;Panama;
07/09/12 20:00;Guatemala City;Guatemala;3:1;Antigua and Barbuda;
07/09/12 20:05;San Jose;Costa Rica;0:2;Mexico;
...
```

Imagine you want to answer the following questions:

◆ How many teams played?

◆ Which team converted most goals?

◆ Which team won all matches it played?

The dataset is not prepared to answer these questions, at least in an easy way. If you want to answer those questions in a simple way, first you will have to normalize the data, that is, convert it to a suitable format before proceeding. Let's work on it.

Time for action – enhancing the matches file by normalizing the dataset

Now, you will convert the matches file to a format suitable for answering the proposed questions as follows:

1. Create a new transformation and read the files by using a **Text file input** step.

2. With a **Split Fields** step, split the `Result` field in two sections: `home_t_goals` and `away_t_goals`. As **Delimiter** use a colon (`:`).

3. From the **Transform** category of steps, drag a **Row Normaliser** step to the canvas.

4. Create a hop from the last step to this new one.

5. Double-click on the Row Normaliser step to edit it and fill in the window as follows:

6. With the Row Normaliser selected, do a preview. You should see this:

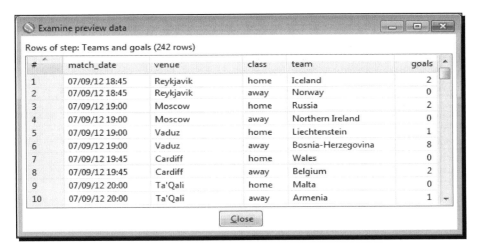

What just happened?

You read the matches file and converted the dataset to a new one, where both the home team and the away team appeared under a new column named `team`, together with another new column named `goals` holding the goals converted by each team. With this new format, it is really easy now to answer the questions proposed at the beginning of the section.

If you take a look at the input file used in the first tutorials of *Chapter 4, Filtering, Searching, and Other Useful Operations with Data*, you will notice that the content is almost the same as the data generated in this tutorial.

Modifying the dataset with a Row Normaliser step

The Row Normaliser Step modifies your dataset so that it becomes more suitable for processing. Usually, this involves transforming columns into rows.

To understand how it works let's take an example file from the tutorial. Here is a diagram showing what we want to have at the end:

	match_date	venue	class	team	goals	
First Match	07/09/12 18:45	Reykjavik	home	Iceland	2	← Home Team
	07/09/12 18:45	Reykjavik	away	Norway	0	← Away Team
Second Match	07/09/12 19:00	Moscow	home	Russia	2	← Home Team
	07/09/12 19:00	Moscow	away	Northern Ireland	0	← Away Team
	...	...	...	...	...	

What we have now is this:

	match_date	venue	home_team	home_t_goals	away_t_goals	away_team
First Match →	07/09/12 18:45	Reykjavik	Iceland	2	0	Norway
Second Match →	07/09/12 19:00	Moscow	Russia	2	0	Northern Ireland
	...	...	...			...

Now, it is just a matter of creating a correspondence between the old columns and the new ones.

Just follow these steps and you will have the work done:

Step	Example
Identify the new desired fields. Give them a name.	`team` and `goals`
Look at the old fields and identify which ones you want to translate to the new fields.	`Home_Team`, `home_t_goals`, `Away_Team`, and `away_t_goals`
From that list, identify the columns that you want to keep together in the same row by creating a sort of classification of the fields. Give each group a name. Also, give a name to the classification.	You want to keep together the fields `Home_Team` and `home_t_goals`. So, you create a group with those fields, and name it `home`. Likewise, you create a group named away with the fields `Away_Team` and `away_t_goals`. Name the classification as `class`.
Define a correspondence between the fields identified earlier, and the new fields.	The old field `Home_Team` goes to the new field team. The old field `home_t_goals` goes to the new field goals. The old field `Away_Team` goes to the new field team. The old field `away_t_goals` goes to the new field goals.
Transcribe all these definitions to the Row Normaliser configuration window as shown in the screenshot in the adjacent column.	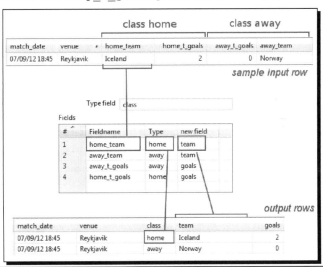

In the fields grid, insert one row for each of the fields that you want to normalize. After normalizing, you will have a new dataset where the fields for the groups that you defined were converted to rows.

The number of rows in the new dataset is equal to the number of groups defined by the number of rows in the old dataset. In the tutorial, the final number is 121 rows x 2 groups = 242 rows.

Note that the fields not mentioned in the configuration of the Row Normaliser (the Match_ Date field in the example), are kept without changes. They are simply duplicated for each new row.

In the tutorial, every group was made by two fields: Home_Team and home_t_goals for the first group, and Away_Team and away_t_goals for the second. When you normalize, any of the groups may have just one field, two as shown in this example, or more than two.

Summarizing the PDI steps that operate on sets of rows

The Row Normaliser and Row denormaliser steps you learned in this chapter are some of the PDI steps that operate on sets of rows, rather than on single rows. The following table gives you an overview of the main PDI steps that fall into this particular group of steps:

Step	Purpose
Group by	Builds aggregates as Sum, Maximum, and so on, on the groups of rows.
Memory Group by	Same as Group by, but doesn't require sorted input.
Analytic Query	Computes lead, lag, first, and last fields over a sorted dataset.
Univariate Statistics	Computes some simple statistics. It complements the **Group by** step. It has less capabilities than that step but provides more aggregate functions, for example median and percentiles.
Split Fields	Splits a single field into more than one. Actually it doesn't operate on a set of rows, but it's common to use it combined with some of the steps in this table. For example: you could use a Group by step to concatenate a field, followed by a **Split Fields** step that splits that concatenated field into several columns.
Row Normaliser	Transforms columns into rows making the dataset more suitable for processing.
Row denormaliser	Moves information from rows to columns according to the values of a key field.
Row flattener	Flattens consecutive rows. You could achieve the same by using a Group by to concatenate the field to flatten, followed by a Split Field step.
Sort rows	Sorts rows based upon field values. Alternatively, it can keep only unique rows.
Split field to rows	Splits a single string field and creates a new row for each split term.
Unique rows	Remove double consecutive rows and leave only unique occurrences.

For examples that use these steps or for getting more information about them, refer to the job entries and steps reference in *Appendix C, Quick reference – Steps and Job Entries*.

Have a go hero – verifying the benefits of normalizing

Extend the transformation and answer the questions proposed at the beginning of the section:

◆ How many teams played?

◆ Which team converted most goals?

◆ Which team won all matches it played?

To answer the third question, you will have to modify the Row Normaliser step as well. If you are not convinced that the normalizer process makes the work easier, you can try to answer the questions without using normalize. That effort will definitely convince you!

Have a go hero – normalizing the Films file

Take the output of the *Time for action – enhancing a films file by converting rows to columns* section. Generate the following output:

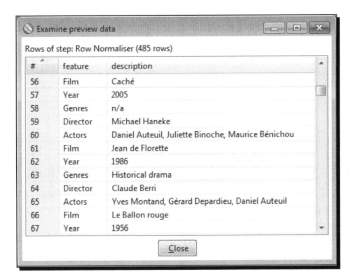

You have two options here:

◆ Modify the tutorial by sending the output to a new file. Then, use that new file to do this exercise.

◆ Extend the stream in the original transformation by adding new steps after the Row Denormaliser step.

After doing the exercise, think about this: does it make sense to denormalize and then normalize again? What is the difference between the original file and the output of this exercise? Could you have done the same without denormalizing and normalizing?

Generating a custom time dimension dataset by using Kettle variables

Dimensions are sets of attributes useful for describing a business. A list of products along with their shape, color, or size is a typical example of dimension. The **time dimension** is a special dimension used for describing a business in terms of when things happened. Just think of time dimension as a list of dates along with attributes describing these dates. For example, given the date 05/08/2009, you know that it is a day of August, it belongs to the third quarter of the year, and it is Wednesday. These are some of the attributes for that date.

In the following tutorial, you will create a transformation that generates the dataset for a **time dimension**, fundamental in any data warehouse. The dataset for a time dimension has one row for every date in a given range of dates and one column for each attribute of the date.

Time for action – creating the time dimension dataset

In this tutorial, we will create a simple dataset for a time dimension.

 In *Chapter 2, Getting Started with Transformations*, you created a transformation that generated a dataset with one row by date in a date range. In this tutorial, we will reuse that work.

First, we will create a stream with the days of the week:

1. Create a new transformation.

2. Press *Ctrl + T* or right-click on the canvas and select **Transformation settings** to access the **Transformation properties** window.

3. Select the **Parameters** tab and fill it as shown in the following screenshot:

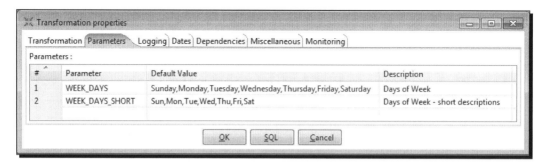

#	Parameter	Default Value	Description
1	WEEK_DAYS	Sunday,Monday,Tuesday,Wednesday,Thursday,Friday,Saturday	Days of Week
2	WEEK_DAYS_SHORT	Sun,Mon,Tue,Wed,Thu,Fri,Sat	Days of Week - short descriptions

4. Expand the **Job** category of the steps.

5. Drag a **Get Variables** step to the canvas, double-click on the step, and fill the window, as shown in the following screenshot:

6. After the **Get Variables** step, add a **Split Fields** step and use it to split the field `week_days` into seven **String** fields named `sun`, `mon`, `tue`, `wed`, `thu`, `fri`, and `sat`. As a **Delimiter** set a comma (,).

7. Add one more **Split Fields** step and use it to split the field `week_days_short` into seven **String** fields named `sun_sh`, `mon_sh`, `tue_sh`, `wed_sh`, `thu_sh`, `fri_sh`, and `sat_sh`. As a **Delimiter** set a comma (,).

8. After this last step, add a **Row Normaliser** step.

9. Double-click on the **Row Normaliser** step and fill it as follows:

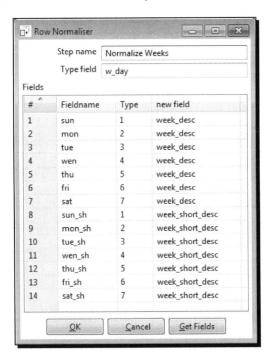

10. Keep the **Row Normaliser** step selected and do a preview. You will see this:

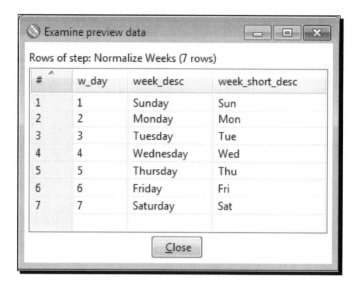

Now, let's build the main stream:

1. Open the transformation created in the *Generating a range of dates and inspecting the data as it is being created* section in *Chapter 2, Getting Started with Transformations*.

2. Right-click on the work area and select **Select All**. Press *Ctrl + C* to copy all steps and hops. Select the tab with the new transformation that you are creating, and press *Ctrl + V* to pass the copied stream.

3. Edit the **Generate rows** step and change the value of the start_date to 2000-01-01.

4. Right-click on the **Delay row** step and select **Detach step**. Then, delete the step. You should have this:

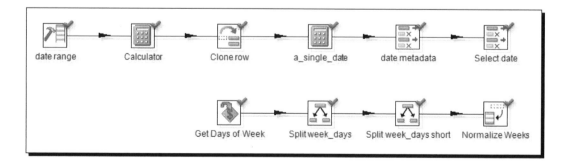

5. Double-click on the second **Calculator** and define the new fields `year`, `month`, `day`, and `week_day`, as shown in the following screenshot:

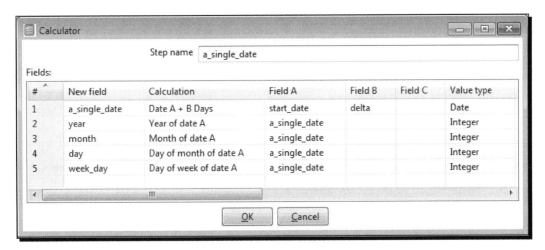

6. Now, double-click on the second **Select values** step and, after the field `a_single_date`, add four new fields. Do a preview on this last step. You will see this:

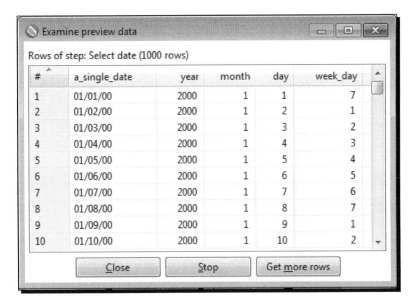

7. After this last **Select values** step, add a **Stream lookup** step.

8. Also, create a hop from the **Row Normaliser** step to the **Stream lookup** step.

9. Double-click on the **Stream lookup** step. In the upper grid, add a row, setting week_day under the **Field** column and w_day under the LookupField column. Use the lower grid to retrieve the **String** fields: week_desc and week_short_desc.

10. Finally, after the **Stream lookup** step add a dummy step. With this step selected, click on the **Preview** button.

11. When the preview window appears click on **Configure**.

12. In the **Parameters** grid of the **Execute a transformation** window, fill the column **Value** as follows:

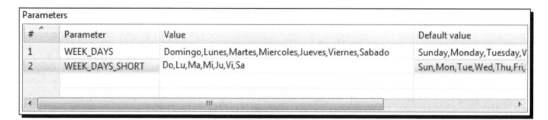

Parameters			
#	Parameter	Value	Default value
1	WEEK_DAYS	Domingo,Lunes,Martes,Miercoles,Jueves,Viernes,Sabado	Sunday,Monday,Tuesday,V
2	WEEK_DAYS_SHORT	Do,Lu,Ma,Mi,Ju,Vi,Sa	Sun,Mon,Tue,Wed,Thu,Fri,

13. Click the **Launch** button. You will see this:

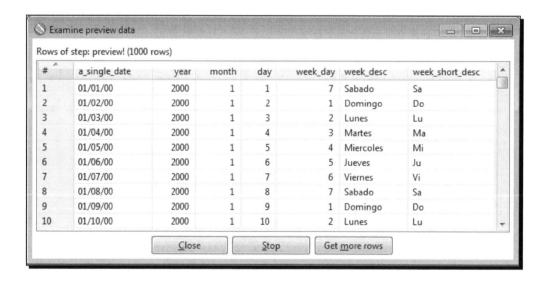

Examine preview data

Rows of step: preview! (1000 rows)

#	a_single_date	year	month	day	week_day	week_desc	week_short_desc
1	01/01/00	2000	1	1	7	Sabado	Sa
2	01/02/00	2000	1	2	1	Domingo	Do
3	01/03/00	2000	1	3	2	Lunes	Lu
4	01/04/00	2000	1	4	3	Martes	Ma
5	01/05/00	2000	1	5	4	Miercoles	Mi
6	01/06/00	2000	1	6	5	Jueves	Ju
7	01/07/00	2000	1	7	6	Viernes	Vi
8	01/08/00	2000	1	8	7	Sabado	Sa
9	01/09/00	2000	1	9	1	Domingo	Do
10	01/10/00	2000	1	10	2	Lunes	Lu

Close   Stop   Get more rows

What just happened?

You generated data for a time dimension with dates ranging from **01/01/2000** to **31/12/2023**. Time dimensions are meant to answer questions related with time, for example: do I sell more on Mondays or on Fridays? Am I selling more this quarter than the same quarter last year? Depending on the kind of question you want to answer, is the list of attributes you need to include in your time dimension. Typical fields in a time dimension are: year, month (a number between 1 and 12), description of month, day of month, weekday, and quarter. In this tutorial, you created few attributes but you could have added much more. Among the attributes included, you had the weekday. The week descriptions were taken from named parameters, which allowed you to set the language of the week descriptions at the time you ran the transformation. In the tutorial, you specified Spanish descriptions. If you had left the parameters grid empty, the transformation would have used the English descriptions that you put as default.

Let's explain how you built the stream with the number and descriptions for the days of the week. First, you created a dataset by getting the variables with the descriptions for the days of the week. After creating the dataset, you split the descriptions and by using the Row Normalize step, you converted that row in a list of rows, including one for every weekday. In other words, you created a single row with all the descriptions for the days of the week. Then, you normalized it to create the list of weekdays.

Getting variables

To create the secondary stream of the tutorial you used a **Get Variables** step. The Get Variables step allows you to get the value of one or more **Kettle variables**.

Remember that we learned about these variables in the *Kettle variables* section in *Chapter 3, Manipulating Real-world Data*.

In this tutorial, you read two variables that had been defined in the **Transformation properties** window.

The variables defined in the **Parameters** tab of the transformation setting window are known as **named parameters**. You will see more on this subject later in the book.

When put as the first step of a stream, in this case, the Get Variables step creates a dataset with one single row and as many fields as read variables.

The following screenshot shows the dataset created by the Get Variables step in the time dimension tutorial:

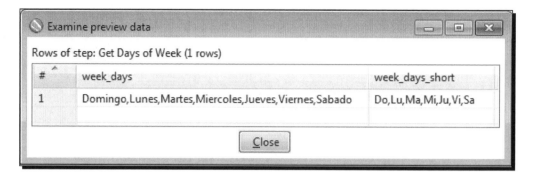

When put in the middle of a stream, this step adds to the incoming dataset as many fields as the variables it reads. Let's see how it works.

Time for action – parameterizing the start and end date of the time dimension dataset

Let's modify the transformation so that the starting and end date depend on variables.

1. Open the transformation you just created.

2. Add a **Get variables** step between the second **Calculator** step and the first **Select values** step.

3. Edit the **Get variables** step and fill it in, as shown in the following screenshot:

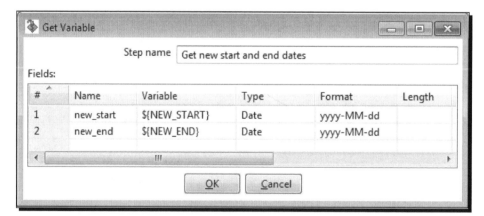

4. After this step, insert a **Filter row** step. Edit the step to add this condition: a_ single_date>=new_start and a_single_date<=new_end.

5. With the Dummy step selected click on **Preview**, and then click on **Configure**.

6. Fill the **Variables** grid, as shown in the following screenshot:

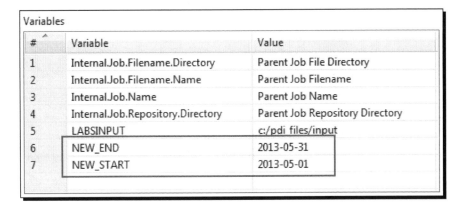

#	Variable	Value
1	Internal.Job.Filename.Directory	Parent Job File Directory
2	Internal.Job.Filename.Name	Parent Job Filename
3	Internal.Job.Name	Parent Job Name
4	Internal.Job.Repository.Directory	Parent Job Repository Directory
5	LABSINPUT	c:/pdi_files/input
6	NEW_END	2013-05-31
7	NEW_START	2013-05-01

7. Click on **Launch**. You will see this:

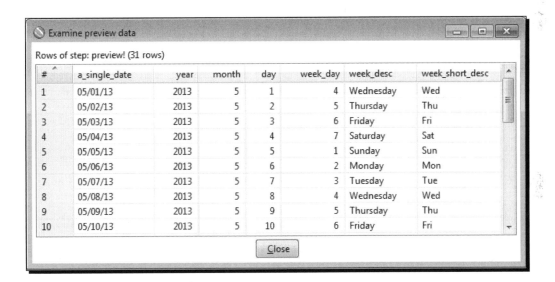

Examine preview data

Rows of step: preview! (31 rows)

#	a_single_date	year	month	day	week_day	week_desc	week_short_desc
1	05/01/13	2013	5	1	4	Wednesday	Wed
2	05/02/13	2013	5	2	5	Thursday	Thu
3	05/03/13	2013	5	3	6	Friday	Fri
4	05/04/13	2013	5	4	7	Saturday	Sat
5	05/05/13	2013	5	5	1	Sunday	Sun
6	05/06/13	2013	5	6	2	Monday	Mon
7	05/07/13	2013	5	7	3	Tuesday	Tue
8	05/08/13	2013	5	8	4	Wednesday	Wed
9	05/09/13	2013	5	9	5	Thursday	Thu
10	05/10/13	2013	5	10	6	Friday	Fri

Close

What just happened?

You modified the transformation that generated data for a time dimension so that the start and end date depend on variables. You read those variables with a **Get Variables** step, generating two new fields. Then, you used them to keep only the dates between those values.

Using the Get Variables step

As you just saw, the Get Variables step allows you to get the value of one or more variables. In the main tutorial, you saw how to use the step at the beginning of a stream. Now, you saw how to use it in the middle. The following screenshot shows the dataset after the Get Variables step for the last exercise:

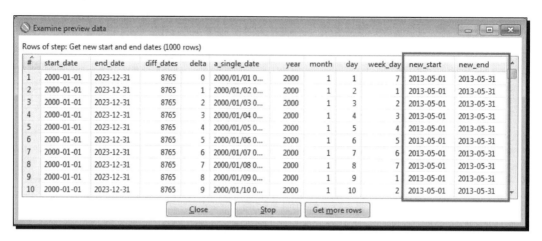

As you can figure out, you could have defined the ${NEW_START} and ${NEW_END} variables as named parameters. Following this method, you could even have set default values for those dates. However, we didn't follow that method on purpose to show you that, with the Get Variables step, you can read any Kettle variable.

Variables defined in the kettle.properties file, internal variables, for example ${user.dir}, named parameters as in the previous tutorial related with time dimension, or other Kettle variables as you did in the last tutorial.

As you know, the type of Kettle variables are String by default. However, at the time you get a variable you can change its metadata. As an example of that, in the previous exercise you converted ${NEW_START} to a Date value by using the yyyy-MM-dd mask.

Note that you specified the variables as ${name of the variable}. You could have used %%name of the variable%% also.

The full specification of the name of a variable allows you to mix variables with plain text. As an example, instead of a date you can use a variable named YEAR. In the Get variables step, you may specify 01/01/${YEAR} as the value. When you execute the transformation this text will be expanded to 01/01/ plus the year you enter when you run the transformation.

Note, that the purpose of using the Get Variable step is to have the values of variables as fields in the dataset. Otherwise, you don't need to use this step when using a variable. You just use it wherever you see a dollar sign icon.

Have a go hero – enhancing the time dimension

Modify the time dimension generation by doing the following:

- Taking as a model the generation of weekdays, add to the dataset the following fields: Name of month, Short name of month, and Quarter.

- Replace the regular variables ${NEW_START} and ${NEW_END} with named parameters: start_year and end_year. Modify the transformation so it only generates dates between those years.

In both cases, make sure you set default values for the variables, so you don't have to type them each time you run the transformation.

Summary

In this chapter, you learned to transform your dataset by applying two magical steps: Row Normaliser and Row Denormaliser. These two steps aren't the kind of steps you use every day as for example a Filter Row or a Select values step. However, when you need to do the kind of task they can achieve, you are really grateful that these steps exist. They do a great task in a quite simple way. You also learned what a time dimension is and how to create a dataset for a time dimension.

Finally, you were introduced to the concept of Named Parameters.

So far, you have been learning how to transform data. In the next chapter, we will start learning to work with databases, a subject that most of you must be waiting for since the *Installing MySQL* section in *Chapter 1, Getting Started with Pentaho Data Integration*.

8
Working with Databases

Database systems are the main mechanism used by most organizations to store and administer organizational data. Online sales, bank-related operations, customer service history, and credit card transactions are some examples of data stored in databases.

This is the first of two chapters fully dedicated to working with databases. Here is a list of the topics that will be covered:

- ◆ Connecting to a database
- ◆ Previewing and getting data from a database
- ◆ Inserting, updating, and deleting data from a database

Introducing the Steel Wheels sample database

As you were told in the first chapter, there is a Pentaho Demo that includes data for a fictional store named Steel Wheels and you can download it from the Internet. This data is stored in a database that is going be the starting point for you to learn how to work with databases in PDI. Before beginning to work on databases, let's briefly introduce the Steel Wheels database along with some database definitions.

 In this book, we will learn about relational databases. You should know that there are several database genres other than relational (big data, document, graph, and more). Not all databases are row/columnar like the relational ones.

A **relational database** is a collection of items stored in tables. Typically, all items stored in a table belong to a particular type of data. The following table lists some of the tables in the Steel Wheels database:

Table	Content
CUSTOMERS	Steel Wheels' customers
EMPLOYEES	Steel Wheels' employees
PRODUCTS	Products sold by Steel Wheels
OFFICES	Steel Wheels' offices
ORDERS	Information about sales orders
ORDERDETAILS	Details about the sales orders

The items stored in the tables represent an entity or a concept in the real world. As an example, the CUSTOMERS table stores items representing customers. The ORDERS table stores items that represent sales orders in the real world.

In technical terms, a **table** is uniquely identified by a name such as CUSTOMERS, and it contains columns and rows of data. You can think of a table as a PDI dataset. You have fields (the columns of the table) and rows (the records of the table)

The **columns**, just like the fields in a PDI dataset, have a metadata describing its name, type, and length. The **records** hold the data for those columns; each record represents a different instance of the items in the table. As an example, the CUSTOMERS table describes the customers with the columns CUSTOMERNUMBER, CUSTOMERNAME, CONTACTLASTNAME, and so forth. Each record of the table CUSTOMERS belongs to a different Steel Wheels' customer.

A table usually has a primary key. A **primary key (PK)** is a combination of one or more columns that uniquely identify each record of the table. In the sample table, CUSTOMERS, the primary key is made up of a single column CUSTOMERNUMBER. This means that there cannot be two customers with the same customer number.

Tables in a relational database are usually related to one another. For example, the CUSTOMERS and ORDERS tables are related to convey the fact that real-world customers have placed one or more real-world orders. In the database, the ORDERS table has a column named CUSTOMERNUMBER with the number of the customer who placed the order. As said, CUSTOMERNUMBER is the column that uniquely identifies a customer in the CUSTOMERS table. Thus, there is a relationship between both tables. This kind of relationship between columns in two tables is called a **foreign key (FK)**.

Connecting to the Steel Wheels database

The first thing you have to do in order to work with a database is tell PDI how to access the database. Let's learn how to do it.

Time for action – creating a connection to the Steel Wheels database

In this first database tutorial, you will download the sample database and create a connection for accessing it from the PDI.

> The Pentaho BI demo includes the sample data. So, if you have already downloaded the demo as explained in *Chapter 1, Getting started with Pentaho Data Integration*, just skip the first three steps. If the Pentaho BI demo is running on your machine, the database server is running as well. In that case, skip the first four steps.

1. Go to the Pentaho Download site `http://sourceforge.net/projects/pentaho/files/`.

2. Under the **Business Intelligence Server | 1.7.1-stable** look for the file named `pentaho_sample_data-1.7.1.zip` and download it.

> This is the only version of the sample database available for downloading alone. Despite being located together with a really outdated version of the Business Intelligence Server, the sample data is the same as the one bundled in recent versions.

3. Unzip the downloaded file in a folder of your choice for example `c:\pentaho\bi-server` or `/opt/pentaho/bi-server`.

4. Run `start_hypersonic.bat` under Windows or `start_hypersonic.sh` under *x operating systems. If you downloaded the sample data, you will find these scripts in the folder named `pentaho-data`. If you downloaded the Pentaho BI server instead, you will find them in the folder named `data`. The database server starts as shown in the following screenshot:

```
start_hypersonic
DEBUG: Using JAVA_HOME
DEBUG: _PENTAHO_JAVA_HOME=C:\Program Files\Java\jdk1.6.0_31
DEBUG: _PENTAHO_JAVA=C:\Program Files\Java\jdk1.6.0_31\bin\java.exe
[Server@187a84e4]: [Thread[main,5,main]]: checkRunning(false) entered
[Server@187a84e4]: [Thread[main,5,main]]: checkRunning(false) exited
[Server@187a84e4]: Startup sequence initiated from main() method
[Server@187a84e4]: Loaded properties from [C:\software\PENTAHO\biserver-ce-4.8.0
\biserver-ce\data\server.properties]
[Server@187a84e4]: Initiating startup sequence...
[Server@187a84e4]: Server socket opened successfully in 28 ms.
[Server@187a84e4]: Database [index=0, id=0, db=file:hsqldb\sampledata, alias=sam
pledata] opened successfully in 1061 ms.
[Server@187a84e4]: Database [index=1, id=1, db=file:hsqldb\hibernate, alias=hibe
rnate] opened sucessfully in 673 ms.
[Server@187a84e4]: Database [index=2, id=2, db=file:hsqldb\quartz, alias=quartz]
 opened sucessfully in 30 ms.
[Server@187a84e4]: Startup sequence completed in 1794 ms.
[Server@187a84e4]: 2013-05-19 22:52:17.415 HSQLDB server 1.8.0 is online
[Server@187a84e4]: To close normally, connect and execute SHUTDOWN SQL
[Server@187a84e4]: From command line, use [Ctrl]+[C] to abort abruptly
```

 Don't close this window. It would cause the database server to stop.

5. Open Spoon and create a new transformation.

6. In the upper-left corner of the screen, click on **View**.

7. Right-click on the **Database connections** option and click on **New**.

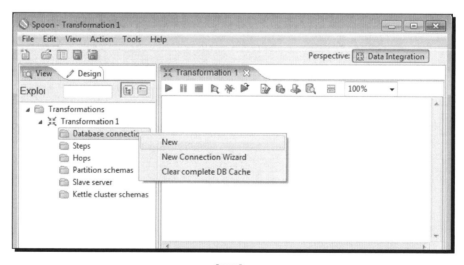

8. Fill the **Database Connection** dialog window as follows:

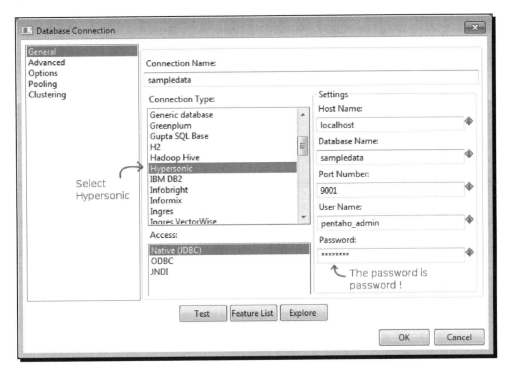

9. Click on the **Test** button. The following window shows up:

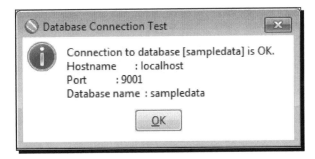

 If you get an error message instead of this, re-check the data you entered in the connection window. Also, verify that the database is running, that is, the terminal window is still open and does not show an error message. If you see an error or if you don't see the terminal, start the database server again as explained at the beginning of the tutorial.

10. Click on **OK** to close the test window.

11. Click on **OK** again to close the database definition window.

12. A new database connection named `sampledata` is added to the tree.

13. Right-click on the created database connection and click on **Share** so the connection is available in all transformations you create from now on.

14. The shared connections are shown in bold letters:

15. Save the transformation.

What just happened?

You created and tested a connection to the Pentaho Sample database. Finally, you shared the connection so it could be reused in other transformations.

Connecting with Relational Database Management Systems

Even if you have never worked with databases, you must have heard of terms such as MySQL, Oracle, DB2, or MS SQL Server. These are just some of the many **Relational Database Management Systems (RDBMS)** on the market. RDBMS is software that lets you create and administer relational databases.

In the tutorial, you worked with **HyperSQL DataBase (HSQLDB)**, another RDBMS that was formerly known as Hypersonic DB. HSQLDB has a small, fast database engine written in Java. HSQLDB is currently being used in many open source projects projects such as OpenOffice. org, as well as in commercial projects and products such as Mathematica. You can get more information about HSQLDB at `http://hsqldb.org/`.

PDI has the ability to connect to both commercial RDBMSes such as Oracle or MS SQL Server, and free RDBMSes such as MySQL. In order to be connected to a particular database you have to define a connection to it.

A database connection describes all the parameters needed to connect PDI to a database. To create a connection, you must give the connection a name and at least fill the general settings as follows:

Setting	Description	SteelWheels sample
Connection Type	Type of database system: HSQLDB, Oracle, MySQL, Firebird, and so on.	`HSQLDB`
Method of access	Native (JDBC), ODBC, JNDI or OCI. The available options depend on the type of database.	`Native (JDBC)`
Host name	Name or IP address for the host where the database is located.	`localhost`
Database name	Identifies the database to which you want to connect.	`sampledata`
Port number	PDI sets as default the most usual port number for the selected type of DB. You can change it of course.	`9001`
User Name/ Password	Name of the user and password to connect to the DB.	`pentaho_admin` `password`

> If you don't find your database engine in the list, you can still connect to it by specifying the **Generic database** option as a **Connection Type**. In that case, you have to provide a connection URL and the driver class name. If you need more help on this, check out the official website for your database engine.

After creating a connection, you can click on the **Test** button to check whether the connection has been defined correctly and that you can reach them from PDI.

The database connections will only be available in the transformation where you defined them unless you shared them for reuse as you did in the tutorial. Normally, you share connections because you know that you will use them later in many transformations. You can also stop sharing the connection: just right-click the database connection, and select **Stop sharing**.

The information about shared connections is stored in a file named `shared.xml` located in the same folder as the `kettle.properties` file.

When you have shared the connections and you save the transformation, the connection information is saved in the transformation itself.

If there is more than one shared connection, all of them will be saved along with the transformation, even if the transformation doesn't use them all. To avoid this, go to the editing options and check the **Only save used connections to XML?** option. This option limits the XML content of a transformation just to the used connections.

Pop quiz – connecting to a database in several transformations

Q1. Which options do you have to connect to the same database in several transformations?

1. Define the connection in each transformation that needs it
2. Define a connection once and share it
3. Any of the above options
4. None of the above options

Have a go hero – connecting to your own databases

You must have access to a database whether local or in the network to which you are logged in. Get the connection information for the database. From PDI create a connection to the database and test it to verify that you can access it from PDI.

Exploring the Steel Wheels database

In the previous section, you learned what RDBMSes are and how to connect to a RDBMS from PDI. Before beginning to work with the data in a database, it would be useful to be familiar with that database. In this section, you will learn to explore databases with the PDI Database Explorer.

Time for action – exploring the sample database

Let's explore the sample database:

1. Open the transformation you just created.
2. Right-click on the connection in the **Database connections** list and select **Explore** in the contextual menu. The database explorer shows up.

3. Expand the **Tables** node of the tree. This is how the explorer looks:

4. Right-click on the CUSTOMERS table and select **View SQL**. The following SQL editor window appears:

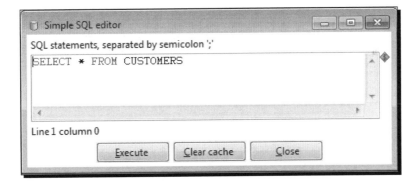

5. Modify the text in there so you have this:

```
SELECT
    CUSTOMERNUMBER
  , CUSTOMERNAME
  , CITY
  , COUNTRY
  FROM CUSTOMERS
```

6. Click on **Execute**. You will see this result:

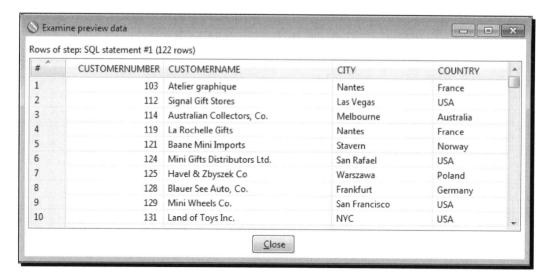

7. Close the **Preview** window—the one that tells the result of the execution - as well as the Results of the SQL statements window—the window that tells us the SQL statements are executed. Finally, close the SQL editor window.

8. Click on **OK** to close the database explorer window.

What just happened?

You explored the Pentaho Sample database with the PDI Database Explorer.

A brief word about SQL

Before explaining the details of the database explorer, it's worth giving you an introduction to SQL, a central topic in relational database terminology.

Structured Query Language (SQL) is the language that lets you access and manipulate databases in a RDBMS.

SQL can be divided into two parts: DDL and DML. The **Data Definition Language (DDL)** is the branch of the language that basically allows the creation or deletion of databases and tables.

The following is an example of DDL. It is the DDL statement that creates the CUSTOMERS table:

```
CREATE TABLE CUSTOMERS
(
  CUSTOMERNUMBER INTEGER
, CUSTOMERNAME VARCHAR(50)
, CONTACTLASTNAME VARCHAR(50)
, CONTACTFIRSTNAME VARCHAR(50)
, PHONE VARCHAR(50)
, ADDRESSLINE1 VARCHAR(50)
, ADDRESSLINE2 VARCHAR(50)
, CITY VARCHAR(50)
, STATE VARCHAR(50)
, POSTALCODE VARCHAR(15)
, COUNTRY VARCHAR(50)
, SALESREPEMPLOYEENUMBER INTEGER
, CREDITLIMIT BIGINT
)
;
```

This DDL statement tells the database to create the CUSTOMERS table with the CUSTOMERNUMBER column that has to be an INTEGER type, the CUSTOMERNAME column that has to be a VARCHAR type with length 50, and so on.

Note that INTEGER, VARCHAR, and BIGINT are HSQLDB types of data, not PDI ones. The **Data Manipulation Language (DML)** allows you to retrieve data from a database. It also lets you insert, update, or delete data from the database.

The statement you typed in the SQL editor is an example of DML:

```
SELECT
  CUSTOMERNUMBER
, CUSTOMERNAME
, CITY
, COUNTRY
 FROM CUSTOMERS
```

This statement is asking the database to retrieve all the rows for the CUSTOMERS table, showing only the CUSTOMERNUMBER, CUSTOMERNAME, CITY and COUNTRY columns. After you clicked on **Execute**, PDI queried the database and showed you a window with the data you had asked for.

If you were to leave the following default query, the window would have showed you all the columns for the CUSTOMERS table:

```
SELECT * FROM CUSTOMERS
```

The SELECT statement allows you to retrieve data from one or more tables. It is the most commonly used DML statement and you're going to use it a lot when working with databases in PDI. You will learn more about the SELECT statement in the next section of this chapter.

Other important DML statements are INSERT, UPDATE, and DELETE.

- The INSERT statement allows you to insert rows in a table
- The UPDATE statement allows you to update the values in rows of a table
- The DELETE statement is used to remove rows from a table

It is important to understand the meaning of these basic statements, but you are not forced to learn them as PDI offers you ways to insert, update, and delete without typing any SQL statement.

Although SQL is standard, each database engine has its own version of the SQL language. However, all database engines support the main commands.

> When you type SQL statements in PDI, try to keep the code within the standard. If you do, your transformations will be reusable in case you have to change the database engine.

If you are interested in learning more about SQL, there are lots of tutorials available on the Internet. The following are a few useful links with tutorials and SQL references:

- http://www.sqlcourse.com/
- http://www.w3schools.com/SQl/
- http://sqlzoo.net/

> Until now, you have used only HSQLDB. In the tutorials to come, you will also work with the MySQL database engine. Thus, you may be interested in the specific documentation for MySQL, which you can find at http://dev.mysql.com/doc/. You can find even more in bookstores as there are plenty of books about both the SQL language and MySQL databases.

Exploring any configured database with the database explorer

The database explorer allows you to explore any configured database. When you open the database explorer, the first thing you see is a tree with the different objects of the database. When you right-click on a database table, a contextual menu appears with several available options for you to explore that table. The following is a full list of options and the purpose of each of them:

Option	Purpose of the option
Preview first 100	Returns the first 100 rows of the selected table, or all the rows if the table has less than 100. Shows all the columns of the table.
Preview x Rows	Same as the previous option but you decide the number of rows you want to show.
Row Count	Tells you the total number of records in the table.
Show Layout	Shows you the metadata for the columns of the table.
DDL | Use Current Connection	Shows you the DDL statement that creates the selected table.
DDL | Select Connection	Lets you select another existent connection, then shows you the DDL just like the previous option. The difference is that the DDL is written with the syntax of the database engine of the selected connection.
View SQL	Lets you edit a SELECT statement to query the table. Here you decide which columns and rows to retrieve.
Truncate Table	Deletes all rows from the selected table.
Data Profile	Collects and displays some statistics for the fields in the selected table: maximum or minimum values, averages, and so on.

 In the tutorial, you opened the database explorer from the contextual menu in the database connections' tree. You can also open it by clicking on **Explore** in the database definition window.

Have a go hero – exploring the sample data in depth

In the tutorial, you only tried the **View SQL** option. Feel free to try other options to explore not only the CUSTOMERS table but also the rest of the tables found in the SteelWheels database.

Have a go hero – exploring your own databases

The *Have a go hero – connecting to your own database* section asked you to connect to your own databases. If you made this connection, use a database connection defined by you and explore the database. See if you can recognize the different objects of the database. Run some previews to verify that everything looks as expected.

Querying a database

So far, you have just connected to a database. You have not yet worked with the data. Now is the time to do it.

Time for action – getting data about shipped orders

Let's continue working with the sample data.

1. Create a new transformation.

2. Select the **Design** view.

3. Expand the **Input** category of steps and drag a **Table input** step to the canvas. Then, double-click on the step.

4. As **Connection**, you should see the `sampledata` connection selected by default. If not, please select it.

5. Click on the **Get SQL select statement...** button. The database explorer window appears.

6. Expand the tables list, select `ORDERS`, and click on **OK**.

7. PDI asks you if you want to include the field names in the SQL. Answer **Yes**.

8. The SQL box type gets filled with a `SELECT` SQL statement:

```
SELECT
    ORDERNUMBER
, ORDERDATE
, REQUIREDDATE
, SHIPPEDDATE
, STATUS
, COMMENTS
, CUSTOMERNUMBER
FROM ORDERS
```

9. At the end of the SQL statement, add the following clause:

```
WHERE STATUS = 'Shipped'
```

10. Click on **Preview** and then **OK**. The following window appears:

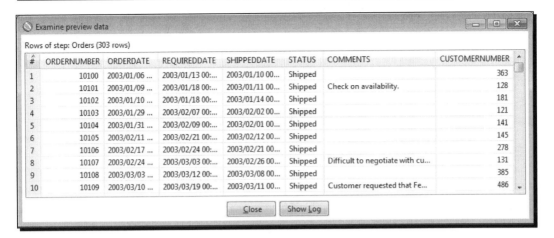

11. Close the window and press **OK** to close the step configuration window.

12. After the **Table input** step, add a **Calculator** step, a **Number range** step, a **Sort rows** step, and a **Select values** step, and link them as follows:

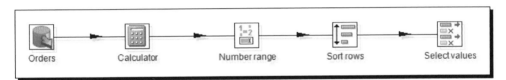

13. With the **Calculator** step, add an **Integer** field to calculate the difference between the shipped date and the required date. Use the calculation **Date A – Date B (in days)** and name the `diff_days` field. Use the **Number range** step to classify the delays in delivery:

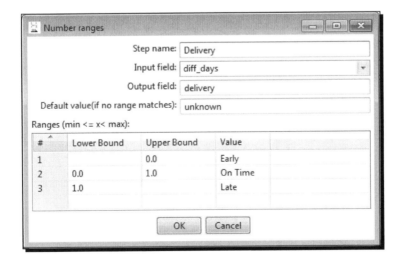

14. Use the **Sort rows** step to sort the rows by the `diff_days` field.

15. Use the **Select values** step to select the fields `delivery`, `ORDERNUMBER`, `REQUIREDDATE`, and `SHIPPEDDATE`.

16. With the **Select values** step selected, do a preview. This is how the final data looks like:

What just happened?

From the sample database, you got information about shipped orders. After you read the data from the database, you classified the orders based on the time it took to do the shipment.

Getting data from the database with the Table input step

The **Table input** step is the main step to get data from a database. In order to use it, you have to specify the connection with the database. In the tutorial, you didn't explicitly specify one because there was just one connection and PDI put it as the default value.

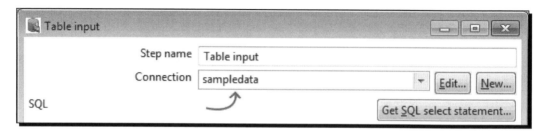

The connection shown in the preceding screenshot was available because you shared it before. If you hadn't, you should have created here again.

The output of a **Table input** step is a regular dataset. Each column of the SQL query leads to a new field and the rows generated by the execution of the query become the rows of the dataset.

As the datatypes of the databases are not exactly the same that the PDI datatypes, when getting data from a table, PDI implicitly converts the metadata of the new fields. For example, consider the ORDERS table. Open the database explorer and look at the DDL definition for the table. Then right-click on the **Table input** step and select **Show output fields** to see the metadata of the created dataset. The following table shows you how the metadata was translated:

Table columns	Database datatype	PDI metadata
ORDERNUMBER and CUSTOMERNUMBER	INTEGER	Integer(9)
ORDERDATE, REQUIREDDATE, and SHIPPEDDATE	TIMESTAMP	Date
STATUS	VARCHAR(15)	String(15)
COMMENTS	TEXT	String(214748364)

Once the data comes out of the Table input step and the metadata is adjusted, PDI forgets that it comes from a database. It treats it just as regular data, no matter whether it came from a database or any other data source.

Using the SELECT statement for generating a new dataset

The SQL area of a Table input is where you write the SELECT statement that will generate the new dataset. As said before, SELECT is the statement that you use to retrieve data from one or more tables in your database.

The simplest SELECT statement is as follows:

```
SELECT <values>
FROM <table name>
```

In the preceding code, <table name> is the name of the table that will be queried to get the resultset and <values> is the list of the desired columns of that table, which are separated by commas.

This is a simple `SELECT` statement:

```
SELECT ORDERNUMBER, ORDERDATE, STATUS
FROM ORDERS
```

If you want to select all columns, you can just put a * here:

```
SELECT *
FROM ORDERS
```

There are some optional clauses you can add to a `SELECT` statement. The most commonly used among the optional clauses are `WHERE` and `ORDER BY`. The `WHERE` clause limits the list of retrieved records, while `ORDER BY` is used to retrieve the rows sorted by one or more columns.

Another common clause is `DISTINCT` that can be used to return only unique records. Let's see some sample `SELECT` statements:

Sample statement	Output
`SELECT ORDERNUMBER, ORDERDATE FROM ORDERS` `WHERE SHIPPEDDATE IS NULL`	Returns the number and order date for the orders that have not been shipped.
`SELECT *` `FROM EMPLOYEES` `WHERE JOBTITLE = 'Sales Rep'` `ORDER BY LASTNAME, FIRSTNAME`	Returns all columns for the employees who work as sales representative, ordered by last name and first name.
`SELECT PRODUCTNAME` `FROM PRODUCTS` `WHERE PRODUCTLINE LIKE '%Cars%'`	Returns the list of products whose product line contains Cars, for example, Classic Cars and Vintage Cars.
`SELECT DISTINCT CUSTOMERNUMBER` `FROM PAYMENTS` `WHERE AMOUNT > 80000`	Returns the list of customer numbers who have made payments with checks above US $80,000. The customers who have paid more than once with a check above US $80,000, appear more than once in the PAYMENTS table, but only once in this resultset.

You can try these statements in the database explorer to check if the resultsets are as explained.

When you add a Table input step, it comes with a default SELECT statement for you to complete:

```
SELECT <values> FROM <table name> WHERE <conditions>
```

If you need to query a single table, you can take advantage of the **Get SQL select statement...** button which generates the full statement for you. After you get the statement, you can modify it at your will by adding, say, the WHERE or ORDER clauses just as you did in the tutorial. If you need to write more complex queries, you definitely have to do it manually.

> You can write any select query as far as it is a valid SQL statement for the selected type of database. Remember that every database engine has its own dialect with slight variants to the language.

Whether simple or complex, you may need to pass the query some parameters. You can do this in a couple of ways. Let's explain this with two practical examples.

Making flexible queries using parameters

One of the ways you can make your queries more flexible is by passing it some parameters. In the following tutorial, you will learn how to do it.

Time for action – getting orders in a range of dates using parameters

Now you will modify your transformation so it shows orders in a range of dates.

1. Open the transformation from the previous tutorial and save it under a new name.

2. From the **Input** category, add a **Get System Info** step.

3. Double-click on it and use the step to get the **command line argument 1** and **command line argument 2** values. Name the fields date_from and date_to respectively. Create a hop from the **Get System Info** step to the **Table input** step.

4. Double-click on the **Table input** step.

5. Modify the SELECT statement as follows:

```
SELECT
    ORDERNUMBER
, ORDERDATE
, REQUIREDDATE
, SHIPPEDDATE
FROM ORDERS
WHERE STATUS = 'Shipped'
AND ORDERDATE BETWEEN ? AND ?
```

6. In the drop-down list to the right of the **Insert data from** step, select **Get System Info** as the incoming step.

7. Click on **OK**.

8. With the **Select values** step selected, click on the **Preview** button.

9. Click on **Configure**.

10. Fill the **Arguments** grid. To the right of the argument **01**, write 2004-12-01. To the right of the argument **02**, write 2004-12-10.

11. Click on **OK**. This window appears:

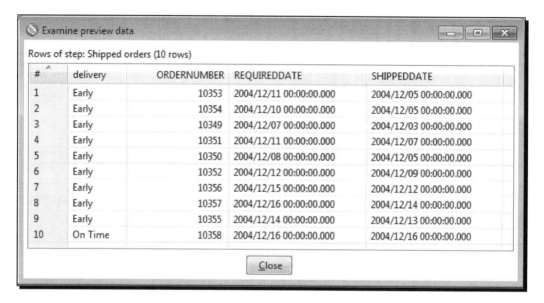

Examine preview data

Rows of step: Shipped orders (10 rows)

#	delivery	ORDERNUMBER	REQUIREDDATE	SHIPPEDDATE
1	Early	10353	2004/12/11 00:00:00.000	2004/12/05 00:00:00.000
2	Early	10354	2004/12/10 00:00:00.000	2004/12/05 00:00:00.000
3	Early	10349	2004/12/07 00:00:00.000	2004/12/03 00:00:00.000
4	Early	10351	2004/12/11 00:00:00.000	2004/12/07 00:00:00.000
5	Early	10350	2004/12/08 00:00:00.000	2004/12/05 00:00:00.000
6	Early	10352	2004/12/12 00:00:00.000	2004/12/09 00:00:00.000
7	Early	10356	2004/12/15 00:00:00.000	2004/12/12 00:00:00.000
8	Early	10357	2004/12/16 00:00:00.000	2004/12/14 00:00:00.000
9	Early	10355	2004/12/14 00:00:00.000	2004/12/13 00:00:00.000
10	On Time	10358	2004/12/16 00:00:00.000	2004/12/16 00:00:00.000

Close

What just happened?

You modified the transformation from the previous tutorial to get orders in a range of dates from the command line.

Adding parameters to your queries

You can make your queries more flexible by adding parameters. Let's explain how you do it.

The first thing to do is to obtain the fields that will be plugged as parameters. In the tutorial, you just used a **Get System Info** step to obtain those fields. However, you can get the fields from any source by using a number of steps, as long as you create a hop from the last step to the **Table input** step.

Once you have the parameters for the query, you have to change the **Table input** step configuration. In the **Insert data from step** option, you have to select the name of the step from which the parameters will come. In the query, you have to put a question mark (?) for each incoming parameter.

When you execute the transformation, the question marks are replaced one by one with the data that comes to the **Table input** step.

> The replacement of the markers respects the order of the incoming fields. When you use question marks to parameterize a query, don't forget that the number of fields coming to a **Table input** must be exactly the same as the number of question marks found in the query.

Let's see how it works in the tutorial. The following is the output of the **Get System Info** step:

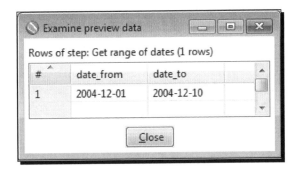

In the SQL statement, you have two question marks. The first is replaced by the value of the date_from field and the second is replaced by the value of the date_to field. After the replacement, the SQL statement becomes:

```
SELECT
    ORDERNUMBER
,   ORDERDATE
,   REQUIREDDATE
,   SHIPPEDDATE
FROM ORDERS
WHERE STATUS = 'Shipped'
AND ORDERDATE BETWEEN '2004-12-01' AND '2004-12-10'
```

In the preceding code, 2004-12-01 and 2004-12-10 are the values you entered as arguments for the transformation.

Making flexible queries by using Kettle variables

Another way you can make your queries flexible is by using Kettle variables. Let's explain how to do it using an example.

Time for action – getting orders in a range of dates by using Kettle variables

In this tutorial, you will do the same as you did in the previous tutorial but another method will be explained.

1. Open the main transformation from the *Time for action – getting data about shipped orders* section, and save it under a new name.

2. Double-click on the **Table input** step.

3. Modify the SELECT statement as follows:

```
SELECT
    ORDERNUMBER
, ORDERDATE
, REQUIREDDATE
, SHIPPEDDATE
FROM ORDERS
WHERE STATUS = 'Shipped'
AND ORDERDATE BETWEEN '${DATE_FROM}' AND '${DATE_TO}'
```

4. Check the **Replace variables in script?** checkbox.

5. Save the transformation.

6. With the **Select values** step selected, click on the **Preview** button.

7. Click on **Configure**.

8. Fill the **Variables** grid in the dialog setting window. To the right of **DATE_FROM,** write 2004-12-01, and to the right of **DATE_TO,** write 2004-12-10.

9. Click on **OK**. The following window appears:

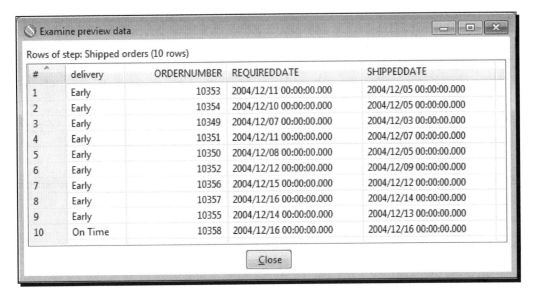

What just happened?

You modified the transformation from the previous tutorial so the range of dates is taken from two variables: DATE_FROM and DATE_TO. The final resultset was exactly the same as the one you got in the previous version of the transformation.

Using Kettle variables in your queries

As an alternative to the use of positional parameters, you can use Kettle variables. Instead of getting the parameters from an incoming step, you check the **Replace variables in script?** option and replace the question marks with the names of variables. The final result is the same.

PDI replaces the name of the variables with their values. Only after that, it sends the SQL statement to the database engine to be executed.

 You can preview the SQL statement in the Table input step, but you have to make sure that the variables already have values. One way for doing that is by using the option **Edit | Set Environment Variables...** available from the main menu.

The advantage of using positional parameters over the variables is quite obvious; you don't have to define the variables in advance.

On the contrary, kettle variables have several advantages over the use of question marks:

♦ You can use the same variable more than once in the same query.

♦ You can use variables for any portion of the query and not just for the values, for example, you could have the following query:

```
SELECT ORDERNUMBER FROM ${ORDER_TABLE}
```

Then the result will vary upon the content of the variable ${ORDER_TABLE}. For this particular example, the variable could be ORDERS or ORDERDETAILS.

♦ A query with variables is easier to understand and less error prone than a query with positional parameters. When you use positional parameters, it's quite common to get confused and make mistakes.

Note that in order to provide parameters to a statement in a Table input step, it's perfectly possible to combine both methods: positional parameters and kettle variables.

Pop quiz – interpreting data types coming from a database

Q1. After you read data from the database with a Table input step, what happens to the datatypes of that data?

1. It remains unchanged.

2. PDI converts the database datatypes to internal datatypes.

3. It depends on how you defined the database connection.

Have a go hero – querying the sample data

Based on the sample data:

♦ Create a transformation to list the offices of Steel Wheels located in the USA. Modify the transformation so the country is entered by a command line.

♦ Create a transformation that lists the contact information of clients whose credit limit is above US$ 100,000. Modify the transformation so the threshold is 100,000 by default but can be modified at the moment you run the transformation. (Hint: Use named parameters.)

♦ Create a transformation that generates two Excel files: one with a list of planes and the other with a list of ships. Include the code, name, and description of the products.

Sending data to a database

By now, you know how to get data from a database. Now you will learn how to insert data into it. For the next tutorials, we will use a MySQL database so before proceeding, make sure you have the MySQL installed and running.

 If you have not installed MySQL yet, refer to *Chapter 1, Getting started with Pentaho Data Integration*. It has basic instructions on installing MySQL both on Windows and Linux operating systems.

Time for action – loading a table with a list of manufacturers

Let's suppose that you love jigsaw puzzles and decided to open a store for selling all kinds of them. You have made all the arrangements and the only missing thing is the software. You have already acquired software to handle your business but you still have a hard task of adding data into the database, that is, loading the basic information about the products you are about to sell in the database.

As this is the first of several tutorials in which you will interact with this database, the first task you have to do is to create the database.

 For MySQL-specific tasks—for example, the creation of a database—we will use **SQuirreL SQL Client**. If you use this tool, make sure you have added a driver for MySQL. For assistance, you can follow this link `http://squirrel-sql.sourceforge.net/user-manual/quick_start.html`. Alternatively, you can do this task using the **MySQL Command Line Client** or any other GUI tool.

1. Download the `js.sql` script file.

 Downloading the example code
You can download the example code files for all Packt books you have purchased from your account at `http://www.packtpub.com`. If you purchased this book elsewhere, you can visit `http://www.packtpub.com/support` and register to have the files e-mailed directly to you.

2. First of all, let's create the database. Open a terminal and log into the MySQL shell as the root user by typing the following:

```
mysql -u root -p
```

3. The `mysql` prompt appears. Type the following:

```
CREATE DATABASE js;
```

4. You will see a message like this:

```
Query OK, 1 row affected (0.01 sec)
```

5. Type `exit` and close the terminal.

6. From now, we will work with SQuirreL, so launch **SQuirreL**.

7. From the main menu, select **Alias | New Alias...** A dialog window appears asking you for the connection information. Fill it in as shown in the following screenshot:

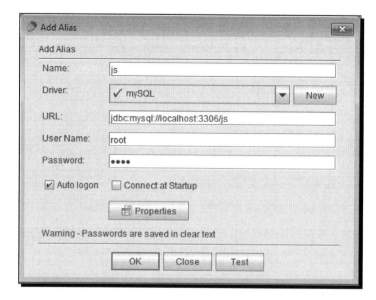

8. Click on **Test** and a window with the message **Connection Successful** should appear.

9. Click on **OK** twice.

10. The new alias will appear to the left in the **Aliases** window. Double-click on it to connect to the created database. You will see the following screenshot:

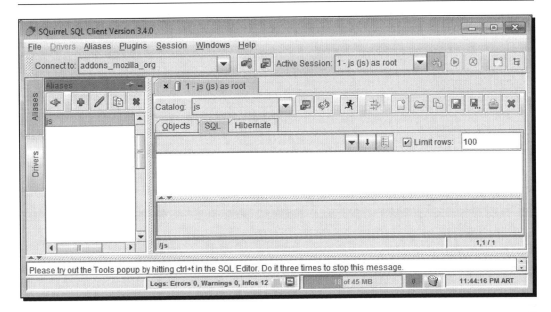

11. Open the `js.sql` file. You can do it by selecting **Session | File | Open** in the main menu, or by clicking on the icon for opening a file available in the toolbar.

12. Select **Session | Run SQL** for running the script. Alternatively, press *Ctrl + Enter* or select the icon for running a query available in the toolbar.

13. Select the **Objects** tab and expand the **js | TABLE** tree. You will see two tables that have just been created: `products` and `manufacturers`.

14. Close the file either from the main menu or from the toolbar.

15. The database has been created but the tables are still empty. Let's load some data into them.

16. From the book's website, download the file `manufacturers.xls`.

17. Open Spoon and create a new transformation.

18. Create a connection to the created database. Under **Connection Type**, select **MySQL**. In the **Settings** frame, put the same values you provided for the connection in Squirrel. As **Host Name**, write `localhost` and as **Database Name** write `js`, which is the database you just created. As **User Name** and **Password,** enter the name and password of the user you created when you installed MySQL. For the other settings in the window, leave the default values. Test the connection to see if it has been properly created.

The main reasons for a failed test can be erroneous data provided in the settings window or that the server is not running. If the test fails, read the error message to find out exactly what the error was, and act accordingly.

19. Right-click on the database connection and share it.

20. Drag a **Microsoft Excel Input** step to the canvas, and use it to read the `manufacturers.xls` file. Fill the **Sheets** tab, indicating that you will read the `manu_list` sheet starting at row 2 and column 0. Fill the **Fields** sheet with the `CODE` and `NAME` fields.

21. Click on **Preview Rows** to check that you are reading the file properly. You should see this:

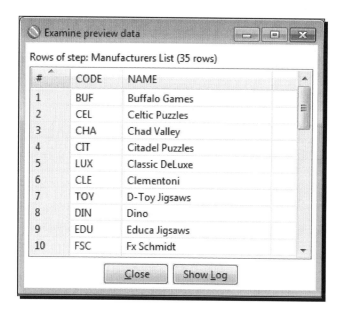

22. From the **Output** category of steps, drag a **Table output** step to the canvas.

23. Create a hop from the **Excel input** step to the **Table output** step.

24. Double-click on the **Table output** step and fill the main setting window as follows:

- As **Connection**, select **js**
- As **Target table,** browse and select the `manufacturers` table or type it
- Check the **Specify database fields** option

It is not mandatory, but recommended in this particular exercise that you also check the **Truncate table** option. Otherwise, the output table will have duplicate records if you run the transformation more than once.

25. Select the **Database fields** tab, fill the grid as shown in the following screenshot, and click on **OK**.

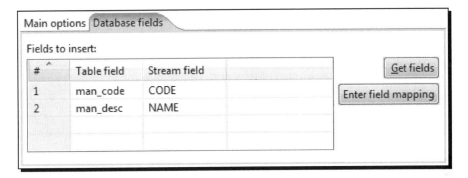

26. After the **Table output** step, add a **Write to log** step.

27. Right-click on the **Table output** step and select **Define error handling...**.

28. Fill the error handling-setting window. As **Target** step, select the **Write to log** step. Check the **Enable the error handling?** option. As **Error descriptions** fieldname, type db_err_desc. As **Error fields** fieldname, type db_err_field. As **Error codes** fieldname, type db_err_cod.

29. Click on **OK**. This is your final transformation:

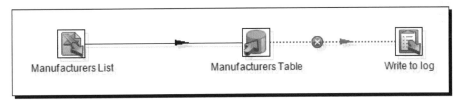

30. Save the transformation and run it.

31. Take a look at the **Steps Metrics** tab window. You will see the following:

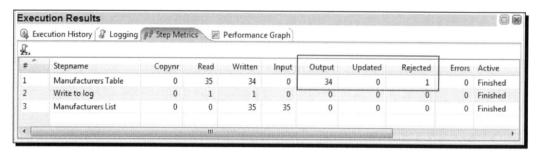

32. Now look at the **Logging** tab window. This is what you see:

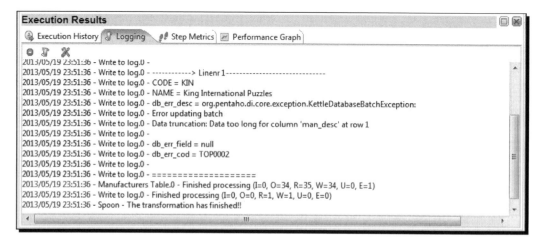

33. Switch to the Squirrel application.

34. In the SQL tab, type:

```
SELECT * FROM manufacturers
```

35. Run the query either from the main menu, the option in the toolbar or by pressing *Ctrl + Enter*. The following resultset is shown:

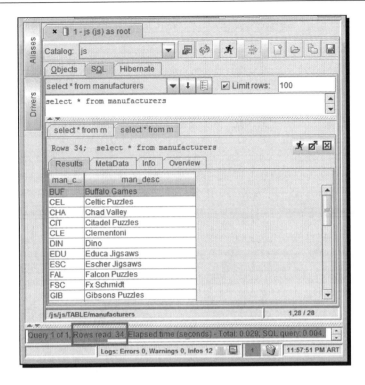

What just happened?

In the first part of the tutorial, you created the Jigsaw Puzzle database. In Spoon, you created a connection to the new database.

Finally, you created a transformation that read an Excel file with a list of puzzle manufacturers and inserted that data into the `manufacturers` table. Note that not all rows were inserted. The row that could not be inserted was informed in the log.

In the data from the Excel file, there was a very long description to be inserted in the table. This was properly reported in the log because you implemented error handling. By doing this, you avoided the abortion of the transformation due to such errors. As you learned earlier in this book, when a row causes an error, is up to you to decide what to do with that row. In this case, the row was sent to the log and was not inserted. Other possible options for you are as follows:

- ◆ Fixing the problem in the Excel file and rerunning the transformation
- ◆ Validating the data and fixing it properly (for example, cutting the descriptions) before the data arrives to the Table output step
- ◆ Sending the full data for the erroneous rows to a file, fixing the date manually in the file, and creating a transformation that inserts only that data

Inserting new data into a database table with the Table output step

The **Table output** step is the main PDI step for inserting new data into a database table.

 Note that in order to insert data to any table or database (generally), the user you specify in the connection must have the privileges to insert into the database.

The use of this step is simple. You have to enter the name of the database connection and the name of the table where you want to insert data. The names for the connection and the table are mandatory, but as you can see, there are some extra settings in the Table output step.

The **Database Field** tab lets you specify the mapping between the dataset stream fields and the table fields. In the tutorial, the dataset had two fields: CODE and NAME. The table has two columns named man_code and man_desc.

As the names are different, you had to explicitly indicate that the CODE field is to be written in the table field named man_code, and that the NAME field is to be written in the table field named man_desc.

The following are some important tips and warnings about the use of the Table output step:

- If the names of the fields in the PDI stream are equal to the names of the columns in the table, you don't have to specify the mapping. In that case, you have to leave the **Specify database fields** checkbox unchecked and make sure that all the fields coming to the Table output step exist in the table.

- Before sending data to a Table output step, check your transformation against the definition for the table. All the mandatory columns that don't have a default value must have a correspondent field in the PDI stream coming to the Table output step.

- Check the datatypes for the fields you are sending to the table. It is possible that a PDI field type and a table column datatype don't match. In that case, fix the problem before sending the data to the table. You can, for example, use the **Metadata** tab of a Select values step to change the datatype of the data.

In the Table output step, you may have noted a button named **SQL**. This button generates the DDL to create the output table. In the tutorial, the output table manufacturers already existed. But, if you want to create the table from scratch, this button allows you to do it based on the database fields you provided in the step.

Inserting or updating data by using other PDI steps

The Table output step provides the simplest but not the only way to insert data into a database table. In this section, you will learn some alternatives for feeding a table with PDI.

Time for action – inserting new products or updating existing ones

So far, you created the jigsaw puzzles database and loaded a list of the puzzles' manufacturers. It's time to begin loading information about the products you will sell, that is, the puzzles.

Suppose that in order to show you what they are selling, the suppliers provide you with lists of products made by the manufacturers themselves. Fortunately, they don't give you the lists in the form of papers, but they give you either plain files or spreadsheets. In this tutorial, you will take the list of products offered by the manufacturer Classic DeLuxe, and load it into the puzzles table.

1. Find the `productlist_LUX_200908.txt` file from the downloaded code bundle and save it in the folder pointed to by your `${LABSINPUT}` variable.

2. Open Spoon and create a new transformation.

3. Add a **Text file input** step and configure it to read the file `productlist_LUX_200908.txt`. As **Separator**, type |. In order to fill in the fields grid, use the **Get Fields** button in the **Fields** tab.

4. Pay attention to the `each` field. It's the price of the product and must be configured as `Number` with format `$0.00`.

5. Preview the file. You should see this:

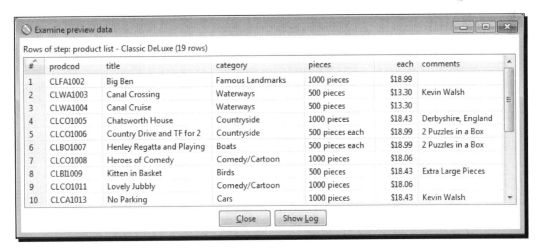

6. In the **Selected Files** grid, replace the text `productlist_LUX_200908.txt` with `${PRODUCTLISTFILE}`.

7. Click on **OK**.

8. After the **Text file input** step, add an **Add constants** step.

9. Use it to add a **String** constant named `man_code` with value LUX.

10. From the **Output** category of steps, drag an **Insert/Update** step to the canvas. Create a hop from the **Add constants** step to this new step.

11. Double-click on the step. As **Connection**, select `js`. As **Target** table, browse and select **products**. In the upper grid of the window, add the conditions `pro_code = prodcod` and `man_code = man_code`.

12. Click on the **Edit mapping** button. The **Mapping** dialog window shows up.

13. Under the **Source fields** list, click on `prodcod`. Under the **Target** fields, click on **pro_code** and then click on the **Add** button. Again, under the **Source fields** list, click on `title`. Under the **Target fields** list, click on `pro_name` and then finally click on **Add**. Proceed with the mapping until you get the following **Mappings**:

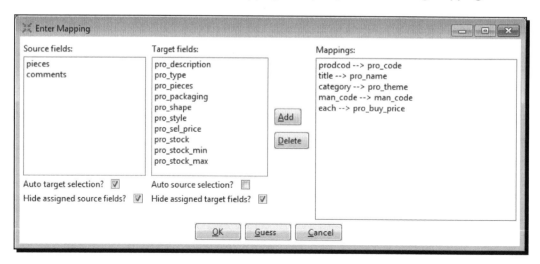

14. Click on **OK**.

15. Fill in the `Update` column for the price row with the value `Y`. Fill in the rest of the column with the value `N`. This is how the final grid will looks:

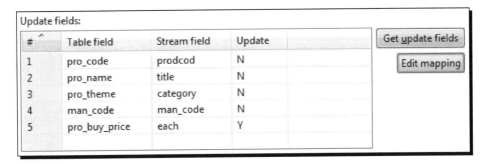

Update fields:

#	Table field	Stream field	Update
1	pro_code	prodcod	N
2	pro_name	title	N
3	pro_theme	category	N
4	man_code	man_code	N
5	pro_buy_price	each	Y

Get update fields

Edit mapping

16. After the **Insert/Update** step, add a **Write to log** step.

17. Right-click on the **Insert/Update** step and select **Define error handling....**

18. Fill the error handling-setting window just as you did in the previous tutorial.

19. Save the transformation and run it by pressing *F9*.

20. In the **Settings** window, assign the `PRODUCTLISTFILE` variable with the `productlist_LUX_200908.txt` value.

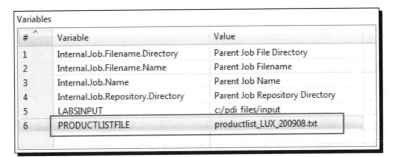

Variables

#	Variable	Value
1	Internal.Job.Filename.Directory	Parent Job File Directory
2	Internal.Job.Filename.Name	Parent Job Filename
3	Internal.Job.Name	Parent Job Name
4	Internal.Job.Repository.Directory	Parent Job Repository Directory
5	LABSINPUT	c:/pdi_files/input
6	PRODUCTLISTFILE	productlist_LUX_200908.txt

21. Click on **Launch**.

22. When the transformation ends, check **Step Metrics**. You will see the following:

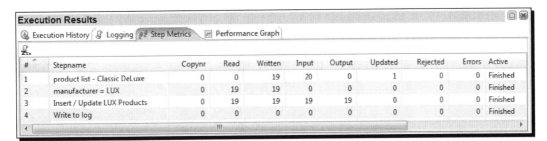

Execution Results

Execution History | Logging | Step Metrics | Performance Graph

#	Stepname	Copynr	Read	Written	Input	Output	Updated	Rejected	Errors	Active
1	product list - Classic DeLuxe	0	0	19	20	0	1	0	0	Finished
2	manufacturer = LUX	0	19	19	0	0	0	0	0	Finished
3	Insert / Update LUX Products	0	19	19	19	19	0	0	0	Finished
4	Write to log	0	0	0	0	0	0	0	0	Finished

23. Switch to Squirrel and type the following query:

```
SELECT * FROM products
```

24. Run the query by pressing *Ctrl + Enter*. The following result set is shown:

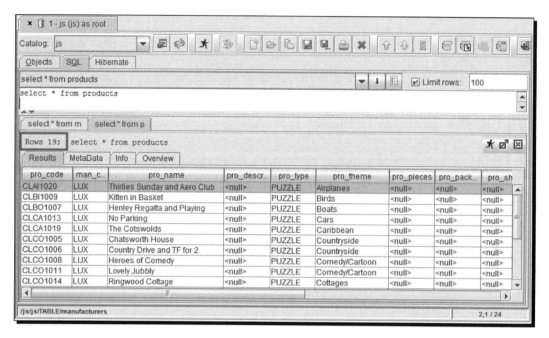

What just happened?

You populated the products table with data found in the text files. To insert the data, you used the **Insert/Update** step.

This was the first time you dealt with the products table. You will notice that before you ran the transformation the table was empty. After running the transformation, you could see how all products in the file were inserted into the table.

Time for action – testing the update of existing products

In the preceding tutorial, you used an Insert/Update step but only inserted records. Let's try the transformation again to see how the update option works.

1. If you closed the transformation, open it.

2. Press *F9* to launch the transformation again.

3. As the value for the `PRODUCTLISTFILE` variable, put `productlist_LUX_200909.txt`.

4. Click on **Launch**.

5. When the transformation ends, check **Step Metrics**. You will see the following:

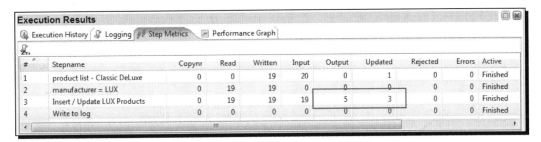

6. Switch to Squirrel and re-run the query. This time you will see the following:

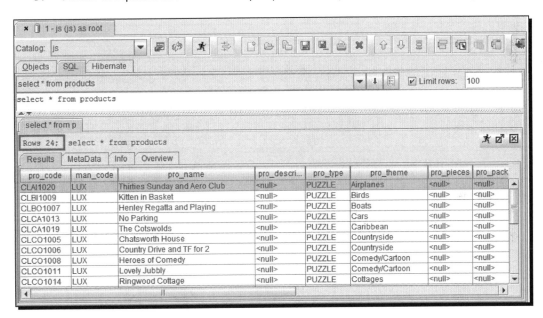

What just happened?

You re-ran the transformation you created in the previous tutorial, this time using a different input file. In this file, there were new products, some products were removed from the list, and some had their descriptions, categories, and prices modified.

When you ran the transformation for the second time, the new products were added to the table. Also, the modified prices of the products were updated. In the **Step Metrics** tab window, you can see the number of inserted records (the **Output** column) and the number of updated ones (the **Update** column).

 Note that as the supplier may give you updated lists of products with different names of files, for the name of the file, you used a variable. Doing so, you were able to reuse the transformation for reading different files each time.

Inserting or updating with the Insert/Update step

While the Table output step allows you to insert brand new data, the Insert/Update step allows you to do both, insert and update data in a single step.

The rows directed to the Insert/Update step can be new data, or can be data that already exists in the table. Depending on the case, the Insert/Update step behaves differently. Let's see each case in detail:

- For each incoming row, the first thing the step does is use the lookup condition you put in the upper grid to check if the row already exists in the table.

- In the tutorial, you wrote two conditions: `pro_code = prodcod` and `man_code = man_code`. By doing so, you told the step to look for a row in the table' products for which the `pro_code` table column is equal to the field `prodcod` of your row, and the `man_code` table column is equal to the field with the same name of your row.

- If the lookup fails, that is, the row doesn't exist, the step inserts the row in the table by using the mapping you put in the lower grid.

The first time you ran the tutorial transformation, the table was empty. There were no rows against which to compare. In this case, all the lookups failed and, consequently, all rows were inserted.

This insert operation is exactly the same as you could have done with a Table output step. This implies that here you also have to be careful about the following:

- All the mandatory columns that don't have a default value must be present in the **Update Field** grid, including the keys you used in the upper grid

- The datatypes for the fields you are sending to the table must match the datatype for the columns of the table

If the lookup succeeds, the step updates the table, replacing the old values with the new ones. This update is made only for the fields where you put `Y` as the value for the **Update** column in the lower grid.

If you don't want to perform any `Update` operation, you can check the **Don't perform any updates** option.

The second time you ran the tutorial, you had two types of products in the file—products that already existed in the database and new products. For example, consider the following row found in the second file:

```
CLTR1001|A Saint at Radley|Trains|500 pieces|$13.30|Peter Webster
```

PDI looks for a row in the table where `prod_code` is equal to `CLTR1001` and `man_code` is equal to `LUX` (the field added with the **Add constants** step). It doesn't find it. Then it inserts a new row with the data coming from the file.

Take another sample row:

```
CLBO1007|Henley Regatta & Playing|Boats|500 pieces each|$19.94|2
Puzzles in a Box
```

PDI looks for a row in the table where `prod_code` is equal to `CLBO1007` and `man_code` equal to `LUX`. It finds the following:

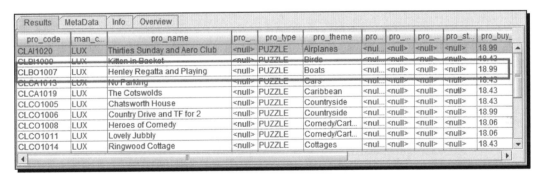

There are two differences between the old and the new versions of the product. Both the name and the price have changed.

As you configured the Insert/Update step to update only the price column, the update operation does so. The new record in the table after the execution of the transformation is as follows:

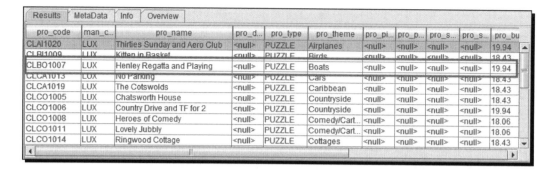

Have a go hero – populating a films database

Download the `films.sql` script from the support page of the Packt website, `www.packtpub.com/support`. Run the script in Squirrel or the GUI tool of your choice. A new database will be created to hold film data.

Browse the folder where you have the files for *Chapter 7, Transforming the Rowset*, and get the `French films` file. You will use it to populate the following tables of the `films` database: GENRES, PEOPLE, and FILMS.

Now follow these instructions:

1. First of all, create a connection to the database.
2. In order to populate the GENRES table, you have to build a list of genres, no duplicates! For the GEN_ID primary key, you don't have a value in the file. Create the key with an **Add sequence** step.
3. The PEOPLE table will have the names of both actors and directors. In order to populate the PEOPLE table, you will have to create a single list of people, no duplicates here either! To generate the primary key, use the same method as before.
4. Finally, populate the FILMS table with the whole list of films found in the file.

Don't forget to handle errors so you can detect bad rows.

Have a go hero – populating the products table

This exercise has two parts. The first is intended to enrich the transformation you created in the tutorial. The transformation processed the product list files supplied by the Classics DeLuxe manufacturer. In the file, there was some extra information that you could put in the table, for example, the number of pieces of a puzzle. However, the data didn't come ready to use. Consider, for example, this text 500 pieces each. In order to get the number of pieces, you need to do some transformation. Modify the Kettle transformation so you can enrich the data in the products table.

The second part of the exercise has to do with populating the products table with products from other manufacturers. Sadly, you cannot expect that all manufacturers share the same structure for the list of products. Not only can the structure change, but also the kind of information they give you can vary. In the code bundle, you have several sample product files belonging to different manufactures. Explore them, analyze them to see if you can identify the different data you need for the products table, and load all the products in the database by using a different transformation for each manufacturer.

Here are some tips:

- ◆ Take the transformation as a model to be used in this section. You may reuse most of it.

- ◆ You don't have to worry about the stock columns or the pro_type column because they already have default values.

- ◆ Use the comments in the file to identify potential values for the pro_packaging, pro_shape, and pro_style columns. Use the pro_packaging field for values as 2 puzzles in a box. Use the pro_shape field for values as or example Panoramic Puzzle or 3D Puzzle. Use the puzzle_type field for values, for example, Glow in the Dark or Wooden Puzzle.

- ◆ You can leave the pro_description empty, or put in it whatever you feel that fits. A fix string such as Best in market! or the full comment found in the file, or whatever your imagination says.

Q1. In the last tutorial you read a file and use an Insert/Update step to populate the products table. Look at the following variant of the transformation:

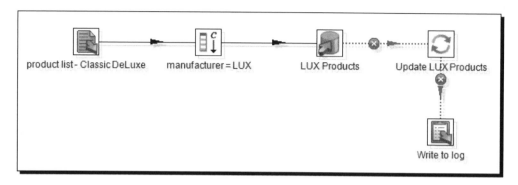

Suppose that you use this transformation instead of the original. Compared to the results you got in the tutorial, after the execution of this version of the transformation the products table will have:

1.   The same number of records

2.   More records

3.   Less records

4.   It depends on the contents of the file

If an incoming row belongs to a product that doesn't exist in the products table, both the Insert/Update step and the Table output step will insert the record.

If an incoming row belongs to a product that already exist in the products table, the Insert/Update step updates it. In this alternative version, the Table output will fail (there cannot be two products with the same value for the primary key) but the failing row goes to the Update step that updates the record.

If an incoming row contains invalid data (for example, a price with a non numeric value), neither of the Insert/Update step, the Table output step, and the Update step would insert or update the table with this product.

Eliminating data from a database

Deleting information from a database is not the most common operation with databases but it is an important one. Now you will learn how to do it with PDI.

Time for action – deleting data about discontinued items

Suppose a manufacturer informs you about the categories of products that will no longer be available. You don't want to have those products in your database that you will not sell. So you use PDI to delete them.

1. Open the `LUX_discontinued.txt` file available in the code bundle.

2. Create a new transformation.

3. With a **Text file input** step, read the file. As **Number of header** lines, type 4. Add a single field of type `String` and name it `category`.

4. Preview the file. You will see the following:

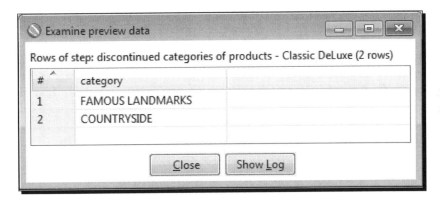

5. After the **Text file input** step, add an **Add constants** step to add a `String` constant named `man_code` with value `LUX`.

6. Expand the **Output** category of steps and drag a **Delete** step to the canvas.

7. Create a hop from the **Add constants** step to the **Delete** step.

8. Double-click on the **Delete** step. As **Connection**, select `js`. As **Target table**, browse and select **products**. In the grid, add the conditions `man_code = man_code` and `pro_theme LIKE category`. After the **Delete** step, add a **Write to log** step.

9. Right-click on the **Delete** step and define the error handling just as you did in each of the previous tutorials in this chapter.

10. Save the transformation.

11. Before running the transformation, open the database explorer.

12. Under the `js` connection, locate the `products` table, right-click on it, and select **View SQL**.

13. In the **Simple SQL** editor type:

```
SELECT pro_theme, pro_name FROM js.products p
ORDER BY pro_theme, pro_name;
```

14. Click on **Execute**. You will see the following resultset:

15. Close the preview data window and the results of the SQL window.

16. Minimize the SQL window. It will be collapsed at the bottom of the Spoon window.

17. Run the transformation.

18. Look at **Step Metrics**. This is what you should see:

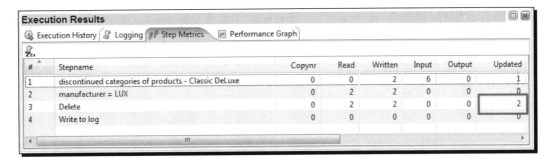

19. Maximize the SQL window.

20. In the SQL editor window, click on **Execute** again. This time you will see this:

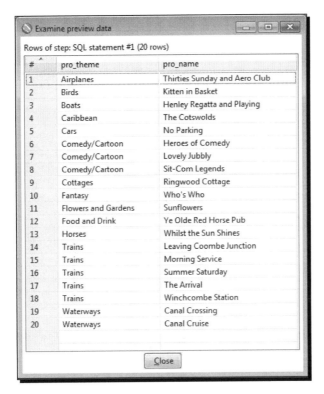

What just happened?

From the `products` table, you deleted all products belonging to the categories found in the file `LUX_discontinued.txt`.

Note that to query the list of products, you used the PDI Database explorer. You could have done this using any GUI tool, for example, Squirrel.

Deleting records of a database table with the Delete step

The **Delete** step allows you to delete records of a database table based on a given condition. For each row that comes to the step, PDI deletes the records that match the condition set in its configuration window.

Let's see how it worked in the tutorial. The following is the dataset that comes to the Delete step:

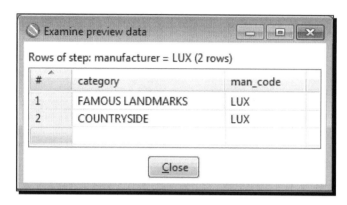

For each of these rows, PDI performs a new delete operation. For the first row, the records deleted from the table products are those where man_code is equal to LUX and pro_ theme is as FAMOUS LANDMARKS.

For the second row, the records deleted from the table products are those where man_ code is equal to LUX and pro_theme is as COUNTRYSIDE. You can verify the performed operations by comparing the result sets you got in the database explorer before and after running the transformation.

Just for your information, you could have done the same task with the following DELETE statements:

```
DELETE FROM products
WHERE man_code = 'LUX' and pro_theme LIKE 'FAMOUS LANDMARKS'

DELETE FROM products
WHERE man_code = 'LUX' and pro_theme LIKE 'COUNTRYSIDE'
```

In the **Step Metrics** result, you may have noticed that the **Updated** column for the **Delete** step has the value 2. This number is the number of delete operations, not the number of deleted records, which was actually a bigger number.

Have a go hero – deleting old orders

Create a transformation that asks for a date from the command line and deletes all orders from the Steel Wheels database whose order dates are prior to the given date.

Have a go hero – creating the time dimension

As the final exercise of this chapter, you're going to finish what you started back in *Chapter 2, Getting started with Transformations*, and continued to develop in the *Time for action – Creating the time dimension dataset* section in *Chapter 7, Transforming the Rowset*.

Open download the `js_dw.sql` script file available in the code bundle. Run the script in Squirrel. A new database named `js_dw` will be created.

Now you are going to modify the transformation created in *Chapter 7, Transforming the Rowset*, to load the time dataset into the `lk_time` table.

The following tips will help you:

♦ Create a connection to the created database

♦ Find a correspondence between each field in the dataset and each column in the `LK_TIME` table

♦ Use a **Table output** to send the dataset to the table

After running the transformation, check if all rows were inserted as expected.

Pay attention to the main field in the time dimension—date. In the transformation, the date is a field whose type is `Date`.

However in the table the type for the `date` field is `CHAR(8)`. This column is meant to hold the date as `String` with the following format YYYYMMDD, for example `20090915`.

As explained, the datatypes of the data you sent to the table have to match the datatypes in the table. In this case, as the types don't match, you will have to use a **Select values** step and change the metadata of the `date` field from `Date` to `String`.

Summary

This chapter discussed how to use PDI to work with databases. Firstly, the chapter introduced the Pentaho Sample Data Steel Wheels—the starting point for you to learn basic database theory. Then you learned how to create connections from PDI to different database engines. After that, you learned to explore databases with the PDI Database Explorer, you were introduced to the basics of SQL, and you learned to perform CRUD (Create, Read, Update, and Delete) operations on databases.

In the next chapter, you will continue working with databases. You will learn some advanced concepts, including data warehouse-specific operations.

9

Performing Advanced Operations with Databases

Performing CRUD operations on databases are just the beginning in your database-learning journey. Besides creating, reading, updating, and deleting data from databases, there are other interesting things that you can do with databases, for example, searching for data, or even more, such as addressing data warehouse concepts.

This chapter explains the different advanced operations with databases. The first part of the chapter includes:

- ◆ Populating the Jigsaw puzzle database so it is prepared for the rest of the activities in the chapter
- ◆ Doing simple lookups in a database
- ◆ Doing complex lookups

The second part of the chapter is fully devoted to data warehouse-related concepts. The list of the topics that will be covered includes:

- ◆ Introducing dimensional modeling
- ◆ Loading dimensions

Preparing the environment

In order to learn the concepts of this chapter, a database with little or no data is useless. Therefore, the first thing that you need to do is populate your Jigsaw puzzle database.

Time for action – populating the Jigsaw database

To load data massively into your Jigsaw database, you must have the Jigsaw database created and the MySQL server running. You already know how to do this. If not, refer to *Chapter 1 Getting started with Pentaho Data Integration*, for the installation of MySQL and to *Chapter 8, Working with Databases*, for the creation of the Jigsaw database.

 This tutorial will overwrite all your data in the js database. If you don't want to overwrite the data in your js database you could simply create a new database with a different name and run the js.sql script to create the tables in your new database.

After checking that everything is in order, follow these instructions:

1. Open the js_data.sql script file available in the code bundle.

 If you created a new database, edit the script and replace the js name by the name of your new database.

2. Run the script by opening a terminal window and typing the following:

```
mysql js < js_data.sql
```

 If you created a new database, replace js with the name of your database. Also, if you are not in the directory where your script is located, you will have to provide its full path, for example, /user/pdi/scripts/js_data.sql.

3. When the script execution ends, verify that the database has been populated. Execute some SELECT statements, for example:

```
SELECT * FROM cities
```

All tables must have records.

Having populated the database, let's prepare the Spoon environment:

1. Edit the `kettle.properties` file located in the PDI home directory. Add the following variables: `DB_HOST`, `DB_NAME`, `DB_USER`, `DB_PASS`, and `DB_PORT`. As values, type the setting for your connection to the Jigsaw database. Use the following lines as a guide:

```
DB_HOST=localhost
DB_NAME=js
DB_USER=root
DB_PASS=1234
DB_PORT=3306
```

2. Add the following variables: `DW_HOST`, `DW_NAME`, `DW_USER`, `DW_PASS`, and `DW_PORT`. As values, type the setting for your connection to the `js_dw` database; the database you created in *Chapter 8, Working with Databases*, to load the time dimension. Here you have some sample lines that you can:

```
DW_HOST=localhost
DW_NAME=js_dw
DW_USER=root
DW_PASS=1234
DW_PORT=3306
```

3. Save the file.

4. In the downloaded code there is a file named `shared.xml`. Copy it to your PDI home directory (the same directory where the `kettle.properties` file is), overwriting the existent file.

> Before overwriting the file, take a backup as this will delete any shared connections you might have created.

5. Launch Spoon. If it was running, restart it so it recognizes the changes in the `kettle.properties` file.

6. Create a new transformation.

> If you don't see the shared database connections `js` and `dw`, verify whether you copied the `shared.xml` file to the right folder.

7. Right-click on the `js` database connection and select **Edit**. In the **Settings** frame, instead of fixed values, you will see variables: `${DS_HOST}` for **Host Name**, `${DS_NAME}` for **Database Name**, and so on.

8. Test the connection.

9. Repeat the steps for the `js_dw` shared connection. Right-click on the database connection and select **Edit**. In the **Settings** frame, you will see the variables that you defined in the `kettle.properties` file: `${DW_HOST}`, `${DW_NAME}`, and so on.

10. Test the `dw_js` connection.

If any of the database tests fail, check whether the connection variables you put in the `kettle.properties` file are correct. Also check that MySQL is running.

What just happened?

In this tutorial, you prepared the environment that you will need for working in the rest of the chapter.

You did two different things:

- First, you ran a script that emptied all the `js` database tables and loaded data into them
- Then, you redefined the database connections to the databases `js` and `js_dw`

Note that the names for the connection don't have to match the name of the databases. This can benefit you in the following way: if you created a database with a different name for the Jigsaw database puzzle, your connection may still be named `js`, and the code you downloaded from the book's website should work without touching anything but the `kettle.properties` file.

You edited the `kettle.properties` file by adding variables with the database connection values: host name, database name, and so on. Then you edited the database connections. There you saw that the database settings didn't have values but variable names—the variables you had defined in the `kettle.properties` file. For shared connections, PDI takes the database definition from the `shared.xml` file.

Note that you didn't save the transformation you created. This was intentional. The only purpose for creating it was to be able to see the shared connections.

Exploring the Jigsaw database model

The information in this section allows you to understand the organization of the data in the Jigsaw database. In the first place, you have an **entity relationship diagram (ERD)**. An ERD is a graphical representation that allows you to see how the tables in a database are related to each other. The following screenshot is the ERD for the js database:

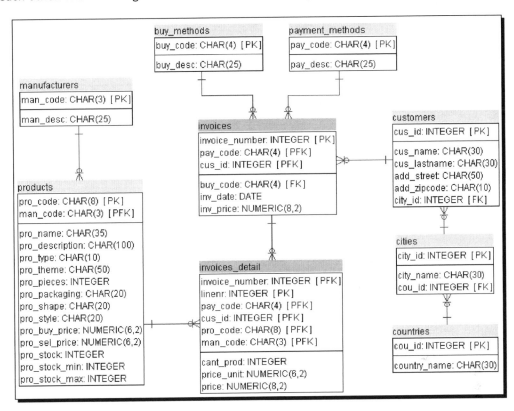

The following table contains a brief explanation of what each table is for:

Table	Content
manufacturers	Information about manufacturers of the products.
products	It is about the products you sell, such as puzzles and accessories. The table has descriptive information and data about prices and stock. The pro_type column has the type of product: puzzle, glue, and so on. Several of the columns only apply to puzzles, for example, shape or pieces.
buy_methods	It contains information about the methods for buying, for example, in store and by telephone.

Table	Content
payment_methods	Information about methods of payment such as cash, check, and credit card.
countries	List of countries.
cities	List of cities.
customers	List of customers. A customer has a number, a name, and an address.
invoices	The header of invoices including date, customer number and total amount. The invoices dates range from 2004 to 2010.
invoices_details	Detail of the invoices including: invoice number, product, quantity and price.

Looking up data in a database

You already know how to create, update, and delete data from a database. It's time to learn how to look up data. Let's call lookup as the act of searching information in a database. You can lookup a column of a single table or you can do more complex lookups. Let's begin with the simplest way of looking up.

Doing simple lookups

Sometimes you need to get information from a database table based on data you have in your main stream. Let's see how you do it.

Time for action – using a Database lookup step to create a list of products to buy

Suppose that you have an online system for your customers to order products. On a daily basis, the system creates a file with the orders information. Now, you will check if you have stock for the ordered products and make a list of the products you'll have to buy:

1. Create a new transformation.

2. From the **Input** category of steps, drag a **Get data from XML** step to the canvas.

3. Use it to read the orders.xml file. In the **Content** tab, fill the **Loop XPath** option with the **/orders/order** string. In the **Fields** tab, get the fields. Also, as the first row insert an integer field named ordernumber. This is an attribute in the file, so as **Xpath**, type @ordernumber.

4. Do a preview. You will see the following:

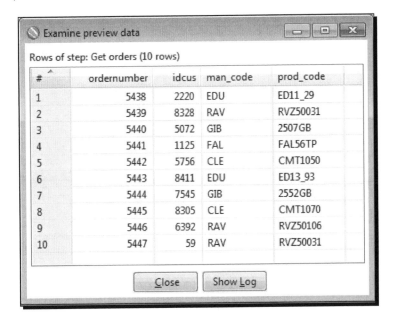

Examine preview data

Rows of step: Get orders (10 rows)

#	ordernumber	idcus	man_code	prod_code
1	5438	2220	EDU	ED11_29
2	5439	8328	RAV	RVZ50031
3	5440	5072	GIB	2507GB
4	5441	1125	FAL	FAL56TP
5	5442	5756	CLE	CMT1050
6	5443	8411	EDU	ED13_93
7	5444	7545	GIB	2552GB
8	5445	8305	CLE	CMT1070
9	5446	6392	RAV	RVZ50106
10	5447	59	RAV	RVZ50031

Close   Show Log

 To keep this exercise simple, the file contains a single product by order.

5. Add a **Sort rows** step, and use it to sort the data by man_code and prod_code.

6. Add a **Group by** step and double-click on it.

7. Use the upper grid for grouping by man_code and prod_code.

8. Use the lower grid for adding a field with the number of orders in each group: write quantity as **Name**, ordernumber as **Subject**, and as **Type**, select **Number of Values (N)**.

9. Expand the **Lookup** category of steps and drag to the canvas a **Database lookup** step. Then, create a hop from the **Group by** step toward this.

10. Double-click on the **Database lookup** step.

11. As **Connection**, select js and in **Lookup table**, browse the database and select products or just type its name.

12. Fill in the grids as follows:

The key(s) to look up the value(s):

#	Table field	Comparator	Field1	Field2
1	man_code	=	man_code	
2	pro_code	=	prod_code	

Values to return from the lookup table :

#	Field	New name	Default	Type
1	pro_name			String
2	pro_stock			Integer

If you don't see both grids just resize the window. This is one of the few configuration steps that lack the scrollbar to the right side.

Also remember that, as in all grids in PDI, you always have the option to populate the grids by using the **Get Fields** and **Get lookup** fields respectively.

13. Click on **OK**.

14. Add a **Filter rows** step to pass only those rows where pro_stock is less than quantity.

15. Add a **Text file output** step to send the manufacturer code, the product code, the product name, and the ordered quantity to a file named products_to_buy.txt.

16. Run the transformation. The file should have this content:

```
man_code;prod_code;pro_name;quantity
EDU;ED13_93;Times Square;1
RAV;RVZ50031;Disney World Map;2
RAV;RVZ50106;Star Wars Clone Wars;1
```

What just happened?

You processed a file with orders. You grouped and counted the ordered products by product code. Then, with the Database lookup step, you looked up the product table for the record belonging to the ordered product. You added to your stream the name and stock for the products. After that, you kept only the rows for which the stock was lower than the units your customers ordered. With the rows that passed, you created a list of products to buy.

Looking up values in a database with the Database lookup step

The database lookup step allows you to lookup values in a database table. In the upper grid of the setting window, you specify the keys to look up. In the example, you look for a record that has the same product code and manufacturer code as the codes coming in the stream.

In the lower grid, you put the name of the table columns you want back. Those fields are added to the output stream. In this case, you added the name and the stock of the product.

The step returns only one row even if it doesn't find a matching record or if it finds more than one. When the step doesn't find a record with the given conditions, it returns null for all the added fields, unless you specify a default value for those new fields.

As a final remark, note that this behavior is quite similar to the Stream lookup step's behavior. You search for a match, and, if a record is found, the step returns the specified fields to you. If not, the new fields are filled with default values. Besides the fact that the data is searched in a database, the new thing here is that you specify the comparator to be used: =, <, >, and so on. The Stream lookup step only looks for equal values.

As all the products in the file existed in your database, the step found a record for every row, adding to your stream two fields: the name and the stock for the product. You can check it by doing a preview on the Database lookup step.

After the Database lookup step, you used a Filter row step to discard the rows where the stock was lower than the required quantity of products. You can avoid adding this step by refining the lookup configuration. In the upper grid, you could add the condition `pro_stock < quantity` and check the **Do not pass the row if the lookup fails** checkbox; doing this will give you a different result. The step will look not only for the product, but also for the condition `pro_stock<quantity`. If it doesn't find a record that matches, that is, the lookup fails, the check **Do not pass the row if the lookup fails** does its work by filtering the row. Doing these changes, you don't have to use the extra Filter rows step, nor add the `pro_stock` field to the stream unless you need it for another use.

As a final remark—if the lookup returns more than a row, only the first is returned. You have the option to abort the whole transformation if this happens; simply check the **Fail on multiple results?** checkbox.

Making a performance difference when looking up data in a database

Database lookups are costly and can severely impact transformation performance. However, performance can be significantly improved by using the cache feature of the Database lookup step. In order to enable the cache feature, just check the **Enable cache?** option.

This is how it works; think of the cache as a buffer of high-speed memory that temporarily holds frequently requested data. By enabling the cache option, Kettle will look first in the cache, and then in the database.

If the table that you look up has few records, you could preload the cache with all of the data in the lookup table. Do this by checking the **Load all data from table** option. This will give you the best performance.

On the contrary, if the number of rows in the lookup table is too large to fit entirely into memory, instead of caching the whole table you can tell Kettle the maximum number of rows to hold in cache. Do this by specifying the number in the **Cache size in rows** textbox. The bigger this number, the faster the lookup process.

The cache options should be set with care. If you have a large table or don't have much memory you risk running out of memory. Another caveat to using the cache is if this lookup data changes frequently; not the typical scenario for lookup data, but a possible pitfall.

Have a go hero – preparing the delivery of the products

Create a new transformation and do the following:

1. Taking as source the orders file create a list of the customers that ordered products.

2. Include their name, last name, and full address.

3. Order the data by country name.

You will need two Database lookup steps: one for getting the customer's information and another to get the name of the country.

Have a go hero – refining the transformation

Modify the original transformation. As the file may have been manipulated, it may contain invalid data. Apply the following treatment:

◆ Verify that there is a customer with the given number. If the customer doesn't exist discard the row. Use the **Do not pass the row if the lookup fails** checkbox.

◆ In the rows that passed, verify that there is a product with the given manufacturer and product codes. If the data is valid check the stock and proceed. If not, make a list so the cases can be handled later by the customer care department.

Performing complex lookups

The Database lookup step is very useful and quite simple, but it lets you search only for columns of a specific table. Let's now try a step that allows you to perform more complex searches.

Time for action – using a Database join step to create a list of suggested products to buy

If your customers ordered a product that is out of stock you don't want to let them down, so you will suggest some alternative puzzles to buy:

1. Open the transformation for the previous tutorial and save it under a new name.

2. Delete the **Text file output** step.

3. Double-click on the **Group by** step and add an aggregated field named customers with the list of customers separated by a comma (,). Under **Subject**, select idcus and select Concatenate strings separated by, as **Type**.

 Pay attention to the type that you choose! This one ends with a comma. There is another one without the separator. Do not confuse them!

4. Double-click on the **Database lookup** step. In the **Values** grid, add the pro_theme field to return from the lookup table. Select String as **Type**.

5. Add a **Select values** step. Use it to select the fields customers, quantity, pro_ theme, and pro_name. Also rename **quantity** as quantity_param and **pro_theme** as theme_param.

6. From the **Lookup** category, drag a **Database join** step to the canvas. Create a hop from the **Select values** step to this step.

7. Double-click on the **Database join** step.

8. Select js as **Connection**.

9. In the **SQL** frame, type the following statement:

```
SELECT man_code
     , pro_code
     , pro_name
FROM     products
WHERE    pro_theme like ?
AND      pro_stock>=?
```

10. In the **Number of rows to return** textbox, type **4**.

11. Fill the grid as shown:

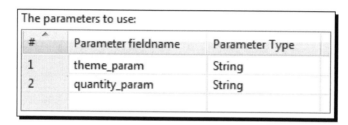

12. Click on **OK**. The transformation will appear as shown in the following screenshot:

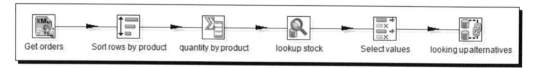

13. With the last step selected, do a preview.

14. You should see this:

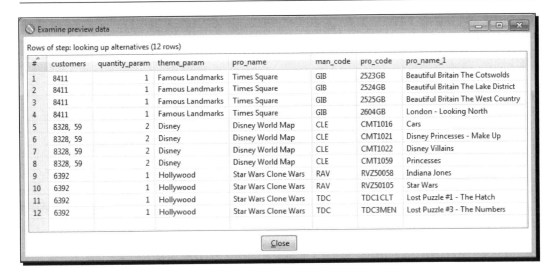

15. In the **Step Metrics** tab, you should see this:

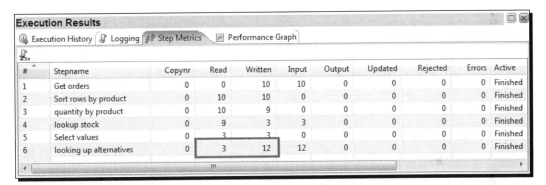

What just happened?

You took the list of orders and filtered those for which you ran out of products. For the customers that ordered those products you built a list of four alternative puzzles to buy.

The selection of the puzzles was based on the theme. To filter the suggested puzzles you used the theme of the ordered product.

The second parameter in the Database join step is the ordered quantity, which was used to offer only alternatives for products for which there is sufficient stock.

Joining data from the database to the stream data by using a Database join step

With the Database join step, you can combine your incoming stream with data from your database, based on given conditions. The conditions are put as parameters in the query that you write in the Database join step.

 Note that this is not really a database join as the name suggests. In fact, it is the joining of data from the database to the stream data.

In the tutorial, you used two parameters —the theme and the quantity ordered. With those parameters, you queried the list of products with the same theme such as:

```
where pro_theme like ?
```

For the preceding theme, you have stock:

```
and pro_stock>=?
```

You set the parameters as question marks. These work like the question marks in the Table input step that you learned in the previous chapter—the parameters are replaced according to the position. The difference is that here you define the list and the order of the parameters. You do it in the small grid at the bottom of the setting window. This means that you aren't forced to use all the incoming fields as parameters, and that you may also change the order.

Just as you do in a Table input step, instead of using positional parameters, you can use Kettle variables by using the $ { } notation and checking the **Replace variables** checkbox.

 You don't need to add the Select values step to discard fields and rename the parameters. You did it just to have fewer fields in the final screenshot so it was easier to understand the output of the Database join step.

The step will give you back the manufacturer code, the product code, and the product name for the matching records.

 As you cannot preview here, you can write and try your query inside a Table input step or in Squirrel for example. When you are done, just copy and paste the query here.

So far, you did the same you could have done with a Database lookup step, that is, looking for a record with a given condition and adding new fields to the stream. However, there is a big difference here—you put 4 in the **Number of rows to return** field. This means for each incoming row, the step will give you back up to four results. The following screenshot shows you this:

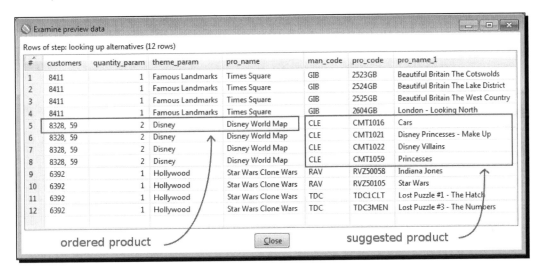

You may need to use a Database join step in several situations:

◆ When, as the result of the lookup, there may be more than a row for each incoming row. This was the case in this section.

◆ When you have to look up in a combination of tables. Look at the following SQL statement:

```
SELECT co.country_name
FROM customers cu
   , cities     ci
   , countries co
WHERE cu.city_id = ci.city_id
AND   ci.cou_id  = co.cou_id
AND   cu.cus_id  = 1000
```

◆ This statement returns the name of the country where the customer having ID as 1000 lives. If you want to look up the countries where a list of customers live, you can do it with a sentence like this by using a Database join step.

♦ When you want to look up for an aggregate result. Look at this sample query:

```
SELECT    pro_theme
        , count(*) quant
FROM      products
GROUP BY  pro_theme
ORDER BY  pro_theme
```

♦ This statement returns the number of puzzles by theme. If you have a list of themes and you want to find out how many puzzles you have for each theme, you can use a query like this by using a Database join step.

The last option in the list can also be developed without using the Database join step. You could execute the SELECT statement with a Table Input step, and then look for the calculated quantity by using a Stream lookup step.

 As you can see, this is another situation where PDI offers more that one way to do the same thing. Sometimes it is a matter of taste. In general, you should test each option and choose the method that gives you the best performance.

Have a go hero – rebuilding the list of customers

Perform the exercise given in the *Have a go hero – preparing the delivery of the products* section again, this time using a Database join step. Try to discover which one is preferable from the performance point of view. If you don't see any difference, try it again with a bigger number of records in the main stream. You will have to create your own dataset for this test.

Introducing dimensional modeling

So far, you have dealt with the Jigsaw puzzles' database; a database used for daily operational work. In the real world, a database like this is maintained by an **On-Line Transaction Processing (OLTP)** system. The users of an OLTP system perform operational tasks; they sell products, process orders, control stock, and so on.

As a counterpart, a data warehouse is a non-operational database; it is a specialized database designed for decision support purposes. Users of a data warehouse analyze the data, and they do it from different points of view.

The most used technique for delivering data to data-warehouse users is dimensional modeling. This technique consists of building a star-like schema with dimension tables surrounding a fact table, making databases simple and understandable.

The primary table in a dimensional model is the fact table. A fact table stores numerical measurements of the business as quantity of products sold, amount represented by the sold products, discounts, taxes, number of invoices, number of claims, and anything that can be measured. These measurements are referred to as **facts**.

A fact is useless without the dimension tables. Dimension tables contain the textual descriptors of the business. Typical dimensions are product, time, customers, and regions. As all surrounding dimension tables get formed in a star-like structure, we often call it a **star schema**.

Data warehouse is a very broad concept. In this book, we will deal with datamarts. While a data warehouse represents a global vision of an enterprise, a **datamart** holds the data from a single business process.

Data stored in data warehouses and datamarts usually comes from different sources; the operational database being the main one. The process that takes the information from the source, transforms it in several ways, and finally loads the data into the datamart or data warehouse is the **ETL process**. PDI is a perfect tool for accomplishing that task. In the rest of this chapter, you will learn how to load dimension tables with PDI. This will build the basis for the final project of the book, that is, loading a full datamart.

Through the tutorials, you will learn more about this. However, the terminology introduced here constitutes just as a preamble to dimensional modeling. It's much more you can learn. If you are really interested in the subject, you should start by reading *The Data Warehouse Toolkit*, *Ralph Kimball and Margy Ross*, *Wiley Computer Publishing*. This book is undoubtedly the best guide to dimensional modeling.

Loading dimensions with data

A dimension is an entity that describes your business; customers and products are examples of dimensions. A very special dimension is the time dimension that you already know. A dimension table, no surprises here, is a table that contains information about a dimension. In this section, you will learn to load dimension tables, that is, fill dimension tables in with data.

Time for action – loading a region dimension with a Combination lookup/update step

In this tutorial, you will load a dimension that stores geographical information.

1. Launch Spoon and create a new transformation.

2. Drag a **Table input** step to the canvas and double-click on it.

3. As **Connection**, select js.

4. In the SQL area, type the following query and click on the **OK** button:

   ```
   SELECT ci.city_id, city_name, country_name
   FROM cities ci, countries co
   WHERE ci.cou_id = co.cou_id
   ```

5. Expand the **Data Warehouse** category of steps.

6. Select the **Combination lookup/update** step and drag it to the canvas.

7. Create a hop from the **Table input** step to this new step.

8. Double-click on the **Combination lookup/update** step.

9. As **Connection**, select dw.

10. As **Target table** browse and select **lk_regions** or simply type it.

11. Change the default **Commit size** to 1.

12. Fill the grid, as shown in the following screenshot:

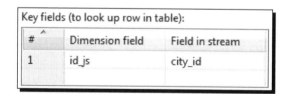

13. As **Technical key field** type id, and as **Date of last update field (optional)** type lastupdate.

14. Click on **OK**.

15. After the **Combination lookup/update** step, add an **Update** step and double-click on it.

16. As **Connection**, select dw and as **Target table**, type lk_regions.

17. Fill the upper grid by adding the condition id = id. The id attribute to the left is the table's ID, while id to the right is the stream ID.

18. Fill the lower grid. Add one row with the **city** and **city_name** values. Add a second row with the **country** and **country_name** values. This will update the table columns `city` and `country` with the values `city_name` and `country_name` coming in the stream.

19. Now create another stream. Add to the canvas a **Generate rows** step, a **Table output** step, and a **Dummy** step.

20. Link the steps in the order you added them.

21. Edit the **Generate rows** step and set **Limit** to `1`.

22. Add four fields in this order. An **Integer** field named `id` with value `0`. A **String** field named `city` with value `N/A`. Another **String** named `country` with value `N/A`. An **Integer** field named `id_js` with the value `0`.

23. Double-click on the **Table output** step.

24. As **Connection**, select `dw`, type `lk_regions` as **Target table**, and then click on **OK**.

25. In the **Table output** step, enable error handling and send the bad rows to the **Dummy** step. The transformation will appear as shown in the following screenshot:

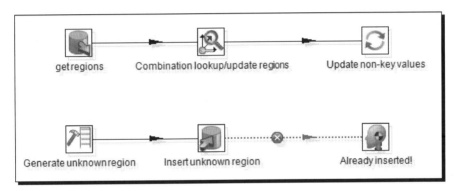

26. Save the transformation and run it. The **Step metrics** tab will appear as shown in the following screenshot:

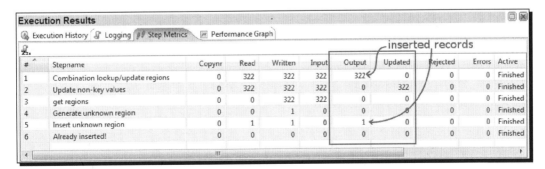

27. Explore the `js_dw` database and preview the `lk_regions` table. You should see this:

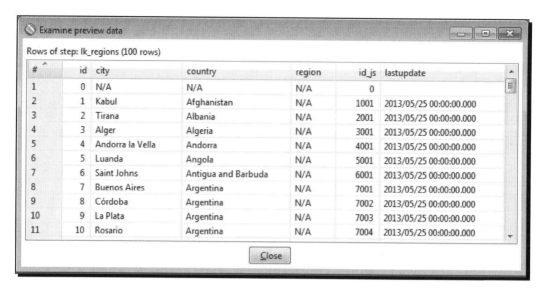

What just happened?

You loaded the region dimension with geographical information—cities and countries.

 Note that you took information from the operational database `js` and loaded a table in another database `js_dw`.

Before running the transformation, the dimension table `lk_region` was empty. When the transformation runs, all cities were inserted in the dimension table. The **Combination lookup/update** step merely inserts the row for each city, whereas, the update adds the city and country information.

 Note that in the **Combination lookup/update** step, we set the commit size to 1. This is the only way in which this transformation will run successfully and reliably every time. There are conflicts in timing if the commit size is larger, as we are attempting to update a row that may not have been committed yet.

Besides the records with cities from the `cities` table, you also inserted a special record with values `N/A` for the descriptive fields. You did it in the second stream added to the transformation.

Note, that the dimension table `lk_regions` has a column named `region` that you didn't update because you don't have data for that column. The column is filled with a default value set in the DDL definition of the table.

Time for action – testing the transformation that loads the region dimension

In the previous tutorial, you loaded a dimension that stores geographical information. You ran it once, causing the insertion of one record for each city and a special record with values `N/A` for the descriptive fields. Let's make some changes in the operational database, and run the transformation again to see what happens.

1. Launch Squirrel and connect to the `js` database.

2. Type the following sentence to change the names of the countries to upper case:

   ```
   UPDATE countries SET country_name = UCASE(country_name)
   ```

3. Execute it. You may do this by clicking on the **Run** button or by pressing *Ctrl + Enter*.

4. If the transformation created in the last tutorial is not open, open it again.

5. Run the transformation.

6. The **Step metrics** tab will appear as shown in the following screenshot:

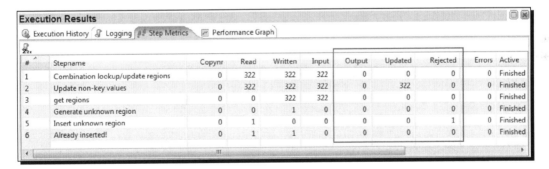

Execution Results

Execution History   Logging   Step Metrics   Performance Graph

#	Stepname	Copynr	Read	Written	Input	Output	Updated	Rejected	Errors	Active
1	Combination lookup/update regions	0	322	322	322	0	0	0	0	Finished
2	Update non-key values	0	322	322	322	0	322	0	0	Finished
3	get regions	0	0	322	322	0	0	0	0	Finished
4	Generate unknown region	0	0	1	0	0	0	0	0	Finished
5	Insert unknown region	0	1	0	0	0	0	1	0	Finished
6	Already inserted!	0	1	1	0	0	0	0	0	Finished

7. Explore the js_dw database again and do preview a of the lk_regions table. This time you will see the following:

What just happened?

After changing the letter case for the names of the countries in the transactional database `js`, you run, again, the transformation that updates the **Regions** dimension. This time the descriptions for the dimension table were updated.

As for the special record with values `N/A` for the descriptive fields, it was created the first time the transformation ran. This time, as the record already existed, the row passed by to the Dummy step.

Describing data with dimensions

A **dimension** table contains descriptions about a particular entity or category of your business. Dimensions are one of the basic blocks of a data warehouse or a datamart. A dimension has the purpose of grouping, filtering, and describing data.

Think of a typical report you would like to have—sales grouped by region, by customer, and method of payment that are ordered by date. The **by** word lets you identify potential dimensions—regions, customers, methods of payment, and dates.

Best practices say that a dimension table must have its own technical key column different to the business key column used in the operational database. This technical key is known as a **surrogate key**. In the `lk_region` dimension table, the surrogate key is the column named `id`.

While in the operational database, the key may be a string, for example the manufacturer code in the `manufacturers` table, surrogate keys are always integers.

Explaining the advantages of having a surrogate key is out of the scope of this book, but it's worth mentioning that one of the main benefits of using a surrogate key is that it often takes less space in the database than key columns in the operational database.

Another good practice is to have a special record for the unavailable data. In the case of the regions example, this implies that besides one record for every city, you should have a record with the key equal to zero, and `N/A` or `unknown`, or something that represents invalid data for all the descriptive attributes.

Having this record, data that is unavailable or invalid in the operation database will not be inserted in the data warehouse; it will be represented by this special record instead.

Along with the descriptive attributes that you save in a dimension, you usually keep the business key so you can match the data in the dimension table with the data in the source database. The following screenshot depicts typical columns in a dimension table:

id	city	country	region	id_js	lastupdate
0	N/A	N/A	N/A	0	
1	Kabul	AFGHANISTAN	N/A	1001	2013/05/25 00:00:00.000
2	Tirana	ALBANIA	N/A	2001	2013/05/25 00:00:00.000
3	Alger	ALGERIA	N/A	3001	2013/05/25 00:00:00.000
4	Andorra la Vella	ANDORRA	N/A	4001	2013/05/25 00:00:00.000
5	Luanda	ANGOLA	N/A	5001	2013/05/25 00:00:00.000
6	Saint Johns	ANTIGUA AND BARBUDA	N/A	6001	2013/05/25 00:00:00.000
7	Buenos Aires	ARGENTINA	N/A	7001	2013/05/25 00:00:00.000
8	Córdoba	ARGENTINA	N/A	7002	2013/05/25 00:00:00.000
9	La Plata	ARGENTINA	N/A	7003	2013/05/25 00:00:00.000
10	Rosario	ARGENTINA	N/A	7004	2013/05/25 00:00:00.000

descriptive fields

surrogate key   *business key*

In the tutorial, you took information from the `cities` and `countries` tables and used that data to load the regions dimension. When there were changes in the transactional database, the changes were translated to the dimension table overwriting the old values. A dimension where changes may occur from time to time is named **Slowly Changing Dimension (SCD)**. If, when you update a SCD dimension, you don't preserve historical values but overwrite the old values, the dimension is called **Type I slowly changing dimension (Type I SCD)**.

Loading Type I SCD with a Combination lookup/update step

In the tutorial, you loaded a Type I SCD by using a Combination lookup/update step. The **Combination lookup/update (Combination L/U)** looks in the dimension table for a record that matches the key fields that you put in the upper grid in the setting window. If the combination exists, the step returns the surrogate key of the found record. If it doesn't exist, the step generates a new surrogate key and inserts a row with the key fields and the generated surrogate key. In any case, the surrogate key is added to the output stream.

> Be aware that in the **Combination lookup/update** step the **Dimension field**, **Technical key field**, and **Date of last update field** options do not refer to fields in the stream, but to columns in the table. In those cases, where you see the word field, you should know that it refers to a column: **Dimension** column, **Technical key** column, and **Date of last update** column.
>
> Also note that the term **Technical** refers to the surrogate key.

Let's see how the Combination lookup/update step works with an example. Look at the following screenshot:

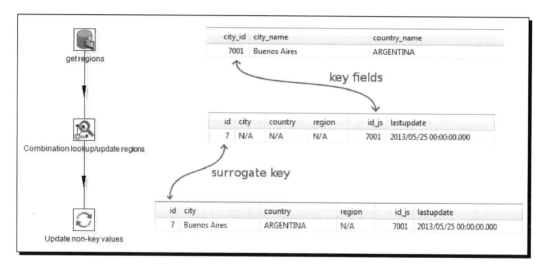

The record to the right of the **Table input** icon is a sample city among the cities that the Table input step gets from the `js` database.

With the Combination L/U step, PDI looks for a record in the `lk_region` table in the `dw` database, where `id_js` is equal to the `city_id` field in the incoming stream, which is 7001. The first time you run the transformation, the dimension table is empty, so the lookup fails. This causes PDI to generate a new surrogate key according to what you put in the **Technical key** field area of the setting's window:

You told PDI that the column that holds the surrogate key is the column named `id`. You also told PDI that in order to generate the key, use the maximum key found in the target table plus one. In this example, it generates a key equal to 7. You may also use a sequence or an auto-increment field if the database engine allows it. If that is not the case, those options are disabled.

Then PDI generates the key and inserts the record you can see to the right of the Combination L/U step in the preceding screenshot. Note that the record contains only values for the **Key** fields and the **Technical key** field.

The Combination L/U step put the returned **Technical key** in the output stream. Then you used that key for updating the descriptions for city and country with the use of an **Update** step. After that step, the record is fully generated, as shown in the record to the right of the Update icon.

> As the Combination L/U only maintains the key information, if you have non-key columns in the table you must update them with an extra Update step.
>
> Note that those values must have a default value or must allow null values. If none of these conditions is true, the insert operation will fail.

After converting all the country names in the source database to uppercase, run the transformation again.

This time the incoming record for the same city is this:

city_id	city_name	country_name
7001	Buenos Aires	ARGENTINA

PDI looks for a record in the `lk_region` table, in the `dw` database, where `id_js` is equal to 7001. PDI finds it. It is the record inserted the first time that you ran the transformation.

Then, the Combination L/U simply returns the key field adding it to the output stream.

Then, use the key that the step added to update the descriptions for city and country. After the Update step, the old values for city and country name are overwritten by the new ones:

id	city	country	region	id_js	lastupdate
7	Buenos Aires	ARGENTINA	N/A	7001	2013/05/25 00:00:00.000

Have a go hero – adding regions to the Region dimension

Modify the transformation that loads the Region dimension to fill the region column. Get the values from the regions.xls file that you will find among the downloaded code for this chapter. To add the region information to your stream, use a Stream lookup step.

> While you are playing with dimensions, you may want to throw away all the inserted data and start all over again. For doing that simply explore the database and use the **Truncate Table** option. You can do the same in Squirrel. For the lk_regions dimension, you could execute any of the following:
>
> ◆ DELETE FROM lk_regions
> ◆ TRUNCATE TABLE lk_regions

Have a go hero – loading the manufacturers dimension

Create a transformation that loads the **manufacturers** dimension: lk_manufacturers.

Here you have the table definition and some guidance for loading:

Column	Description
id	Surrogate key.
name	Name of the manufacturer.
id_js	Business key. Here you have to store the manufacturer's code (the man_code field of the source table manufacturers).

Storing a history of changes

The Region dimension is a typical Type I SCD dimension. If some description changes as the country names did, it makes no sense to keep the old values. The new values simply overwrite the old ones. This is not always the best choice. Sometimes you would like to keep a history of the changes. Now you will learn how to load a dimension that keeps a history.

Time for action – keeping a history of changes in products by using the Dimension lookup/update step

Let's load a puzzles dimension along with the history of the changes in puzzles attributes:

1. Create a new transformation.

2. Drag a **Table input** step to the work area and double-click on it.

3. As **Connection**, select js.

4. In the SQL area type the following query:

```
SELECT pro_code
     , man_code
     , pro_name
     , pro_theme
FROM   products
WHERE pro_type LIKE 'PUZZLE'
```

5. Click on **OK**.

6. Add an **Add constants** step, and create a hop from the **Table input** step toward it.

7. Use the step to add a **Date** field named changedate. As format, type dd/MM/yyyy and as value, type 01/10/2009.

8. Expand the **Data Warehouse** category of steps.

9. Select the **Dimension lookup/update** step and drag it to the canvas.

10. Create a hop from the **Add constants** step to this new step.

11. Double-click on the **Dimension lookup/update** step.

12. As **Connection**, select dw.

13. As **Target table**, type lk_puzzles.

14. Fill the **Key** fields, as shown in the following screenshot:

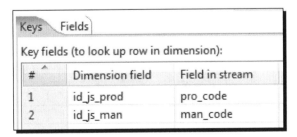

15. As **Technical key** field, select `id`.

16. In the **Creation of technical key** frame, leave the default **Use table maximum + 1**.

17. As **Version field**, select **version**.

18. As **Stream Datefield**, select `changedate`.

19. As **Date range start field**, select `start_date`.

20. As **Table daterange end**, select `end_date`.

21. Select the **Fields** tab and fill it in with the following information shown in the screenshot: :

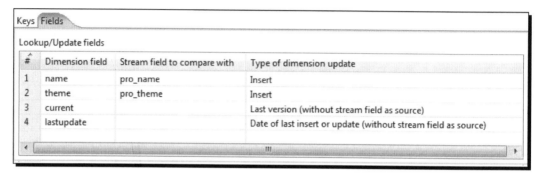

#	Dimension field	Stream field to compare with	Type of dimension update
1	name	pro_name	Insert
2	theme	pro_theme	Insert
3	current		Last version (without stream field as source)
4	lastupdate		Date of last insert or update (without stream field as source)

22. Close the setting window.

23. Save the transformation and run it.

24. Explore the `js_dw` database and do a preview of the `lk_puzzles` table. You should see this:

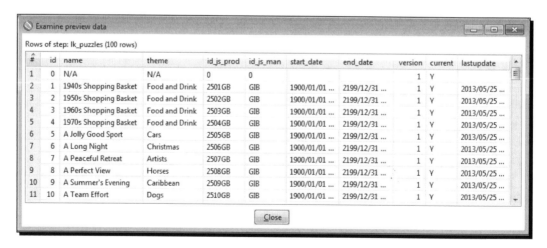

What just happened?

You loaded the puzzle dimension with the name and theme of the puzzles you sell. The dimension table has the usual columns for a dimension—technical ID (field `id`), fields that store the key fields in the table of the operational database (`prod_code` and `man_code`), and columns for the puzzle attributes (`name` and `theme`). It also has some extra fields specially designed to keep history.

When you ran the transformation, all records were inserted in the dimension table. Also a special record was automatically inserted for unavailable data.

So far, there is nothing new except for a few extra columns with dates. In the next section, you will learn more about those columns.

Time for action – testing the transformation that keeps history of product changes

In the preceding section, you loaded a dimension with products by using a Dimension lookup/update step. You ran the transformation once, caused the insertion of one record for each product, and a special record with values `N/A` for the descriptive fields. Let's make some changes in the operational database, and run the transformation again to see how the Dimension lookup/update step stores history.

1. Among the downloaded material locate the `update_jumbo_products.sql` script and run it.

2. Switch to Spoon.

3. If the transformation created in the last tutorial is not open, open it again.

4. Run the transformation.

5. Explore the `js_dw` database again. Right-click on the `lk_puzzles` table and click on **View SQL**. Modify the proposed statement so it looks like the following:

```
SELECT    *
FROM      lk_puzzles
WHERE     id_js_man = 'JUM'
ORDER BY id_js_prod
        , version
```

You will see this:

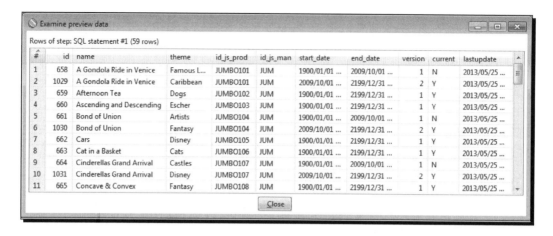

What just happened?

After making some changes in the operational database, you ran the transformation for a second time. The modifications you made caused the insertion of new records recreating the history of the puzzles attributes.

Keeping an entire history of data with a Type II slowly changing dimension

Type II SCDs differs from Type I SCDs. A Type II SCD keeps the whole history of the data of your dimension. Some typical examples of attributes for which you would like to keep history are sales territories that change over time, categories of products that are reclassified from time to time, promotions that you apply to products which are valid in a given range of dates.

There are no rules that dictate whether or not you keep the history in a dimension. It's the final user who decides this based on his requirements.

In the puzzle dimension, you kept information about the changes for the name and theme attributes. Let's see how the history is kept for this sample dimension.

Each puzzle is to be represented by one or more records, each with the information valid during certain period of time, as shown in the following screenshot:

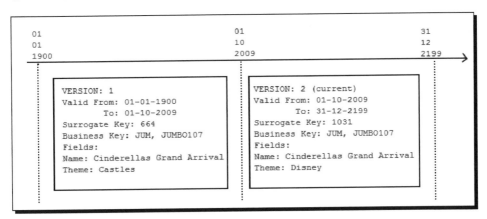

The history is kept in three extra fields in the dimension table—version, date_from, and date_to. The version field is an automatically incremented value that maintains a revision number of the records for a particular puzzle. The date range is used to indicate the period of applicability of the data.

In this section, you also had a current field that acted as a flag to know if a record is the record valid in the present day.

The sample puzzle, Cinderellas Grand Arrival, was classified in the category Castles until 1st October 2009. After that date, the puzzle was reclassified as a Disney puzzle. This is the second version of the puzzle as indicated by the column version. It's also the current version as indicated by the column current.

In general, if you have to implement a Type II SCD dimension with PDI, your dimension table must have the first three fields—version, date_from, and date_to. The current flag is optional.

Loading Type II SCDs with the Dimension lookup/update step

Type II SCDs can be loaded by using the Dimension lookup/update step, or Dimension L/U for short. The main difference between this step and the Combination lookup/update step that you saw before is the Dimension L/U step's ability to keep a history of changes in data.

The Dimension lookup/update step looks in the dimension for a record that matches the information you put in the **Keys** grid of the setting window.

If the lookup fails, it inserts a new record. If a record is found, the step inserts or updates records depending on how you configured the step.

Let's explain how the Dimension L/U step works with the following sample puzzle in the `js` database:

pro_code	man_code	pro_name	pro_des...	pro_type	pro_theme
JUMBO107	JUM	Cinderellas Grand Arrival		PUZZLE	Castles

The first time you run the transformation, the step looks in the dimension for a record where `id_js_prod` is equal to `JUMBO107`, and `id_js_man` is equal to `JUM`. The period from `start_date` to `end_date` of the found record must contain the value of the stream `datefield` which is `01/10/2009`.

Because you never loaded this table before, the table was empty so the lookup failed. As a result, the step inserts the following record:

id	name	theme	id_js_prod	id_js_man	start_date	end_date	version	current	lastupdate
664	Cinderellas Grand Arrival	Castles	JUMBO107	JUM	1900/01/01 ...	2199/12/31 ...	1	Y	2013/05/25 00:

Note the values that the step put for the special fields. The version for the new record is `1`, the current flag is set to `true`, and the `start_date` and `end_date` fields take as values the dates you put in the **Min. year** and **Max. year**, that is, `01/01/1900` and `31/12/2199` in this case.

After making some modifications in the operational database, you ran the transformation again. Look at the following screenshot:

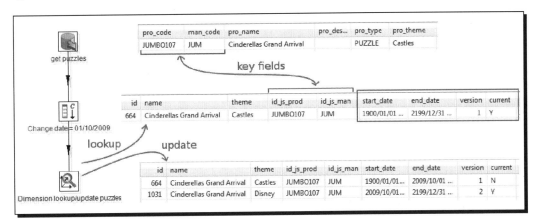

The puzzle information has changed. As you see to the right of the Table input step, the puzzle is now classified as a Disney puzzle.

This time the lookup succeeds. There is a record for which the keys match and the period from `start_date` to `end_date` of the found record; `01/01/1900` to `31/12/2199` obviously contain the value of the `stream datefield`, that is, `01/10/2009`.

Once found, the step compares the fields you put in the **Fields** tab `name` and `theme` in the dimension table against `pro_name` and `pro_theme` in the incoming stream.

As there is a difference in the `theme` field, the step inserts a new record, and modifies the current—it changes the validity dates and sets the current flag to `false`. Now this puzzle has two versions in the dimension table, as you see below the Dimension L/U icon in the preceding screenshot. These update and insert operations are made for all records that changed.

For the records that didn't change, dimension records are found but as nothing changed, nothing is inserted nor updated.

Refer to the stream date. The field you put here is key to the loading process of the dimension, as its value is interpreted by PDI as the effective date of the change. In this section, you put a fixed date 01/10/2009. In real situations, you should use the effective or last changed date of the data, if that date is available. If it is not available, leave the field blank. PDI will use the system's date.

In this example, you filled the **Type** column of dimension update with the **Insert** option for every field. By doing this, you loaded a pure Type II dimension, that is, a dimension that keeps track of all changes in all fields.

In the sample puzzles dimension, you kept history of changes both in the theme and in the name. For the sample puzzle, the theme was changed from **Castles** to **Disney**. If, after some time, you query the sales and notice that the sales for that puzzle increased after the change, then you may conclude that the customers are more interested in Disney puzzles than in Castle puzzles. The possibility of doing these kind of reports is a good reason for maintaining a Type II SCD.

On the other hand, if the name of the puzzle changes, you may not be so interested in knowing what the name was before. Fortunately, you may change the configuration and create a **Hybrid SCD**. Instead of selecting Insert for every field, you may select Update or Punch through:

♦ When there is a change in a field for which you chose Update, the new value overwrites the old value in the last dimension record version that is the usual behavior in Type I SCDs.

♦ When there is a change in a field for which you chose Punch through, the new data overwrites the old value in all record versions.

Note that you select Punch through for all the fields, the Dimension L/U step allows you to load a Type I SCD dimension. As for a Type I, you are not interested in range dates so you can leave the **Stream Datefield** textbox empty. The current date is assumed by default.

In practice, we use both Type I and Type II along with Hybrid SCD. The choice of the type of SCD depends on the business needs.

Besides all those insert and update operations, the Dimension L/U step automatically inserts the record for unavailable data in the dimension.

In order to insert the special record with a key that equals zero, all fields must have default values or should allow nulls. If none of these conditions are true, the automatic insertion will fail.

In order to load a dimension with the Dimension L/U step, your table has to have columns for the version, date from, and date to. The step automatically maintains those columns. You simply have to put their names into the right textbox in the setting window.

Besides those fields, your dimension table may have a column for the `current` flag, and another column for the date for the last insert or update. To fill those optional columns, you have to add them in the **Fields** tab as you did in the tutorial.

Have a go hero – storing a history just for the theme of a product

Modify the loading products dimension so that it only keeps a history of the theme. If the name of the product changes, just overwrite the old values. Modify some data in the `js` database and run your transformation to confirm that it works as expected.

Have a go hero – loading the Regions dimension as a Type II SCD

As you saw in the *Have a go hero – adding regions to the Region dimension* section, the countries were grouped in three: Spain, Rest of Europe, and Rest of the World.

As the sales rose in several countries of the world, you decided to regroup the countries in more than three groups. However, you want to do this starting in 2008. For older sales, you prefer to keep seeing the sales grouped by the original categories.

This is what you will do; use the table named `lk_regions_2` to create a Type II Regions Dimension. Here you have a guide to follow. Create a transformation that loads the dimension. You will take the stream date (the date you use for loading the dimension), from the command line. If the command-line argument is empty, use the present date.

As name for the sheet with the region definition, use a named parameter.

Stream date

If the command-line argument is present, remember to change it to date before using it. You do this using a Select values step.

Note that you have to define the format of the entered data in advance. Suppose that you want to enter as an argument the date January 1, 2008. If you chose the format `dd-mm-yyyy`, you'll have to enter the argument as `01-01-2008`.

In case the command-line argument is absent, you can get the default one with a Get System Info step. Note that the system date you add with this step is already a Date field.

Let us now perform these steps:

1. Run the transformation by using the `regions.xls` file. Don't worry about the command-line argument. Check that the dimension was loaded as expected. There has to be a single record for every city.

2. Run the transformation again. This time use the `regions2008.xls` file as a source for the region column. As command line, enter January 1, 2008. Remember to insert the date in the expected format (check the preceding tip). Explore the dimension table. There has to be two records for each country: one valid before 2008 and one valid after that date.

3. Modify the sheet to create a new grouping for the American countries. Use your imagination for this task! Run the transformation for the third time. This time use the sheet you created, and as date, type the present day (or leave the argument blank). Explore the dimension table. Now each city for the countries you regrouped has to have three versions, where the current one is the version you created. The other cities should have two versions each, because nothing related to those cities has changed.

Pop quiz – implementing a Type III SCD in PDI

Type III SCD are dimensions that store the immediately preceding and current value for a descriptive field of the dimension. Each entity is stored in a single record. The field for which you want to keep the previous value has two columns assigned in the record: one for the current value and other for the old. Sometimes it is possible to have a third column holding the date of effective change.

Type III SCD are appropriate to use when you don't want to keep all of the history, and mainly when you need to support two views of the attribute simultaneously—the previous and the current. Suppose that you have an Employees dimension. Among the attributes you have their position. People are promoted from time to time and you want to keep these changes in the dimension; however, you are not interested in knowing all the intermediate positions the employees have been through. In this case you may implement a Type III SCD.

Q1. How would you load a Type III dimension with PDI?

1. With a Dimension L/U step configuring it properly.

2. By using a Database lookup step to get the previous value. Then with a Dimension L/U step or a Combination L/U step insert or update the records.

3. You can't load Type III dimensions with PDI.

Have a go hero – loading a mini dimension

As the final exercise of this chapter, you will load a mini-dimension. A **mini dimension** is a dimension where you store the frequently analyzed or frequently changing attributes of a large dimension. Look at the products in the Jigsaw puzzles database. There are several puzzles attributes you may be interested in, for example, when you analyze the sales, that is, number of puzzles in a single pack, number of pieces of the puzzles, material of the product, and so on. Instead of creating a big dimension with all puzzles attributes, you can create a mini dimension that stores only a selection of attributes. There would be one row in this mini dimension for each unique combination of the selected attributes encountered in the products table, not one row per puzzle.

In this exercise, you'll have to load a mini dimension with puzzles attributes. Here you have the definition of the table that will hold the mini-dimension data:

Column	Description
id	Surrogate key
glowsInDark	Y/N
is3D	Y/N
wooden	Y/N
isPanoramic	Y/N
nrPuzzles	Number of puzzles in a single pack
nrPieces	Number of pieces of the puzzle

Take as a starting point the following query:

```
SELECT DISTINCT pro_type
              , pro_packaging
              , pro_shape
              , pro_style
FROM   products
WHERE  pro_type = 'PUZZLE'
```

Use the output stream for creating the fields you need for the dimension, for example, for the field is3D, you'll have to check the value of the pro_shape field.

Once you have all the fields you need, insert the records in the dimension table by using a Combination L/U step. In this mini dimension, the key is made by all the fields of the table. As a consequence, you don't need an extra Update step.

Summary

In this chapter, you learned to perform some advanced operations on databases. Firstly, you populated the Jigsaw database in order to have data for the activities in the chapter. Then, you learned how to do simple and complex searches in a database.

After that, you were introduced to dimensional concepts, learned what dimensions are, and how to load them with PDI. You learned about Type I, Type II, Type III SCDs, and mini dimensions. You still have to learn when and how to use those dimensions. You will do so in *Chapter 12, Developing and Implementing a Simple Datamart*.

The steps you learned in this and the last chapter are far from being the full list of steps that PDI offers to work with databases. However, taking into account all that you learned, you are now ready to use PDI for implementing most of your database requirements.

In the next chapter, you will switch to a very different yet core subject needed to work with PDI: jobs.

10
Creating Basic Task Flows

So far, you have been working with data. Basically, you got data from a file, a sheet, or a database, transformed it somehow, and sent it back to some file or table in a database. You did it by using PDI transformations. A PDI transformation does not run in isolation. Usually, it is embedded in a bigger process. Here are some examples:

- Download a file, clean it, load the information of the file in a database, and fill an audit file with the result of the operation.
- Generate a daily report and transfer the report to a shared repository.
- Update a data warehouse. If something goes wrong, notify the administrator by e-mail.

All these examples are typical processes in which a transformation is only a part. These types of processes can be implemented by PDI jobs. In this chapter, you will learn how to build basic jobs. These are the topics that will be covered:

- Introduction to jobs
- Executing tasks upon conditions
- Working with arguments and named parameters

Introducing PDI jobs

A PDI job is an analogous process. As with processes in real life, there are basic jobs and there are jobs that do really complex tasks. Let's start by creating a job in the first group.

Time for action – creating a folder with a Kettle job

In this tutorial, you will create a very simple job, so that you can get an idea of what jobs are about:

1. Open Spoon.

2. Navigate to **File** | **New** | **Job** or press *Ctrl+Alt+N*. A new job is created.

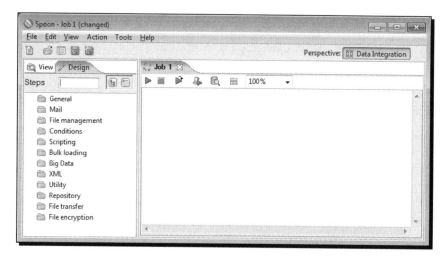

3. Press *Ctrl + J*. The **Job properties** window appears. Give the job a name and description as shown in the following screenshot:

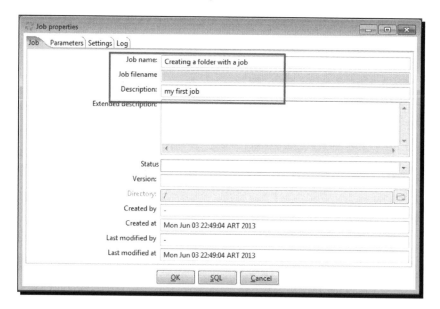

4. Press *Ctrl + S* to save the job.

5. To the left of the screen, there is a tree with job entries. Expand the **General** category of job entries, select the **START** entry, and drag it to the work area, as shown in the following screenshot:

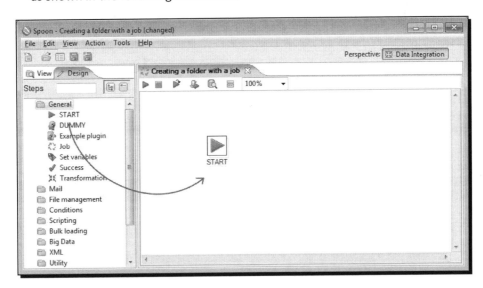

6. Expand the **File management** category, select the **Create a folder** entry, and drag it to the canvas.

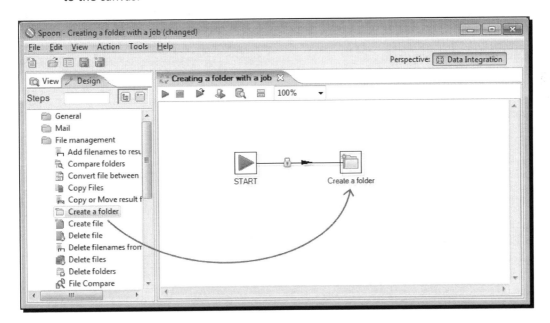

7. Select both entries. With the mouse cursor over the second entry, right-click and select **New hop**. A new hop is created.

> Just like in a transformation, you have several ways to create hops. For more detail, please refer to the *Time for Action – creating a hello world transformation* section in *Chapter 1, Getting started with Pentaho Data Integration*, where hops were introduced, or to *Appendix D, Spoon shortcuts*.

8. Double-click on the **Create a folder** icon.

9. In the text box next to the **Folder name** option, type `${LABSOUTPUT}/chapter10` and click on **OK**.

10. Press *Ctrl + S* to save the job, and then press *F9* to run the job. The following window appears:

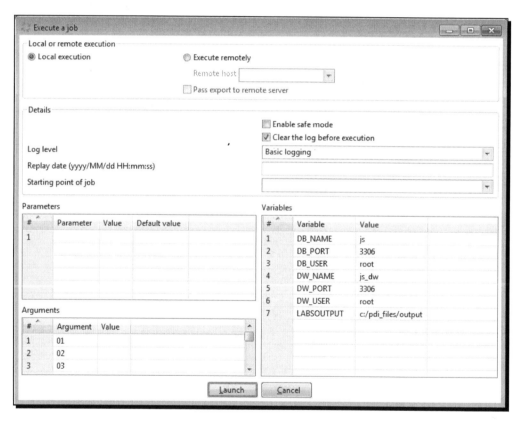

Remember that in the earlier chapters, you defined the LABSOUTPUT variable in the kettle.properties file. You should see its value in the **Variables** grid. If you removed the variable from that file, provide a value here.

11. Click on **Launch**.

12. At the bottom of the screen, you will see the **Execution results** section. The **Job metrics** will appear as follows:

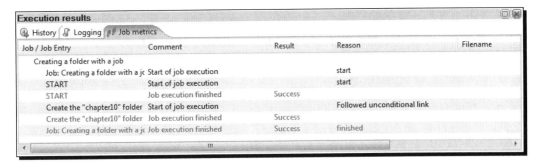

13. Select the **Logging** tab. It appears as the following screenshot:

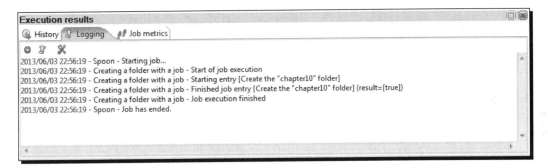

14. Explore the folder pointed by your ${LABSOUTPUT} variable, for example, c:/pdi_files/output. You should see a new folder named chapter10.

What just happened?

You created a PDI job whose purpose was to create a folder named chapter10 inside the directory pointed by the ${LABSOUTPUT} variable.

You ran the job and the chapter10 folder was created.

Executing processes with PDI jobs

A job is a PDI entity designed for the execution of processes. In the preceding section, you ran a very simple process that created a folder. A more complex example could be one that truncates all the tables in a database and loads data in all the tables from a set of text files. Other examples involve sending e-mails, transferring files, and executing shell scripts.

The unit of execution inside a job is a **job entry**. In Spoon, you can see the entries grouped into categories according to the purpose of the entries. In the preceding section, you used job entries from two of those categories: **General** and **File management**.

Most of the job entries in the **File management** category have a self-explanatory name as the one you used in the tutorial, **Create a folder**, and their use is quite intuitive. Feel free to experiment with them!

As to the **General** category, it contains many of the most used entries. Among them is the **START** job entry that you used. A job must begin with a **START** job entry.

 Don't forget to start your sequence of job entries with **START**. A job can have any mix of job entries and hops, as long as they start with this special kind of job entry.

A hop is a graphical representation that links two job entries. The direction of the hop defines the order of execution of the job entries it links. Besides, the execution of the destination job entry does not begin until the job entry that precedes it has finished. This is distinctly different from transformation executions. While the execution of a transformation is parallel and synchronous in nature, a job executes in a sequential and asynchronous way.

A hop connects only two job entries. However, a job entry may be reached by more than one hop. Also, more than a hop may leave a job entry.

A job, just as a transformation, is neither a program nor an executable file. It is simply plain XML. The job contains metadata which tells the Kettle engine, which processes to run and the order of execution of those processes. Therefore, it is said that a job is flow control oriented.

Using Spoon to design and run jobs

As you just saw, with Spoon you not only create, preview, and run transformations, but you also create and run jobs.

You are already familiar with this graphical tool, so you don't need too much explanation about the basic work areas. So let's do a brief review:

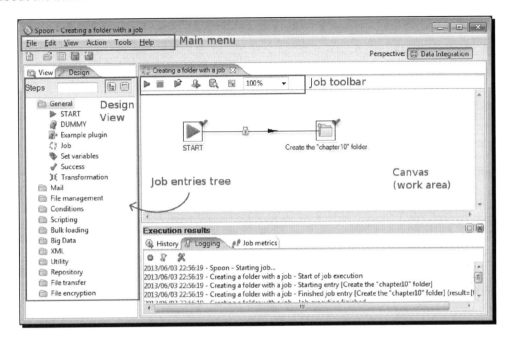

The following table describes the main differences you will notice while designing a job, compared to designing a transformation:

Area	Description
Design tree	You don't see a list of steps but a list of job entries (despite on top of the list you see the word **Steps**).
Job toolbar	You no longer see some options that only make sense while working with datasets. One of them is the **Preview** button. It makes no sense to preview data in jobs.
Job metrics tab (**Execution results** window)	Instead of a **Step Metrics**, you have this tab. Here you can see metrics for each job entry.

If you click on the **View** icon in the upper-left hand corner of the screen, the tree will change to show the structure of the job currently being edited:

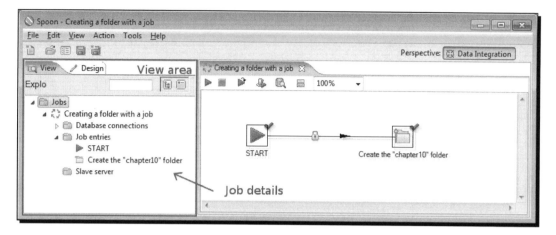

Pop quiz – defining PDI jobs

Q1. A job is:

1.   A big transformation that groups smaller transformations
2.   An ordered group of task definitions
3.   An unordered group of task definitions

Q2. A job allows you to send e-mails:

1.   True
2.   False

Q3. A job allows you to compare folders:

1.   True
2.   False

Q4. A job allows you to run transformations:

1. True

2. False

Q5. A job allows you to truncate database tables:

1. True

2. False

Q6. A job allows you to transfer files with FTP:

1. True

2. False

Designing and running jobs

In the previous section, you created and ran a very simple job. In this section, you will get familiar with the design process of a job by enriching that job.

Time for action – creating a simple job and getting familiar with the design process

Now you will create a job similar to the one you just created, but a little more elaborate. You will add some extra tasks in order to avoid unexpected errors.

1. Run Spoon and open the job you created in the previous tutorial. Save it under a different name.

 We are assuming that you already ran the job, so the `chapter10` folder already exists. If not, please run it or create the folder by hand.

2. Run the job. You should see this:

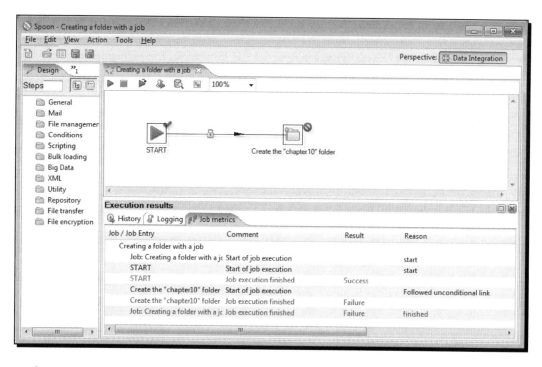

3. It's not good to receive this kind of unexpected errors! Let's modify the job so that it's more friendly. First of all, let's start over by deleting the `chapter10` folder.

4. Now expand the **Conditions** category of entries and select the **Checks if files exist** entry.

5. Drag the entry to the canvas and drop it over the hop that leaves the **START** entry. When asked for splitting the hop answer **Yes**. This is how your job looks like:

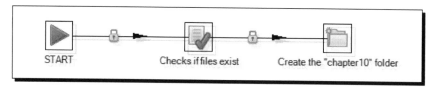

6. Double-click on the new entry, and in the first row of the grid, in the **File/Folder** column, type `${LABSOUTPUT}/chapter10`.

7. Click twice on the lock of the second hop. It will become green after the first click, and red after the second one.

8. From the **Utility** category of steps, drag to the canvas a **Write To Log** entry.

9. Create a new hop from the **Checks if files exist** entry to this new entry. The hop should be green.

10. Double-click on the **Write to Log** entry and fill it as shown:

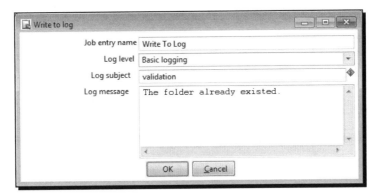

11. Close the window. Your job looks like:

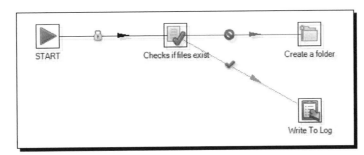

12. Save it and run it. The `chapter10` folder should have been created again.

13. In the **Execution results** window, you will see the following:

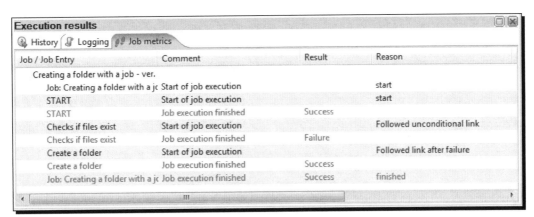

14. Run the job again and this time you will see the following:

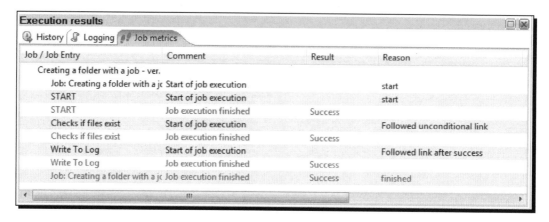

What just happened?

You created a more advanced version of your first job. The new job evaluates whether the chapter10 folder already exists. If it does, this fact is reported to the Kettle log. If not, the folder is created. With these changes, you avoided unexpected errors.

A job may contain any number of entries. Not all of them execute always. Some of them execute depending on the result of previous entries in the flow.

Changing the flow of execution on the basis of conditions

The execution of any job entry either succeeds or fails. For example, a Mail entry succeeds if Kettle can send the message, but it may fail if the specified SMTP host is unknown. As another example, a ZIP file entry succeeds if Kettle can zip the specified files, but will fail if the ZIP file existed and you configured the entry for failing in case Kettle hit that condition. In particular, the job entries under the Conditions category just evaluate something and succeed or fail upon the result of the evaluation. That is the case of the **Checks if files exist** entry you used in the tutorial.

Whichever the job entry, you can use the result of its execution to decide which of the entries following it execute and which don't.

In the tutorial, you included an entry that evaluates the existence of a folder. If the condition evaluates to true, the entry succeeds. Then the execution follows the green hop toward the **Write to Log** entry which will report it in the Kettle log.

If the condition evaluates to false, that is, the folder does not exist, the entry fails. Then the execution follows the red path toward the **Create a folder** entry.

So, when you create a job, you not only arrange the entries and hops according the expected order of execution, but also specify under which condition each job entry runs.

You define the conditions in the hops. You can identify the different hops either by looking at the color of the arrow or at the small icon on it. The following table lists the possibilities:

A hop that looks...	And had the following icon...	Represents...	Which means that...
Black		Unconditional execution	The destination entry executes no matter what the result of the previous entry is.
Green		Execution upon success	The destination entry executes only if the previous job entry was successful.
Red		Execution upon failure	The destination entry executes only if the previous job entry failed.

At any hop, you can define the condition under which the destination job entry will execute. In most cases, the first hop that leaves an entry is created green. The second hop is created red. You can change the color, that is, the behavior of the hop. Just right-click on the hop, select **Evaluation**, and then the condition.

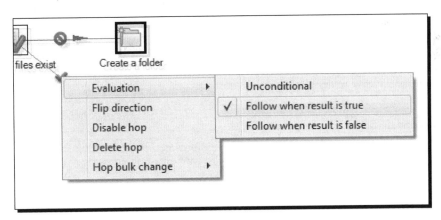

Or easier than that, you click on the small icon on the arrow as you did in the tutorial. Each time you click on it, the type of hop changes.

One exception is the hop or hops that leave the **START** entry. You cannot edit them; the destination job entries always execute unconditionally.

Another exception is the special entry **Dummy** which does nothing; it doesn't even allow you to decide if the job entries after it run or not. They always run.

No matter if an entry fails or succeeds, you can force the job to change this result.

Suppose that you expect that the chapter10 folder doesn't exist, or if it exists, there are no files in it. You can evaluate this with Kettle. If you find out that the condition is not true, you can write a message to the log, and force an abortion just by appending an **Abort job** entry and the end of the flow. In general, you can append an **Abort job** entry to any entry forcing the job to fail.

On the contrary, if you append a **Success** entry after any entry, you are ignoring the error in case that entry fails.

Looking at the results in the Execution results window

The **Execution results** window shows you what is happening while you run a job. As said, the difference compared to the same window in the case of having a transformation is that you have a **Job metrics** tab instead of the **Step Metrics** one.

The Logging tab

The **Logging** tab shows the execution of your job. By default, the level of the logging detail is Basic, but you can choose among the following options: **Nothing at all, Error logging only, Minimal logging, Basic logging, Detailed logging, Debugging or Rowlevel (very detailed)**. The list is the same one that you learned back in *Chapter 2, Getting Started with Transformations*, when you started working with transformations. In order to change the log level, you just select the proper option in the drop-down list available in the **Execute a job** window. Just as you do when you run transformations, you should choose the option depending on the level of detail that you want to see.

The Job metrics tab

The **Job metrics** tab shows, for each entry of the job, several status and information columns. For us, the most relevant columns in this tab are:

Column	Description
Comment	Status of the execution, for example, Start of job execution.
Result	Result of the execution as explained above. Possible values are Success or Failure.
Reason	The reason why this entry is being executed, for example, Followed link after success.

Note that the content of both **Logging** and **Job metrics** tabs are color-coded. When there is an error, you see the lines in red. When an entry succeeds, you can see the details in green. The rest of the information is shown in a black font.

Besides, the result of the execution of individual entries is represented with small ticks on top of the icons as shown in the following screenshot:

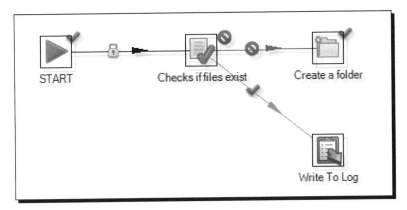

Running transformations from jobs

In the previous tutorials, you created simple jobs and learned some basics about working with Spoon during the design process of a job. Now you are ready to learn one of the most common tasks people do with jobs, running transformations.

Time for action – generating a range of dates and inspecting how things are running

In this tutorial, you will run the transformation you created in the tutorial, *Time for action – generating a range of dates and inspecting the data as it is being created* from *Chapter 2, Getting Started with Transformations*. The novelty here is that you will run it from a job as shown:

1. Run Spoon and create a new job.

2. Expand the **General** category of entries and drag a **START** and a **Transformation** entry to the canvas.

3. Create a hop form the **START** entry to the **Transformation** entry.

4. Save the job.

5. Before continuing, look for the transformation that generated a date range—the one that you created back in *Chapter 2, Getting Started with Transformations*. Copy it to a folder named `transformations` inside the folder where you just saved your job. Rename it as `generating_date_range.ktr`.

6. Now double-click on the **Transformation** entry.

7. Position the cursor in the **Transformation filename:** textbox, press *Ctrl* + Space, and select **${Internal.Job.Filename.Directory}**.

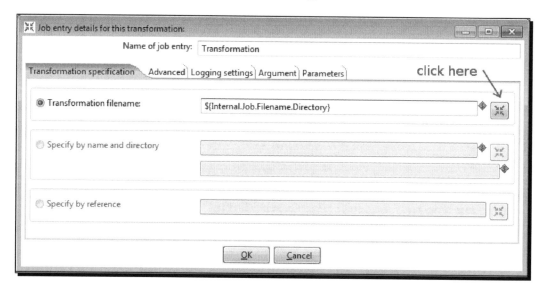

This variable is the counterpart to the variable `{Internal.Transformation.Filename.Directory}` you already know. `{Internal.Job.Filename.Directory}` evaluates the directory where the job resides.

8. Then click on the icon to the left of the textbox. A window appears that let you search for the transformation file in your system file.

9. As you can see, the `{Internal.Job.Filename.Directory}` variable provides a convenient starting place for looking up the transformation file. Select the transformation **generating_date_range.ktr** and click on **OK**.

10. Now the **Transformation filename:** textbox has the full path to the transformation. Replace the full job path back to **${Internal.Job.Filename.Directory}** so the final text for the **Transformation filename:** field is as shown in the following screenshot:

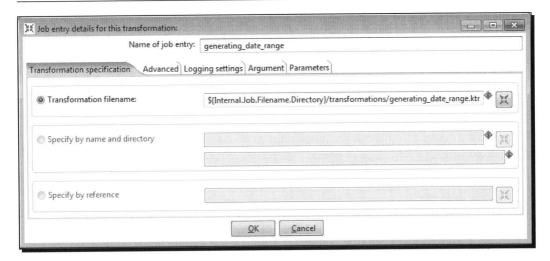

11. Click on **OK**.

12. Save the job and run it.

13. While running, a special tick appears on top of the Transformation icon, meaning that the transformation is being executed.

14. While running, right-click on the transformation icon and select **Open Transformation**. The transformation will be opened, and you will see how it is being executed.

As usual, you could do sniff test. Remember that you do it by right-clicking on any step and selecting any of the **Sniff** test during execution options in the contextual menu. For more details on this, please refer to *Chapter 2, Getting Started with Transformations*.

15. Select the job tab again. You will see that the log also displays information about the execution of the transformation that is called by the job.

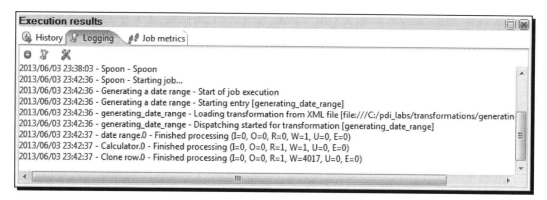

What just happened?

You created a job that called the transformation that generated a range of dates. You ran the job and tried a Kettle feature named drill-down. While the transformation was running, you right-clicked on the entry and opened the transformation. Then, you could see what was going on inside it.

After drilling-down you also run some sniff-testing, that is, inspected the data that was being generated by the transformation.

Using the Transformation job entry

The **Transformation job** entry allows you to call a transformation from a job.

There are several situations where you may need to use a **Transformation job** entry.

Sometimes, the job just keeps your work organized. Consider the transformations that loaded the dimension tables for the `js` database. As you will usually run them together, you can embed them into a single job as shown in the following screenshot:

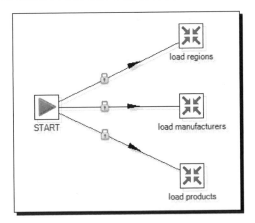

The only task done by this job is to keep the transformations together. Although the picture implies that the entries are run in parallel, that is not the case.

 Job entries typically execute sequentially, this being one of the central differences between jobs and transformations.

When you link two entries with a hop, you force an order of execution. On the contrary, when you create a job as the shown in the preceding screenshot, you need not give an order and the entries still run in sequence, one entry after another depending on the creation sequence.

Launching job entries in parallel

As the transformations that load dimensions are not depending on each other, as an option, you can ask the **START** job entry to launch them simultaneously. To do that, right-click on the **START** entry and select **Launch next entries in parallel**. Once selected, the arrows to the next job entries will be shown in dashed lines.

This option is available in any entry, not just in the START entry.

The jobs explained earlier are just two examples of how and when you use a **Transformation job** entry. Note that many transformations perform their tasks by themselves. That is the case of the transformation you ran in the tutorial that generated a range of dates. In this case, we created a job with just a **START** entry, followed by a **Transformation job** entry in order to show you how to run transformations from jobs, and also to apply the drill-down feature. In general, you will not do this. If it makes sense to run the transformation alone, you can do it. You are not forced to embed it into a job.

On the other side, not all jobs involve transformations. You already saw examples of that in the first tutorials in this chapter. Other examples are jobs that copy or move files, run external scripts, run bulk loading processes, and more.

Have a go hero – loading the dimension tables

Create a job that loads the main dimension tables in the jigsaw database: manufacturers, products, and regions. Test the job.

Receiving arguments and parameters in a job

Jobs, as well as transformations, are more flexible when receiving parameters from outside. You already learned to parameterize your transformations by using named parameters and command-line arguments. Let's extend these concepts to jobs.

Time for action – generating a hello world file by using arguments and parameters

In this tutorial, you will use all that you have learned so far, and at the same time, you will learn how to send arguments and parameters form a job to a transformation.

In the first place, let's create a new version of the Hello world transformation you created in *Chapter 1, Getting Started with Pentaho Data Integration*.

1. Create a new transformation.

2. Press *Ctrl + T* to bring the **Transformation properties** window.

3. Select the **Parameters** tab and add a named parameter. Call it HELLOFOLDER. As default value, type chapter10 and click on **OK**.

4. Drag a **Get System Info** step to the canvas.

5. Double-click on the step and add a field named `yourname`. As **Type**, select `command-line argument 1`.

6. Click on **OK** and add a **UDJE** step.

7. Use the step to add a `String` field named message. As **Java expression**, type `"Hello, " + yourname + "!"`.

8. Finally, add a **Text file output** step.

9. Use the step to send the message data to a file. As file name, type `${LABSOUTPUT}/${HELLOFOLDER}/hello`.

10. Save the transformation in the `transformations` folder that you created in the previous tutorial, under the name `hello_world_param.ktr`.

11. Close it.

The transformation is ready. Now let's create the main job:

1. Create a job named `hello_world_param.kjb`.

2. Add a **START**, **Create a folder**, and **Transformation** entries, and link them in that order.

3. Press *Ctrl + J* to open the **Job properties** window.

4. Select the **Parameters** tab and add the same named parameter that you added in the transformation. Then click on **OK**.

5. Double-click on the **Create a folder** entry.

6. In the **Folder name** textbox content type `${LABSOUTPUT}/${HELLOFOLDER}`.

7. Uncheck the **Fail if folder exists:** switch, and click on **OK** to close the window.

8. Double-click on the **Transformation** entry.

9. Change the **Transformation filename:** textbox to point to the new transformation: `${Internal.Job.Filename.Directory}/transformations/hello_world_param.ktr`. Then click on **OK**.

10. Save the job in the same directory as the transformations folder and press *F9* to run the job.

11. Fill the dialog window with a value for the named parameter and a value for the command-line argument as shown in the following screenshot. Then click on **Launch**.

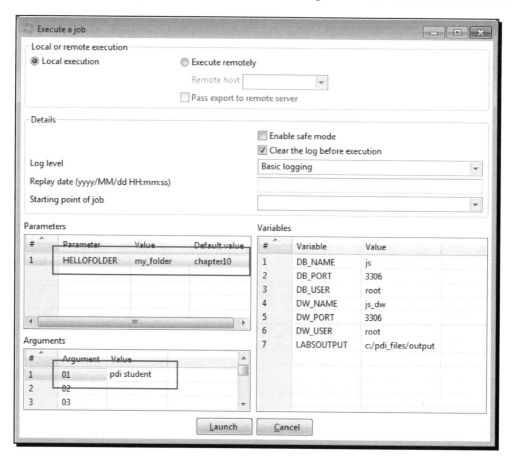

12. When the execution finishes, check the output folder. The folder named `my_folder` that you specified as named parameter was created.

13. Inside that folder there should be a file named `hello.txt`. This time the content of the file has been customized with the name you provided:

```
Hello, pdi student!
```

What just happened?

You created a transformation that generated a Hello file in the folder given as named parameter. The content of the file is a customized "Hello" message that gets the name of the reader from the command-line.

In the main job, you also defined a named parameter, the same that you defined in the transformation. The job needs the parameter to create the folder.

When you run the job, you provided both the command-line argument and the named parameter in the job dialog window that shows up when you launch the execution. After that, a folder was created with the name you gave, and a file was generated customized with the name you typed as argument.

Using named parameters in jobs

You can use named parameters in jobs in the same way you do in transformations. You define them in the **Job properties** window. You provide names and default values, and then you use them just as regular variables. The places where you can use variables, just as in a transformation, are identified with a dollar sign to the right of the textboxes. In the tutorial, you used the name parameter in the **Create a folder** job entry. In this particular example, you used the same named parameter both in the main job and in the transformation called by the job. So, you defined the named parameter HELLOFOLDER in two places—in the **Job settings** window and in the **Transformation properties** window.

Have a go hero – backing up your work

Suppose you want to back up regularly your output files, that is, the files in your ${LABSOUTPUT} directory. Build a job that creates a ZIP file with all your output files. For the name and location of the ZIP file, use two named parameters.

Use the **Zip file** job entry located in the **File management** category.

Running jobs from a terminal window

In the main tutorial of this section, both the job and the transformation called by the job used a named parameter. The transformation also required a command-line argument. When you executed the job from Spoon, you provided both the parameter and the argument in the job dialog window. You will learn to launch the job and provide that information from a terminal window.

Time for action – executing the hello world job from a terminal window

In order to run the job from a terminal window, follow these instructions:

1. Open a terminal window.

2. Go to the directory where Kettle is installed.

   ❑ On Windows systems, type:

   ```
   C:\pdi-ce>kitchen /file:c:/pdi_labs/hello_world_param.kjb
   Maria
       -param:"HELLOFOLDER=my_work" /norep
   ```

   ❑ On Unix, Linux, and other Unix-like systems type:

   ```
   /home/yourself/pdi-ce/kitchen.sh
       /file:/home/yourself/pdi_labs/hello_world_param.kjb Maria
       -param:"HELLOFOLDER=my_work" /norep
   ```

3. If your job is in another folder, modify the command accordingly. You may also replace the name `Maria` with your name, of course. If your name has spaces, enclose the whole argument within `" "`, for example in `"Maria R"`.

4. You will see how the job runs, showing you the log in the terminal:

```
 C:\windows\system32\cmd.exe

INFO  03-06 23:51:20,081 - Kitchen - Start of run.
INFO  03-06 23:51:20,198 - hello_world_param - Start of job execution
INFO  03-06 23:51:20,203 - hello_world_param - Starting entry [Create folder $(HELLOFOLDER
>]
INFO  03-06 23:51:20,207 - hello_world_param - Starting entry [hello_world_param]
INFO  03-06 23:51:20,209 - hello_world_param - Loading transformation from XML file [file:
///c:/pdi_labs/transformations/hello_world_param.ktr]
INFO  03-06 23:51:20,318 - hello_world_param - Dispatching started for transformation [hel
lo_world_param]
INFO  03-06 23:51:20,422 - Get your name - Finished processing (I=0, O=0, R=1, W=1, U=0, E
=0)
INFO  03-06 23:51:20,790 - Hello Message - Finished processing (I=0, O=0, R=1, W=1, U=0, E
=0)
INFO  03-06 23:51:20,793 - hello file - Finished processing (I=0, O=1, R=1, W=1, U=0, E=0)

INFO  03-06 23:51:20,821 - hello_world_param - Finished job entry [hello_world_param] (res
ult=[true])
INFO  03-06 23:51:20,822 - hello_world_param - Finished job entry [Create folder $(HELLOFO
LDER)] (result=[true])
INFO  03-06 23:51:20,824 - hello_world_param - Job execution finished
INFO  03-06 23:51:20,827 - Kitchen - Finished!
INFO  03-06 23:51:20,828 - Kitchen - Start=2013/06/03 23:51:20.003, Stop=2013/06/03 23:51:
20.828
INFO  03-06 23:51:20,829 - Kitchen - Processing ended after 0 seconds.
```

5. Go to the output folder, the folder pointed by your LABS_OUTPUT variable.

6. A folder named `my_work` should have been created.

7. Check the content of the folder. A file named `hello.txt` should be there. Edit the file. You should see the following:

```
Hello, Maria!
```

What just happened?

You ran the job with **Kitchen**, the program that executes jobs from a terminal window.

After the name of the command, `kitchen.bat` or `kitchen.sh`, depending on the platform, you provided the following:

- The full path to the job file: `/file:c:/pdi_labs/hello_world_param.kjb`
- A command-line argument: `Maria`
- A named parameter: `-param:"HELLOFOLDER=my_work"`
- The switch `/norep` to tell Kettle not to connect to a repository

After running the job, you could see that the folder had been created and a file with a custom "Hello" message had been generated.

Here you used some of the options available when you ran Kitchen. *Appendix B, Pan and Kitchen – Launching Transformations and Jobs from the Command Line*, tells you all the details about using Kitchen for running jobs.

Have a go hero – experiencing Kitchen

Run the `hello_world_param.kjb` job from Kitchen with and without providing arguments and parameters. See what happens in each case.

Using named parameters and command-line arguments in transformations

As you know, transformations accept both arguments from the command line and named parameters. When you run a transformation from Spoon, you supply the values for arguments and named parameters in the transformation dialog window that shows up when you launch the execution. From a terminal window, you provide those values in the Pan command line. Remember from *Chapter 3, Manipulating Real-world Data*, that Pan is the program that runs transformations from a terminal window.

In this chapter, you have learned to run a transformation embedded in a job. Here the methods you have for supplying named parameters and arguments needed by the transformation are quite similar. From Spoon, you supply the values in the job dialog window that shows up when you launch the job execution. From the terminal window, you provide the values in the Kitchen command line.

Whether you run a job from Spoon or from Kitchen, the named parameters and arguments you provide are unique, and shared by the main job and all transformations called by that job. Each transformation, as well as the main job, may or may not use them according to their needs.

There is still another way in which you can pass parameters and arguments to a transformation. Let's understand it by some examples.

Time for action – calling the hello world transformation with fixed arguments and parameters

In this tutorial, you will call the parameterized transformation from a new job.

1. Open the `hello_world_param.kjb` job you created in the previous tutorial and save it as `hello_world_fixedvalues.kjb`.

2. Double-click on the **Create a folder** job entry.

3. Replace the `${HELLOFOLDER}` string with the string `fixedfolder`.

4. Double-click on the **Transformation job** entry and fill the **Argument** tab as follows:

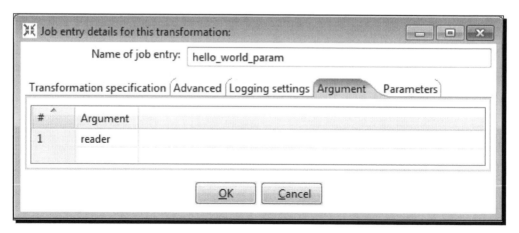

5. Click on the **Parameters** tab and fill it as follows:

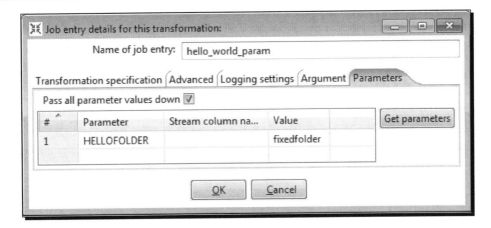

6. Click on **OK** and save the job.

7. Open a terminal window and go to the directory where Kettle is installed.

   ❏ On Windows systems type:

```
C:\pdi-ce>kitchen /file:c:/pdi_labs/hello_world_param.kjb
   /norep
```

   ❏ On Unix, Linux, and other Unix-like systems type:

```
/home/yourself/pdi-ce/kitchen.sh
   /file:/home/yourself/pdi_labs/hello_world_param.kjb /
norep
```

8. When the executions finishes, check the output folder. A folder named `fixedfolder` has been created.

9. In that folder, there is a file `hello.txt` with the following content:

```
Hello, reader!
```

What just happened?

You reused the transformation that expects an argument and a named parameter from the command line. This time you created a job that called the transformation and set both the parameter and the argument in the **Transformation job** entry setting window.

Then you ran the job from a terminal window without typing any arguments or parameters. It didn't make a difference for the transformation. Whether you provide parameters and arguments from the command line or you set constant fixed values in a **Transformation job** entry, the transformation does its job—creating a file with a custom message in the folder with the name given by the ${HELLOFOLDER} parameter.

Instead of running from the terminal window, you could have ran the job by pressing *F9* and then clicking **Launch**, without typing anything in either the parameter or the argument grid. The final result should be exactly the same.

Have a go hero – saying hello again and again

Modify the `hello_world_param.kjb` job so it generates three files in the default `${HELLOFOLDER}`, each saying "hello" to a different person.

After the creation of the folder, use three transformation job entries. Provide different arguments for each.

Run the job to see that it works as expected.

Have a go hero – loading the time dimension from a job

Earlier in the book, namely in *Chapter 2, Getting Started with Transformations*, *Chapter 7, Transforming the Row Set*, and *Chapter 8, Working with Databases*, you built a transformation that created the data for a time dimension and loaded it into a time dimension table.

The transformation had several named parameters, one of them being `START_DATE`. Create a job that loads a time dimension with dates starting at `01/01/2000`. In technical words, create a job that calls your transformation and passes a fixed value for the `START_DATE` parameter.

Deciding between the use of a command-line argument and a named parameter

Both command-line arguments and named parameters are means for creating more flexible jobs and transformations. The following table summarizes the differences and reasons for using one or the other. In the first column, the word argument refers to the external value you will use in your job or transformation. That argument could be implemented as a named parameter or as a command-line argument.

Situation	Solution using named parameters	Solution using arguments
It is desirable to have a default for the argument.	Named parameters are perfect in this case. You provide default values at the time you define them.	Before using the command-line argument, you have to evaluate if it was provided in the command line. If not, you have to set the default value at that moment.
The argument is mandatory.	You don't have means to determine if the user provided a value for the named parameter.	To know if the user provided a value for the command-line argument, you just get the command-line argument and compare it to a null value.
You need several arguments but it is probable that not all of them are present.	If you don't have a value for a named parameter, you are not forced to enter it when you run the job or transformation.	Let's suppose that you expect three command-line arguments. If you have a value only for the third, you still have to provide empty values for the first and the second.
You need several arguments and it is highly probable that all of them are present.	The command-line would be too long. It will be clear the purpose for each parameter, but typing the command line would be tedious.	The command line is simple as you just list the values one after the other. However, there is a risk—you may unintentionally enter the values unordered, which could lead to unexpected results.
You want to use the argument in several places.	You can do it, but you must assure that the value will not be overwritten in the middle of the execution.	You can get the command-line argument by using a **Get System Info** step as many times as you need.
You need to use the value in a place where a variable is needed.	Named parameters are ready to be used as Kettle variables.	First, you need to set a variable with the command-line argument value. Usually this requires creating additional transformations to be run before any other job or transformation.

Depending on your particular situation, you would prefer one or the other solution. Note that you can mix both as you did in the previous tutorials.

Have a go hero – analyzing the use of arguments and named parameters

In the *Time for Action - generating a hello world file by using arguments and parameters* section, you created a transformation that used an argument and a named parameter. Based on the preceding table, try to understand why the folder was defined as named parameter and the name of the person you want to say Hello to was defined as a command-line argument. Would you have applied the same approach?

Summary

In this chapter, you have learned the basics about PDI jobs—what a job is, what you can do with a job, and how jobs are different from transformations. In particular, you have learned to use a job for running one or more transformations.

You also saw how to use named parameters in jobs, and how to supply parameters and arguments to transformations when they are run from jobs.

In the next chapter, you will learn to create jobs that are a little more elaborate than the jobs you created here, which will give you more power to implement all types of processes.

11
Creating Advanced Transformations and Jobs

When you design and implement jobs in PDI, you not only want certain tasks to be accomplished, but also want a clean and organized work; a work that can be reused, easy to maintain, and more. In order to accomplish these objectives, you still need to learn some advanced PDI techniques.

This chapter is about learning techniques for creating complex transformations and jobs. Among other things, you will learn to:

◆   Create subtransformations

◆   Implement process flows

◆   Nest jobs

◆   Iterate the execution of jobs and transformations

You already are quite an expert with Spoon! Therefore, in this chapter we will not give much space to details such as how to configure a **Text file input** step. Instead, we will focus on more generic procedures, in order to focus on the techniques you will learn.

 If you get into trouble, you can refer to earlier chapters, browse the Wikipedia page for a specific step or job entry, or simply download the material for the chapter from the book's site.

Re-using part of your transformations

In occasions you have bunches of steps that do common tasks and you notice that you will want to use them in other contexts, that is, you would copy, paste, and reuse part of your work. This is one of the motivations for the use of subtransformations—a concept that you will learn in this section.

Time for action – calculating statistics with the use of a subtransformations

Suppose that you are responsible to collect the results of an annual examination that is being taken in a language school. The examination evaluates English, Mathematics, Science, History, and Geography skills. Every professor gives the exam paper to the students, the students take the examination, the professors grade the examinations on a scale of 0-100 for each skill, and write the results in a text file, like the following:

```
student_code;name;english;mathematics;science;history_and_geo
80711-85;William Miller;81;83;80;90
20362-34;Jennifer Martin;87;76;70;80
75283-17;Margaret Wilson;99;94;90;80
83714-28;Helen Thomas;89;97;80;80
61666-55;Maria Thomas;88;77;70;80
00647-35;David Collins;88;95;90;90
```

All the files follow that pattern.

In this section and in the sections to come, you will use these files to run different kinds of transformations. Before starting, get the sample files from the book site.

Now, let's start by calculating some statistics on the data.

1. Open Spoon and create a new transformation.
2. Create a named parameter to create a parameter named FILENAME and set the following default value: ${LABSINPUT}\exam1.txt.
3. Read the file by using a **Text file input** step. As filename, type ${FILENAME}.

> The **Text file input** preview and the **Get fields** functions will not be able to resolve the named parameter, If you want to preview the file or get the fields, you can hardcode the path first, get the fields, then replace the explicit path with the named parameter.

✱ STUDENT_NAME

4. After reading the file, add a **Sort rows** step to sort the rows by the `english` field in descending order.

5. Then add an **Add sequence** step and use it for adding a field named `seq`.

6. With a **Filter rows** step, keep the first ten rows. As filter, enter `seq <= 10`.

7. Add a **Group by** step. So far, you have this:

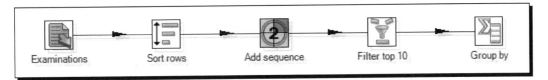

8. Double-click on the **Group by** step and configure it as shown:

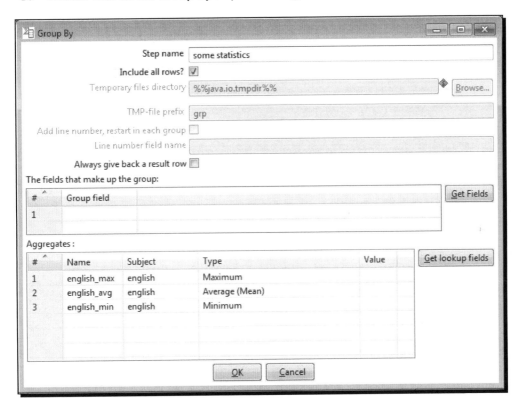

9. Do a preview on the last step. You will see the following statistics about the `english` field, that is, the scores that the students got in English:

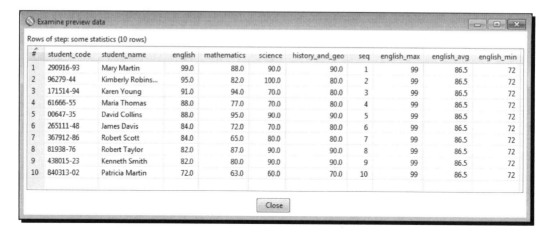

#	student_code	student_name	english	mathematics	science	history_and_geo	seq	english_max	english_avg	english_min
1	290916-93	Mary Martin	99.0	88.0	90.0	90.0	1	99	86.5	72
2	96279-44	Kimberly Robins...	95.0	82.0	100.0	80.0	2	99	86.5	72
3	171514-94	Karen Young	91.0	94.0	70.0	80.0	3	99	86.5	72
4	61666-55	Maria Thomas	88.0	77.0	70.0	80.0	4	99	86.5	72
5	00647-35	David Collins	88.0	95.0	90.0	90.0	5	99	86.5	72
6	265111-48	James Davis	84.0	72.0	70.0	80.0	6	99	86.5	72
7	367912-86	Robert Scott	84.0	65.0	80.0	80.0	7	99	86.5	72
8	81938-76	Robert Taylor	82.0	87.0	90.0	90.0	8	99	86.5	72
9	438015-23	Kenneth Smith	82.0	80.0	90.0	90.0	9	99	86.5	72
10	840313-02	Patricia Martin	72.0	63.0	60.0	70.0	10	99	86.5	72

Note that we have checked the **Include all rows?** flag. This means that along with the statistics, we have kept the original rows with their values.

So far you have calculated some statistics on the top ten English scores. Nothing new so far. Now suppose that you want to see the same statistics, but for the Mathematics scores. You should replace the `english` field with the `math` field in several places. Not only that, you also want the same statistics for the rest of the subjects—Science, History, and Geography. You can do many changes, but there is a more convenient approach:

1. Create a new transformation and give it the name `map_statistics`.

2. From the **Mapping** category of steps drag to the work area a **Mapping input specification** and a **Mapping output specification**.

3. Double-click on the **Mapping input specification** step and fill it as shown:

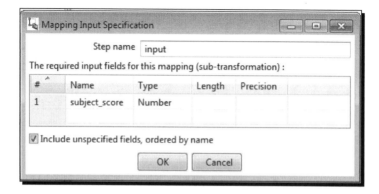

4. Select the transformation you created previously, copy all steps but the **Text file input** step, and paste them in the new transformation. Link the steps so that you have the following:

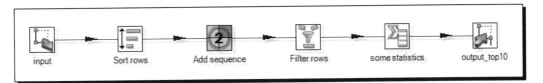

5. Modify the configuration of the **Sort rows** step in order to sort by the subject_ score field.

6. In the **Group by** field, replace all occurrences of the english field with subject_ score. Also, replace the names of the new fields with score_max, score_avg, and score_min in that order.

7. Save the transformation.

8. Select the transformation you created previously and remove all steps, but the **Text file input** step.

9. From the **Mapping** category of steps, drag to the work area a **Mapping (sub-transformation)** step. Create a link from the **Text file input** step towards this new step.

10. Double-click on the Mapping step for configuring it. Maximize the window so that you can see clearly all the available options.

11. Under **Use a file for the mapping transformation** in the **Mapping transformation** frame, type ${Internal.Transformation.Filename.Directory}/map_ statistics.ktr.

12. Select the **Input** tab, and fill the grid as shown:

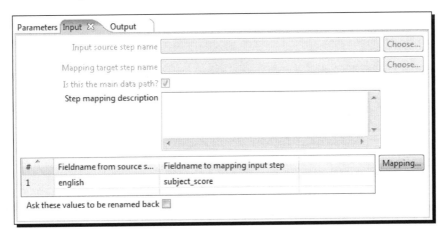

13. Select the **Output** tab, and fill the grid as shown:

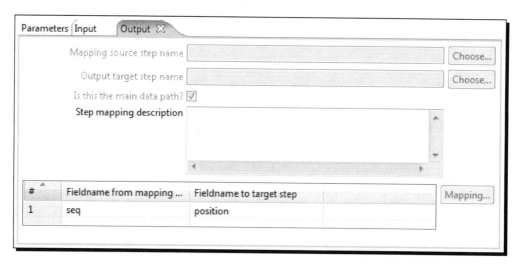

14. Close the window.

15. Do a preview on the Mapping step. If everything runs as expected, you should see the same result as before, except for the name of the `english` column:

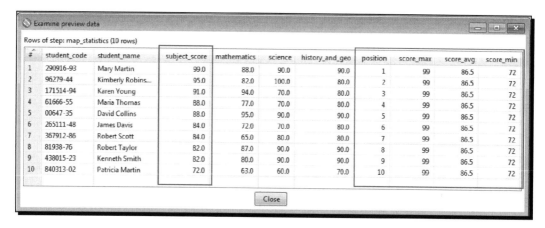

So far, you have the same final data you had in the first part of the section. Now, you have two transformations instead of just one! What is the advantage? Let's see:

1. Double-click on the **Mapping** step, select the Input step, and modify the grid, replace `english` with `mathematics`.

2. Do a preview and you will see the following screenshot:

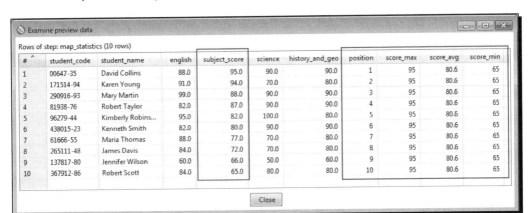

#	student_code	student_name	english	subject_score	science	history_and_geo	position	score_max	score_avg	score_min
1	00647-35	David Collins	88.0	95.0	90.0	90.0	1	95	80.6	65
2	171514-94	Karen Young	91.0	94.0	70.0	80.0	2	95	80.6	65
3	290916-93	Mary Martin	99.0	88.0	90.0	90.0	3	95	80.6	65
4	81938-76	Robert Taylor	82.0	87.0	90.0	90.0	4	95	80.6	65
5	96279-44	Kimberly Robins...	95.0	82.0	100.0	80.0	5	95	80.6	65
6	438015-23	Kenneth Smith	82.0	80.0	90.0	90.0	6	95	80.6	65
7	61666-55	Maria Thomas	88.0	77.0	70.0	80.0	7	95	80.6	65
8	265111-48	James Davis	84.0	72.0	70.0	80.0	8	95	80.6	65
9	137817-80	Jennifer Wilson	60.0	66.0	50.0	60.0	9	95	80.6	65
10	367912-86	Robert Scott	84.0	65.0	80.0	80.0	10	95	80.6	65

3. Repeat these last steps, replacing `mathematics` with `science`.

4. Do it one more time, now using the last field `history_and_geo`. Each time you will get a different result.

What just happened?

You read a file with the scores obtained by students in different subjects. Then you calculated some statistics.

First of all, you calculated and previewed some statistics, namely maximum, average, and minimum over the top ten scores for a particular subject, English.

Then you wanted the same figures, but for the rest of the subjects—Mathematics, Science, History, and Geography. In order to avoid doing too many changes here and there, you moved the calculations to a special transformation—a subtransformation.

The subtransformation received a field, `subject_score`, and calculated the different statistics based on the value of that field. In the main transformation, you simply use a mapping step for executing that subtransformation. By creating a correspondence between the `english` field in your main transformation and the `subject_score` in the subtransformation, you got the same results.

You changed the correspondence between each score field and the `subject_score` field three more times, once for each subject. Doing it this way, you could preview the different statistics just by changing a simple mapping in the **Input** tab of the mapping step.

Creating and using subtransformations

Subtransformations are, as the name suggests, transformations inside transformations.

> The PDI proper name for a subtransformation is mapping. However, as the word mapping is also used with other meanings in PDI—an example of that is the mapping of table fields with stream fields in a **Table output** step, we will use the more intuitive name sub-transformation.

In the section, you created a subtransformation to isolate a task that you needed to apply four times. This is a common reason for creating subtransformation—to isolate functionality that is likely to be needed more than once. Then you called the subtransformation by using a single step.

Let's see how subtransformations work. A subtransformation is like a regular transformation but it has input and output steps that connect it to the transformations that use it.

The **Mapping input specification** step defines the entry point to the subtransformation. You specify here just the fields needed by the subtransformations. In particular, you specify the fields that are subject to change. The **Mapping output specification** step simply defines where the flow ends.

> The presence of the **Mapping input specification** and **Mapping output specification** steps is the only fact that makes a subtransformations different from a regular transformation.

In the sample subtransformation you created in the previous section, you defined a single field named subject_score. Then you added a bunch of steps in order to calculate the different statistics over the value of that field.

You call or execute a subtransformation by using a **Mapping (sub-transformation)** step. In order to execute the subtransformation successfully, you have to establish a relationship between your fields and the fields defined in the **Mapping input specification** step in the subtransformation.

Let's see first how you define the relationship between your data and the input specification. For the sample subtransformation, you have to define which of your fields is to be used as the input field subject_score defined in the input specification. You do it in an **Input** tab in the Mapping step dialog window. The first time you tried the mapping step, you told the subtransformation that uses the field english as its subject_score field.

If you look at the output fields coming out of the mapping step, you will no longer see the `english` field, but a field named `subject_score`. It is the same field, `english`, that was renamed. If you don't want your fields to be renamed, simply check the **Ask these values to be renamed back on output?** option found in the **Input** tab. This will cause the field to be renamed back to its original name, `english` in this example.

Now let's see now how you define the relationship between your data and the output specification. If the subtransformation creates new fields, you may or may not want to add them to your main dataset. To add to your dataset, a field created in the subtransformation, you use an **Output** tab of the Mapping step dialog window. In the previous section, you added several fields, but in the **Output** tab, you only defined one of them, `seq`. You did this to rename the field named `seq` in the subtransformation as position in the main transformation. Note that the rest of the fields—`max_score`, `avg_score`, and `min_score`—were also added with the same name as they were created in the subtransformation.

If you want the subtransformation to simply transform the incoming stream without adding new fields, or if you are not interested in the fields added in the subtransformation, you don't need to create an **Output** tab.

The following drawing summarizes what is explained above. The upper and lower grids show the datasets before and after the stream has flown through the subtransformation.

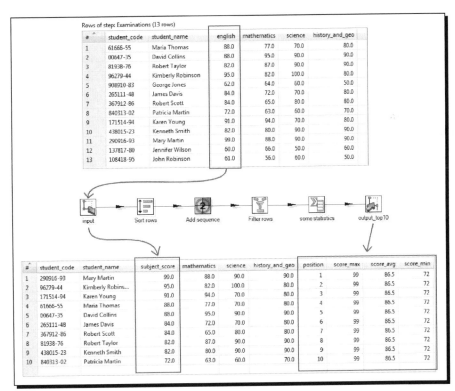

The subtransformation in the section allowed you to reuse a bunch of steps that you wanted to use several times with different arguments—namely the name of the score field. This way, you avoided doing the same task several times. Another common situation where you may use subtransformations is the one where you have a transformation with too many steps. If you can identify a subset of steps which accomplish a specific purpose, you may move those steps to a subtransformation. Doing so, your transformation will become cleaner and easier to understand.

> While you are designing a subtransformation, you can provisionally substitute the **Mapping input specification** step with a step that provides some fictional data, for example, a **Data Grid** step. This way you can test it before calling it from a main transformation.

You can have subtransformations without Mapping input or Mapping output specifications. You can also have more than one Mapping input or Mapping output specification in a subtransformation. We will not learn those particular cases in this book. If you are interested in learning more, you can find examples and more background on subtransformations in the book *Pentaho Data Integration Cookbook* by Packt Publishing.

Have a go hero – calculating statistics for all subjects

Modify the main transformation you created in the section in the following way:

Generate four files—one for each different subject. Each file will have the student name and score for the top ten students in each subject—English, Mathematics, and so on.

> You can do this in a single transformation. Just call the subtransformation four times.

Have a go hero – counting words more precisely (second version)

Combine the following exercises from *Chapter 4, Filtering, Searching, and Performing Other Useful Operations with Data*:

- *Have a go hero – playing with filters*
- *Have a go hero – counting words more precisely*

Create a subtransformation that receives a string value and cleans it. Remove extra signs that may appear as part of the string, for example, . ,) or ". Then convert the string to lower case.

Also, create a flag that tells if the string is a valid word. Remember that the word is valid if:

- Its length is at least three, or it is in a list of words you don't want to exclude, such as sun
- It is not in a given list of common words

Retrieve the modified word and the flag.

Modify the main transformation by using the subtransformation. After the subtransformation step, filter the words by looking at the flag.

Creating a job as a process flow

In this new section and the rest of the chapter, we will continue working with the examination files, but using and transforming the data in different ways.

Despite being very simple, the following section will serve you to learn a very useful technique for letting the data flow from one transformation to another. In other words, you will learn to create a very simple process flow. Let's see how to do it.

Time for action – generating top average scores by copying and getting rows

In this section, we will split our work into two different transformations:

- The first for reading the examination data and preparing it for further processing
- The second for picking that prepared data and do some work with it

As said, you will need the same input files you've been working with. Once you have the files, you are ready for work:

1. Open Spoon and create a new transformation.

2. Just as you did in the previous section, define a named parameter with the name of the file to read, and read the examination file with a **Text file input** step.

 It's not mandatory to use the named parameter, but we do it for two reasons: first, for getting the habit of creating reusable transformations and second, because we will use that parameter in the last sections of this chapter.

3. Use a **Java Filter** step to filter the students with low scores. As a filter enter the following:

```
(english<75)&&(mathematics<75)&&(science<75)&&(history_and_
geo<75)
```

4. Expand the **Job** category of steps and drag to the canvas a **Copy rows to result** step.

5. Create a hop from the filter towards this step. When asked for the kind of hop, select **Main output of step**.

6. Save the transformation as `prepare_data.ktr`. It should look as shown:

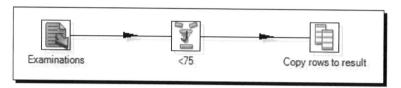

7. Create a new transformation.

8. From the **Job** category, drag to the canvas a **Get rows from result** step.

 Please be careful when selecting and dragging the step. Do not choose the **Get files from result** step which is just next to it, but serves a totally different purpose!

9. Double-click on the step and fill the window as follows:

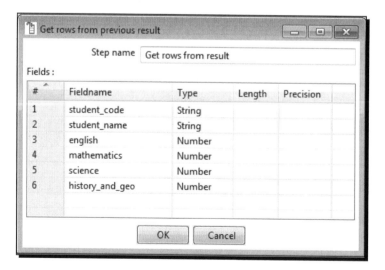

10. Close the window.

11. After this step, add a **User Defined Java Expression** and use it to create a new field with the average of the scores. Give the file the name `avg`, as **Java expression** type `(english+mathematics+science+history_and_geo)/4`, and as **Value type** select **Number**.

12. Add a **Sort rows** step and use it to sort the `avg` field in descending order.

13. Finally, send the results to a file: By using a **Text file output** step, configure the output to generate a file in `${LABSOUTPUT}/students_by_average_desc.txt`. As field, select `student_code, student_name` and `avg`.

14. Save the transformation as `process_data.ktr`. This transformation will look as shown:

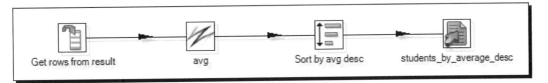

15. Now create a job.

16. Drag to the canvas a **START** and two **Transformation** job entries.

17. Link the entries so that you have the following:

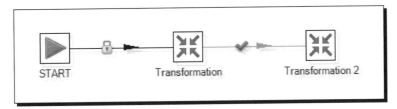

18. Configure the first **Transformation** entry to run the `prepare_data.ktr` transformation and the second to run the `process_data.ktr` transformation.

19. Define a named parameter identical to the one you defined in the `prepare_data.ktr`, that is, a parameter named `FILENAME` with `${LABSINPUT}\exam1.txt` as its default value.

20. Save the job and run it.

> If you experience problems with data types when attempting this exercise, make sure that you used number types instead of integer when reading the file.

 FIELD

21. Check the ${LABSOUTPUT} folder. You should see a new file named `students_by_average_desc.txt` with the following content:

```
student_code;student_name;avg
840313-02;Patricia Martin;66.25
908910-83;George Jones;59
137817-80;Jennifer Wilson;59
108418-95;John Robinson;56.75
```

What just happened?

You created a simple process flow. You created a job that runs two transformations, one after the other. The first of the transformations read a file with scores and prepared the data for processing—in this case, it simply filtered out the data you were not interested in. At the end of the stream, it copied the data for being processed later. The second transformation received that data already filtered and after calculating the average of the scores, sent the information to an output file. By using the **Copy rows to result** step, you sent the flow of data outside the transformation. By using **Get rows from result**, you picked that data to continue with the flow.

 Notice that you could have obtained exactly the same result if you put everything in a single transformation without using the copy rows/get rows steps. However, as you will learn in a bit, there are some benefits of doing things this way.

As a final remark, please note that in the main job, we defined a named parameter identical to the one needed for the first transformation. The way we have for passing the named parameters—the FILENAME parameter in this case—to the subtransformation is by selecting the check named **Pass all parameter values down to the sub-transformation** in the **Parameters** tab of the **Transformation** job entries. This check is selected by default. Therefore, the `prepare_data.ktr` transformation received the value of the FILENAME parameter, that is, the name of the file to process.

Transferring data between transformations by using the copy/get rows mechanism

The copy/get rows mechanism allows you to transfer data between two transformations, creating a process flow. The following figure shows you how it works:

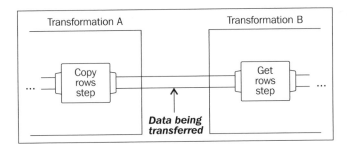

The **Copy rows to result** step transfers your rows of data to the outside of the transformation. Then you can pick that data by using a **Get rows from result** step. By calling the transformation that gets the rows right after the transformation that copy the rows, you get the same result as having all steps in a single transformation.

The copy of the dataset is made in the memory. It's useful when you have small datasets. For bigger datasets, you should prefer saving the data in a temporary file or database table in the first transformation, and then create the dataset from the file or table in the second transformation.

The **Serialize to file/De-serialize from file** steps are very useful for this since the data and the metadata are saved together.

There is no limit in the number of transformations that can be chained using this mechanism. Look at the following figure:

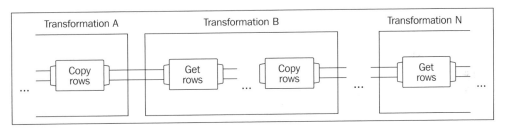

As you can see, you may have a transformation that copy the rows, followed by another that gets the row and copy again, followed by a third transformation that gets the rows, and so on.

Have a go hero – modifying the flow

Modify the last exercise in the following way:

♦ Include only the students who had an average score above 70

> Note that you have to modify just the transformation that prepares the information, without caring what the second process does with that data.

♦ Generate only the top five average scores

> Note that you have to modify just the transformation that processes the information, without caring how the list of students was built.

Iterating jobs and transformations

It may happen that you develop a job or a transformation to be executed several times, one for a different row of your data. Suppose, for example, you have to send a custom email to a list of customers. Then you would build a job that, for a given customer, gets the relevant data as name or e-mail account and send the e-mail. Then you would run the job manually several times, once for each customer. Instead of doing that, PDI allows you to execute the job automatically once for each customer in your list.

The same applies to transformations. If you have to execute the same transformation several times, once for each row of a set of data, you can do it by iterating the execution. The next section shows you how to do it.

Time for action – generating custom files by executing a transformation for every input row

Suppose that 75 is the threshold below which a student must retake the examination. Let's find out the list of students with at least one score below 75, that is, those who didn't succeed. Then, let's create one file per student telling him/her about this.

If you did the previous sections successfully, you should know that you already have half the work done! The `prepare_data.ktr` transformation builds the list of students. If not, before proceeding, please go back and create that transformation; you will need it now.

1. Create a new transformation.
2. Drag to the canvas a **Get rows from result** step.

3. Double-click on the **Get rows from result** step and use it to define two string fields: a field named `student_code` and another field named `student_name`.

4. Add a **User Defined Java Expression** step and create a hop from the **Get rows from result** step to this new step.

5. Double-click on the step and configure it as shown:

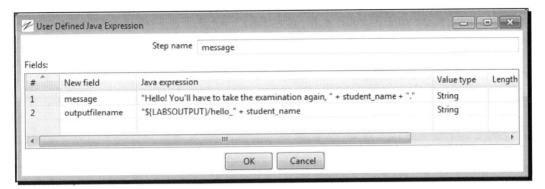

6. After that step, add a **Text file output** step, and double-click on the step to configure it.

7. Click on **Accept file name from field?**. As the filename field, select or type `outputfilename`, the field you just created.

8. In the content tab, uncheck **Header**. As field, select the field `message`.

9. Save the transformation under the name `hello_student.ktr`.

 You can't test this transformation alone. If you want to test it, just replace temporarily the **Copy rows from result** step by a **Generate rows** step, generate a single row with fixed values for the fields, and run the transformation.

10. Now create a job.

11. Drag to the canvas a **START**, a **Delete files** and two **Transformation** entries, and link them one after the other as shown:

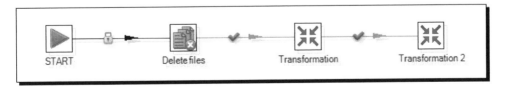

12. Save the job.

13. Double-click on the **Delete files** step. Fill the **Files/Folders:** grid with a single row. Under **File/Folder** type `${LABSOUTPUT}` and under **Wilcard (RegExp)** type `hello_.*\.txt`. This regular expression includes all `txt` files in the `${LABSOUTPUT}` folder whose name starts with `hello_`.

14. Configure the first **Transformation** entry to run the `prepare_data.ktr` transformation.

15. Double-click on the second **Transformation** entry. As **Transformation filename** type `${Internal.Job.Filename.Directory}/hello_student.ktr`.

16. On the **Advanced** tab, check the option **Execute for every input row?** and click on **OK**.

17. Save the job with the name `process_for_each_student.kjb` and press *F9* to run it.

18. When the execution finishes, explore the folder pointed by your `${LABSOUTPUT}` variable. You should see one file for each student in the list. The files are named `hello_<student_name>.txt`. The generated files look like the following:

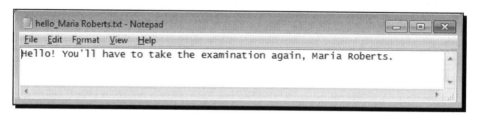

What just happened?

You reused a transformation that built a list of students that had to retake the examination. Then, for each student, you generated a file with a custom message.

In this section, you used the copy/get rows mechanism in a slightly different way compared to the previous section. In this case, the second transformation, the one that gets rows from results, runs once for every copied row, that is, once for each student in the list. Each time the transformation gets the rows from the result, it gets a single row with information about a single student and generates a file with the message for that student.

Executing for each row

The **execute for every input row?** option that you have in the **Transformation** entry setting window allows you to run the transformation once for every row copied in a previous transformation by using the **Copy rows to result** step. PDI executes the transformation as many times as the number of copied rows, one after the other. Each time the transformation executes, when it gets the rows from result, it gets a different row.

Note that in the transformation you don't limit the number of incoming rows. You simply assume that you are receiving a single row. If you forget to set the **execute for every input row?** switch in the job, the transformation will run but you will get unexpected results.

If you look at the log in the section, you can see it working:

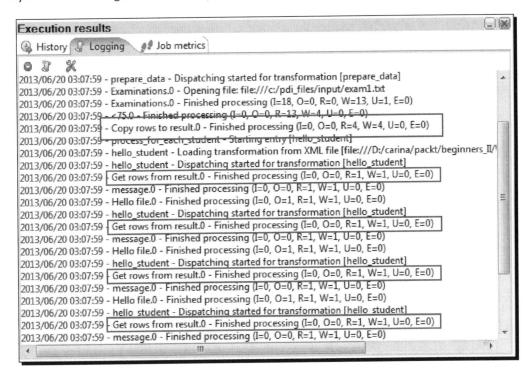

The transformation that builds the list of students copies four rows to results. Then, the main job executes the second transformation four times, once for each of those students.

This mechanism of executing for every input row also applies to jobs. To execute several times a single job, once for every copied row, you have to check the **execute for every input row?** option in the **Job** entry setting window.

In PDI 5, the latest PDI version, there is a new concept named executors. With an executor, you can achieve this same kind of loop over a list of rows, but in a much simpler way.

Have a go hero – building lists of products to buy

This exercise is related to the JS database.

Create a transformation to find out the manufacturers for the products you've sold best in the current month. Take the first three manufacturers in the list.

Create another transformation that for every manufacturer in that list, builds a file with a list of products that are out of stock.

 The first transformation must copy the rows to result. The second transformation must execute for every input row. Start the transformation with a **Get rows from result**, then a **Table Input** step that receives as parameter a code of manufacturer. The SQL to use could be something as shown:

```
SELECT *
FROM products
WHERE code_man LIKE '?' AND pro_stock<pro_stock_min
```

Enhancing your processes with the use of variables

Throughout the different chapters, you had the opportunity of using different Kettle variables including predefined ones, and those defined in the `kettle.properties` file. Now it is time to create your own variables which will lead to more versatile transformations. That is the subject of this section.

Time for action – generating custom messages by setting a variable with the name of the examination file

All the sections in this chapter read an examination file whose name was defined as a named parameter. So far, you run the transformations and jobs without modifying that parameter— you always read the file defined as default. Now it is time to get advantage of that parameter and set a new value at real time. For this section, you will need the examination files in the input folder, and also the job you created in the last section, `process_for_each_student.kjb`.

1. Open Spoon and create a new transformation.
2. Use a **Get System Info** to get the first command-line argument. Name the field `exam_filename`.

3. Add a **Filter rows** step and create a hop from the **Get System Info** step toward this step.

4. From the **Flow** category, drag to the canvas an **Abort** step and from the **Job** category of steps, drag a **Set Variables** step.

5. Create a hop from the **Filter rows** step towards the **Abort** step. As the kind of hop to create, select **Result is FALSE**.

6. Now create a hop from the **Filter rows** step towards the **Set Variables** step. This time, select **Result is TRUE**.

7. Double-click on the **Abort** step. As the **Abort** message put `File name is mandatory`.

8. Double-click on the **Set Variables** step and click on **Get Fields**. The window will be filled as shown:

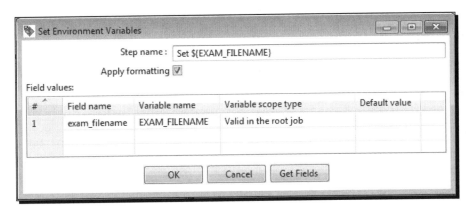

#	Field name	Variable name	Variable scope type	Default value
1	exam_filename	EXAM_FILENAME	Valid in the root job	

Step name : Set ${EXAM_FILENAME}
Apply formatting ☑
Field values:

9. Click on **OK**.

10. Double-click on the **Filter rows** step. Add the following filter: `exam_filename IS NOT NULL`. Close the window.

11. The final transformation looks as shown:

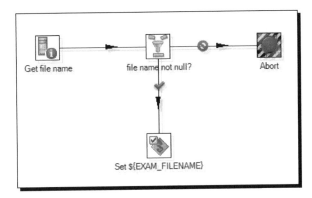

12. Save the transformation in the `transformations` folder under the name `getting_filename.ktr`.

13. Create a new job.

14. From the **General** category, drag to the canvas a **START** entry and a **Transformation** entry. Link them.

15. Save the job as `examinations.kjb`.

16. Double-click on the **Transformation** entry. As **Transformation filename**, put the name of the first transformation you created, `${Internal.Job.Filename.Directory}/getting_filename.ktr`, and click on **OK**.

> Remember that you can avoid typing that long variable name by pressing *Ctrl*-Space and selecting the variable from the list.

17. From the **Conditions** category drag to the canvas a **File Exists** entry, and create a hop from the **Transformation** entry to this new one.

18. Double-click on the **File Exists** entry.

19. In the **Filename** textbox, write `${LABSINPUT}\${EXAM_FILENAME}`, and click on **OK**.

20. Add a new **Job** entry and create a hop from the **File Exists** entry towards this one. Make sure the hop is green, that is, the job should execute if the **File Exists** entry evaluates to true.

21. Double-click on the entry and as **Job filename** put the name of the job you created in the last section, `${Internal.Job.Filename.Directory}/ process_for_each_student.kjb`.

22. Select the **Parameters** tab, and fill it as shown:

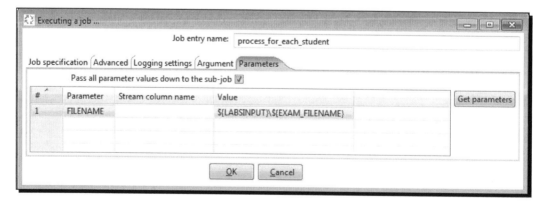

23. Add an **Abort** entry, and create a hop from the **File Exists** entry towards this. Make sure the hop is red.

24. Double-click on the entry and, as **Message**, type `The file ${LABSINPUT}\${EXAM_FILENAME} doesn't exist.`

25. Save the job and press *F9* to run the job.

26. Set the level log to **Minimal logging**, and click on **Launch**.

27. The job fails. This is what you should see in the **Logging** tab in the **Execution results** window:

```
2013/06/19 23:47:04 - 4 validate_and_process - Start of job
   execution
2013/06/19 23:47:04 - Abort.0 - ERROR (version 4.4.0, build 1
   from 2012-09-29 08.22.14 by buildguy) : Row nr 1 causing
      abort : []
2013/06/19 23:47:04 - Abort.0 - ERROR (version 4.4.0, build 1
   from 2012-09-29 08.22.14 by buildguy) : File name is
      mandatory
2013/06/19 23:47:04 - get_filename - get_filename
```

28. Press *F9* again.

29. In the arguments grid, write the name of a fictitious file, for example, `nofile.txt`. Click on **Launch**. This is what you see now in the log tab window:

```
2013/06/19 23:45:20 - Spoon - Starting job...
2013/06/19 23:45:20 - 4 validate_and_process - Start of job
execution
2013/06/19 23:49:20 - File doesn't exist - ERROR (version 4.4.0,
build 1 from 2012-09-29 08.22.14 by buildguy) : The file c:/pdi_
files/input\nofile.txt doesn't exist
2013/06/19 23:45:20 - 4 validate_and_process - Job execution
finished
2013/06/19 23:45:20 - Spoon - Job has ended.
```

30. Press *F9* for the third time. Now provide a real examination filename, for example, `exam2.txt`. Click on **Launch**. This time you see no errors. In the folder pointed to the `${LABSOUTPUT}` variable, you should see a single file named `hello_Maria Roberts.txt`, given that she is the only student in the `exam2.txt` file with a score below 75.

What just happened?

This time you embedded the job, you created in the earlier section, in an outer job that gets and validates the filename from a terminal window. First, a transformation checks that the argument is not null. In that case, it sets a variable with the name provided. The main job verifies that the file exists. If everything is all right, the main job is called to do its main task, generating the hello files based on the data in the given exam file.

As the inner job defined the examination filename as a named parameter, you provided the name in the **Parameters** tab of the **Job** job entry.

Note that the first two times that you ran the job, you changed the log level to minimal because you were just interested in seeing the error messages.

 You may choose any log level you want, depending on the details of information you want to see.

Setting variables inside a transformation

So far you have only defined variables in the `kettle.properties` file or inside Spoon while you were designing a transformation. In the previous exercise, you learned to define your own variables at runtime. You set a variable with the name of the file provided as a command-line argument. You used that variable in the main job to check if the file existed. Then you used the variable to provide a value for the named parameter of the inner job. There you used it as the name of the file to read.

This example showed you how to set a variable with the value of a command-line argument. This is not always the case. The value you set in a variable can be originated by any other means. It can be a value coming from a table in a database, a value defined with a **Generate rows** step, a value calculated with a **Formula** or **Calculator** step, and so on.

The variables you define with a **Set variables** step can be used in the same way and in the same places where you use any Kettle variable. Just take precautions to avoid using these variables in the same transformation where you have set them.

The variables defined in a transformation are not available for use until you leave that transformation.

Running a job inside another job with a Job job entry

The **Job** job entry allows you to run a job inside a job. Just like any job entry, this entry may end successfully or may fail. Upon that result, the main job decides which of the entries that follow it will execute. None of the entries following the job entry start until the nested job ends its execution. There is no limit to the levels of nesting. You may call a job that calls a job that calls a job and so on. Usually, you will not need more than two or three levels.

As with a **Transformation** job entry, you must specify the location and name of the job file. If the job (or any transformation inside the nested job) uses arguments or has defined named parameters, you have the possibility of providing fixed values just as you do in a **Transformation** job entry by filling the **Arguments** and **Parameters** tabs.

Understanding the scope of variables

By nesting jobs, you implicitly create a relationship among the jobs. Look at the following screenshot:

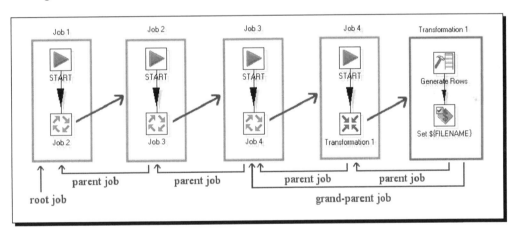

Here you can see how a job and even a transformation may have parents and grandparents. The main job is called **root-job**. This hierarchy is useful to understand the scope of variables. When you define a variable, you have the option to set the scope, that is, define the places where the variable is visible.

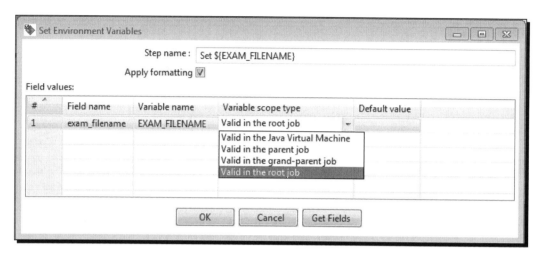

The following table explains which jobs and transformations can access the variable depending on the variable's scope:

Variable scope type	Visibility of the variable
Valid in the parent job	Can be seen by the job that called the transformation and any transformation called by this job.
Valid in the grandparent job	Can be seen by the job that called the transformation, the job that called that job, and any transformation called by any of these jobs.
Valid in the root job	Can be seen by all the jobs in the chain starting with the main job, and any transformation called by any of these jobs.
Valid in the Java Virtual Machine	Seen by all the jobs and transformations that run from the same Java Virtual Machine. For example, suppose that you define a variable with scope in the Java Virtual Machine. If you run the transformation from Spoon, the variable will be available in all jobs and transformations you run from Spoon as long as you don't exit Spoon.

Have a go hero – processing several files at once

Modify the first section, *Time for action – calculating statistics with the use of a subtransformation*, in the following way:

- Modify the main transformation, so that at the end it saves the calculated statistics to a file.
- Create a transformation that gets from the command line the name of a folder. Abort if the user did not supply a name, or if the folder does not exist.
- If the folder exists, list the files in that folder.
- Create a job that, after running the preceding transformation, runs the transformation that calculates the statistics. The transformation should run once for each listed file.

You can use the following hint. Create a transformation that instead of validating that the parameter is a file, validates that it is a folder. In order to do so, use the **File exists** step inside the **Lookup** category of steps.

If the folder exists, use a **Get File Names** step. That step allows you to retrieve the list of filenames in a given folder, including the attributes for those files. To define which files to get, use the options in the **Filenames from field** box. Copy the names to results.

The main transformation should be executed for every input row. The name of the file comes from the **Copy rows to result** step, but in the transformation, you expect a named parameter. This is how you pass the name to the transformation:

- In the **Transformation** job entry, select the **Advanced** tab and check the **Copy previous results to parameters?** box.
- Then select the **Parameters** tab and fill the grid shown as follows:

  As **Parameter**, type FILENAME (the name of the name parameter), and as the **Stream** column name, type the name of the field coming from the previous transformation and that holds the name of the file.

Have a go hero – enhancing the jigsaw database update process

In the *Time for action – inserting new products or updating existent ones* in *Chapter 8, Working with Databases*, you read a file with a list of products belonging to the manufacturer Classic DeLuxe. The list was expected as a named parameter. Enhance that process; create a job that first validates the existence of the provided file. If the file does not exist, put the proper error message in the log. If it exists, process the list. Then move the processed file to a folder named processed.

You don't need to create a transformation to set a variable with the name of the file. As it is expected as a named parameter, it is already available as a variable.

Have a go hero – executing the proper jigsaw database update process

In the *Have a go hero – populating the products table* section in *Chapter 8, Working with Databases*, you created different transformations for updating the products, one for each manufacturer. Now you will put all that work together.

Create a job that accepts two arguments, the name of the file to process and the code of the manufacturer to which the file belongs.

Create a transformation that validates that the code provided belongs to an existent manufacturer. If the code exists, set a variable named TRANSFORMATION_FILE with the name of the transformation that knows how to process the file for that manufacturer.

The transformation also must check that the name provided is not null. If it is not null, set a variable named FILENAME with the name supplied.

Then in the job check that the file exists. If it exists and the manufacturer code was valid, run the proper transformation. In order to do so, put ${TRANSFORMATION_FILE} as the name of the transformation in the **Transformation** job entry dialog window.

Test your job.

Pop quiz – deciding the scope of variables

Q1. In the previous section you created a transformation that set a variable with the name of a file. For the scope you left the default value, **Valid in the root job**. Which of the following scope types could you have chosen getting the same results (you may select more than one):

1.   Valid in the parent job
2.   Valid in the grand-parent job
3.   Valid in the Java Virtual Machine

 In general, if you have doubts about which scope type to use, you can use **Valid in the root job** and you will be good. Simply ensure that you are not using the same name of variable for different purposes.

Summary

In this chapter, you learned techniques to combine jobs and transformations in different ways.

First, you learned to isolate part of a transformation as a subtransformation. You also learned to implement process flows by copying and getting rows.

Then, you learned to nest jobs and to iterate the execution of jobs and transformations.

Finally, you learned to define your own variables at runtime. You defined variables in one transformation and then used them in other jobs and/or transformations. You also learned to define different scopes for those variables.

By using all these PDI capabilities, your work will look cleaner and will be more organized.

Let's say that this was a really productive chapter. By now, you should feel that you are ready to use PDI for developing most of your requirements. And you are indeed.

You are now ready for the next chapter, where you will develop the final project that will allow you to review a little of everything you have learned throughout the book.

12
Developing and Implementing a Simple Datamart

In this chapter, you will implement a simple but complete process of loading a datamart. The sections will not only teach you about this interesting subject and how PDI can help in the process, but will also allow you to review all concepts learned through the book. Even more, following the step-by-step instructions in this chapter will help you be confident that you master the tool.

This chapter will cover the following:

+ Introduction to a sales datamart based on the Jigsaw puzzles database
+ Loading the dimensions of the sales datamart
+ Loading the fact table for the sales datamart
+ Automating what has been done

Exploring the sales datamart

In *Chapter 9, Performing Advanced Operations with Databases*, you were introduced to star schemas. In a few words, a star schema consists of a central table known as the fact table, surrounded by dimension tables. While the fact has indicators of your business, for example, sales in dollars, the dimensions have descriptive information about the attributes of your business such as time, customers, and products.

A star that addresses a specific department's needs or that is built for use by a particular group of users is called a **datamart**. You could have datamarts focused on customer relationship management, inventory, human resources management, budget, and more. In this chapter, you will load a datamart focused on sales.

Sometimes the term "datamart" is confused with "data warehouse". However, datamarts and data warehouses are not the same.

> The main difference between datamarts and data warehouses is that data warehouses address the needs of the whole organization, whereas datamarts addresses the needs of a particular department, for example, marketing, sales, personnel, and so on.

Data warehouses contain information from multiple subject areas allowing you to have a global vision of your business. Thus, they are oriented to the company's staff such as executives or managers.

The following star represents your sales datamart—a central fact named **SALES**, surrounded by six dimensions:

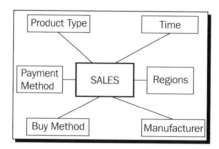

The following is a brief description for the dimensions in your SALES star:

Dimension	Description
Time	The date on which the sales occurred
Regions	The geographical area where the products were sold
Manufacturers	The name of the manufacturers that build the products that were sold
Payment method	Cash, check, and so on
Buy method	Internet, by telephone, and so on
Product type	Puzzle, glue, frame, and so on

In real models, you may find two kinds of dimensions related to time: a dimension holding calendar day attributes and a separate dimension with attributes as hours, minutes, and seconds.

Let's now look at the **Entity Relationship Diagram (ERD)** for the database that represents this model. The table named **FT_SALES** is the fact table. The others are the dimension tables.

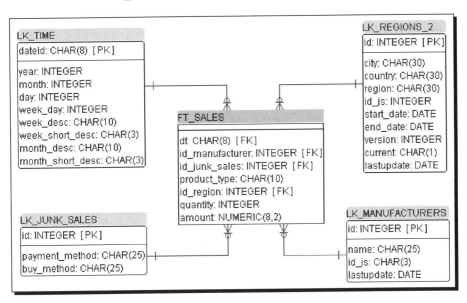

The following table shows you the correspondence between the dimensions in the model and the tables in the database:

Dimension	Table
Manufacturers	lk_manufacturer
Time	lk_time
Regions	lk_regions_2
Payment method	lk_junk_sales
Buy method	lk_junk_sales
Product type	None

As you can see, there is no one-to-one relationship between the dimensions in the model and the tables in the database.

A one-to-one relationship between a dimension and a database table is not required, but may coincidentally exist.

The first three dimensions have their corresponding tables.

The payment and buy method dimensions share a junk dimension. A **junk dimension** is an abstract dimension that groups unrelated low-cardinality flags, indicators, and attributes. Each of those items could technically be a dimension on its own, but grouping them into a junk dimension has the advantage of keeping your database model simple. It also saves space and contributes to better performance.

The last dimension, product type, doesn't have a separate table. It is so simple that it isn't worth creating a dimension table. Instead, its values are stored in a dedicated field in the fact table. This kind of dimension is called **degenerate dimension**.

Deciding the level of granularity

The level of detail in your star model is called **grain**. The granularity is directly related to the kind of questions you expect your model to answer. Let's see some examples:

The product-related information your model has is the manufacturer and the kind of product (puzzle, glue, and so on). Thus, it allows you to ask questions such as the following:

◆ Beyond puzzles, which kind of product is the best sold?

◆ Do you sell more products manufactured by Ravensburger than products manufactured by Educa Jigsaws?

What if you want to know the names of the top ten products sold? You simply cannot, because that level of detail is not stored in the model. For answering this type of question, you need a lower level of granularity. You could have that by adding a product dimension where each record represents a particular product.

Now let's see the time dimension. Each record in that dimension represents a particular calendar day. This allows you to answer questions such as, how many products did you sell every day in the last four months?

If you were not interested in daily, but in monthly information, you could have designed a model with a higher level of granularity by creating a time dimension with just one record per month.

Understanding the level of granularity of your model is a key to the process of loading the fact table, as you will see when you load the sales fact table.

Loading the dimensions

As you saw, the SALES star model is made by a fact surrounded by the dimension tables. In order to load the star, first you have to load the dimensions. You already learned to load dimension tables. Here you will load the dimensions for the SALES star.

Time for action – loading the dimensions for the sales datamart

In this section, you will load each dimension for the sales datamart and enclose them into a single job. Before starting, check the following things:

- Check that the database engine is up and that both the `js` and the `js_dw` databases are accessible from PDI.

- If your time dimension table `lk_time` has data, truncate the table. Remember that you can do it by right-clicking on the table in the database explorer and selecting the **Truncate Table** option.

 You may reuse the `js_dw` database in which you have been loading data in previous chapters. There is no problem with that. However, dropping the database and creating the tables again is preferred so that you can see how the entire process works.

The explanation will be focused on the general process. For details on creating a transformation that loads a particular type of dimension, please refer to *Chapter 9, Performing Advanced Operations with Databases*. You can also download the full material for this chapter where the transformations and jobs are ready to browse and try.

1. Create a new transformation and use it to load the manufacturer dimension. This is a Type I SCD, that is, a dimension where you don't preserve historical values. The data for the dimension comes from the `manufacturers` table in the `js` database. The dimension table in `js_dw` is `lk_manufacturer`. Use the following screenshot as a guide:

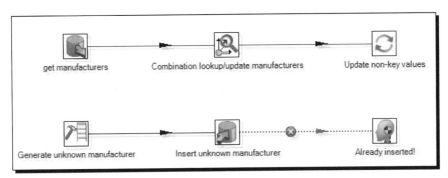

2. Save the transformation in a folder named `lk_transformations`.

3. Create a new transformation, and use it to load the regions dimension.

 You already loaded this dimension in the *Time for action – loading a region dimension with a Combination lookup/update step* section in *Chapter 9, Performing Advanced Operations with Databases*. If you performed the *Have a go hero – loading the Regions dimension as a Type II SCD* section in that chapter, you may skip this step.

4. The region dimension is a Type II SCD. The data for the dimension comes from the `city` and `country` tables. The information about regions is in Excel files that you can download from the Packt website. The dimension table in `js_dw` is `lk_regions_2`. Use the following screenshot as a guide:

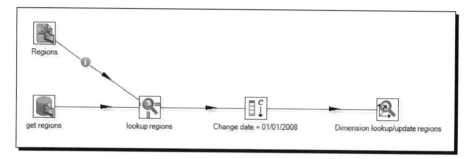

5. Save the transformation in the `lk_transformations` folder.

6. Create a new transformation, and use it to load the time dimension.

 You started to create a dataset for the time dimension in *Chapter 2, Getting Started with Transformations*, and continued enriching the dataset in *Chapter 7, Transforming the Rowset*. Then in *Chapter 8, Working with Databases*, the loading of the data into a table was part of the *Have a go hero – creating the time dimension* section. If you did it, you may skip this step.

7. The dimension table in `js_dw` is `lk_time`.

8. Save the transformation in the `lk_transformations` folder.

Now you will create a job to put it all together:

1. Create a new job and save it in the same folder where you created the `lk_transformations` folder.

2. Drag to the canvas a **START** and two **Transformation** job entries.

3. Create a hop from the **START** entry to each of the transformation entries. You have the following:

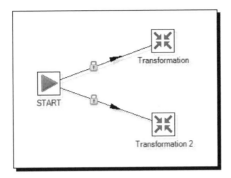

4. Use one of the transformation entries to execute the transformation that loads the manufacturer dimension.

5. Use the other transformation entry to execute the transformation that loads the region dimension.

6. Add an **Evaluate rows number in a table** entry to the canvas. You'll find it under the **Conditions** category.

7. Create a hop from the **START** entry toward this new entry.

8. Double-click on the new entry and fill it as shown:

9. After this entry, add another transformation entry and use it to execute the transformation that loads the time dimension.

10. Finally, from the **General** category, add a **Success** entry.

11. Create a hop from the **Evaluate...** step to this entry. The hop should be red, meaning that this step executes when the evaluation fails.

12. Your final job looks like this:

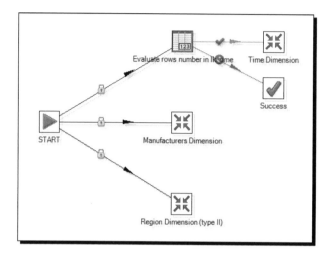

13. Save and run the job. The manufacturer and regions dimensions should be loaded. You can verify it by exploring the tables from the database explorer or in any other GUI tool, for example, Squirrel.

14. In the logging window, you'll see that the evaluation succeeded and so the time dimension is also loaded:

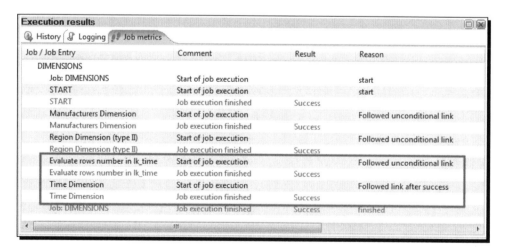

15. You can check it by exploring the table from the database explorer. Remember that you can access it by right-clicking on the database and selecting **Explore**:

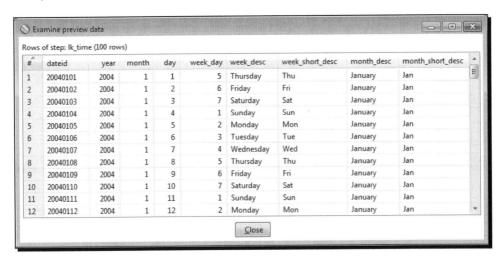

16. Run the transformation again. This time the evaluation fails and the transformation that loads the time dimension is not executed.

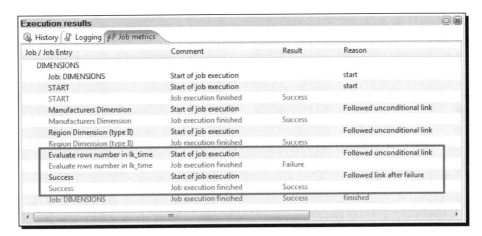

What just happened?

You created the transformations to load the dimensions you need for your sales star.

As already explained in *Chapter 10, Creating Basic Task Flows*, the job entries connected to the **START** entry run one after the other, not in parallel as the arrangement in the work area might suggest.

As for the time dimension, once it is loaded, you don't need to load it again. Therefore, you put an evaluation entry to check if the table had already been loaded. The first time you ran the job, there were no records, so the time dimension was loaded. The second time, the time dimension had already been loaded. This time the evaluation failed avoiding the execution of the transformation that loaded the time dimension.

 Note that you put a **Success** entry to avoid the job failing after the failed evaluation.

Extending the sales datamart model

You may, and you usually have, more than one fact table sharing some of the dimensions.

Look at the following figure:

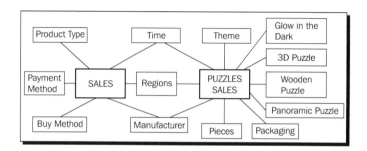

It shows two stars sharing three dimensions: **Regions**, **Manufacturer**, and **Time**. The star model to the left is the **SALES** star model you already know. The star model to the right does not have data for accessories but has more detail for puzzles, for example, the number of pieces they have or the category or theme they belong to. When you have more than one fact table sharing dimensions as here, you have what is called a **constellation**.

The following table summarizes the dimensions added to the datamart:

Dimension	Description
Pieces	Number of pieces of the puzzle, grouped in the following ranges: 0-25, 26-100, and so on
Theme	Classification of the puzzle in any of the following categories: Fantasy, Castles, Landscapes, and so on
Glows in the Dark	Yes/No
3D Puzzle	Yes/No
Wooden Puzzle	Yes/No

Dimension	Description
Panoramic Puzzle	Yes/No
Packaging	Number of puzzles packed together: 1, 2, 3, 4

The following is the updated ERD for the database that represents the model:

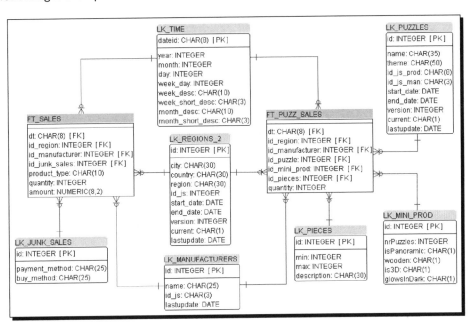

The new fact table is represented by a table named `ft_puzz_sales`.

The following table shows you the correspondence between the dimensions added to the model and the tables in the database.

Dimension	Table
Pieces	lk_pieces
Theme	lk_puzzles
Glows in the Dark	lk_mini_prod
3D Puzzle	lk_mini_prod
Wooden Puzzle	lk_mini_prod
Panoramic	lk_mini_prod
Packaging	lk_mini_prod

The following section allows you to practice what you learned in this section, but this time applied to the puzzle star model.

Have a go hero – loading the dimensions for the puzzle star model

In this section, you will load some of the dimensions that were added to the model.

- Create a transformation that loads the `lk_pieces` dimension. You may create any range you want. The following table may help you in the creation:

Minimum	Maximum	Description
0	25	Less than 25
26	100	26-100
101	1000	101-1000
1001	2000	1001-2000
2000	99999	Greater than 2000

- Create another transformation that loads the `lk_puzzles` dimension. This is Type II SCD, and you already loaded it in *Chapter 9, Performing Advanced Operations with Databases*. If you have the transformation that does it, half of your work is done.

- Finally, modify the job in the section by adding the execution of these new transformations. Note that the `lk_pieces` dimension has to be loaded just once.

Loading a fact table with aggregated data

Now that you have data in your dimensions, you are ready to load the sales fact table. In this section, you will learn how to do it.

Time for action – loading the sales fact table by looking up dimensions

Let's load the sales fact, `ft_sales`, with sales information for a given range of dates. Before performing this section, be sure that you have already loaded the dimensions. You did it in the previous section.

Also, check that the database engine is up and that both the `js` and the `js_dw` databases are accessible from PDI. If everything is in order, you are ready to start:

1. Create a new transformation.
2. Drag a **Table input** step to the canvas.
3. Double-click on the step. As **Connection**, select **js** – the connection to the operational database.
4. In the SQL frame, type the following query:

```
SELECT  i.inv_date
       ,d.man_code
       ,cu.city_id
       ,pr.pro_type        product_type
       ,b.buy_desc
       ,p.pay_desc
       ,sum(d.cant_prod) quantity
       ,sum(d.price)     amount
FROM    invoices          i
       ,invoices_detail   d
       ,customers         cu
       ,buy_methods       b
       ,payment_methods   p
       ,products          pr
WHERE i.invoice_number = d.invoice_number
  AND         i.cus_id   = cu.cus_id
  AND         i.buy_code = b.buy_code
  AND         i.pay_code = p.pay_code
  AND         d.pro_code = pr.pro_code
  AND         d.man_code = pr.man_code
  AND i.inv_date BETWEEN cast('${DATE_FROM}' as date)
                    AND cast('${DATE_TO}'   as date)
GROUP BY i.inv_date
        ,d.man_code
        ,cu.city_id
        ,pr.pro_type
        ,b.buy_desc
        ,p.pay_desc
```

5. Check the **Replace variables in script?** option and click on **OK**.

Let's retrieve the surrogate key for the manufacturer:

1. From the **Lookup** category, drag a **Database lookup** step to the canvas.

2. Create a hop from the **Table input** step to this new step.

3. Double-click on the **Database lookup** step.

4. As **Connection**, select **dw** – the connection to the datamart database.

5. Click on **Browse...** and select the lk_manufacturers table.

6. Fill the upper grid with the condition id_js = man_code.

7. Fill the lower grid—under **Field** type id, as **New name** type id_manufacturer, as **Default** type 0, and as **Type** select **Integer**.

8. Click on **OK**.

Now you will get the surrogate key for the region:

1. From the **Data Warehouse** category drag to the canvas a **Dimension L/U** step.
2. Create a hop from the **Database lookup** step to this new step.
3. Double-click on the **Dimension L/U** step.
4. As **Connection**, select dw.
5. Browse and select the lk_regions_2 table.
6. Fill the **Keys** grid as shown:

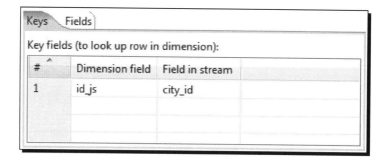

7. As **Technical key field**, select id. In the **new name** textbox, type id_region.
8. As **Stream Datefield** select inv_date.
9. As **Date range star field** and **Table daterange end**, select start_date and end_date respectively.
10. Select the **Fields** tab and fill it as shown:

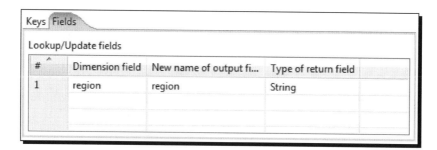

Now it's time to generate the surrogate key for the junk dimension:

1. From the **Data Warehouse** category, drag a **Combination L/U** step to the canvas.
2. Create a hop from the **Dimension L/U** step to this new step.

3. Double-click on the **Combination L/U** step.

4. As **Connection**, select dw.

5. Browse and select the lk_junk_sales table.

6. Fill the grid as shown:

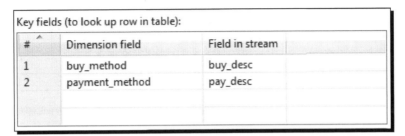

7. As **Technical key field**, type id. In the **Creation of technical key** frame, leave the default value **Use table maximum + 1**. Then click on **OK**.

8. Add a **Select values** step and use it to rename the field id to id_junk_sales.

Finally, let's do some adjustments and send the data to the fact table:

1. Add another **Select values** step to change the metadata of the inv_date field as shown:

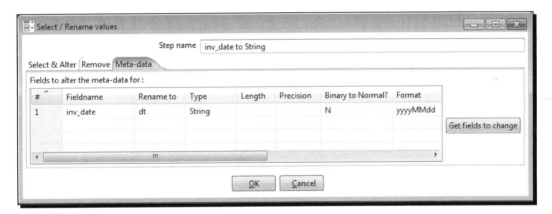

2. Add a **Table output** step and double-click on it.

3. As **Connection**, select dw.

4. Browse and select the ft_sales table.

5. Check the **Specify database fields** option, select the **Database fields** grid, and fill it as shown:

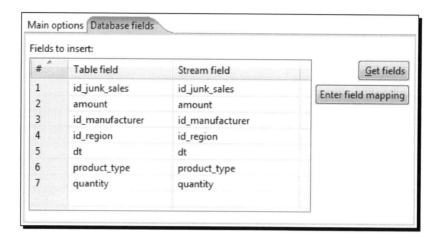

 Remember that you can avoid typing by using the **Get fields** button that populates the grid automatically.

6. Click on **OK**. The following is your final transformation. Press *Ctrl + S* to save it.

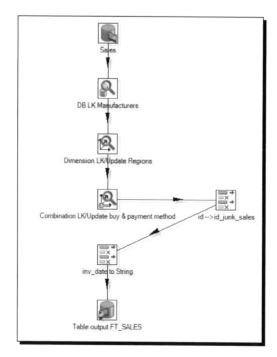

7. Press *F9* to run it.

8. In the setting window, provide some values for the date range:

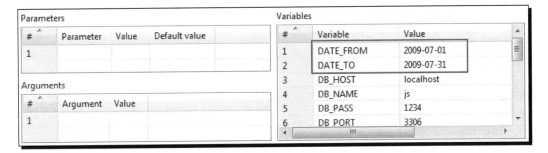

9. Click on **Launch**.

10. The fact table should have been loaded. To check it, open the database explorer and run the following query:

```
SELECT * FROM ft_sales
```

You will get this:

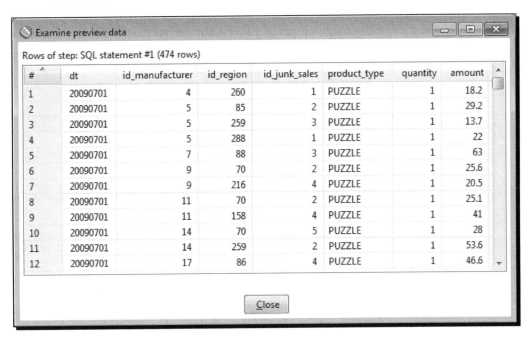

11. To verify that only the sales between the provided dates were processed, run the following query:

```
SELECT MIN(dt), MAX(dt) FROM ft_sales
```

You will get this:

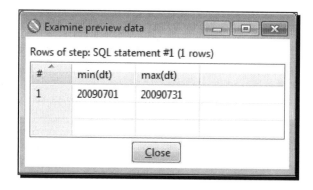

What just happened?

You loaded the sales fact table with the sales in a given range of dates.

First of all, you got the information from the source database. You did it by typing a SQL command in a **Table input** step. You already know how a **Table input** works.

As said, a fact table has foreign keys to the primary key of the dimension tables. Note that this is why you loaded the dimensions before the fact table! The query you wrote gave you the business keys. So, after getting the data from the source, you translated the business keys into surrogate keys. You did it in different ways depending on the kind of each related dimension.

Finally, you inserted the obtained data into the fact table `ft_sales`.

Getting the information from the source with SQL queries

You already know how to use a **Table input** to get information from any database. However, the query in the section may have looked strange or long compared with the queries you wrote in previous chapters. There is nothing mysterious in that query, it's simply a matter of knowing what to put in it. Let's explain it in detail.

In order to load the fact table, you have to look at the grain.

As mentioned at the beginning of the chapter, the grain, or level of detail, of the fact is implicitly expressed in terms of the dimension.

Looking at the model, you can see the following dimensions, along with their level of detail:

Dimension	Level of detail (most atomic data)
Manufacturers	manufacturer
Regions	city
Time	day
Product Type	product type
Payment method	payment method
Buy method	buy method

Does this have anything to do with loading the fact? Well, the answer is yes. This is because the numbers you have to put as measures in the numeric fields must be aggregated accordingly to the dimensions. These are the measurements—quantity representing the number of products sold, and Sales representing the amounts.

So, in order to feed the table, what you need to take from the source is the sum of quantity and the sum of sales for every combination of manufacturer, day, city, product type, payment method, and buy method.

In SQL terms, you do it with a query as the one you wrote in the **Table input** step. The query is not as complicated as it may seem at first. Let's dissect the query, beginning with the FROM clause:

```
FROM    invoices          i
        ,invoices_detail   d
        ,customers         cu
        ,buy_methods       b
        ,payment_methods   p
        ,products          pr
```

These are the tables where you need to take the information from. The word following the name of the table, for example, pr for the table products is an alias for the table. The **alias** is used to distinguish fields that have the same name but are in different tables, and we have several cases in our model. As an example, there is a field named man_code both in the invoices_detail table and in the products table. We refer to those fields as d.man_code and pr.man_code respectively.

The database engine takes all the records for all the listed tables, side-by-side, and creates all the possible combinations of records where each new record has all the fields for all the tables.

```
WHERE i.invoice_number = d.invoice_number
  AND      i.cus_id    = cu.cus_id
```

```
AND        i.buy_code = b.buy_code
AND        i.pay_code = p.pay_code
AND        d.pro_code = pr.pro_code
AND        d.man_code = pr.man_code
```

These conditions represent the join between tables. A **join** limits the number of records you have when combining tables as explained above. For example, the following condition:

```
i.cus_id = cu.cus_id
```

The condition implies that out of all the records, the engine keeps only those where the customer ID in the table `invoices` is the same that of the customer ID in the table `customers`.

```
AND i.inv_date BETWEEN cast('${DATE_FROM}' as date)
                   AND cast('${DATE_TO}'   as date)
```

This simply filters the sales in the given range. The `cast` function converts a `string` to a `date`.

> Different engines have different ways to cast or convert fields from one data type to another. If you are using an engine different from MySQL, you may have to check your database documentation and adapt this part of the query.

```
GROUP BY i.inv_date
         ,d.man_code
         ,cu.city_id
         ,pr.pro_type
         ,b.buy_desc
         ,p.pay_desc
```

By using the `GROUP BY` clause, you ask the SQL engine that for each different combination of the listed fields, it should return just one record.

Finally, look at the fields following the `SELECT` clause:

```
SELECT i.inv_date
       ,d.man_code
       ,cu.city_id
       ,pr.pro_type        product_type
       ,b.buy_desc
       ,p.pay_desc
       ,sum(d.cant_prod)  quantity
       ,sum(d.price)      amount
```

These fields are the business keys you need—date of sale, manufacturer, city, and so on—one for each dimension in the sales model. Note the word `product_type` after the `pro_type` field. This is an alias for the field. By using an alias, the field is renamed in the output. Also, `quantity` and `amount` are aliases for the new fields that are calculated in the query.

As you can see, with the exception of the highlighted fields, the fields you put after the `SELECT` clause are exactly the same as you put in the `GROUP BY` clause. When you have a `GROUP BY` clause in your sentence, after the `SELECT` clause you can put only those fields listed in the `GROUP BY` clause or aggregated functions as the following:

```
,sum(d.cant_prod)  quantity
,sum(d.price)      amount
```

`sum()` is an aggregate function that gives you the sum of the column you put in brackets. Therefore, these last two fields are the sum of the `cant_prod` field and the sum of the `price` field for all the grouped records. These two fields give you the measures for your fact table.

To confirm that the `GROUP BY` clause works as explained, let's explore one example. Remove from the query, `sum()` functions leaving just the fields, and also remove the `GROUP BY` clause. Do a preview setting `2009-07-07` both as `start_date` and `end_date`. You will see the following:

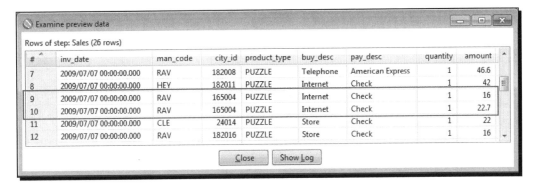

As you can see, in the same day, in the same city, you sold two products of the same type made by the same manufacturer, by using the same payment and buy method. In the fact table, you will not save two records, but will save a single record. Restore the original query and do a preview. You will see the following:

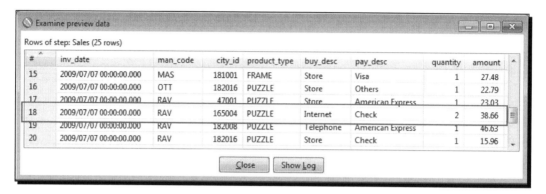

Here you can see that the GROUP BY clause has grouped those two records into a single one. For quantity and amount it summed the individual values.

Notice that the GROUP BY clause, along with the aggregate functions, does the same as you could have done by using a **Sort rows** step to sort by the listed fields, followed by a **Group by** step to get the sum of the numeric fields.

 Wherever the database can do the operations, for performance reasons it's recommended that you allow the database engine to do it.

Translating the business keys into surrogate keys

You already have the transactional data for the fact table. But that data contains business keys. Look at the field's definition for your fact table:

```
dt CHAR(8) NOT NULL,
id_manufacturer INT(10) NOT NULL,
id_region INT(4) NOT NULL,
id_junk_sales INT(10) NOT NULL,
product_type CHAR(10) NOT NULL,
quantity INT(6) DEFAULT 0 NOT NULL,
amount NUMERIC(8,2) DEFAULT 0 NOT NULL
```

`id_manufacturer`, `id_region`, and `id_junk_sales` are foreign keys to surrogate keys. So, before inserting the data into the fact, for each business key you have to find the proper surrogate key. Depending on the kind of dimensions referenced by the IDs in the fact table, you get those IDs in a different way. Let's see in the following section, how you do in each case:

Obtaining the surrogate key for Type I SCD

For getting the surrogate key in case of a Type I SCD as the Manufacturer one, you used a **Database lookup** step. You are already familiar with this step so understanding how to use it is easy:

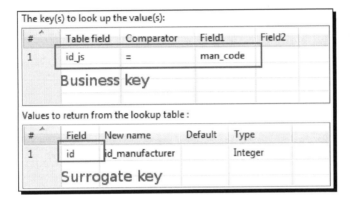

In the first grid, you provided the business keys. The key to look up in the incoming stream is `man_code`, whereas the key to look up in the dimension table is stored in the field `id_js`.

With the **Database lookup** step, you returned the field named `id`, which is the field that stores the surrogate key. You renamed it to `id_manufacturer`, as this is the name you need for the fact table.

If the key is not found, you use `0` as default, that is, the record in the dimension reserved for unknown values.

The following screenshot shows you how it works:

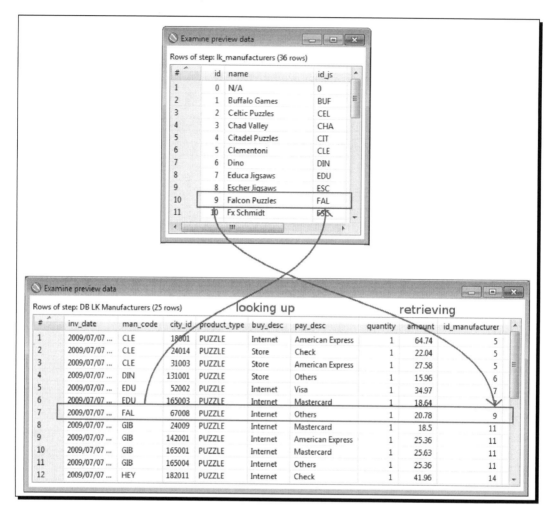

Obtaining the surrogate key for Type II SCD

In the case of a Type II SCD as the Region dimension, you used the same step that you used to load the table dimension—a **Dimension L/U** step. The difference is that here you unchecked the **Update the dimension?** option. By doing that, the step behaves quite as a database lookup—you provide the keys to look up and the step returns the fields you put both in the **Fields** tab and in the **Technical key field** option. The difference with that step is that here you have to provide time information. By using that time information, PDI finds and returns from the Type II SCD, the proper record in time:

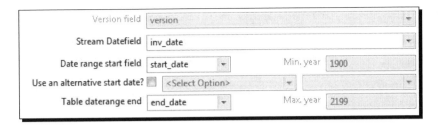

Here you give PDI the names of the columns that store the data ranges—start_date and end_date. You also give it the name of the field stream to use in order to compare the dates—in this case inv_date, that is, the date of the sell.

Look at the following image to understand how the lookup works:

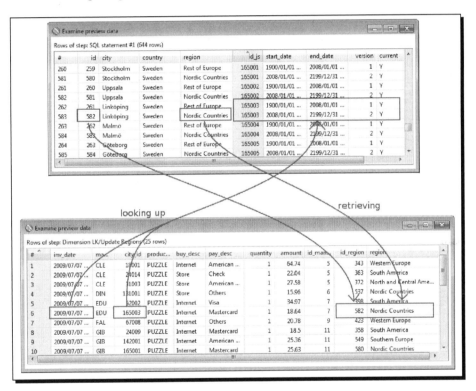

The step has to get the surrogate key for the city with ID 261. There are two records for that city. The key is in finding the proper record, the record valid on 07/07/2009. So, PDI compares the date provided against the start_date and end_date fields and returns the surrogate key 582, for which the city is classified as belonging to the Nordic Countries region.

If no record is found for the given keys on the given date, the step retrieves the ID 0, which is used for the unknown data.

Obtaining the surrogate key for the Junk dimension

The payment and buy methods are stored in a Junk dimension. A Junk dimension can be loaded by using a **Combination L/U** step. You learned how to use this step in the *Time for action – loading a region dimension with a Combination lookup/update step* section in *Chapter 9, Performing Advanced Operations with Databases*. As all the fields in a junk dimension are part of the primary key, you don't need an extra **Update** step to load it.

In the previous section, you loaded the dimension at the same time you loaded the fact. You know from *Chapter 9, Performing Advanced Operations with Databases*, that when you use a **Combination L/U** step, the step returns you the generated key. So, the use of the step here for loading and getting the key at the same time fits perfectly.

 If the dimension had been loaded previously, instead of a **Combination L/U** step you could have used a **Database lookup** step by putting the key fields in the upper grid and the key in the lower grid of the Database lookup configuration window.

Obtaining the surrogate key for the Time dimension

You already obtained the surrogate keys for Type I and Type II SCDs and for the Junk dimension. Finally, there is a Time dimension. As for the key, you use the date in string format; the method for getting the surrogate key is simply changing the metadata from date to string by using the proper format. Once again, if you had used a regular surrogate key instead of the date for getting the surrogate key, you would have to use a **Database lookup** step.

The following table summarizes the different possibilities:

Dimension type	Method for getting the surrogate key	Sample dimension
Type I SCD	**Database lookup** step	Manufacturer
Type II SCD	**Dimension L/U** step	Regions
Junk and Mini	**Combination L/U** step if you load the dimension at the same time as you load the fact (as in the section).	Sales Junk dimension
	Database lookup step if the dimension is already loaded.	
Degenerate	As you don't have a table or key to translate, you just store the data as a field in the fact. You don't have to worry about getting surrogate keys.	Product type
Time	Change the metadata to the proper format if you use date as the key (as in the section).	Time
	Dimension L/U step if you use a normal surrogate key.	

Pop quiz – creating a product type dimension

Suppose that you decided to create a new table for the product type dimension. The table will have the following columns: id, product_type_description, and product_type. As data you would have, for example, 1, puzzle, puzzle for the product type puzzle, or 2, glue, accessory for the product type glue.

Q1. As field with the foreign key in the fact table:

1. You reuse the product_type field.
2. You create a new field.

Q2. For getting the surrogate key:

1. You use a Combination lookup/update step
2. You use a Dimension lookup/update step
3. You use a Database lookup/update step

> The product_type field is a string; it's not the proper field for referencing a surrogate key from a fact table, so you have to define a new field for that purpose. For getting the right key, you use a **Database lookup** step.

Have a go hero – loading a puzzles fact table

In the *Have a go hero – loading the dimensions for the puzzles star model* section, you were asked to load the dimensions for the puzzle star model. Now you will load the fact table.

To load the fact table you will need to build a query taking data from the source. Try to figure out how the query looks like. Then you may try writing the query by yourself, or you may cheat; this query will serve you as a starting point:

```
SELECT
        i.inv_date
      , d.man_code
      , cu.city_id
      , pr.pro_theme
      , pr.pro_pieces
      , pr.pro_packaging
      , pr.pro_shape
      , pr.pro_style
      , SUM(d.cant_prod)  quantity
```

```
FROM   invoices         i
      ,invoices_detail d
      ,customers       cu
      ,products        pr
WHERE i.invoice_number = d.invoice_number
  AND       i.cus_id   = cu.cus_id
  AND       d.pro_code = pr.pro_code
  AND       d.man_code = pr.man_code
  AND pr.pro_type like 'PUZZLE'
  AND i.inv_date BETWEEN cast('${DATE_FROM}' as date)
                    AND cast('${DATE_TO}' as date)
GROUP BY i.inv_date
        ,d.man_code
        ,cu.city_id
        ,pr.pro_theme
        ,pr.pro_pieces
        ,pr.pro_packaging
        ,pr.pro_shape
        ,pr.pro_style
```

After that, look for the surrogate keys for dimensions of Type I and II.

Here you have a mini-dimension. You may load it at the same time you load the fact as you did in the section with the Junk dimension. Also, make sure that you properly modify the metadata for the time field.

Insert the data into the fact, and check whether the data was loaded as expected.

Getting facts and dimensions together

Loading the star involves both loading the dimensions and loading the fact. You already loaded the dimensions and the fact separately. In the following two sections, you will put it all together.

Time for action – loading the fact table using a range of dates obtained from the command line

Now you will get the range of dates from the command line and load the fact table using that range:

1. Create a new transformation.

2. With a **Get system info** step that you will find in the **Input** category of steps, get the first two arguments from the command line and name them `date_from` and `date_to`.

3. By using a couple of steps, check that the arguments are not null, have the proper format (yyyy-mm-dd), and are valid dates.

4. If something is wrong with the arguments, abort.

5. If the arguments are valid, use a **Set variables** step to set two variables named `DATE_FROM` and `DATE_TO`.

6. Save the transformation in the same folder, where you saved the transformation that loads the fact table.

7. Test the transformation by providing valid and invalid arguments to see that it works as expected.

8. Create a job and save it in the same folder in which you saved the job that loads the dimensions.

9. Drag to the canvas a **START** and two transformation job entries, and link them one after the other.

10. Use the first transformation entry to execute the transformation you just created.

11. Use the second transformation entry to execute the transformation that loads the fact table.

12. This is how your job should look like:

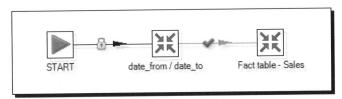

13. Save the job and press *F9* to run the job.

14. Fill the job setting window as follows and click on **Launch**:

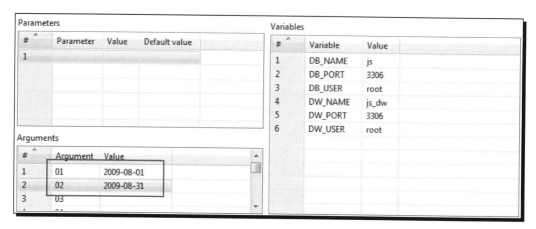

15. When the execution finishes, explore the database to check that the data for the given dates was loaded in the fact table. You will see the following:

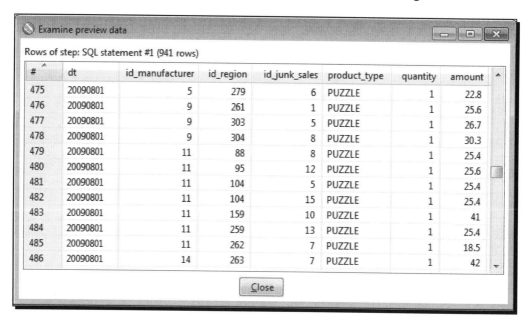

What just happened?

You built a main job that loads the sales fact table. First, it reads from the command line the range of dates to be used for loading the fact and validates it. If they are not valid, the process aborts. If they are valid, the fact table is loaded for the dates in that range.

Time for action – loading the SALES star

You already created a job for loading the dimensions and another job for loading the fact.

In this section, you will put them together in a single main job:

1. Create a new job in the same folder in which you saved the mentioned jobs. Name this job `load_dm_sales.kjb`.

2. Drag to the canvas a **START** and two **Job** job entries, and link them one after the other.

3. Use the first job entry to execute the job that loads the dimensions.

4. Use the second job entry to execute the job you just created for loading the fact table.

5. Save the job. This is how it looks:

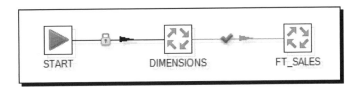

6. Press *F9* to run the job.

7. As arguments, provide a new range of dates: `2009-09-01`, `2009-09-30`. Then press **Launch**.

8. The dimensions will be loaded first, followed by the loading of the fact table.

9. The **Job metrics** tab in the **Execution results** window shows you the whole process running. As usual, you may drill-down and do sniff-testing to see that everything is running as you expect.

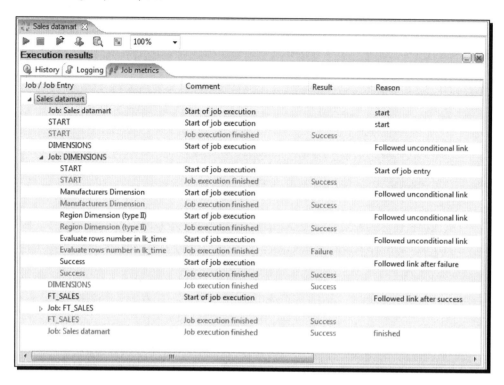

10. Exploring the database you'll see once again the data updated:

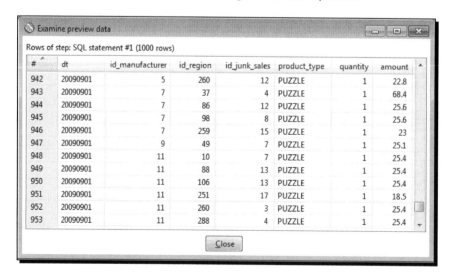

What just happened?

You built a main job that loads the sales datamart. First, it loads the dimensions. After that, it loads the fact table by filtering sales in a range of dates coming from the command line.

Have a go hero – enhancing the loading process of the sales fact table

Facts tables are rarely updated. Usually, you just insert new data. However, after loading a fact, you may detect that there were errors in the source. Or it could also happen that some data arrives late to the system. In order to take into account those situations, you should have the possibility to reprocess data that has already been processed. To avoid duplicates in the fact table, do the following modification to the loading process:

After getting the start and end date and before loading the fact table, delete the records that may have been inserted in a previous execution for the given range of dates.

Have a go hero – loading the puzzle sales star

Modify the main job so it also loads the puzzle fact table.

Make sure that the job that loads the dimensions includes all the dimensions needed for both fact tables. Also, pay attention to not read and validate the arguments twice.

Have a go hero – loading the facts once a month

Modify the whole solution so the loading of the fact tables is made once a month. Don't modify the model! You still want to have daily information in the fact tables; what you want to do is simply replace the daily updating process with a monthly process. Ask for a single parameter as `yyyymm` and validate it. Replace the old parameters `START_DATE` and `END_DATE` with this new one, wherever you use them.

Automating the administrative tasks

The solution you built through the chapter loads both dimensions and the fact in a star model for a given range of dates. Now suppose that you want to keep your datamart always updated. Would you sit every day in front of your computer, and run the same job over and over again? You probably would, but you know that it would not be a good idea. There are better ways to do this. Let's see how you can get rid of that task.

Time for action – automating the loading of the sales datamart

Suppose that every day you want to update your sales datamart by adding the information about the sales for the day before. Let's do some modifications to the jobs and transformations you created, so that the job can be run automatically.

In order to test the changes, you will have to change the date for your system. Set the current date to `2009-10-02`.

1. Create a new transformation.

2. Drag to the canvas a **Get system info** step and fill it as shown:

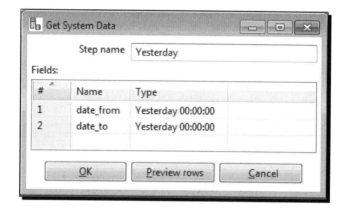

3. With a **Select values** step, change the metadata of both fields. As type, put `String` and as format, `yyyy-MM-dd`.

4. Add a **Set variables** step and use the two fields to create two variables named `START_DATE` and `END_DATE`.

5. Save the transformation in the same folder where you saved the transformation that loads the fact.

6. Modify the job that loads the fact so that instead of executing the transformation that takes the range of dates from the command line, it executes this one. The job looks as shown:

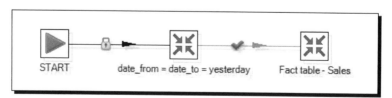

7. Save it.

Now let's create the scripts for executing the job from the command line:

1. Create a folder named `log` in the folder of your choice.

2. Open a terminal window.

3. Create a new file with your favorite text editor.

4. Under Windows systems, type the following in the new file:

```
for /f "tokens=1-3 delims=/- " %%a in ('date /t') do set
    XDate=%%c%%b%%a
for /f "tokens=1-2 delims=: " %%a in ('time /t') do set
    XTime=%%a.%%b

set path_etl=C:\pdi_labs
set path_log=C:\logs

c:\
cd ..
cd pdi-ce
kitchen.bat /file:%path_etl%\load_dm_sales.kjb /level:Detailed
    >> %path_log%\sales_"%Xdate% %XTime%".log
```

5. Save the file as `dm_sales.bat` in a folder of your choice.

6. Under Linux, Unix, and similar systems, type the following:

```
UNXETL=/pdi_labs
UNXLOG=/logs

cd /pdi-ce
kitchen.sh /file:$UNXETL/load_dm_sales.kjb /level:Detailed >>
    $UNXLOG/sales_'date +%y%m%d-%H%M'.log
```

7. Save the file as `dm_sales.sh` in a folder of your choice.

 Irrespective of your system, please replace the names of the folders in the highlighted lines with the names of your own folders, that is `path_etl` (the folder where your main job is), `path_log` (the folder you just created), and `pdi-ce` (the folder where PDI is installed).

Now let's test what you've done:

1. Execute the batch you created.

   Under Windows, type:

   ```
   dm_sales.bat
   ```

   Under Unix-like systems, type:

   ```
   sh dm_sales.sh
   ```

2. When the prompt in the command window is available, it means that the batch ended. Check the log folder. You'll find a new file with the extension `log`, named `sales` followed by the date and hour, for example, `sales_0210Fri 06.46.log`.

3. Edit the log. You will see the full log for the execution of the job. Among the lines you'll see these:

   ```
   INFO   02-10 17:46:39,015 - Set Variables DATE_FROM and
      DATE_TO.0 - Set variable DATE_FROM to value [2009-10-01]
   INFO   02-10 17:46:39,015 - Set Variables DATE_FROM and
      DATE_TO.0 - Set variable DATE_TO to value [2009-10-01]
   ```

4. Also check the fact table. The fact should have the data for the sales made yesterday:

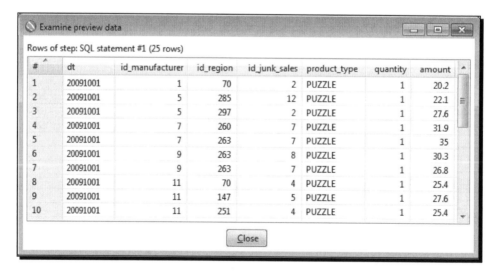

 Don't forget to restore the date in your system!

What just happened?

You modified the job that loads the sales datamart so it always loads the sales from the day before. You also created a script that embedded the execution of the Kitchen command and sent the result to a log. The name of the log is different for every day; this allows you keep a history of logs.

 To understand exactly the full Kitchen command line you put into the scripts, please refer to *Appendix B, Pan and Kitchen – Launching Transformations and Jobs from the Command Line*.

Doing all this, you don't have to worry about providing dates for the process, nor running Spoon, nor remembering the syntax of the Kitchen command. Not only that, if you use a system utility as a cron in Unix or the scheduler in Windows to schedule this script to run every day after midnight, you are done. You got rid of all the administrative tasks!

Have a go hero – creating a backup of your work automatically

Choose a folder where you use to save your work (it could be, for example, the `pdi_labs` folder). Create a job that zips your work under the name `backup_yyyymmdd.zip`. where `yyyymmdd` represents the system date. Test the job.

Then create a `.bat` or `.sh` file that executes your job by sending the log to a file. Test the script.

Finally, schedule the script to be executed weekly.

Have a go hero – enhancing the automation process by sending an email if an error occurs

Modify the main job so if something goes wrong, it sends you an e-mail reporting the problem. Doing so, you don't have to worry about checking the daily log to see if everything went fine. Unless there is a problem with the e-mail server, you'll be notified whenever some error occurs.

 For sending an e-mail, you have to use the **Mail** job entry. For details about how to configure the entry, you can visit `http://wiki.pentaho.com/display/EAI/Mail`.

Summary

In this chapter, you created a set of jobs and transformations that loads a sales datamart. Specifically, you learned how to load a fact table and to embed that process into a bigger one—the process that loads a full datamart.

You also learned to automate PDI processes that is useful to get rid of tedious and repetitive manual tasks. In particular, you automated the loading of your sales datamart.

Beyond that, you must have found this chapter useful for reviewing all you learned since the first chapter.

I hope you enjoyed reading the book and learning PDI, and will start using the tool to solve all your data requirements.

A

Working with Repositories

Spoon allows you to store your transformations and jobs under two different configurations: file-based and database repository. In contrast to the file-based configuration that keeps the transformations and jobs in XML format as `*.ktr` *and* `*.kjb` *files in the local filesystem, the database repository configuration keeps the same information in tables in a relational database.*

Although working with the file-based system is simple and practical, the database repository method can be convenient in some situations.

The following is a list of some of the distinctive repository features:

- Repositories implement security. In order to work with a repository, you need credentials.

- Repositories are, by their nature, prepared for basic team development. The elements you create (transformations, jobs, database connections, and so on) are shared by all the repository users as soon as you create them.

- The Enterprise Repository is a Java content repository capable of more robust and scalable collaborative functions such as version control, locking, and more.

Before you decide on working with a repository, you have to be aware of the file-based system benefits you lose. Here are some examples:

- When working with the database repository-based system, you need access to the repository database. If for some reason you cannot access it (for example, network problems), you will not be able to work. You don't have this restriction when working with files, where you only need the software and the transformation and job files, that is, the .ktr and .kjb files.

- When working with the database repositories, it is difficult to keep track of the changes. Working with the filesystem, it is easier to know which jobs or transformations were modified. If you use Subversion or Git, you even have a control version that allows you to examine the history of changes and to recover older versions of your work if necessary.

- Suppose that you want to search and replace some text in all the jobs and transformations. If you are working with repositories, you would have to do it for each table in the repository database. Whereas working with the file-based system, this task is quite simple. For example, you could create a Sublime project - available for downloading at www.sublimetext.com - open the root directory of your jobs and transformations, and do the task by using the Sublime utilities.

As explained in *Chapter 1, Getting Started with Pentaho Data Integration*, there is a third method, File repository, that is a mix of the two mentioned earlier. It's a repository of jobs and transformations stored in the filesystem.

 The use of the File repository is similar to the database repository. Therefore, we will not explain it in this appendix. You should not have any difficulty in trying it once you understand how to work with the database repository.

This appendix shows you how to create a database repository and how to work with it. You can try repositories and decide for yourself which method, database repository-based or file-based, suits you best.

Creating a database repository

If you want to work with the database repository method, you have to create a database repository in advance.

Time for action – creating a PDI repository

To create a repository, follow these steps:

1. Open the MySQL command-line client.

2. In the command window, type the following command:

   ```
   CREATE DATABASE PDI_REPO;
   ```

3. Open Spoon.

4. Unless a repository dialog appears, open the repository dialog from the **Tools | Repository | Connect...** menu.

5. Click on the plus icon to create a new repository. A window with two options appears: Select the **Kettle database repository** option, as shown in the following screenshot:

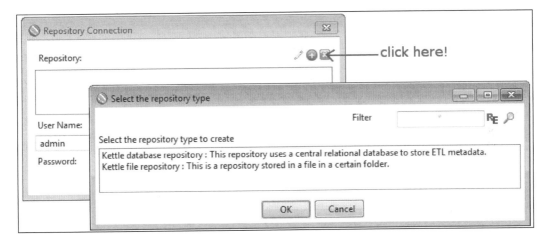

6. The **Repository information** dialog shows up. Click on **New** to create a new database connection.

7. The database connection window appears. Define a connection to the database you have just created and give the connection the name PDI_REPO_CONN.

> In order to create the database connection, refer to the *Time for Action – creating a connection to the Steel Wheels database* recipe in *Chapter 8, Working with Databases*.

8. Test the connection to see that it is properly configured.

9. Click on **OK** to close the database connection window. The **Select Database Connection** box will show the created connection.

10. Give the repository an **ID** and a **Name**, for example, kettle_repo and My First Repo.

11. Click on **Create or Upgrade**.

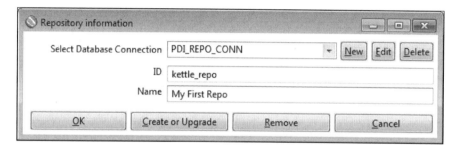

12. PDI will ask you if you are sure you want to create the repository on the specified database connection. Answer **Yes** (if you are sure of the settings you entered of course).

13. A dialog appears asking if you want to do a dry run to evaluate the generated SQL before execution. Answer **No**, unless you want to preview the SQL that will create the repository.

14. A progress window appears showing you the progress while the repository is being created.

15. Finally, you see a window with the message **Kettle created the repository on the specified connection**. Close the dialog window.

16. Click on **OK** to close the **Repository information** window. You will be back in the repository dialog, this time with a new repository available in the repository list.

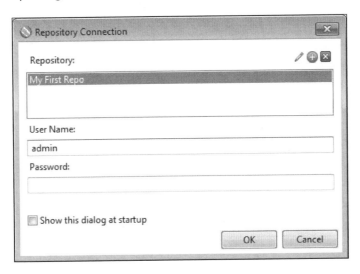

17. If you want to start working with the created repository, refer to the *Working with the repository storage system* section. If not, click on **Cancel**. This will close the window.

What just happened?

In MySQL, you created a new database named PDI_REPO. Then, you used that database to create a PDI database repository.

Creating a database repository to store your transformations and jobs

A Kettle database repository is a database that provides a storage system for your transformations and jobs. The repository is the alternative to the *.ktr and *.kjb file-based system.

In order to create a new database repository, a database must have been created previously. In that section, the repository was created in a MySQL RDBMS. However, you can create your repositories in any JDBC compliant RDBMS.

 The PDI repository database should be used exclusively for its purpose!

Note that if the repository has already been created from another machine or by another user, which means another profile in the operating system, you don't have to create the repository again. In that case, just define the connection to the repository but don't create it again. In other words, follow all the instructions but don't click on the **Create or Upgrade** button.

Once you have created a repository; its name, description, and connection information are stored in a file named `repositories.xml`, located in the PDI home directory. The repository database is populated with a bunch of tables with the familiar names of `transformation`, `job`, `steps`, and `steps_type`.

Note that you may have more than one repository—different repositories for different projects, different repositories for different versions of a project, a repository just for testing new PDI features, and another for serious development, and so on. Therefore, it is important that you give the repositories meaningful names and descriptions so you don't get confused if you have more than one.

Working with the repository storage system

In order to work with a database repository, you must have created at least one. If you didn't, please refer to the section, *Creating a database repository*.

If you already have a repository and you want to work with it, the first thing you have to do is to log in to it. The next tutorial teaches you how to do it.

Time for action – logging into a database repository

To log on into an existent database repository, follow these instructions:

1. Launch Spoon.
2. If the repository dialog window doesn't show up, select **Tools | Repository | Connect...** from the main menu. The repository dialog window appears.
3. In the list, select the repository you want to log in.
4. Type your username and password. If you didn't create a user, use the default `admin`/`admin`, and click on **OK**.

5. You are logged into the repository. You will see the name of the repository in the upper-left corner of Spoon:

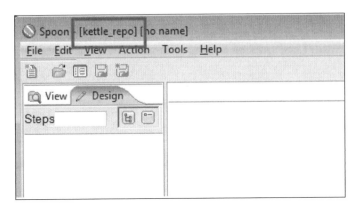

What just happened?

In the preceding section, you opened Spoon and logged into a database repository.

Logging into a database repository using credentials

If you want to work with the repository storage system, you have to log in to the repository before starting to work. In order to do that, you have to choose the repository and provide a repository username and password.

The repository dialog that allows you to log into repository can be opened from the main Spoon menu. If you intend to log into the repository often, you'd better select **Tools | Options...** and check the general option **Show repository dialog at startup?**, which will cause the repository dialog to always show up when you launch Spoon.

It is possible to log into the repository automatically. Suppose you have a repository named MY_REPO, and you use the default user. By adding the following lines to the kettle.properties file, the next time you launch Spoon you will log into the repository automatically:

```
KETTLE_REPOSITORY=MY_REPO
KETTLE_USER=admin
KETTLE_PASSWORD=admin
```

For details on the `kettle.properties` file, refer to the *Kettle variables* section in *Chapter 3, Manipulating Real-world Data*.

As a final note, take into account that the log information is exposed and as such, autologin is not recommended.

Creating transformations and jobs in repository folders

In a repository, the jobs and transformations are organized in folders. A folder in a repository fulfills the same purpose as a folder in your drive—it allows you to keep your work organized. Once you create a folder, you can save both transformations and jobs in it.

While connected to a repository, you can design, preview, and run jobs and transformations just as you do with files. However, there are some differences when it comes to opening, creating, or saving your work. So let's summarize how you do those tasks when logged into a repository:

Task	Procedure
Open a transformation/job	Select **File	Open**. The repository explorer shows up. Navigate the repository until you find the transformation or job you want to open, then double-click on it.
Create a folder	Select **Tools	Repository	Explore ...**, expand the transformation or job tree, locate the parent folder, right-click on it and create the folder.
Create a transformation	Select **File	New	Transformation** or press *Ctrl + N*.
Create a job	Select **File	New	Job** or press *Ctrl + Alt + N*.
Save a transformation	Press *Ctrl + T*. Give the transformation a name. In the **Directory** textbox, select the folder where the transformation is going to be saved. Press *Ctrl + S*. The transformation will be saved in the selected directory under the given name.
Save a job	Press *Ctrl + J*. Give the job a name. In the **Directory** textbox, select the folder where the job is going to be saved. Press *Ctrl + S*. The job will be saved in the selected directory under the given name.

Creating database connections, users, servers, partitions, and clusters

Besides jobs and transformations, there are some additional PDI elements that you can define:

Element	Description
Connections	This element defines connections to relational databases. These are covered in *Chapter 8, Working with Databases*.
Security	This element provides security to the users. They are needed to log into the repository. There are two predefined users: `admin` and `guest`.

You can also define some elements not covered in this book, but worth mentioning:

Element	Description
Slaves	Slave servers are the servers installed in remote machines to execute jobs and transformations remotely.
Partitions	Partitioning is a mechanism by which you can send individual rows to different copies of the same step, for example, based on a field value.
Clusters	Clusters are a group of slave servers which collectively execute a job or a transformation.

All the elements can also be created, modified, and deleted from the repository explorer. Once you create any of these elements, they are automatically shared by all repository users.

Designing jobs and transformations

You shouldn't have any difficulty in designing jobs and transformations under a database repository-based method. The way you work is exactly the same as the way you learned through all the chapters while working under the file-based method. The main change, besides the way you open and save your work, is the way you refer to other jobs and transformations. Here you have a list of the main situations:

Task	File-based method	Database repository-based method
Providing the name of the job to run in a Job-job entry	You provide the full path of the `.kjb` file or a relative path, eventually using the `${Internal.Job.Filename.Directory}` variable.	You should fill the **Repository: specify by name** option. You may eventually use a relative location using the `${Internal.Job.Repository.Directory}` variable.
Providing the name of the transformation to run in a Transformation-job entry	You provide the full path of the `.ktr` file or a relative path, eventually using the `${Internal.Job.Filename.Directory}` variable.	You should fill the **Specify by name and directory** option. You may eventually use a relative location using the `${Internal.Job.Repository.Directory}` variable.
Providing the name of the transformation to run as a subtransformation using a Mapping step	You provide the full path of the `.ktr` file or a relative path, eventually using the `${Internal.Transformation.Filename.Directory}` variable.	You should fill the **Use a mapping transformation from the repository** option. You may eventually use a relative location using the `${Internal.Transformation.Repository.Directory}` variable.
Providing the name of a file whose location is relative to the location of a job or a transformation	You provide the relative path using `${Internal.Job.Filename.Directory}` in a job or `${Internal.Transformation.Filename.Directory}` in a transformation.	In a database repository-based system, you can create a folder tree as you do in the filesystem. However, you are not able to specify relative paths.

Backing up and restoring a repository

You may regularly back up your database repository in the same way as you would do with any database. You do it by using the utilities provided by the RDBMS, for example, `mysqldump` in MySQL. However, PDI offers you a method for creating a backup in an XML file.

- You create a backup from the **Tools | Repository | Export Repository...** option. You will be asked for the name and location of the XML file that will contain the backup data. To backup a single folder, open the Repository explorer and right-click on the name of the folder.

- You restore a backup from the **Tools | Repository | Import Repository...** option. You will be asked for the name and location of the XML file that contains the backup.

Both in the export and the import operations, Kettle offers you the possibility to apply some rules to make sure that the transformations and jobs adhere to the given standards.

As an example, suppose that you want to make sure that there are no disabled hops in your jobs. One of the rules that Kettle offers does this verification—the name of the rule is 'Job has no disabled hops'. The list of available rules is quite limited but still useful for meeting some basic requirements.

Examining and modifying the contents of a repository with the Repository Explorer

The Repository Explorer (completely redesigned in PDI 4.0) shows you a tree view of the repository to which you are connected. From the main Spoon menu, select **Tools | Repository | Explore...** and you get to the explorer window. Alternatively, you can open it with the shortcut *Ctrl + E*, or by clicking on the explore repository icon in the main toolbar. The following screenshot shows you a sample **Repository explorer** screen:

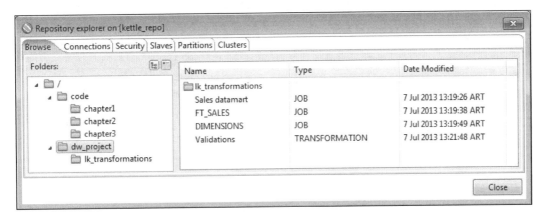

As mentioned earlier, besides jobs and transformations, there are additional tabs for exploring connections, partitions, and more.

The repository explorer not only shows you these elements, but also allows you to create, modify, and delete them. All these operations are executed using the toolbar at the upper right-hand corner of the **Repository explorer**.

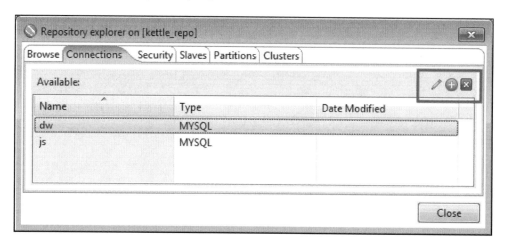

The following table summarizes the available actions:

Action	Toolbar option	Procedure
Create a new element (any but transformations and jobs)	⊕	Click on the plus icon. A window will show-up for you to fill in the different properties of the new element.
Open an element for inspecting or editing	✎	Select the item and click on the pencil icon. A window will show-up displaying the current values for the selected item and allowing you to change them.
Delete an element	☒	Select the item you want to delete and click on the cross icon.

Migrating from file-based system to repository-based system and vice versa

No matter which storage system you are using, file-based or database repository, you may want to move your work to the other system just to try it or for taking advantage of the benefits of the other system, mentioned at the beginning of this appendix. The following table summarizes the procedure for doing that (migrating from a file-based configuration to a database repository):

PDI element	Procedure for migrating from file to repository
Transformations or jobs	From **File | Import from an XML file**, browse to locate the `.ktr/.kjb` file to import, and open it. Once the file has been imported, you can save it into the repository as usual.
Database connections, Partition schemas, Slaves, and Clusters	When importing from an XML file, job, or transformation that uses the database connection, the connection is imported as well. The same applies to partitions, slave servers, and clusters.

There is also a command-line tool that will allow you to bulk import jobs and transformations into a repository. This is the **Import tool**, which you can find in the PDI installation directory as `import.sh` or `import.bat`.

For examples and a full description of the use of the Import utility, you can visit the website `http://wiki.pentaho.com/display/EAI/Import+User+Documentation`.

The following table summarizes the procedure for migrating from database repository to file-based configuration:

PDI element	Procedure for migrating from repository to file
Single transformation or job	Open the job or transformation, select **File | Export to an XML file**, browse the disk to find the folder where you want to save the job or transformation and save it. Once it has been exported, it will be available to work with the under-the-file storage method, or to import from another repository.
All transformations saved in a folder	In the **Repository explorer**, right-click on the name of the folder and select **Export transformations**. You will be asked to select the directory where the folder and all its subfolders and transformations will be exported. If you right-click on the name of the repository or the root folder in the transformation tree, you can export all the transformations.

PDI element	Procedure for migrating from repository to file
All jobs saved in a folder	In the **Repository explorer**, right-click on the name of the folder and select **Export Jobs**. You will be asked to select the directory where the folder and all its subfolders and jobs will be exported.
	If you right-click on the name of the repository or the root folder in the Job tree, you can export all the jobs.
Database connections, Partition schemas, Slaves and Clusters	When exporting to an XML file a job or transformation that uses the database connection, the connection is exported as well (it's saved as part of the .ktr/.kjb file). The same applies to partitions, slave servers, and clusters.

 You have to be logged into the repository in order to do any of the explained operations.

If you share a database connection, a partition schema, a slave server, or a cluster; it will be available to use from both a file and a repository as the shared elements are always saved in the shared.xml file in the Kettle home directory.

Summary

This appendix covered the basic concepts for working with repositories. Besides the topics covered here, working with repositories is pretty much the same as working with files.

Although the tutorials in this book were explained assuming that you work with files, all of them can be implemented under a repository-based configuration with minimal changes, as explained in the *Designing jobs and transformations* section earlier. You should not have any trouble in developing and testing the exercises.

Whether you decide to work with repositories or not, you will find the next appendix very useful. It explains in detail how to launch transformations and jobs from the command-line, both from a file-based and a database repository-based system.

B

Pan and Kitchen – Launching Transformations and Jobs from the Command Line

Despite having used Spoon as the tool for running jobs and transformations, you may also run them from a terminal window. Many transformations and jobs you design in Spoon end up being used as part of batch processes, for example, processes that run every night in a scheduled fashion. When it comes to running them in that way, you need Pan and Kitchen.

Pan is a command-line program which lets you launch the transformations designed in Spoon, both from the `.ktr` *files and from a repository.*

The counterpart to Pan is Kitchen, which allows you to run jobs both from `.kjb` *files and from a repository.*

This appendix shows you the different options you have to run these commands.

Running transformations and jobs stored in files

In order to run a transformation or a job stored as a .ktr file or a .kjb file follow these steps:

1. Open a terminal window.

2. Go to the **Kettle installation** directory.

3. Run the proper command according to the following table:

Task	Windows	Unix-based system
Running a transformation	`pan.bat /file:<ktr file name>`	`pan.sh /file:<ktr file name>`
Running a job	`kitchen.bat / file:<kjb file name>`	`kitchen.sh /file:<kjb file name>`

 When specifying the `.ktr` or `.kjb` filename you must include the full path. If the name contains spaces, surround it with double quotes.

Here you have some examples:

♦ Suppose that you work with Windows and that your Kettle installation directory is `c:\pdi-ce`. In order to execute a transformation stored in the file `c:\pdi_labs\hello.ktr`, you have to type the following commands:

```
C:
cd \pdi-ce
pan.bat /file:"c:\pdi_labs\hello.ktr"
```

♦ Suppose that you work with a Unix-based system and that your **Kettle installation** directory is `/home/yourself/pdi-ce`. In order to execute a job stored in the file `/home/pdi_labs/hellojob.kjb`, you have to type the following commands:

```
cd /home/yourself/pdi-ce
kitchen.sh /file:"/home/yourself/pdi-ce/hellojob.kjb"
```

 If you have a repository with autologin (see *Appendix A, Working with Repositories*), as part of the command add `/norep`. This will avoid the PDI log into the repository.

Running transformations and jobs from a repository

In order to run a transformation or job stored in a repository, follow these steps:

1. Open a terminal window.
2. Go to the Kettle installation directory.
3. Run the proper command according to the following table:

Task	Windows	Unix-based system
Running a transformation	`pan.bat /rep:<value>` `/user:<user>` `/pass:<value>` `/trans:<value>` `/dir:<value>`	`pan.sh /rep:<value>` `/user:<user>` `/pass:<value>` `/trans:<value>` `/dir:<value>`
Running a job	`kitchen.bat /rep:<value>` `/user:<user>` `/pass:<value>` `/job:<value>` `/dir:<value>`	`kitchen.sh /rep:<value>` `/user:<user>` `/pass:<value>` `/job:<value>` `/dir:<value>`

In the Windows column of the preceding table:

- `rep` is the name of the repository to log into
- `user` and `pass` are the credentials to log into the repository
- `trans` and `job` are the names of the transformation or job to run
- `dir` is the name of the directory where the transformation or job is located

> The parameters are shown in different lines so that you can clearly identify all of the options.
> When you type the command, you have to write all of the parameters in the same line.

Suppose you work in Windows, you have a repository named MY_REPO and you log into the repository with user PDI_USER and password 1234. To run a transformation named Hello located in a directory named MY_WORK in that repository, type the following code:

```
pan.bat /rep:"MY_REPO" /user:"PDI_USER" /pass:"1234" /trans:"Hello"
/dir:"/MY_WORK/"
```

> If you have defined an autologin you don't need to provide the repository information, that is, the rep, user, and pass command-line parameters, as part of the command.

Specifying command-line options

In the examples provided in this appendix, all options are specified by using the syntax /option:value, as for example /trans:"Hello".

Instead of a slash (/) you can also use a hyphen (-). Between the name of the option and the value you can also use an equal to (=). This means that the option /trans:"Hello" and -trans="Hello" are equivalents.

You may use any combination of a slash (/) and a hyphen (-) or a colon (:) and an equal to (=).

> As in Windows the use of - and = may cause problems, it's recommended that you use the /option:value syntax.

As for the values, if spaces are present you can use quotes (") or double quotes ("") to keep the value together. If there are not spaces, the quotes are optional.

Kettle variables and the Kettle home directory

As explained in the *Kettle Variables* section in *Chapter 3, Manipulating Real-world Data* you can define Kettle variables in the kettle.properties file. This file is located in the .kettle folder in your home directory. Pan and Kitchen recognize the variables defined in this file in the same way that Spoon does. The .kettle folder is referred to as the Kettle home directory.

If you want to run a job or a transformation for a particular set of variables that are different from those defined in the default Kettle home directory, you may want to create a copy of this folder in a different place, define your variables in the new `kettle.properties` file, and change the value of the `KETTLE_HOME` variable. Supposing that the new location is `/opt/pentaho_test`, you can change the value by running `export KETTLE_HOME=/opt/pentaho_test` before running Pan or Kitchen.

Checking the exit code

Both Pan and Kitchen return an error code based on how the execution went. To check the exit code of Pan or Kitchen under Windows after running the command, type:

```
echo %ERRORLEVEL%
```

To check the exit code of Pan or Kitchen under Unix-based systems, type:

```
echo $?
```

If you get a zero, it means that there are no errors. A value greater than zero means a failure. The following table shows the meaning of the possible exit codes:

Exit Code	Meaning
0	The transformation/job ran without problem
1	Errors occurred during processing
2	An unexpected error occurred during loading/running of the transformation/job
3	Unable to prepare and initialize the transformation (only in Pan)
7	The transformation/job couldn't be loaded from XML or the repository
8	Error loading steps or plugins (error in loading one of the plugins mostly)
9	Command-line usage printing

Providing options when running Pan and Kitchen

When you execute a transformation or a job with Spoon, you have the option to provide additional information, for example, named parameters. The following Spoon dialog window shows you an example of that:

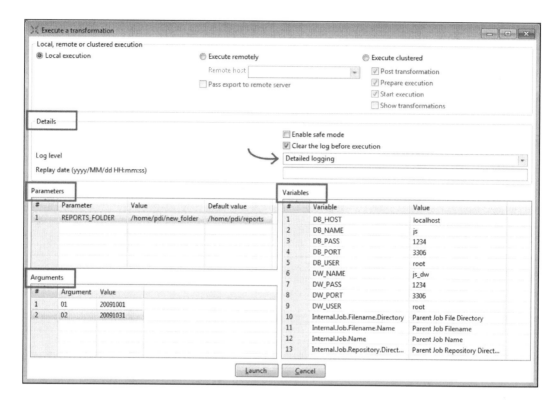

When you execute the transformation or job with Pan or Kitchen respectively, you provide this same information as options in the command line. This is how you do it compared side-by-side with Spoon:

◆ Log **Details**

The following table compares providing the log **Details** when executing a transformation or a job with Spoon versus Pan/Kitchen:

Spoon	Pan/Kitchen option	Example

You specify the log level in the drop-down list inside the **Details** box.
 	
When the transformation or job runs, the log is shown in the **Execution Results** window.
	`/level:<logging level>`
	
	where the logging level can be one of the following:
	
	`Error, Nothing, Minimal, Basic, Detailed, Debug, or Rowlevel.`
		`/level:Detailed`
		
		The log appears in the terminal window but you use the command language of your operating system to redirect it to a file.

◆ Named **Parameters**

The following table compares providing the named **Parameters** when executing a transformation or a job with Spoon versus Pan/Kitchen:

Spoon	Pan/Kitchen option	Example

You specify the named parameters in the **Parameters** box. The window shows you the name of the defined named parameters for you to fill the values or leave the defaults.	`/param:`
	
	`<parameter name>=`
	
	`<parameter value>`
		`/param:`
		
		`"REPORT_FOLDER=`
		
		`c:\my_rep\"`

◆ **Arguments**

The following table compares providing the **Arguments** when executing a transformation or a job with Spoon versus Pan/Kitchen:

Spoon	Pan/Kitchen option	Example

You specify the command-line arguments in the **Arguments** grid. Each line corresponds to a different argument.	You type them in order as part of the command.	`20091001`
		
		`20091031`

◆ **Variables**

The following table compares providing the **Variables** when executing a transformation or a job with Spoon versus Pan/Kitchen:

Spoon	Pan/Kitchen option
The grid named **Variables** shows the variables used in the transformation/ job as well as their current values. At the time of the execution you can type different values.	You cannot set variables in the Pan nor in the Kitchen command. The variables have to exist. You may define them in the `kettle. properties` file.

Suppose that the sample transformation shown in the screenshot is located at `c:\pdi_labs\sales_report.ktr`. Then the following Pan command executes the transformation with the same options shown in the screenshot:

```
pan.bat /file:"c:\pdi_labs\sales_report.ktr" 20091001 20091031 … /
level:Detailed > c:\pdi_labs\logs\sales_report.log
```

You should not continue a sentence in this manner- write the sentence before the code in full and start a new one after the code has been inserted. The command redirects the log to the file `c:\pdi_labs\logs\sales_report.log`.

Besides these, both Pan and Kitchen have additional options. For a full list and more examples, visit the Pan and Kitchen documentation at `http://wiki.pentaho.com/ display/EAI/Pan+User+Documentation`, and `http://wiki.pentaho.com/ display/EAI/Kitchen+User+Documentation` respectively.

Summary

This appendix explained in detail how to run jobs and transformations from a terminal window, by using the Kitchen and Pan command-line programs respectively.

You learned how to run jobs and transformations both from files or from a repository, and also saw the most commonly used command-line options available.

C

Quick Reference – Steps and Job Entries

This appendix summarizes the purpose of the steps and job entries used in the tutorials throughout the book. For each of them you can see the name of the Time for Action section where it was introduced and also a reference for the chapters where you can find more examples that use it.

How to use this reference?

Suppose that you are inside Spoon editing a transformation. If the transformation uses a step that you don't know and you want to understand what it does or how to use it, double-click on the step and take a note of the title of the settings window. That title is the name of the step. Then, search for that name in the transformation steps reference table. The steps are listed in alphabetical order so you can find them quickly. The last column will take you to the place in the book where the step is explained.

The same applies to jobs. If you see in a Job an unknown entry, double-click on the entry and take a note of the title of the setting window. That title is the name of the entry. Then, search for that name in the job entries reference table. The job entries are also listed in alphabetical order.

Transformation steps

The following table includes all of the transformation steps used in the book. For a full list of the steps and their descriptions, select **Help | Step information...** in Spoon's main menu.

Also visit the website `http://wiki.pentaho.com/display/EAI/`
`Pentaho+Data+Integration+Steps`.

There you will find a full step reference and some examples as well.

Icon	Name	Purpose	Time for action
	Abort	Aborts a transformation.	*Generating custom messages by setting a variable with the name of the examination file (Chapter 11, Creating Advanced Transformations and Jobs). Also in Chapter 12, Developing and Implementing a Simple Datamart.*
	Add constants	Adds one or more constants to the input rows.	*Gathering progress and merging all together (Chapter 5, Controlling the Flow of Data). Also in Chapter 8, Working with Databases, Chapter 9, Performing Advanced Operations with Databases, and Chapter 12, Developing and Implementing a Simple Datamart.*
	Add sequence	Gets the next value from a sequence.	*Assigning tasks by distributing (Chapter 5, Controlling the Flow of Data). Also in Chapter 11, Creating Advanced Transformations and Jobs, and Chapter 12, Developing and Implementing a Simple Datamart.*
	Append streams	Appends two streams in an ordered way.	*Giving priority to Bouchard by using Append Stream (Chapter 5, Controlling the Flow of Data).*
	Calculator	Creates new fields by performing simple calculations.	*Avoiding errors while converting the estimated time (Chapter 2, Getting started with Transformations). Also in Chapter 3, Manipulating Real-world Data, Chapter 4, Filtering, Searching, and Performing Other Useful Operations with Data, Chapter 5, Controlling the Flow of Data, Chapter 7, Transforming the Rowset, Chapter 8, Working with Databases, Chapter 10, Creating Basic Task Flows, and Chapter 12, Developing and Implementing a Simple Datamart.*
	Clone row	Clones a row as many times as needed.	*Generating a range of dates and inspecting (Chapter 2, Getting started with Transformations). Also in Chapter 7, Transforming the Rowset, and Chapter 10, Creating Basic Task Flows.*

Icon	Name	Purpose	Time for action
	Combination lookup/update	Updates a junk dimension in a data-warehouse. Alternatively, looks up information in this dimension.	*Loading a region dimension with a Combination lookup-update step (Chapter 9, Performing Advanced Operations with Databases). Also in Chapter 12, Developing and Implementing a Simple Datamart.*
	Copy rows to result	Writes rows to the executing job. The information will then be passed to the next entry in the job.	*Generating top average scores by copying and getting rows (Chapter 11, Creating Advanced Transformations and Jobs).*
	Data Grid	Allows you to create rows of static data in a grid, usually for testing, reference, or demo purposes.	*Avoiding errors while converting the estimated time (Chapter 2, Getting started with Transformations). Also in Chapter 5, Controlling the Flow of Data.*
	Database join	Executes a database query using stream values as parameters.	*Using a Database join step to create a list of suggested products to buy (Chapter 9, Performing Advanced Operations with Databases).*
	Database lookup	Looks up values in a database using field values.	*Using a Database lookup step to create a list of products to buy (Chapter 9, Performing Advanced Operations with Databases). Also in Chapter 12, Developing and Implementing a Simple Datamart.*
	Delay row	Outputs each input row after a delay.	*Generating a range of dates and inspecting (Chapter 2, Getting started with Transformations) Also in Chapter 10, Creating Basic Task Flows.*
	Delete	Deletes data in a database table based upon keys.	*Deleting data about discontinued items (Chapter 8, Working with Databases).*
	Dimension lookup/ update	Updates a slowly changing dimension in a data-warehouse. Alternatively, look up information in this dimension.	*Keeping a history of changes in product by using the Dimension lookup-update step (Chapter 9, Performing Advanced Operations with Databases). Also in Chapter 12, Developing and Implementing a Simple Datamart.*

Icon	Name	Purpose	Time for action
	Dummy (do nothing)	This step type doesn't do anything. It's useful however when testing, or in certain situations where you want to split streams.	*Creating a hello world transformation (Chapter 1, Getting started with Pentaho Data Integration). Also in Chapter 3, Manipulating Real-world Data, Chapter 4, Filtering, Searching, and Performing Other Useful Operations with Data, Chapter 6, Transforming your Data by Coding, Chapter 7, Transforming the Rowset, Chapter 9, Performing Advanced Operations with Databases, Chapter 11, Creating Advanced Transformations and Jobs, and Chapter 12, Developing and Implementing a Simple Datamart.*
	Filter rows	Filters rows using simple equations.	*Counting frequent words by filtering (Chapter 4, Filtering, Searching, and Performing Other Useful Operations with Data). Also in Chapter 5, Controlling the Flow of Data, Chapter 7, Transforming the Rowset, Chapter 9, Performing Advanced Operations with Databases, Chapter 11, Creating Advanced Transformations and Jobs, and Chapter 12, Developing and Implementing a Simple Datamart.*
fx	Formula	Calculates a formula using Pentaho's `libformula`.	*Generating custom files by executing a transformation for every input row (Chapter 11, Creating Advanced Transformations and Jobs).*
	Generate random value	Generates random values.	*Have a go Hero – measuring the performance of input steps (Chapter 3, Manipulating Real-world Data).*

Icon	Name	Purpose	Time for action
	Generate Rows	Generates a number of empty or equal rows.	*Creating a hello world transformation (Chapter 1, Getting started with Pentaho Data Integration). Also in Chapter 2, Getting started with Transformations, Chapter 3, Manipulating Real-world Data, Chapter 7, Transforming the Rowset, Chapter 9, Performing Advanced Operations with Databases, Chapter 10, Creating Basic Task Flows, and Chapter 12, Developing and Implementing a Simple Datamart.*
	Get data from XML	Gets data from an XML file by using `XPath`. This step also allows you to parse XML defined in a previous field.	*Getting data from an XML file with information about countries (Chapter 3, Manipulating Real-world Data). Also in Chapter 4, Filtering, Searching, and Performing Other Useful Operations with Data, and Chapter 9, Performing Advanced Operations with Databases.*
	Get rows from result	Reads rows from a previous entry in a job.	*Generating top average scores by copying and getting rows (Chapter 11, Creating Advanced Transformations and Jobs).*
	Get System Info	Gets information from the system such as system date, arguments, and so on.	*Reading and writing matching files with flexibility (Chapter 3, Manipulating Real-world Data). Also in Chapter 8, Working with Databases, Chapter 10, Creating Basic Task Flows, Chapter 11, Creating Advanced Transformations and Jobs, and Chapter 12, Developing and Implementing a Simple Datamart.*
	Get Variables	Determines the values of certain (environment or Kettle) variables and puts them in field values.	*Creating a time dimension dataset (Chapter 7, Transforming the Rowset). Also in Chapter 12, Developing and Implementing a Simple Datamart.*
	Group by	Builds aggregates in a group by fashion. This works only on a sorted input. If the input is not sorted, only double consecutive rows are handled correctly.	*Calculating football matches statistics by grouping data (Chapter 4, Filtering, Searching, and Performing Other Useful Operations with Data). Also in Chapter 5, Controlling the Flow of Data, Chapter 9, Performing Advanced Operations with Databases, and Chapter 11, Creating Advanced Transformations and Jobs.*

Icon	Name	Purpose	Time for action
	If field value is null	Sets a field value to a constant if it is null.	*Enhancing a films file by converting rows to columns (Chapter 7, Transforming the Rowset).*
	Insert/Update	Updates or insert rows in a database based upon keys.	*Inserting new products or updating existent ones (Chapter 8, Working with Databases).*
	Java Filter	Filters rows using Java code.	*Generating top average scores by copying and getting rows (Chapter 11, Creating Advanced Transformations and Jobs).*
	Mapping (subtransformation)	Run a subtransformation, use `MappingInput` and `MappingOutput` to specify the fields interface.	*Calculating statistics with the use of a subtransformation (Chapter 11, Creating Advanced Transformations and Jobs).*
	Mapping input specification	Specifies the input interface of a mapping.	*Calculating statistics with the use of a subtransformation (Chapter 11, Creating Advanced Transformations and Jobs).*
	Mapping output specification	Specifies the output interface of a mapping.	*Calculating statistics with the use of a subtransformation (Chapter 11, Creating Advanced Transformations and Jobs).*
	Microsoft Excel Input	Reads data from Excel and OpenOffice Workbooks (`.xls`, `.xlsx`, and `.ods`).	*Browsing new features of PDI by copying a dataset (Chapter 5, Controlling the Flow of Data). Also in Chapter 8, Working with Databases, and Chapter 12, Developing and Implementing a Simple Datamart.*
	Microsoft Excel Output	Stores records into an Excel (`.xls`) document.	*Getting data from an XML file with information about countries (Chapter 3, Manipulating Real-World Data). Also in Chapter 5, Controlling the Flow of Data.*
	Modified JavaScript Value	Allows you to code JavaScript to modify or create new fields.	*Counting frequent words by coding in JavaScript (Chapter 6, Transforming your Data by Coding). Also in Chapter 7, Transforming the Rowset.*

Icon	Name	Purpose	Time for action
	Number range	Creates ranges based on a numeric field.	*Creating a simple transformation (Chapter 2, Getting Started with Transformations). Also in Chapter 8, Working with Databases.*
	Regex Evaluation	Evaluates a field using a regular expression. It can also extract new fields out of an existing field with capturing groups.	*Loading the fact table using a range of dates (Chapter 12, Developing and Implementing a Simple Datamart).*
	Replace in string	Replaces all occurrences of a word in a string with another word.	*Fixing words before counting them (Chapter 4, Filtering, Searching, and Performing Other Useful Operations with Data).*
	Row denormaliser	Denormalizes rows by looking up key-value pairs and assigning them to new fields in the output rows. This method aggregates and needs the input rows to be sorted on the grouping fields.	*Enhancing a films file by converting rows to columns (Chapter 7, Transforming the Rowset).*
	Row Normaliser	Denormalized information can be normalized using this step-type.	*Enhancing the matches files by normalizing the dataset (Chapter 7, Transforming the Rowset). Also in Chapter 12, Developing and Implementing a Simple Datamart.*
	Select values	Selects, reorders, or removes fields. Optionally, allows you to change the metadata: type, length, and precision.	*Avoiding errors while converting the estimated time (Chapter 2, Getting Started with Transformations). Also in Chapter 3, Manipulating Real-World Data, Chapter 4, Filtering, Searching, and Performing Other Useful Operations with Data, Chapter 5, Controlling the Flow of Data, Chapter 7, Transforming the Rowset, Chapter 8, Working with Databases, Chapter 9, Performing Advanced Operations with Databases, Chapter 10, Creating Basic Task Flows, and Chapter 12, Developing and Implementing a Simple Datamart.*

Icon	Name	Purpose	Time for action
	Set Variables	Sets Kettle variables based on a single-input row.	*Generating custom messages by setting a variable with the name of the examination file (Chapter 11, Creating Advanced Transformations and Jobs). Also in Chapter 12, Developing and Implementing a Simple Datamart.*
	Sort rows	Sorts rows based upon field values (ascending or descending).	*Sorting information about matches (Chapter 4, Filtering, Searching, and Performing Other Useful Operations with Data). Also in Chapter 5, Controlling the Flow of Data, Chapter 7, Transforming the Rowset, Chapter 8, Working with Databases, Chapter 9, Performing Advanced Operations with Databases, and Chapter 11, Creating Advanced Transformations and Jobs.*
	Split field to rows	Splits a single string field by delimiter and creates a new row for each split term.	*Counting frequent words by filtering (Chapter 4, Filtering, Searching, and Performing Other Useful Operations with Data). Also in Chapter 6, Transforming your Data by Coding.*
	Split Fields	Splits a single string field into two or more.	*Aggregating football matches data with the Row denormaliser step (Chapter 7, Transforming the Rowset). Also in Chapter 12, Developing and Implementing a Simple Datamart.*
	Stream lookup	Looks up values coming from another stream in the transformation.	*Finding out which language people speak (Chapter 4, Filtering, Searching, and Performing Other Useful Operations with Data). Also in Chapter 7, Transforming the Rowset, and Chapter 12, Developing and Implementing a Simple Datamart.*
	Switch/Case	Switches a row to a certain target step based on the case value in a field.	*Assigning tasks by filtering priorities with the Switch Case step (Chapter 5, Controlling the Flow of Data).*
	Table input	Reads data from a database table.	*Getting data about shipped orders (Chapter 8, Working with Databases). Also in Chapter 9, Performing Advanced Operations with Databases, and Chapter 12, Developing and Implementing a Simple Datamart.*

Icon	Name	Purpose	Time for action
	Table output	Writes data onto a database table.	*Loading a table with a list of manufacturers (Chapter 8, Working with Databases). Also in Chapter 9, Performing Advanced Operations with Databases, and Chapter 12, Developing and Implementing a Simple Datamart.*
	Text file input	Reads data from a text file.	*Reading results of football matches from files (Chapter 3, Manipulating Real-world Data). Also in Chapter 4, Filtering, Searching, and Performing Other Useful Operations with Data, Chapter 6, Transforming your Data by Coding, Chapter 7, Transforming the Rowset, Chapter 8, Working with Databases, and Chapter 11, Creating Advanced Transformations and Jobs.*
	Text file output	Writes data to a text file.	*Sending the results of matches to a plain file (Chapter 3, Manipulating Real-world Data). Also in Chapter 4, Filtering, Searching, and Performing Other Useful Operations with Data, Chapter 9, Performing Advanced Operations with Databases, Chapter 10, Creating Basic Task Flows, and Chapter 11, Creating Advanced Transformations and Jobs.*
	Unique rows	Removes double rows leaving unique occurrences.	*Have a go hero – listing the last match played by each team (Chapter 4, Filtering, Searching, and Performing Other Useful Operations with Data).*
	Update	Updates data in a database table based upon keys.	*Loading a region dimension with a Combination lookup-update step (Chapter 9, Performing Advanced Operations with Databases) Also in Chapter 12, Developing and Implementing a Simple Datamart.*
	User Defined Java Class	Allows you to program a step using Java code.	*Counting frequent words by coding in Java (Chapter 6, Transforming your Data by Coding).*

Icon	Name	Purpose	Time for action
	User Defined Java Expression	Calculates the result of a Java Expression using Janino.	*Creating a simple transformation (Chapter 2, Getting Started with Transformations). Also in Chapter 10, Creating Basic Task Flows, and Chapter 11, Creating Advanced Transformations and Jobs.*
	Value Mapper	Maps values of a certain field from one value to another.	*Browsing new features of PDI by copying a dataset (Chapter 5, Controlling the Flow of Data).*
	Write to log	Writes data to the log.	*Avoiding errors while converting the estimated time (Chapter 2, Getting started with Transformations). Also in Chapter 5, Controlling the Flow of Data, and Chapter 8, Working with Databases.*

Job entries

The following table includes all of the job entries used in the book. For a full list of job entries and their descriptions, select **Help | Job Entry Information...** in Spoon's main menu.

Also visit the website `http://wiki.pentaho.com/display/EAI/Pentaho+Data+Integration+Job+Entries`. There you will find a full job entries reference and some examples as well.

Icon	Name	Purpose	Time for action
	Abort job	Aborts the job.	*Generating custom messages by setting a variable with the name of the examination file (Chapter 11, Creating Advanced Transformations and Jobs).*
	Checks if files exist	Checks if the files exist.	*Creating a simple job and getting familiar with the design process (Chapter 10, Creating Basic Task Flows).*
	Create a folder	Creates a folder.	*Creating a folder with a Kettle job (Chapter 10, Creating Basic Task Flows).*

Icon	Name	Purpose	Time for action
	Delete files	Deletes the files.	*Generating custom files by executing a transformation for every input row (Chapter 11, Creating Advanced Transformations and Jobs).*
	Evaluate rows number in a table	Evaluates the content of a table. You can also specify an SQL query.	*Loading the dimensions for the sales datamart (Chapter 12, Developing and Implementing a Simple Datamart).*
	File Exists	Checks if a file exists.	*Generating custom messages by setting a variable with the name of the examination file (Chapter 11, Creating Advanced Transformations and Jobs).*
	Job	Executes a job.	*Generating custom messages by setting a variable with the name of the examination file (Chapter 11, Creating Advanced Transformations and Jobs). Also in Chapter 12, Developing and Implementing a Simple Datamart.*
	Mail	Sends an email.	*Have a go hero – enhancing the automate process by sending an email if an error occurs (Chapter 12, Developing and Implementing a Simple Datamart).*
	Special entries	START job entry; mandatory at the beginning of a job.	*Creating a folder with a Kettle job (Chapter 10, Creating Basic Task Flows). Also in Chapter 11, Creating Advanced Transformations and Jobs, and Chapter 12, Developing and Implementing a Simple Datamart.*
	Success	Forces the success of a job execution.	*Loading the dimensions for the sales datamart (Chapter 12, Developing and Implementing a Simple Datamart).*
	Transformation	Executes a transformation.	*Generating a range of dates (Chapter 10, Creating Basic Task Flows). Also in Chapter 11, and Chapter 12, Developing and Implementing a Simple Datamart.*

Icon	Name	Purpose	Time for action
	Write To Log	Writes a message to the Kettle log.	*Creating a simple job and getting familiar with the design process (Chapter 10, Creating Basic Task Flows).*

> Note that this appendix is just for a quick reference. It's not meant at all for learning to use the PDI. In order to learn from scratch, you should read the book starting from the first chapter.

Summary

PDI has hundreds of steps and job entries available for designing jobs and transformations. In this book, you have only learned a subset of them. This appendix served as a quick reference to that subset of steps and job entries, but also gave you web references so you can investigate further on the Internet.

D

Spoon Shortcuts

The following tables summarize the main Spoon shortcuts. Have this appendix handy; it will save you a lot of time while working with Spoon.

 If you are a Mac user, be aware that a mixture of Windows and Mac keys are used. In general, the *Ctrl* key should be replaced with the *command* key, and you use the name *option* for referring to the *Alt* key. For example, for copying, you do not use *Ctrl + C* but *command + C*; instead of creating a job with *Ctrl + Alt + N*, you do it with *command + option + N*. That said, in order to avoid confusion, Windows and Mac OS shortcuts are listed in separate columns.

General shortcuts

The following table lists the general Spoon shortcuts:

Action	Windows shortcut	Mac OS shortcut
New job	Ctrl + Alt + N	command + option + N
New transformation	Ctrl + N	command + N
Open a job/transformation	Ctrl + O	command + O
Open recently opened job(s)/ transformation(s)	Ctrl + 1, Ctrl + 2, Ctrl + 3, and so on	command + 1, command + 2, command + 3, and so on
Save a job/transformation	Ctrl + S	command + S

Action	Windows shortcut	Mac OS shortcut
Close a job/transformation	*Ctrl + W*	*command + W*
Close all (transformations and jobs)	*Shift + Ctrl + W*	*shift + command + W*
Run a job/transformation	*F9*	*fn + F9*
Preview a transformation	*F10*	*fn + F10*
Debug a transformation	*Shift + F10*	*shift + fn + F10*
Verify a transformation	*F11*	*fn + F11*
Job settings	*Ctrl + J* or double-click on job in the Job tree in the **View** tab	*command + J* or double-click on job in the Job tree in the **View** tab
Transformation settings	*Ctrl + T* or double-click on transformation in the Transformation tree in the **View** tab	*command + T* or double-click on transformation in the Transformation tree in the **View** tab
Search metadata	*Ctrl + F*	*command + F*
Set environment variables	*Ctrl + Alt + J*	*command + option + J*
Show used environment variables	*Ctrl + L*	*command + L*
Show arguments	*Ctrl + Alt + U*	*command + option + U*
Edit the `kettle.properties` file	*Ctrl + Alt + P*	*command + option + P*

Designing transformations and jobs

The following are shortcuts that help with the designing of transformations and jobs:

Action	Windows shortcut	Mac OS shortcut
New step/job entry	Drag the step/job entry icon to the work area and drop it there	
Edit step/job entry	Double-click or Edit option in the mouse over assistance toolbar	
Edit step description	Double-click on the middle mouse button	
New hop	Click on a step and drag it towards the second step while holding down the middle mouse button, or while pressing the *Shift* key and holding down the left mouse button, or select the Input/Output connector in the mouse over assistance toolbar	
Edit a hop	Double-click on transformations, right-click on jobs	
Enable/disable a hop	Left-click on the hop	

Action	Windows shortcut	Mac OS shortcut
Change the evaluation (only available in jobs)	Left-click on the small hop icon	
Split a hop	Drag a step over the hop until it gets wider	
Select some steps/job entries	*Ctrl + click*	
Select all steps	*Ctrl + A*	*command + A*
Clear selection	*Esc* or click on anywhere outside the selection	*fn + esc* or click on anywhere outside the selection
Copy selected steps/job entries to clipboard	*Ctrl + C*	*command + C*
Paste from clipboard to work area	*Ctrl + V*	*command + V*
Delete selected steps/job entries	*Delete*	
Align selected steps/job entries to top	*Ctrl + up arrow*	*command + up arrow*
Align selected steps/job entries to bottom	*Ctrl + down arrow*	*command + down arrow*
Align selected steps/job entries to left	*Ctrl + left arrow*	*command + left arrow*
Align selected steps/job entries to right	*Ctrl + right arrow*	*command + right arrow*
Distribute selected steps/job entries horizontally	*Alt + right arrow*	*option + right arrow*
Distribute selected steps/job entries vertically	*Alt + up arrow*	*option + up arrow*
Zoom in	*Page Up*	
Zoom out	*Page Down*	
Zoom 100 percent	*Home*	
Snap to grid	*Alt + Home*	*option + Home*
Undo	*Ctrl + Z*	*command + Z*
Redo	*Ctrl + Y*	*command + Y*
Show output stream (only available in transformations)	Position the mouse cursor over the step; then press *Space bar*	
List variables (in a textbox where the dollar sign is present)	*Ctrl + Space bar*	

In Mac OS, the *control + Space bar* key combination is reserved for the launching the Spotlight application. You may either deactivate that predefined behavior, or use *Shift + command + Space bar* instead.

Grids

The following shortcuts are useful when editing grids:

Action	Windows shortcut	Mac OS shortcut
Move a row up	*Ctrl + up arrow*	
Move a row down	*Ctrl + down arrow*	
Resize all columns to see the full values (header included)	*F3*	*fn + F3*
Resize all columns to see the full values (header excluded)	*F4*	*fn + F4*
Select all rows	*Ctrl + A*	
Clear selection	*Esc*	*fn + esc*
Copy selected lines to clipboard	*Ctrl + C*	
Paste from clipboard to grid	*Ctrl + V*	
Cut selected lines	*Ctrl + X*	
Delete selected lines	*Delete*	
Keep only selected lines	*Ctrl + K*	
Undo	*Ctrl + Z*	
Redo	*Ctrl + Y*	

Repositories

The following are the available shortcuts for working with repositories:

Action	Windows shortcut	Mac OS shortcut
Connect to repository	*Ctrl + R*	*command + R*
Disconnect repository	*Ctrl + D*	*command + D*
Explore repository	*Ctrl + E*	*command + E*
Edit current user	*Ctrl + U*	*command + U*

Database wizards

The following are some shortcuts for dealing with databases:

Action	Windows shortcut	Mac OS shortcut
Create database connection	*F3*	*fn + F3*
Copy table	*F4*	*fn + F4*
Copy tables	*Ctrl + F10*	*command + fn + F10*

Summary

This appendix summarized the main Spoon shortcuts for designing, running, editing, and more. This will help you by saving you a lot of time while working with the tool.

E

Introducing PDI 5 Features

While writing the second edition of this book, Version 5 was still under development. Most of the novelties in this new release are quite advanced or have to do with concepts that are out of the scope of this book, for example, Carte—a simple web server that allows you to execute transformations and jobs remotely.

There are, however, some features that may interest you. This appendix will quickly introduce you to those features.

Welcome page

PDI 5 comes with a new welcome page full of links to web resources, blogs, forums, books on PDI, and more. Following those links, you will be able to learn more and become active in the Pentaho community. Remember that this window is opened by default when you launch Spoon for the first time. Alternatively, you can open it from the main menu by navigating to the **Help | Welcome Screen** option.

Usability

The first thing you will notice while working with PDI 5, is the **Help** button on steps and job entries, as shown in the following screenshot:

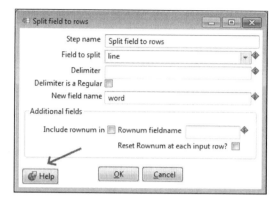

After clicking on that button, if available, the wiki page for the step will show up to help you understand the purpose of the entry of step.

One interesting improvement regarding usability, is the continuous preview mode. If you are designing and testing a transformation, instead of running previews of individual steps, you have the option of running the transformation and seeing the output of individual steps in the **Preview data** tab of the **Execution Results** window, as shown in the following screenshot:

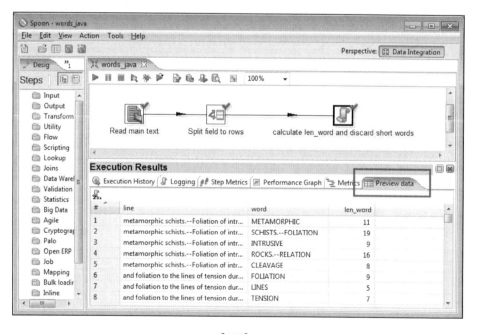

The preceding screenshot shows you an example of the continuous preview mode. The **Preview data** tab displays the output of the selected step, in this case, the **User Defined Java Class (UDJC)**.

Solutions to commonly occurring situations

Among several common use-cases in PDI, there are three that have been specially addressed in PDI 5: restartability, database transactions, and looping.

Restartability has to do with the ability of restarting a job after an interruption. To keep track of the status of an execution, you define **checkpoints**. Checkpoints ensure that the status variable, arguments, files, and rows from the result set are serialized. This way, the execution of a failed job can be easily resumed in a safe state after the following job entry of the last successful checkpoint.

The second common requirement that was introduced is the database transaction across transformations and jobs. This differs from previous versions of PDI where the scope of a transaction was a single transformation or job.

Finally, a very interesting feature included in PDI 5 is the possibility of including subjobs in transformations, through the use of executors. For a long time PDI developers used to ask, "Can I run a job inside a transformation?". The answer was definitely a no. In order to solve the requirement, the solution was to create jobs and transformations nested in complex ways. Now you can avoid all that unnecessary work by looping-over data or files in an easier way. There is a **job executor** step that can easily be configured to loop-over the rows in a dataset. Not only is the loop easier to implement, but also there is a bonus: the step returns the execution results (number of rows read, number of errors, and so on), the result rows, and the result files. Analogous to this, there is also a **transformation executor**.

Backend

Finally, there are new backend features. One of them is the gathering of low-level statistics. For evaluating the performance of your work, you can see the full execution lineage in a new tab of the **Execution Results** window: the **Metrics** tab. The following screenshot shows you a sample of these metrics:

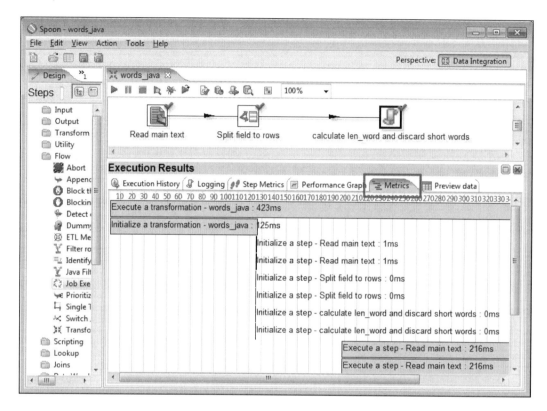

Summary

This appendix introduced you some of the main features included in Kettle 5.0. As I've already said, there are many other features not mentioned here. You always have the option of downloading Pentaho Kettle 5.0 and exploring the tool by yourself to get familiar with it and to take advantage of the new features.

All the explanations and exercises in this book have been developed, explained, and tested in the latest stable version 4.4. This does not prevent you from trying all of the examples and exercises given in this book in Kettle 5.0. You should not have any difficulties.

Best Practices

*This appendix gives you some advice to take into account in your daily work
with PDI. If you intend to work seriously with PDI, knowing how to accomplish
different tasks is just not enough.*

Here you have some guidelines that will help you to go in the right direction:

- Outline your ideas on paper before creating a transformation or a job. Don't drop
  steps randomly on the canvas trying to get things to work, otherwise you will end
  up with a transformation or a job that is difficult to understand and might not be
  of any use.

- Document your work. Write at least a simple description in the transformation and
  job setting windows. Replace the default names of the steps and the job entries with
  meaningful ones. Use notes to clarify the purpose of the transformations and the
  jobs. Color-code your notes for a better effect; for example, use a color for notes
  explaining the purpose of a transformation, and a different color or font for technical
  notes. By doing this, your work will be well documented.

- Make your jobs and transformations clear to understand. Arrange the elements
  in the canvas so that it does not look like a puzzle to solve. Memorize the shortcuts
  for arrangement and alignment and use them regularly. You will find a full list in
  Appendix D, Spoon Shortcuts.

- Organize the PDI elements in folders. Don't save all of the transformations and
  jobs in the same folder. Organize them according to the purpose they have.

◆ Make your work flexible and reusable. Make use of arguments, variables, and named parameters. If you identify tasks that are going to be used in several situations, create subtransformations.

◆ Make your work portable (ready for deployment). Do whatever you can so that even if you move your work to another machine or another folder, or the path to source or destination files change, or the connection properties to the databases change, everything keeps working without or with minimal changes. In order to do that, don't use fixed names but variables. If you know the values for the variables beforehand, define the variables in the `kettle.properties` file. For the name of the transformations and jobs use the relative paths (use the `${Internal.Job.Filename.Directory}`, and `${Internal.Transformation.Filename.Directory}` variables).

◆ Avoid overloading your transformations. A transformation should do a precise task. If it doesn't, think of splitting it into two or more, or create subtransformations. Doing so, your transformation will be clearer and in the case of subtransformations, also reusable.

◆ Handle errors. Try to figure out the kind of errors that may occur and trap them by validating, handing errors, and acting accordingly—fixing data, taking alternative paths, sending friendly messages to the log files, and so on.

◆ Do everything you can to optimize the PDI performance. You can find a full checklist at `http://wiki.pentaho.com/display/COM/PDI+Performance+tuning+check-list`.

For tracking the performance of individual steps in a transformation, you can look up the details at `http://wiki.pentaho.com/display/EAI/Step+performance+monitoring`.

◆ Keep a track of jobs and transformations history. You can use a versioning system, such as Subversion or Git. In doing so, you can recover older versions of your jobs and transformations or examine the history of how they changed. For more on Subversion, visit the site `http://subversion.tigris.org/`. For more on Git visit the official site `http://git-scm.com/`. Also, consider upgrading to EE, where versioning is a repository feature.

◆ Bookmark the the forum page and visit it frequently. The PDI forum is available at `http://forums.pentaho.org/forumdisplay.php?f=135`. If you are stuck with something, search for a solution in the forum. If you don't find what you're looking for, create a new thread, expose your doubts or scenario clearly and you'll get a prompt answer as the Pentaho community and particularly the PDI one is quite active. Alternatively you can meet Pentaho people on IRC server `www.freenode.net`, channel #pentaho. On the channel, people discuss all kinds of issues related to all the Pentaho tools, and not just Kettle.

Summary

Knowing how to accomplish different tasks with PDI is as important as doing it in the right way. This appendix has the purpose of guiding you in that direction. Following the guidelines proposed here, your work will be useful, easy to maintain, reusable, and of high quality.

G

Pop Quiz Answers

Chapter 1, Getting Started with Pentaho Data Integration

Pop quiz – PDI data sources

Q1	5

Pop quiz – PDI prerequisites

Q1	3

Pop quiz – PDI basics

Q1	2 (because Spoon is the only graphical tool)
Q2	1
Q3	2 (because Spoon doesn't generate code, but interprets metadata saved in KTR or KJB files whose content is plain XML)
Q4	2 (because the grid size is intended to line up steps in the screen)
Q5	2 (as an example the transformation in this chapter created the rows of data from scratch; it didn't use external data)

Chapter 2, Getting Started with Transformations

Pop quiz – generating data with PDI

Q1	3
Q2	3
Q3	1

Chapter 3, Manipulating Real-world Data

Pop quiz – providing a list of text files using regular expressions

Q1	Both are true
Q2	1. False
	2. False (It is possible, but there are limitations. For example, you cannot specify footer lines. As a consequence, the step will read the whole file and it will be your task to remove that invalid data later in the transformation).
	3. True
	4. True

Chapter 4, Filtering, Searching, and Performing Other Useful Operations with Data

Pop quiz – formatting output fields

Q1	Possible answers are 1 and 2. The field is already a Number, so you may define the output field as a Number, taking care of the format you apply. If you define the output field as a String and you don't set a format, Kettle will send the field to the output as 0.0, 1.0, 2.0, 3.0, and so on, which clearly is not the same as the input you had. Just to confirm this, modify the transformation to see the results for yourself.

Chapter 5, Controlling the Flow of Data

Pop quiz – deciding between a Number range step and a Switch/Case step

Q1	3
	The answer is 3, as both 1 and 2 solve the situation. You can use a Number range step that maps the number of people that speak the language to the number of interpreters. Then you can Switch/Case based on the number of interpreters. This would be option 1. Alternatively, you can use just a Switch/Case step based not on the number of interpreters but on the number of people. This would be option 2.

Pop quiz – understanding the difference between copying and distributing

Q1	3
	In the second transformation the rows are copied, so all the unassigned rows reach the dummy step. In the first transformation, the rows are distributed, half of the rows arrive at the filter step. When you do the preview, you see only the unassigned tasks for this half; you don't see the unassigned tasks that went to the other stream.
	Option 3 may be true depending in the data and depending on how the data is distributed

Chapter 6, Transforming Your Data by Coding

Pop quiz – choosing a scripting language for coding inside a transformation

Q1	2. False
	You can perfectly have one or more MJSV as well as one or more UDJC steps in the same transformation, and everything should work.
Q2	2. False
	There is an experimental step named Script (you can see this under the category named Experimental), that will provide support for other scripting languages such as Ruby, Python, Groovy, and so on. You can check the status of this step in Jira (`http://jira.pentaho.com/browse/PDI-3035`).

Q3	2. False
	Despite not being recommended for all situations, coding in JavaScript is useful and there are no plans for deprecating the JavaScript step.

Chapter 8, Working with Databases

Pop quiz – connecting to a database in several transformations

Q1	3

Pop quiz – interpreting data types coming from a database

Q1	2

Pop quiz – interpreting data types coming from a database

Q1	1
	If an incoming row belongs to a product that doesn't exist in the products table, both the Insert/Update step and the Table output step will insert the record.
	If an incoming row belongs to a product that already exist in the products table, the Insert/Update step updates it. In this alternative version, the Table output will fail (there cannot be two products with the same value for the primary key), but the failing row goes to the Update step that updates the record.
	If an incoming row contains invalid data (for example, a price with a non-numeric value), neither the Insert/Update step, the Table output step, and the Update step would insert or update the table with this product.

Chapter 9, Performing Advanced Operations with Databases

Pop quiz – implementing a Type III SCD in PDI

Q1	2

(1) is not a valid option. The Dimension L/U by itself is not prepared to maintain the previous value and the current value in the same record automatically.

There are very few things you cannot do with PDI if you have to work with data, so (3) is out of discussion.

The right answer is (2). With a Database lookup to get the current value stored in the dimension. If there is no data in the dimension table, the lookup fails and returns null; that is not a problem. After that, you compare the found data with the new one and set the proper values for the dimension columns. Then, you load the dimension either with a Combination L/U or with a Dimension lookup, just as you do for a regular Type I SCD.

It's worth saying that type III SCD are used rather infrequently and cannot always be automated. Sometimes they are used to represent human-applied changes and the implementation has to be made manually.

Chapter 10, Creating Basic Task Flows

Pop quiz – defining PDI jobs

Q1	2
Q2	1
Q3	1
Q4	1
Q5	1

Q6	1

Chapter 11, Creating Advanced Transformations and Jobs

Pop quiz – deciding the scope of variables

Q1	All the options are valid. In the section, you had just a transformation and its parent job that is also the root job. So option 1 is valid. The grand-parent job scope includes the parent job, so option 2 is valid too. Option 3 includes all the other options, so it is a valid option too.

Chapter 12, Developing and Implementing a Simple Datamart

Pop quiz – creating a product type dimension

Q1	2
Q2	3

Index

transformation, previewing
  Execution Results pane 47
trap detector 163
Type II SCD
  about 310
  history of data, storing with 310, 311
  loading, with Dimension L/U step 312-316
  surrogate key,obtaining for 402, 403
  vs, Type I SCD 310, 311
Type I SCD
  about 303
  loading, Combination L/U step used 304-306
  surrogate key,obtaining for 401
  vs, Type II SCD 310, 311

U

Ubuntu
  MySQL, installing 34, 35
UDJC
  about 190
  usability 459
UDJC step
  used, for inserting Java code 191, 192
unstructured files
  parsing, with JavaScript 180-182
  reading, with JavaScript 180-182
UPDATE statement 244
User Defined Java Class. *See* **UDJC**
User Defined Java Expression step 199
users
  creating 425

V

variables
  scope 373-376
  scope type 374
  setting, inside transformation 372
  used, for enhancing processes 368-372
variables, scope type
  visibility 374

W

Weka Project 10
welcome page, PDI 5 457
WHERE clause 250
Windows
  MySQL, installing 31, 33
writeToLog() function 177
Written column 48

X

XML
  about 96
  URL, for more info 96
XML files
  about 91-95
  data, getting from 97
  data getting, XPath used 97
XML step
  Get data, configuring from 98
XPath
  about 97
  URL,for more info 98
  used, for getting data from XML files 97

Thank you for buying
Pentaho Data Integration Beginner's Guide, Second Edition

About Packt Publishing

Packt, pronounced 'packed', published its first book "*Mastering phpMyAdmin for Effective MySQL Management*" in April 2004 and subsequently continued to specialize in publishing highly focused books on specific technologies and solutions.

Our books and publications share the experiences of your fellow IT professionals in adapting and customizing today's systems, applications, and frameworks. Our solution based books give you the knowledge and power to customize the software and technologies you're using to get the job done. Packt books are more specific and less general than the IT books you have seen in the past. Our unique business model allows us to bring you more focused information, giving you more of what you need to know, and less of what you don't.

Packt is a modern, yet unique publishing company, which focuses on producing quality, cutting-edge books for communities of developers, administrators, and newbies alike. For more information, please visit our website: www.packtpub.com.

About Packt Open Source

In 2010, Packt launched two new brands, Packt Open Source and Packt Enterprise, in order to continue its focus on specialization. This book is part of the Packt Open Source brand, home to books published on software built around Open Source licences, and offering information to anybody from advanced developers to budding web designers. The Open Source brand also runs Packt's Open Source Royalty Scheme, by which Packt gives a royalty to each Open Source project about whose software a book is sold.

Writing for Packt

We welcome all inquiries from people who are interested in authoring. Book proposals should be sent to author@packtpub.com. If your book idea is still at an early stage and you would like to discuss it first before writing a formal book proposal, contact us; one of our commissioning editors will get in touch with you.

We're not just looking for published authors; if you have strong technical skills but no writing experience, our experienced editors can help you develop a writing career, or simply get some additional reward for your expertise.

[PACKT] open source
PUBLISHING
community experience distilled

Pentaho 5.0 Reporting by Example: Beginner's Guide

ISBN: 978-1-782162-24-7   Paperback: 342 pages

Create high-quality, professional, standard reports using today's most popular open source reporting tool

1. Install and configure PRD in Linux and Windows

2. Produce reports with groups, aggregate functions, parameters, graphics, and sparklines

3. Create and publish your own Java web application with parameterized reports and an interactive user interface

4. Install and configure Pentaho BI Server to execute PRD reports

Instant Pentaho Data Integration Kitchen

ISBN: 978-1-849696-90-6   Paperback: 68 pages

Explore the world of Pentaho Data Integration command-line tools which will help you use the Kitchen

1. Learn something new in an Instant! A short, fast, focused guide delivering immediate results

2. Understand how to discover the repository structure using the command line scripts

3. Learn to configure the log properly and how to gather the information that helps you investigate any kind of problem

4. Explore all the possible ways to start jobs and learn transformations without any difficulty

Please check **www.PacktPub.com** for information on our titles

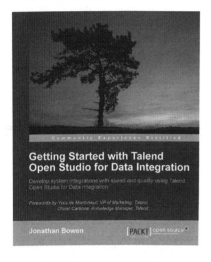

Getting Started with Talend Open Studio for Data Integration

ISBN: 978-1-849514-72-9   Paperback: 320 pages

Develop system integrations with speed and quality using Talend Open Studio for Data Integration

1. Develop complex integration jobs without writing code

2. Go beyond "extract, transform and load" by constructing end-to-end integrations

3. Learn how to package your jobs for production use

Pentaho Data Integration 4 Cookbook

ISBN: 978-1-849515-24-5   Paperback: 352 pages

Over 70 recipes to solve ETL problems using Pentaho Kettle

1. Manipulate your data by exploring, transforming, validating, integrating, and more

2. Work with all kinds of data sources such as databases, plain files, and XML structures among others

3. Use Kettle in integration with other components of the Pentaho Business Intelligence Suite

4. Each recipe is a carefully organized sequence of instructions packed with screenshots, tables, and tips to complete the task as efficiently as possible

Please check **www.PacktPub.com** for information on our titles

19731302R00287

Made in the USA
San Bernardino, CA
10 March 2015